THE MOVEMENT FOR REPRODUCTIVE JUSTICE

SOCIAL TRANSFORMATIONS IN AMERICAN
ANTHROPOLOGY
General Editor: Ida Susser

The Sounds of Latinidad: Immigrants Making Music and Creating Culture in a Southern City
Samuel K. Byrd

Mobile Selves: Race, Migration, and Belonging in Peru and the U.S.
Ulla D. Berg

Citizen, Student, Soldier: Latina/o Youth, JROTC, and the American Dream
Gina M. Pérez

Empire in the Air: Airline Travel and the African Diaspora
Chandra D. Bhimull

The Movement for Reproductive Justice: Empowering Women of Color through Social Activism
Patricia Zavella

The Movement for Reproductive Justice

Empowering Women of Color through Social Activism

Patricia Zavella

NEW YORK UNIVERSITY PRESS
New York

NEW YORK UNIVERSITY PRESS
New York
www.nyupress.org

References to Internet websites (URLs) were accurate at the time of writing. Neither the author nor New York University Press is responsible for URLs that may have expired or changed since the manuscript was prepared.

Library of Congress Cataloging-in-Publication Data
Names: Zavella, Patricia, author.
Title: The movement for reproductive justice : empowering women of color through social activism / Patricia Zavella.
Description: New York : New York University Press, [2020] | Series: Social transformations in American anthropology | Includes bibliographical references and index.
Identifiers: LCCN 2019029660 | ISBN 9781479829200 (cloth) |
ISBN 9781479812707 (paperback) | ISBN 9781479878505 (ebook) |
ISBN 9781479887071 (ebook)
Subjects: LCSH: Reproductive rights—United States. | Minority women—Political activity—United States. | Women political activists—United States. | Women in community organization—United States. | Minority women—United States—Social conditions. | Social movements—United States. | Social justice—United States.
Classification: LCC HQ1236.5.U6 Z348 2020 | DDC 320.082/0973—dc23
LC record available at https://lccn.loc.gov/2019029660

New York University Press books are printed on acid-free paper, and their binding materials are chosen for strength and durability. We strive to use environmentally responsible suppliers and materials to the greatest extent possible in publishing our books.

Manufactured in the United States of America

10 9 8 7 6 5 4 3 2 1

Also available as an ebook

This work is dedicated to the memory of my mother, Isabel Martínez Zavella Schnebelen, who raised twelve children and taught us the values of equality, compassion, and social justice, and to my grandchildren, Max and Ben Schneider and Sofia Gonzales

CONTENTS

Color plates appear as an insert following page 146.

ABBREVIATIONS

ACA Patient Protection and Affordable Care Act
AFLA Adolescent Family Life Act
BMMA Black Mamas Matter Alliance
COLOR Colorado Organization for Latina Opportunity and
Reproductive Rights
CLRJ California Latinas for Reproductive Justice
DACA Deferred Action for Childhood Arrivals
ICAH Illinois Caucus for Adolescent Health
ICE Immigration and Customs Enforcement
LAN Latina Advocacy Network, organized by NLIRH
LIPS Latinas Increasing Political Strength, organized by COLOR
LOV Latinas of Vision, organized by COLOR
MALCS Mujeres Activas en Letras y Cambio Social
MFG Maximum Family Grant rule
NAPAWF National Asian Pacific American Women's Forum
NLIRH National Latina Institute for Reproductive Health
PNA Parental Notification of Abortion Act
PRWORA Personal Responsibility and Work Opportunity
Reconciliation Act
RJ reproductive justice
SAFIRE Sisters in Action for Reproductive Empowerment, organized
by Forward Together
SISTERSONG SisterSong Women of Color Reproductive Justice
Collective
TWA Tewa Women United
VAWA Violence Against Women Act
WADRJ Women of African Descent for Reproductive Justice
WSC Western States Center
YPAR youth participatory action research
YWU Young Women United

I always say, the movement for reproductive justice found me. As I was completing my last book, I was struggling with an array of emotions about the research, mainly sadness and anger at neoliberal immigration policies, as I grappled with making sense of Latinxs' daily experiences with migration and poverty that often had such painful outcomes. Out of nowhere I received an email inviting me to a presentation on comprehensive sex ed to be presented by adolescent Latinxs, a man and a woman, using the reproductive justice approach in Fresno, California. This meant that these young people probably came from farmworker backgrounds since Fresno is in the middle of the San Joaquin Valley, where the largest employers are in agribusiness and so many of the workers are migrants. I was intrigued by the reproductive justice approach that involved young men and gratified that these young people were actively trying to change conditions related to their well-being. I resolved to look into the reproductive justice movement, and eventually my interests blossomed into a full-scale research project. I was drawn to researching this movement in part because the participants use an approach based in intersectionality, which I have used in my own research and teaching.

As I conducted research on this movement, so many memories of my own experiences being a young parent came bubbling up. I was the first generation in my Mexican American family to attend university and grew up in poverty, the oldest of twelve children. I knew firsthand the shame directed at women of color with "too many" children. I worked and gained scholarships to support myself since my working-class parents could not afford to contribute to my education. As one of a few students of color in 1974, graduate school felt alienating, which was exacerbated when I became pregnant during my second year of classes. Questions were raised about whether I could keep my fellowship, and I was told the faculty debated this idea during a department meeting.

My adviser assured me afterward that the faculty decided I could. He chuckled, "We practically affirmed motherhood and apple pie!" ignoring that male students who were parents did not have their commitment to their careers questioned. Months later a mentor told me about another debate that took place behind closed doors during deliberations for a prestigious national fellowship, in which some faculty suggested that my pregnancy raised questions about my commitment to academia. Her intervention assured that the deliberations were based on merit, so I landed that fellowship, which allowed me to remain in school and finish my dissertation. When I got my first academic position in 1983, it was unusual at the time to be a woman professor with two children. I experienced the discomfort imposed by those who think women of color get pregnant "too early." The reticence I felt about being a young parent is part of what reproductive justice advocates call reproductive oppression, and parenting continues to be seen as a woman's issue in academia.[1] I see myself as an ally to those who are working on reproductive justice and introduced myself as such when I met and conducted interviews or focus groups with participants in this social movement.

I completed this book after thirty-four years as a professor at the University of California in Santa Cruz. During my tenure at UCSC, I had taught a course in the Feminist Studies Department about women of color and was familiar with Cherríe Moraga's provocative statement, "The *idea* of Third World feminism has proved to be much easier between the covers of a book than between real live women."[2] UCSC supports interdisciplinary work as well as collaboration between faculty and graduate students through research clusters. In 1991, Angela Davis, my colleague in Feminist Studies, organized a research cluster called "Women of Color in Collaboration and Conflict" that sponsored talks by invited guests and members as well as other activities such as writing groups, the Women of Color Film Festival, and hosting an INCITE! conference called "The Color of Violence: Violence against Women of Color" in 2000. The cluster was active as late as 2017. The notion that we should problematize collaboration by women of color was foundational to the cluster and shaped my approach to this research project on women of color in the movement for reproductive justice. Initially I was sympathetic to the movement's goals but skeptical about collaboration by women of color. However, in the end I was impressed by the ways in which reproductive justice activists mindfully negotiate across their many differences as they work with sister organizations and with others.

I had not planned to write about self-care or spirituality when I designed this project; but in the course of conducting research these issues came up repeatedly, so I had to come to terms with them. I was raised Catholic and have loving memories of attending weekly Mass with my grandmother when I was a child, even though she would discipline me for fidgeting by pinching my arm. My mother and grandmother were devoted Catholics; we participated in all the Days of Obligation and sacraments, and they even gave money to the church regularly despite our poverty. Over time I drifted away from the church due to its perpetration of various forms of violence during the conquest and thereafter, its rigid stance on contraception and abortion, and ongoing social problems related to abuse of minors and women. Yet I often joked that I was a "recovering Catholic" since, in honor of my relatives' devotion, I would attend religious ceremonies without question when visiting my grandmother and I was shaped by Catholic tenets related to being a good person, contributing community service, and working toward social justice. I came to identify with Elisa Facio's concept "cultural Catholicism," in which participants take part in Mexican religious expressions out of respect for family members while maintaining a critique of the Catholic Church's shortcomings even as it continues to shape their subjectivity.[3] This concept helped me to see how many activists negotiate spirituality in relation to their respective religious traditions even if they are not practicing religion directly.

This book explores the often overlooked story in which women of color supported women's access to health information, expressed in the landmark publication *Our Bodies, Our Selves*, and more generally the women's health movement that pushed for greater access to culturally sensitive health care.[4] The social movement for reproductive justice takes health advocacy further by pushing for women's *human right* to access health care with dignity and to express their full selves, including their spiritual beliefs, as well as policies that address social inequalities.

Introduction

The Movement for Reproductive Justice

Reproductive justice is more than a term, it is a movement.
—NativeYouthSexHealth, tweet posted on November 7, 2014

When I interviewed "Lola," a community outreach worker in a reproductive justice organization, she insisted on beginning by telling me her life story (in Spanish).[1] In brief, it was a heartbreaking narrative about crossing the US-Mexico border with a smuggler, without authorization. She had climbed the border fence holding a rosary, which caught when she jumped down and ripped off the tip of her finger, which bled profusely. With no options for seeking health care in the United States, Lola immediately returned to Mexico, where she was unable to disclose exactly how she was injured since the smuggler threatened to kill her if she revealed his identity. She recalled, "I think the worst part of the story was how the medical personnel treated me. The doctor said, 'I don't understand why you came from your town only to risk your life.' He told me if my finger got infected, they would have to cut off my hand and maybe my arm or I might die. After the surgery, no one cared that I was crying and crying." After a long period of recuperation with help from women she met in the border town, Lola reentered the United States without authorization and began working at various low-paying jobs. As an undocumented worker, she had no medical insurance, so she received no health-care services for a number of years. Lola was well aware that it was risky to seek contraception, and she became pregnant.[2] It was not until she landed a job as a community organizer with a nonprofit devoted to reproductive justice that she had regular access to health care. Over the years as her colleagues marveled about her strength and resiliency, she came to identify with Wonder Woman and has a collection of figurines on her desk. However, without a driver's license she cannot board planes to travel out of state for her work. These experiences shaped Lola's desire to continue working for reproductive justice on behalf of immigrants since she knows their struggles firsthand. We both teared up as she declared, "That's why I have to do something big in this life because I didn't die when I crossed. . . . And when we give talks about our reproductive justice work, we have to talk about *everything* we do because people without documents won't qualify for anything related to health."

Lola's story illustrates the trauma, structural vulnerability, and struggles undocumented women experience on a daily basis.[3] Her experience raises concern about why the right to health care seems elusive in the United States for women of color with low incomes. Lola's story also illustrates how the reproductive justice activism that now grounds her daily life is different from other social movements since it views her structural vulnerabilities as an undocumented racialized woman with a low income as interconnected. This book explores how vulnerable women like Lola participate in a social movement that takes an intersectional approach and that claims that she has the human right to health care with dignity and engages her in a process of empowerment.

Women of color have been organizing on behalf of women's reproductive health since the 1970s.[4] The Black Women's Health Imperative was founded in 1984, and soon thereafter other organizations such as National Latina Health Organization, the Native American Women's Health Education Resource Center, and Asian Pacific Islanders for Choice were formed and eventually developed nonprofit organizations. These organizations later coalesced into the SisterSong Women of Color Reproductive Justice Collective in 1997.[5] The term "reproductive justice" (RJ), a neologism that "spliced reproductive rights and social justice," was coined in 1994 by a group of Black women who formed Women of African Descent for Reproductive Justice in Chicago.[6] The national debut of reproductive justice as a strategy for building a movement of indigenous women and women of color occurred in 2003.[7] SisterSong defines reproductive justice as "the human right to maintain personal bodily autonomy, have children, not have children, and parent the children we have in safe and sustainable communities."[8] This statement critiques the history of sterilization abuse and contraceptive experimentation on women of color—documented in scholarly work and exposed in the award-winning documentary *No Más Bebés*.[9] This definition also insists on the right to the preconditions of health as well as access to health care.

Reproductive justice activists address multiple forms of reproductive oppression or injustice, ranging from women never receiving basic anatomy instruction to alarmingly high Black maternal mortality rates. In an interview, Laura Jimenez, executive director of California Latinas for Reproductive Justice, pointed out, "Reproductive justice is a struggle in opposition to what we call reproductive oppression, which all of our communities—the Latino community, African American / Black communities, Asian American communities, Native American communities—have been doing since the time of contact and before." In a shadow report for the UN Committee on the Elimination of Racial Discrimination, the Center for Reproductive Rights, National Latina Institute for Reproductive Health, and SisterSong critique four dimensions of reproductive injustice, which include "lack of information about sexuality and sexual health; discrimination in the health care system; lack of access to sexual and reproductive health care; and poor quality of sexual and reproductive health information and services."[10]

There is ample scholarship that analyzes various forms of reproductive oppression: Dorothy Roberts argues that there has been a sustained campaign to punish Black women for having children and expressing their concerns in ways that are unintelligible to health-care practitioners.[11] Arachu Castro and Virginia Savage, Rogelio D'Gregorio, Lydia Dixon, Iris Lopez, and Rebecca Martínez critique human rights violations through "obstetric violence" that health institutions perpetrate against women, especially indigenous women, including unnecessary cesarean sections as well as cultural insensitivity and racism through which women are pressured to become sterilized, take long-term contraceptives, give birth under traumatizing conditions, or forgo abortions.[12] Khiara Bridges demonstrates how the medicalization of social problems reproduces racial stereotypes and governs the bodies of low-income women of color.[13] Alysha Gálvez analyzes processes of subjectification of Latina immigrants who are systematically directed toward medicalizing their births, conforming to particular regimens of prenatal care, and abandoning their own healthy practices.[14] Lynn Paltrow and Jeanne Flavin document the hundreds of cases in which women, particularly low-income women of color, perceived to have deliberately harmed fertilized eggs, embryos, or fetuses, were subject to attempts to restrict their liberty.[15] Flavin also documents the multiple ways in which American women who live in poverty or are incarcerated face stigma and even legal procedures in efforts to force them to become the "right" kind of mothers.[16] Jennifer Denbow illustrates how the notion of autonomy and technological innovations mask the plethora of regulations and surveillance of women's reproductive health and decision-making.[17] Charlene Galameau argues that migrant women farmworkers' poor reproductive health is rooted in poverty, with low wages, few benefits, hazardous work conditions (including sexual assault and pesticide exposure), and weak labor and safety regulations limiting those hazards, as well women's double day, in which they perform domestic chores after their work days.[18] The Brown Boi Project and National Latina Institute for Reproductive Health find that LGBTQ and gender-nonconforming, masculine of center, and trans people of color are often excluded from reproductive health care.[19] Barbara Gurr argues convincingly, "medicine serves an imperialist purpose in the State's double discourse of care for and neglect of Native people, and . . . the reproductive body is a primary site for this imperialism through the State's exercise of biopower."[20] Clearly reproductive oppression toward women of color takes many forms, depending on social context, and induces needless social suffering.

The causes of reproductive oppression range from institutional violence that subjects women to various forms of trauma from social workers, health-care practitioners, or religious leaders to discursive approbation by kin or friends for "inappropriate" behavior or inquiries into their personal circumstances, leaving women feeling judged. As the human rights scholar-activist Alicia Ely Yamin points out, "there may be no area where narratives of 'sin' and 'transgression' are more clearly embedded in policies and laws than sexual and reproductive health."[21] More chilling, conservative forces have increasingly waged a war on women's reproductive and sexual rights in the United States. The conservative movement has curtailed abortion through legislation in states by targeted regulation of abortion providers, mandating pre-abortion wait times and viewing fetal ultrasounds, and pushing legislation for parental consent for minors seeking abortions.[22] They also promulgate anti-abortion films, support bogus "crisis pregnancy centers," introduce legislation regarding "fetal personhood," and pass laws that ban abortion when embryonic cardiac activity can be detected even though women often are unaware they are pregnant at that point.[23] These are forms of "reproductive governance" in which various actors use "legislative controls, economic inducements, moral injunctions, direct coercion, and ethical incitements to produce, monitor, and control reproductive behaviours and practices."[24]

Reproductive justice advocates contest reproductive governance using a holistic approach. They advocate for communities free from state violence expressed through colonialism, neoliberalism, poverty, criminalization, or policies related to child welfare, environmental regulation, immigration, or education that impede women's rights.[25] By including the right to bodily autonomy, reproductive justice critiques the politics of place, where access to health care as well as to parks and open space are linked to the ability to earn a living wage, afford healthy food and quality child care, and express spiritual and cultural traditions.[26] Advocates also make pointed critiques of "pregnancy crisis centers" that claim to provide reproductive health services but instead offer misinformation and discourage women from seeking abortions, often for religious reasons.[27] Reproductive justice advocates agree with Iris Lopez, who argues for changing conditions to enable women's full reproductive freedom, so that "women and men have viable alternatives from which to choose, and that the best possible social and political conditions exist that allow women to decide, free from coercion or violence, if, when, and how many children to have."[28]

Most organizations using the reproductive justice framework are racially specific. There are, for example, Asian American women's groups, Black women's groups, groups that serve Latinx women, and so forth. Yet reproductive justice advocates work in impressive ways to honor solidarity and difference. The women involved in these movements support one another, they build coalitions, and they share resources, even though they largely remain organized within their racially or ethnically specific groups. This book explores how the women involved with these reproductive justice organizations frame their identities as they are influenced by this work and by these interconnections with women in other communities, and it also examines how they conceptualize and reframe the racist and sexist ideologies used against them by conservative politicians in their joint work for social justice. It argues that this movement, with its effective collaboration among like-minded groups all working toward similar goals, offers a model for other social movements.

There are over thirty reproductive justice nonprofit organizations in the United States (with one in Canada) that frame their work around intersectionality and human rights.[29] Most of them have small staffs and, as nonprofits, apply for funding from a variety of foundations and donors. I conducted interviews with staff and participants working in thirteen reproductive justice organizations or independent programs located across the United States that were founded at different times: Black Women for Wellness (Los Angeles, 1997), California Latinas for Reproductive Justice (CLRJ, Los Angeles, 2004), Colorado Organization for Latina Opportunity and Reproductive Rights (COLOR, Denver, 1998), Forward Together (Oakland, 1989), Illinois Caucus for Adolescent Health (ICAH, Chicago, 1977), National Asian Pacific American Women's Forum (NAPAWF, Brooklyn, 1995), National Latina Institute for Reproductive Health (NLIRH, New York and Washington, DC, 2002), Los Angeles Coalition for Reproductive Justice (Los Angeles, 1980), Strong Families Network (Oakland, 2005), Strong Families New Mexico (Albuquerque, 2012), Tewa Women United (TWU, Española, NM, 1989), Western States Center (WSC, Portland, OR, 1987), and Young Women United (YWU, Albuquerque, 1999)—see appendix A for information about the reproductive justice organizations with which I conducted research.[30] I analyze specific campaigns by these reproductive justice organizations to illustrate the movement's dynamism.

Social movements are "groups of individuals who collectively challenge authorities over a sustained period of time, often using public means to express their grievances and resistance."[31] The scholarship on social movements often focuses on three different processes with which social movements engage—identity formation, the organization of protests (including their communication strategies), and policy advocacy—and it often ignores the struggles and activism of women of color like Lola.[32] Reproductive justice advocates organize their share of mass protests—I happened to interview executive directors of NLIRH and NAPAWF, who co-organized a 2013 demonstration to push for comprehensive immigration reform as they prepared to leave for the DC protest—and they use varied forms of media.[33] However, the work cultivating long-term social transformation by reproductive justice activists is distinct from other social movements. This book explores the ways in which reproductive justice advocates characterize their movement as honoring solidarity *and* difference by sharing resources and supporting one another through particular struggles or campaigns, in ways that are generally unlike their collaborations with other movements, even as they simultaneously negotiate the challenges involved when members of different social categories approach issues with distinct perspectives.

In this book I propose that we analyze women of color's empowerment using the analytic of *poder* (power) that signals the ability of structurally vulnerable people to develop skills or capabilities and aspire to better conditions or even wellness. I build on the anthropologists Ann Bookman and Sandra Morgen's suggestion that empowerment begins when women "change their ideas about the causes of the powerlessness, when they recognize the systemic forces that oppress them, and when they act to change the conditions of their lives."[34] This perspective suggests that empowerment connotes "a spectrum of political activities that range from acts of individual resistance to mass political mobilization that aim to challenge the basic power relations in society."[35] Thus, "empowerment is a *process* aimed at consolidating, maintaining, or changing the nature and distribution of power in a particular cultural context."[36]

This approach to empowerment is helpful for analyzing the reproductive justice movement's praxis, "reflection and action directed at the structures to be transformed," especially related to youth empowerment projects.[37] Yet Bookman and Morgen's notion of empowerment was part of the scholarship that highlighted working-class women's activism in the late 1980s. Since then, we have witnessed some progressive change as well as unexpected social transformations that seem retrograde. What has activism by low-income women of color looked like since then?

During the Obama administration, there was ongoing activism related to opposing a well-funded conservative movement that successfully imposed restrictions on women's access to abortion in the states.[38] Reproductive justice activists also agitated against the detention of unauthorized migrants and deportation policies by the "deporter in chief." Actually President Obama had worked to decrease apprehensions and deportations of undocumented immigrants with established roots in US communities who had no criminal records and he issued an executive order on Deferred Action for Childhood Arrivals, which protected un-documented youth. Obama inherited a robust immigration-enforcement regime, as congressional funding for immigration enforcement had increased in the post-9/11 era. Between 2009 and 2016, his administration prioritized national security threats, noncitizens apprehended at the border, gang members, and noncitizens convicted of felonies or aggravated felonies, and his administration abandoned worksite enforcement.[39] Nonetheless, with a total of 12,290,905 deportations under Bill Clinton, 10,328,850 under George W. Bush, and 5,281,115 under Obama, state violence has had devastating effects in communities of color.[40] As Obama's tenure ended, there was much unfinished organizing work related to growing class inequality, ongoing racial tensions particularly evident in voter suppression and the need for comprehensive immigration reform, and providing full access to health care through the Patient Protection and Affordable Care Act (ACA) regardless of legal status (critical for unauthorized migrants living in the United States), to name a few.[41] The heightened political polarization made such efforts extremely difficult.

Increasingly health care is market driven for consumers rather than rights administered through social policy. The Trump political agenda represented a culmination and more transparent version of neoliberalism that entails a "massive disinvestment in families and communities."[42] Neoliberalism encourages individual responses to social problems and characterizes those who struggle, particularly people of color, as deficient and somehow responsible for their own misfortunes.[43] Under the guise of health promotion, subjects are exhorted to engage in healthy behaviors, reduce their risks, and consume appropriately, with the implication that noncompliance raises questions about whether they are taking responsibility for their own health, thus silencing the needs of the poor and justifying their exclusion from state-funded health care.

This book helps to shed light on whether reproductive justice activities implicitly advocate individual neoliberal as opposed to community health rights. The movement for reproductive justice has a long history of activism in which activists mobilize *poder*, multiple forms of capacity building that engage women in policy advocacy and culture shift on behalf of low-income women. We will see that *empoderamiento* (empowerment) is a complex process in which women form political subjectivity and embrace their identities as powerful women.

The Movement for Reproductive Justice

When formed in 1997, SisterSong consisted of sixteen organizations representing the major racial-ethnic groups in the United States: Blacks/African Americans, Latinas/Hispanics, Native Americans/Indigenous peoples, and Asian/Pacific Islanders, as well as Arab and Muslim women.[44] Initially it was challenging to organize women of diverse commitments—Loretta Ross, one of the founders of SisterSong, tried five times to form a national coalition before SisterSong was formed. Indeed, there was opposition and doubt that women of color could build a movement centered on women's lived experience—what Cherríe Moraga calls "theory in the flesh" that emphasizes women's skin color, place, and sexuality.[45] However, these reproductive justice advocates mindfully navigate collaboration. They acknowledge the relationality of racial categories in the United States, in which, as Laura Pulido argues, "the status and meanings associated with one group are contingent upon those of another."[46] Specifically, reproductive justice organizers are concerned about well-known racial inequalities that are manifest in social determinants of health and limit access to health care.[47] Simultaneously, they recognize "differential racialization," in which, Pulido suggests, "various racial/ethnic groups are racialized in unique ways and have distinct experiences of racism."[48] Thus, some reproductive justice organizations work with particular racial-ethnic categories—for example, Black Women for Wellness (which works with women from the African diaspora), California Latinas for Reproductive Justice (which works mainly with Latinas), and Tewa Women United (a multiracial organization whose constituencies are predominantly Native American women). Women of color complicate the notion of differential racialization by pointing out how race is coconstitutive with gender, class, sexuality, ethnicity, age, embodiment, legal status, ability, religion, and other power relations in changing historical contexts that shape women's everyday lives and their identities. Other reproductive justice organizations emphasize the collaboration of women of color in their organizations' names, like Young Women United or SPARK Reproductive Justice NOW. Further, virtually all of them have participants who are not members of their racial-ethnic group—TWU, for example, works with Latinas; YWU, an organization focused on women of color, had a white woman who participated regularly in their activities; COLOR had an Arab Muslim woman working with them during one season, and so on. As we will see, the identity "women of color" is contingent and deployed strategically in relation to external forces and internal organizational dynamics in which movement activists value cultural capital.[49] This book explores the following questions: What are the benefits and tensions related to collaborating as women of color on reproductive justice while working locally in organizations that are largely racially-ethnically specific? How do organizational staff and participants, particularly young women, experience collaboration across difference?

Like so many social movements around the globe that work on behalf of women's rights, not all reproductive justice advocates identify publicly with feminism.[50] While every reproductive justice organization with which I conducted staff interviews are women centered and include women in their mission statements, none of them identify as feminist *organizations*, although many individuals working in reproductive justice organizations call themselves feminists. The tension related to identifying as a feminist as a woman of color has a long history, since feminism is associated with racial, class, and heterosexual privilege. Indeed, some women prefer using the term "Third World women" to signify their transnational solidarity with struggles in the Global South.[51] The writer Alice Walker suggests the term "womanist," and the artist Ester Hernández uses the Spanish form, *mujerista*, for those who advocate on behalf of women's rights but do not identify as feminist.[52] The Native American sociologist Luana Ross prefers "indigenous/feminism," which is "grassroots, in-the-trenches, and activist." She elaborates: "My notion of indigenous/feminism seeks to empower communities. It includes female, male, and other genders. My indigenous/feminism privileges storytelling as a way to decolonize and empower our communities."[53] I never heard anyone in the reproductive justice movement identify as womanist or as *mujerista*. I did hear plenty of ambivalence toward mainstream feminist leaders and organizations. We will see how reproductive justice activists practice a form of unnamed feminism in which they frame advocacy on behalf of women of color by distancing themselves from white feminism and, as the indigenous scholar Dion Million says, "choosing strategies and language that locates them within the heart of their own experiences."[54] As one RJ activist told me, "I consider myself a feminist but don't claim that identity. It doesn't make sense to place that label [feminist] on us, and 'women of color' captures our politics in a way that doesn't negate any of our identities." It seems that "women of color" is a phrase that reflects low-income racialized women's political subjectivity even as they retain strong racial-ethnic-national, gendered, sexual, and other identities.

An important turning point in the movement for reproductive justice took place in 2004, when women of color refused to join a national march initially using the word "choice," which seemed to limit the politics to abortion and excluded non-English speakers. Loretta Ross recalled, "We women of color felt that the abortion framework, the choice framework, was just too narrow a vessel to talk about the threat to women's lives. We were dealing with the [George W.] Bush administration, an immoral and illegal war in Iraq, the Patriot Act, poverty—all these things would not be challenged by just talking about freedom of choice. I mean, if we made abortion totally accessible, totally legal, totally affordable, women would still have other problems. And so reducing women's lives down to just whether or not choice is available, we felt was inadequate."[55] Jessica González-Rojas, executive director of NLIRH, pointed out, "You can't even translate that word [choice] into Spanish in the same context. Sometimes you say 'pro derechos' [pro rights], but it's just not the same; not everyone knows what you mean. Like when you say 'pro-choice' [in English], everyone knows what you mean. So, there were a lot of cultural things that we were putting into that conversation." Indeed, these activists would agree with Iris Lopez's critique: "The ideology of choice is the basis of the fundamental ideal underpinning American society: that we live in a free society, that as individuals we have an infinite number of options from which to choose, and that because all individuals are presumed to be created equally, regardless of race, class, or gender, we all therefore must have equal opportunity to choose."[56] After threatening to boycott the march, women of color negotiated their participation in what became the March for Women's Lives, in which over a million people demonstrated on behalf of women's rights.[57] Mindful of the power of framing, reproductive justice activists take care when using the phrase "reproductive rights," which they see as often representing the mainstream, that is, the experiences of white, middle-class women.[58] Cristina Aguilar, former executive director of COLOR, clarified how reproductive justice framing is important: "Reproductive justice asserted that women of color and low income women, marginalized groups, do not have the power that 'choice' implies and that we needed the movement that was working to eradicate the barriers that get in front of women's ability to enact 'choice.'"

A key process of reframing also occurred in a position paper issued in 2005 by Asian Communities for Reproductive Justice (which later changed its name to Forward Together) and SisterSong.[59] They offered an expanded definition of reproductive justice: "reproductive justice will be achieved when women and girls have the economic, social and political power and resources to make healthy decisions about our bodies, sexuality and reproduction for ourselves, our families and our communities in all areas of our lives."[60] This definition emphasizes the structural bases of inequality experienced by women and girls of color and challenges neoliberal thinking about "individualized and independent notion of access" to reproductive health care and "instead views access as collective and interdependent."[61] Eveline Shen, executive director of Forward Together, recalled, "At that time the national movement was starting to consolidate. Reproductive justice groups were saying, 'We're pretty different in terms of how we're doing reproductive rights.' That paper was really saying, 'Actually we're pretty different in terms of how we define the problem, the solutions, and who are our primary constituencies, and we need to work together.' That [report] catapulted us to the national scene. We got a lot of requests to talk about reproductive justice and to partner." The position paper clarified that reproductive justice organizations differ from two other sectors working on women's reproductive health: those providing reproductive health *services*, such as access to contraception, prenatal care, birthing support, or abortion provided by organizations such as Planned Parenthood, and those working on reproductive health *policy*, such as efforts for comprehensive sex education in schools or to change legislation related to abortion, such as those promoted by NARAL Pro-Choice America.[62] Reproductive justice advocates often collaborate with those who are working on reproductive health services and reproductive health policy; indeed, many reproductive justice organizations include those who work in reproductive health policy and reproductive health services on their boards of directors.[63] Cristina Aguilar pointed out the importance of clarifying the unique approach offered by reproductive justice: "What's really important for us is that we're defining it every time we use it to ensure that it is something that is lifted up as an empowering term." Indeed, as we will see, a strengths-based approach is key to reproductive justice organizing. Several prominent reproductive health organizations, such as Planned Parenthood, now use the term "reproductive justice," rather than "reproductive rights," according to the sociologist Zakiya Luna, "suggesting a continued impact [of the reproductive justice movement] on the women's movement."[64]

Asian Communities for Reproductive Justice and SisterSong included an image in their paper that represents how reproductive justice intersects with other social justice movements (see plate 1).[65] This image reminds me of a Tibetan prayer wheel and indicates the ways in which the reproductive justice movement pivots so as to collaborate with other social movements. The ongoing efforts to join forces with other social movements is exemplified in the webinar series Collective Voices, which Monica Simpson, executive director of SisterSong, characterized as "moving our framework further, wider and deeper, looking on the intersection of reproductive justice and other social justice issues."[66]

By 2017, Forward Together expanded the definition of reproductive justice so it was even more inclusive: "All people having the social, political, and economic power and resources to make healthy decisions about their gender, bodies, sexuality, and families for themselves and their communities."[67] Other organizations followed suit and explicitly began including men. In 2017 SisterSong announced its #WECOMMIT project, "A Declaration of Response and Responsibility from men regarding rape culture, racism, and toxic masculinity, led by a cis gender male staff member."[68] Black Women for Wellness organizes an annual "Bring a Brother to Breakfast" event that gives awards to men for their hard work in the Black community. And Forward Together and ICAH include young men in their youth programs, while CLRJ and TWU explicitly reach out to men.

When I conducted interviews with staff working in nonprofit organizations and activists who focus on reproductive justice, I asked whether there were organizing models or concepts they followed. I heard time and again that they do not follow specific theories of change—one executive director even said, "I hate the idea, theory of change!" Instead, they incorporate two broad approaches to praxis that engage human rights with the theoretical/political framework of intersectionality that feminists of color in the United States began articulating in the 1960s and 1970s.[69] Women's publications at the time reported on women's and liberation movements in the Third World and celebrated International Women's Year in 1975, linking local struggles to those abroad.[70] While women have participated in many international fora, the United Nations World Conference on Women in Beijing in 1995 was pivotal, as was the United Nations World Conference against Racism in 2001 and the United Nations Committee to Eliminate Racial Discrimination in 2008.[71] At these conferences, women of color collaborated with activists from the Global South who were using a framework that linked racism, xenophobia, violence, and poverty with gender discrimination and homophobia. They recognized that human rights activism should be enacted in the United States as well.[72] Indeed, the National Asian and Pacific American Women's Forum was founded, according to former executive director Miriam Yeung when participants in Beijing realized that "there was no organized voice for Asian or Pacific Islander women from the United States to participate in the official UN conference," and they formed the multi-issue NAPAWF in 1996.[73] Reproductive justice activists followed the path that Amitra Basu observed: "the UN international conferences enabled women from around the world to meet and collaborate, forming relationships that lasted long after the conferences ended."[74] The need for situating women of color within a global perspective on women's rights is articulated by Loretta Ross and colleagues: "Whether through the neglect of health care delivery systems or through aggressive population control strategies, the reproductive health rights of women of color are constantly compromised by poverty, racism, sexism, homophobia, and injustice."[75]

The reproductive justice social movement integrates human rights and intersectionality to make political claims in three ways. First, it engages in the Gramscian war of position, which entails long-term countermovement by civil society with the goal of subverting mechanisms of ideological diffusion.[76] This work includes base-building, in which reproductive justice nonprofits conduct grassroots organizing in communities of color. As we will see, particular campaigns reach out to specific categories of women—such as undocumented Latinas, minors, or Black women—and may last for several years, or campaigns may arise in response to proposed legislation. Reproductive justice organizations build their bases through community education, training low-income women of color regarding their human right to access health care through forums and curricula presented in workshops, institutes, or *cafecitos* (coffee klatches), where the setting is smaller and informal, which allows for deeper engagement. Some reproductive justice organizations have set up chapters or paid membership bases. Organizational supporters or members can be mobilized for lobbying events, demonstrations, or other activities like get-out the-vote campaigns or cultural activities. Activists in the movement for reproductive justice take great pride in their grassroots organizing; indeed, they see this work as distinguishing them from those who are working on reproductive rights or reproductive health policy.

A second line of reproductive justice organizing is "culture shift work," which begins with critiques of deficit thinking and negative representations about people of color. Instead, reproductive justice activists situate their work in a framework that also draws on the strength, resiliency, and spirituality of people of color. Culture shift work also includes working with artists to strategically offer alternative theories, narratives, or representations about women of color in specific campaigns in which the goal is to educate the public, including particular communities. Again, drawing on Gramsci, culture shift work entails knowing oneself in the context of history; practitioners name and expand on individual concerns and strategize for their collective experience.[77]

The third level of work by reproductive justice organizations is policy advocacy at the federal, state, or local levels. Policy work includes crafting legislation and working with legislators to sponsor and shepherd bills through legislative bodies, conducting research, writing position papers, submitting amicus briefs for lawsuits, or testifying before legislative bodies or for court cases. Reproductive justice organizations also lobby public officials for implementation of policies already on the books or to support the allocation of resources to make those policies effective.

There is a great deal of overlap, so that grassroots organizing, culture shift work, and policy advocacy are linked by reproductive justice organizations. Indeed, several organizations conduct primary research to understand the views of women of color on reproductive health issues or to identify the issues they deem important, and then use those findings to inform their community education, culture shift work, or policy advocacy. González-Rojas emphasized the movement's overall goal: "When you say community mobilization, policy advocacy, and education through culture shift—we're building power. That's what we're doing, and we are going to use that language moving forward. . . . Our role is to be agents of change."

Like other social movements, reproductive justice activists self-consciously construct a collective identity that emerges through the actions they take together. The term "women of color" emerged in the 1980s and is associated with the path-breaking book *This Bridge Called My Back: Writings by Radical Women of Color*, edited by Cherríe Moraga and Gloria Anzaldúa.[78] Through poetry and self-reflexive essays in this book, women of quite diverse identities powerfully expressed their pain and the ways they cope with oppression. "Women of color" signals "a political identity, a way of acknowledging our interconnections, reflecting upon our common contexts of struggle, and recognizing the *different* ways that structures impose violence, separation, and war on each of us."[79] Indeed, identifying as women of color is a step toward consciousness-raising and seeking the empowerment of communities of color.

Collective identity also emerges out of common experiences that distinguish women of color from the dominant society, such as being targets of policing practices, as in the case of the #SayHerName movement, which raises awareness for Black female victims of police brutality and anti-Black violence in the United States or the xenophobia that views immigrant women's fertility as a threat to the nation.[80] In addition to forming a collective political identity out of social action and differential treatment, collective public identity also is dynamic since it requires engagement with participants' multiple identities. Like some other social movements, reproductive justice constructs a public collective identity around the logic of inclusiveness. Thus, this intersectionality approach leads reproductive justice activists to use the term "women of color," which has a long history of embracing women of quite diverse racial, ethnic, national, gender, or sexual identities. The use of "women of color" is visible in Facebook posts by different organizations as well as in different reproductive justice convenings.

Simultaneously, many reproductive justice organizations honor historically specific racial and ethnic identities such as Native American, Asian American, African American, and Latina. Yet within these collective identities there are political impulses to problematize them.[81] The movement recognizes internal diversity by national origin for migrants. For example, Senait Admassu, founder of the African Communities Public Health Coalition, which works with the African diaspora, presented at a reproductive justice conference. She pointed out that African migrants hail from fifty-four different countries in Africa, "which makes linguistic and cultural sensitivity hard." The movement is also attentive to the particular experiences of indigenous peoples as well as Blacks and those of mixed race.

Activists also began using "Latinx" rather than "Latina/o" to signal the questioning of binaries related to gender and sexuality and to include those whose sexual or gender identity is fluid. Strong Families New Mexico cited an article explaining the significance of using "Latinx": "The x makes Latino, a masculine identifier, gender-neutral. It also moves beyond Latin@–which has been used in the past to include both masculine and feminine identities—to encompass genders outside of that limiting man-woman binary."[82] Activists and scholars have debated the emergence of the term "Latinx" or the more general "womanx." Some view "Latinx" as gender inclusive, foregrounding gender-nonconforming people;[83] others argue that it silences gender struggles;[84] and a third group of scholars see "Latinx" as demonstrating "a continuity of internal shifting group dynamics and disciplinary debates."[85] Similarly, some organizations, like Tewa Women United, deliberately avoid gender-neutral language, according to executive director Corrine Sanchez:

> We're gender-inclusive in recognizing the LGBTQIA spectrum and continuum of identities and sexualities; however, we've been challenged because in reproductive justice and identity politics, our transgender siblings want us to be gender neutral; we push back because our experiences are not neutral in any way, shape or form. We've experienced what we've experienced as Native women *because* we're Native women, and to erase

that and put a gender-neutral frame on that is erasing our experiences again. It is a hard conversation, and, to me holds a lot of privilege. In other words, in this conversation you have the privilege of saying, "I'm going to be X" or "I'm not going to be this and that." Whereas, as Native women, we've never had that privilege to say we're not women; and the truth is, our violence is happening to us *because* we are women.[86]

Informed by the passion and logic of these debates, in this book I use "Latinx" in place of "Latina/o" and use "Latina" when discussing women-specific issues.

The movement is also attentive to other differences within racial-ethnic communities, such as age (some programs are oriented to youth, while others honor the elders) or educational level (those with college degrees approach reproductive justice differently from immigrants with limited formal education). Thus, organizations continually strategize how to recruit particular constituents. Christina Lares, former community engagement manager of CLRJ, points out that they continually ask, "What is the best way to reach out to the community? How should we work with different groups?" Their strategies include deciding which language to use—Spanish or English. Reproductive justice organizations also must vet the location of venues depending on the specific audience they are trying to reach, whether it is accessible by public transportation, and how those who live in rural communities have different needs from those who live in big cities. As we will see, like Latinx activists, Native American, Asian American, and African American reproductive justice activists are attuned to differences within racial-ethnic categories related to age, national origins, language, location, or legal status. This movement's attention to diversity, then, is not about bringing outsiders into previously white institutions but about ensuring that activists are continually paying attention to the specific needs of all women of color and fine-tuning their organizing methods accordingly.

The movement for reproductive justice goes far beyond advocating identity politics. Reproductive justice activists recruit those who are marginalized by institutions—low-income women, women of color, LGBTQ people, the undocumented, rural women, or youth who have limited legal rights—for purposes of accessing the human right to health care and advocating for social justice.[87] Reproductive justice activists especially work on behalf of the structurally vulnerable who experience state violence directly. Indeed, there are calls to queer reproductive justice by making explicit how LGBTQ people also need an array of reproductive health-care services as well as bodily autonomy and freedom to express their sexual identities.[88] Yet each of the thirteen reproductive justice organizations with which I conducted research incorporates LGBTQ issues into its work, and five of the executive directors are lesbians. Through community organizing, policy advocacy, and culture shift work, the RJ movement moves beyond vague notions of racial disparities by pursuing specific rights and resources that would fundamentally restructure societal treatment of all women of color.[89]

To analyze the activism of women of color within the movement for reproductive justice, I build on the scholarship that emphasizes women's flexibility and skilled navigation of multiple social fields or borderlands.[90] These are women whom the lesbian writer-theorist Gloria Anzaldúa calls "Nepantleras" since they contend with borders between nation-states or categories of power as well as spiritual syncretism constructed when hegemonic cultures are imposed through violence.[91] This scholarship demonstrates women's ability to negotiate multiple forms of subjugation and the formation of coalitional consciousness—concrete practices intended to sustain collaboration despite members' differences in identities, constituencies, and resources.[92] Indeed, Angela Moreno, board member of SisterSong, says, "What draws me to RJ is the Nepantla of it: that it is continuously in motion; that it is in between even though it has room for absolutes; and the way that it is a map and also a continuous confirmation that nothing is static and everything is relational and interdependent. So, in a world where systems cause harm, applying RJ principles prevents this from being made monolithic. It requires that all of us are seen and heard for our great complexities." The activists working in the movement for reproductive justice develop organizing skills and coalitional consciousness as well as teach us how to construct strategic collaboration by problematizing difference within structural conditions.

In the current era in which resistance by diverse participants seems to flourish in mainstream politics, reproductive justice advocates take care to acknowledge that they have a long history of negotiating difference among participants.[93] Further, reproductive justice proponents take care to distinguish themselves from other social movements by focusing on women of color. As Marsha Jones puts it, "Part of being unapologetic is not asking permission to do the work."[94]

The Praxis of Intersectionality

Intersectionality has been a capacious theoretical framework for understanding political praxis that includes legal and policy advocacy to remedy discrimination based simultaneously on race and gender. Kimberlé Crenshaw, widely attributed as having coined the term "intersectionality," states, "While the primary intersections that I explore here are between race and gender, the concept [intersectionality] can and should be expanded by factoring in issues such as class, sexual orientation, age, and color."[95] Intersectionality illuminates social movements that engage with multiple forces, as well as how women's subjectivities, identities, and emotions shape their expressions of agency.[96] Key texts that analyze politics using an intersectional approach illustrate the flexibility that activists must cultivate as they negotiate dynamics of difference and sameness in relation to axes of power around gender, race, or sexuality in local movement contexts even when activism takes place in international venues.[97]

An intersectional approach includes four major components: (1) Intersectionality is an epistemological practice that looks for alternative sources of knowledge to help fill the gaps in understanding and silences in the historical record, legal documents, scholarship, and discourses about citizenship and human rights that ignore women of color. Besides drawing on primary research, reproductive justice advocates also draw on spirituality, cultural practices, vernacular knowledge, and the senses in their analyses of social problems and expressions of identity. (2) Intersectionality is also an ontological project that accounts for multiple identities and complex subjectivity and reconceptualizes agency while acknowledging the simultaneity of privilege and oppression.[98] Reproductive justice activists are quick to highlight the needs and agency of those who are structurally vulnerable within communities of color, such as gender-nonconforming or trans people or undocumented immigrants, and call on those who have privileges—such as advanced educational degrees—to advocate on behalf of everyone. (3) Intersectionality engages in coalitional politics grounded in solidarity rather than sameness, which is strategically constructed while working to eradicate inequalities. (4) Intersectionality is also a resistant imaginary that disrupts dominant social discourses about people of color and intervenes in historical memory, often using artwork or narratives.[99] The feminist scholar Vivian May adroitly sums up how an intersectional approach to reproductive justice addresses a broad range of issues including "widespread poverty and an ever-increasing wage gap; environmental hazards and pollution in poor rural and urban areas; increased disparities in access to health care and in life span and rates of illness; immigration and citizenship policies which unduly impact women; ongoing anti-natalist policies and practices with regard to disability; race, poverty, and citizenship; endemic and escalating forms of violence against women, much of which remains underreported and unaddressed; and intensified rates and forms of incarceration and their gendered politics and implications."[100] Emphasizing the simultaneous coconstruction of race with gender, class, and sexuality places reproductive justice advocates at odds with those who see race as primary.[101] As TWU environmental justice manager Beata Tsosie-Peña observed during a presentation on reproductive justice, "It's important that we bring our *whole* selves into these spaces and these movements."[102] In an interview, Cristina Aguilar affirmed, "In reproductive justice, you're not checking any identities at the door; in fact, you're really invited to do the opposite, to show up in *all* of your identities, your hopes, your dreams."

Women of color theorists also see intersectionality as rooted in a colonial matrix of power, which has multiple implications.[103] The Peruvian sociologist Anibal Quijano argues, "What is termed globalization is the culmination of a process that began with the constitution of America and colonial/modern Eurocentered capitalism as a new global power. One of the fundamental axes of the model of power is the social classification of the world's population around the idea of race, a mental construction that expresses the basic experience of colonial domination and pervades the more important dimensions of global power, including its specific rationality, Eurocentrism."[104] The sociologist and feminist philosopher Maria Lugones makes a critical intervention to this formulation by pointing out that coloniality of power glosses patriarchal and heteronormative discourses imposed by colonialism and calls for critiques of racialized, capitalist, and gender oppression.[105] The Bolivian feminist subaltern theorist Silvia Rivera Cusicanqui argues, "the possibility of a profound cultural reform in our society depends on the decolonization of our gestures and acts and the language with which we name the world."[106] Indeed, the feminist theorist Laura Pérez further suggests that "feminist queer of color critical thought is central to the work of decolonization," and "we must undertake [the critique] collectively, in solidarity, and alongside the critique of our own subject formations."[107] By theorizing the origins of social constructs related to race, class, gender, and sexuality in coloniality rather than bodies, the movement directs attention to the anthropologists Jonathan Rosa and Yarimar Bonilla's observation that modern colonialism is a "practice of violence, assemblage, superordination, exploitation, and segregation," as well as the interdisciplinary scholar Maylei Blackwell's insight that the coloniality of power also generates new forms of organizing.[108]

It is vital to consider the importance of place and focus on organizations that include the perspectives of those who are multiply marginalized by institutions, women of color with low incomes like Lola.[109] I analyze how women of color in reproductive justice organizations contest structural processes of power within particular contexts in relation to one another and simultaneously see activism on behalf of women as integral to the well-being of all.[110] I also illustrate how women of color construct political strategies and identities while attempting to end reproductive injustice.

The Human Right to Health

The notion that those who are marginalized by society in the United States deserve human rights and that these rights were linked to the Declaration of Independence and the Constitution was first articulated by the social reformer Frederick Douglass in the 1850s. He also argued that access to economic, social, and cultural rights should accompany human rights.[111] Yet it was not until the post–World War II era that the United Nations issued guidelines for government activity related to human rights.[112] The Constitution of the World Health Organization declared in 1946 that the right to health includes public health, sanitation, occupational and environmental conditions, education and nutrition, and medical treatment provided in a nondiscriminatory manner, expressing the idea that human rights are inextricably intertwined.[113] Women have pushed for the notion that "women's rights are human rights," a slogan first used at the UN World Conference on Human Rights in Vienna in 1993. The United States ratified three international human rights treaties that protect women's reproductive rights: the International Covenant on Civil and Political Rights, the International Convention on the Ratification of All Forms of Racial Discrimination, and the Convention against Torture. The United States also signed the Convention on the Elimination of All Forms of Discrimination against Women and the International Covenant on Economic, Social, and Cultural Rights, which confer important reproductive rights such as the right to health.[114] However, there is no right to be healthy under international or national law.[115] The right to health care is not mentioned in the US Constitution, and states are not required to pay medical expenses of indigents, though most provide some health coverage for the elderly and people with disabilities.[116] Nonetheless, the World Health Organization's definition of optimal health care was a critical intervention, a "step toward denaturalizing the suffering produced by social causes."[117]

Increasingly, social movements have taken up the cause of ensuring that states provide access to health care for all, which includes confirming that health facilities, goods, and services are available, sensitive to ethnic and cultural concerns, of high quality, and based on scientific evidence.[118] The moral foundations of health systems that provide universal coverage— seen as the highest standard of health-care delivery—are solidarity, community, equity, and dignity: "Respect for human dignity demands that no one refrain from seeking medical care due to fear of the consequences of doing so, and that no one suffer financial adversity as a result of having sought care."[119] This view was also expressed by Pope Francis, who declared, "health care is a right, not a privilege."[120] However, evoking human rights in the United States often carries more moral authority than legal efficacy when international agreements are unenforceable.[121]

Activists attempting to further the human right to health care aim to foster understanding of social problems that contribute to human rights violations and their moral implications as well as to mobilize shame so as to generate change in policies and practice.[122] The scholarship on human rights directs our attention to "the governments, armies, corporations, or other entities that are violating rights," yet the political scientist Rosalind Petchesky reminds us that "today 'human rights' covers a much broader swathe of issues than egregious . . . crimes."[123] The study of human rights by ethnographers initially focused on debates about whether universal rights were salient in relation to particular cultural groups and historically specific conditions.[124] Given the variability and historical specificity of human rights claims, ethnographers have moved toward an understanding of human rights as "a type of politically consequential normative framework that is constituted through social practice."[125] Ethnographers encourage us to present descriptive analyses in a framework where people build what the anthropologist Meg McLagan calls a "formidable transnational communications infrastructure through which 'local' actors' claims . . . are formatted into human rights 'issues.'"[126] Thus scholars should specify what human rights mean for different social actors and how they relate to transnational assemblages—material, collective, and discursive relationships in which "the forms and values of individual and collective existence are problematized . . . so they are subject to technological, political, and ethical reflection and intervention."[127]

Human rights activism is a key reframing in the movement for reproductive justice. As the human rights activist Malika Dutt clarifies, "understanding human rights as the *right to be human* underscores the fact that the paradigm is not a language game but a mechanism through which we understand that we cannot take rights seriously without taking human suffering seriously."[128] Further, according to the feminist historian Jennifer Nelson, "A human rights discourse moves the conversation beyond the dichotomy of the 'right to choose' abortion or carry a pregnancy to term versus the absence of that choice to an understanding that real choices require economic, cultural, and social environments that ensure a real range of options."[129] Indeed, Rosalind Petchesky argues that human rights, reproductive health, and economic justice are indivisible and that "reproductive and sexual rights for women will remain unachievable if they are not connected to a strong campaign for economic justice and an end to poverty."[130]

Thus, reproductive justice advocates emphasize the historically specific conditions in which different categories of women of color are denied access to health care and other rights and push for accountability by the state and relevant social actors.[131] Loretta Ross and her colleagues affirm, "rights are legal articulations of claims to meet human needs and protect human freedoms."[132]

There are tensions related to melding an intersectionality framework, which highlights structurally based inequalities that disproportionately affect vulnerable people, and human rights discourse that often uses neoliberal logic seeking redress for the universal individual subject.[133] Native Americans, for example, are the beneficiaries of the United Nations Declaration on the Rights of Indigenous Peoples (UNDRIP), passed in 2006, that supports human and civil rights. However, that declaration does not have the force of law and only establishes a "moral high ground" where signatories are obliged to uphold the standards of the UNDRIP for indigenous people seeking cultural, political, or economic goals, but implementation takes place within nation-states that may not honor indigenous sovereignty.[134] Further, UNDRIP does not define indigeneity or recognize political self-government from indigenous nations, which limits their ability to consent to upholding human rights protections.[135]

These tensions are problematic in the United States, where settler colonists claimed that indigenous peoples, African slaves, and other groups were racially inferior and treaty rights with Native Americans have not been honored.[136] Further, in the contemporary era there are debates about whether people have the right to health or to health care that take place in a context in which legislation, the marketplace, medical training and research institutions, and "alternative" medicine shape how care is delivered.[137] Indeed, pushing for the human right to health care may seem quixotic when many Americans would lose coverage through repeal of the ACA, designed with the belief, according to Barack Obama, "that health care is not a privilege for a few, but a right for all."[138] The ACA included coverage of reproductive health care (contraception, mammograms, and annual gynecological exams) without copayments, ended the insurance-industry rating system that charged women more than men, banned insurers from refusing coverage to people with preexisting conditions, and included preventative health services like screening for colon cancer for adults over fifty, well-child visits, flu shots for all children and adults, and many more services.[139] However, an estimated eleven million undocumented immigrants in the United States were barred from Medicaid and the Children's Health Insurance Program, and the undocumented (along with those with Temporary Protected Status and Deferred Action for Childhood Arrivals) could not purchase private insurance from health insurance exchanges. In a study done in 2014 with thirty-three independent health agencies across nineteen states, one in four American Indian and Alaska Native people under age sixty-five had no health insurance, a rate three times higher than that for non-Hispanic whites, and the rate of uninsured youth was over three times higher than the rate of non-Hispanic white children.[140] These exclusions were rarely mentioned in the national debates about the ACA.[141]

Another tension in using a human rights framework is that some activists may feel pulled to concentrate their efforts within international venues such as the United Nations, which may detract from their local work. The "NGO-ization" of social movements or reliance on the "nonprofit industrial complex" may lead to diminished immersion in grassroots organizing.[142] Indeed, human rights may become "the specialized language of a select professional cadre with its own rites of passage and methods of certification."[143] However, a human rights framework provides the basis for seeking redress on behalf of structurally vulnerable people to lead healthy lives with *dignity*.[144] Malika Dutt clarifies, "When one moves to define rights as fundamental human rights, one claims the notion of a self in relation to others, a claim which, for historically disempowered groups of people, is an important step in declaring their humanity."[145] Moreover, social activists work as cultural translators; according to the anthropologist Sally Engle Merry, they "present their initiatives in cultural terms that will be acceptable to at least some of the local community" by translating "local grievances . . . into the powerful language of transnational human rights."[146] A key component in human rights training is capacity building with structurally vulnerable populations.[147] Cultural translators help to forge symbols, ideologies, or organizational forums in which participants are trained in the human rights framework and provide a means for their implementation. As community members become aware of human rights violations related to health, they may experience a profound shift in their subjectivities.

As we will see, the reproductive justice movement is innovative in its use of human rights and emphasizes its radical implications. It builds on the thinking of indigenous human rights activists who embrace a collectivist view toward human rights, which according to the cultural theorist Rosa-Linda Fregoso, "long spearheaded the transformation of existing human rights norms to incorporate more complex and flexible understandings of human rights."[148] The notion of the right to have rights extends to nature as well, such that bodies of water, forests, or mountains should be protected along with humans.[149] Reproductive justice activists also claim women's right to cultural citizenship and to use their preferred language and cultural expressions in public.[150] Reproductive justice activists collaborate proactively at different scales—local, state, national, and international—regarding the interconnections of multiple human rights issues.[151] They craft alternative meanings about the rights of women, focusing on women of color, and mobilize the enactment of policies, practices, and narratives that ensure that those rights are realized. As Loretta Ross and her colleagues clarify, "Intersectionality is our process; human rights are our goals."[152] By emphasizing that different social categories become structurally vulnerable while simultaneously asserting the claim to equality, freedom, and dignity, these activists construct a politics rooted in difference. Further, the movement for reproductive justice self-consciously and strategically problematizes collaboration and advocates wholeness of body/mind/spirit among activists and participants. The approach to change constructed by advocates of reproductive justice, situated in intersectionality and human rights praxis, is fluid and complex and leads them to craft particular strategies.

My Research

I situate my work in the tradition of feminist activist research, in which we commit to the people with whom we work and engage *with* them on behalf of shared political goals.[153] Further, I do not presume that I am the sole bearer of knowledge generated through research. I agree with the sociologist Manisha Desai that "research is an ethical and epistemological stance where the scholar is one of many producers of social change oriented knowledge."[154] Given my research questions and my interest in how multiple organizations collaborate and negotiate the tensions around difference and similarity, I conducted participant observation in multiple sites. Instead of seeing the reproductive justice movement as somehow connected through some global force as suggested by the term "multi-sited ethnography,"[155] I came to see how organizations advocate for reproductive justice in light of shifting politics at local, regional, national, and transnational levels and how activists build skills related to collaboration. Eveline Shen captured this evolution nicely: "When I first came in the movement, a lot of the work that reproductive justice groups were doing was very, very local. Over time, however, reproductive justice organizations constructed an infrastructure that strategically incorporated innovative ways to collaborate with one another across multiple scales." While reproductive justice activists in different parts of the country share similar visions and practices and frequently collaborate on particular campaigns, they also craft local praxis. I do not want to leave the impression that there is a homogeneous reproductive justice worldview. These activists are working in states with very different policies, including those related to health-care access or immigrant rights, and with particular racial demographics and regional cultures. Mindful of the importance of these differences, at a reproductive justice conference, Black Lives Matter cofounder Patrisse Khan-Cullors reminded us, "We *have* to ground down locally."[156] Given the large number of reproductive justice organizations, it would not be possible to do justice to all of their processes of collaboration. Therefore, this book focuses on particular organizations' campaigns that illustrate their grassroots organizing, policy advocacy, and culture shift work that are part of the reproductive justice movement yet express local work.

I have had ongoing negotiations with reproductive justice organizations that set the terms for my participation in their work. In most instances, executive directors were remarkably generous and allowed me to conduct participant observation, including with their youth projects, and welcomed me into the fold. I agree with the anthropologist Shannon Speed that the social dynamics of the research process should be open to an ongoing dialogue with many interlocutors.[157] Such transparency respects the multiple perspectives among the people with whom we work and leads to multilayered knowledge, which encourages ethnographers to maintain some humility and self-reflexivity.[158]

Over time as reproductive justice advocates came to know and trust me, I became integrated into a dynamic system of knowledge production as new issues came up. The research for this project was processual—"a spiraling cumulative progression"[159]—that covered multiple sites and incorporated several techniques: My research, conducted in 2013–18, spanned the second administration of President Obama and the beginning of the Trump administration. During this time, I did participant observation at sixty-seven workshops, conferences, training institutes, lobbying efforts, political events, and webinars organized by reproductive justice organizations. I also conducted sixty-eight interviews with staff working at thirteen reproductive justice organizations, all but two face-to-face, and several more than once, as well as with community members who participated in reproductive justice organizations. I sent transcripts of the interviews to most of the staff I interviewed and gave them the opportunity to elaborate or refine their thoughts or to delete sensitive material.[160] I also interviewed sixteen allies: activists or advocates in social justice organizations that support people working on reproductive justice, funders of reproductive justice organizations, or people working in programs that provide reproductive health education. I did these latter interviews early in the research process as a means of identifying what was unique about the reproductive justice approach and to gauge how other organizations work with youth. In addition, I conducted twelve focus groups with twenty-three staff members and forty-one participants in the reproductive justice movement. Virtually all of the reproductive justice organizations with which I conducted staff interviews are led by women of color, as are the participants in these organizations' youth projects. In some instances, these categories overlap. For example, all the staff in YWU are under thirty-five years old and the organization recruits young women participants; several others have mostly young women on their staff. I also had numerous informal conversations with reproductive justice activists at events, over coffee or meals, or on the phone, where I received updates and clarifications about their ongoing activities, and several individuals shared internal documents with me. Throughout my research, I was open about my engaged participation rather than passive observation.

In line with the growing scholarship on the Internet as a key site for ethnographic research,[161] I also examined reproductive justice organizations' strategic use of websites and social media (mainly Facebook and Twitter) to advertise events or disseminate their framing of issues.[162] I "liked" or "followed" as many reproductive justice organizations as I could, and I became a member of two organizations, Black Women for Wellness and SisterSong. Through these means I received information about their campaigns pretty much on a daily basis. I admit at times I felt overwhelmed by the frequent calls for political action, especially after Trump was elected president.

As I came to see, the executive directors and much of their staff in reproductive justice organizations are quite accomplished. Most have completed college, and many have advanced degrees—master's degrees, law degrees, or doctorates—in such fields as ethnic studies, film, feminist studies, justice studies, Latin American studies, public health, and sociology.[163] Thus, they are knowledgeable about intersectionality theory and other analytic approaches to social justice. Many individual activists have received accolades for their work in the nonprofit world.[164] Philanthropedia has recognized three organizations—Forward Together, National Network of Abortion Funds, and National Latina Institute for Reproductive Health—for their leadership in reproductive justice organizing and the Center for Reproductive Rights and Justice honored CLRJ for their activism related to repealing caps on social welfare.[165] Thus, the leadership of the movement for reproductive justice has a great deal of experience moving between the worlds of academia, activism, and policy making. I often found the interviews with staff to be analytically nuanced and revelatory. Simultaneously, these leaders had firsthand understanding of the skills needed to work with their communities and were particularly sensitive to language use and the importance of engaging community members in ways they felt comfortable.

My own positionality related to power and privilege brought up some challenges while I conducted the research. Some of these advocates were familiar with my scholarship and voiced their appreciation for my contributions. Others, however, either were apprehensive about having a researcher in close contact or were hesitant to allow my participation in private organizational projects. As we discussed my possible involvement in a new network of organizations focusing on reproductive justice, for example, one staff member voiced every ethnographer's nightmare: "Just the gravitas of having you sitting in the room gives me pause," she said and declined my request. Another organization insisted on vetting my focus-group guide and consent form before I was invited to work with its members. In a few other instances, with my ability to travel and talk with staff from multiple organizations, I observed tensions over collaboration. For example, one organization thought about moving into a state where there were already several reproductive justice organizations, and in another instance a RJ leader publicly questioned why there was no work being done along the US-Mexico border when a sister organization had been working there for years. Also, I was privy to gossip about activists or organizations that are challenging to work with and to leaders' struggles with stress and burnout associated with activism as well as conflict with mainstream organizations or leaders. I always indicated that I would honor the need to keep organizational processes confidential if need be. Thus, in instances of delicate relationships between organizations over territory, acknowledgment of leadership in campaigns, political conflict, or personality differences, I remained neutral. I reminded interviewees that I would not write about confidential issues and would share my writing with them if they desired, and several did give me feedback on my work in progress.

I occasionally collaborated with reproductive justice organizations and bonded with the staff and, after attending multiple events by one organization, was regarded "like family." My collaboration included codesigning and helping to administer an evaluation form for a day-long workshop by CLRJ. Also, I was asked to sign the "Open Letter to Planned Parenthood," in which reproductive justice organizations critiqued the silencing of women of color activism, which I did. I organized a twenty-fifth-anniversary celebration and fundraiser at my house for Forward Together. I gave copies of my field notes and photographs to staff at ICAH, COLOR, and CLRJ about specific activities when the organizations indicated that these materials would be helpful. I made modest donations to several reproductive justice organizations during fundraising campaigns or moments of crisis. I organized a keynote plenary panel, "The Movement for Reproductive Justice in the Southwest," that included representatives from four reproductive justice organizations for a conference sponsored by Mujeres Activas en Letras y Cambio Social (Activists Women in Letters and Social Change) in 2015 and another panel in 2018. With the support of COLOR executive director Cristina Aguilar, I designed and administered two focus groups as part of the organization's successful campaign against a constitutional amendment on personhood in Colorado. Aguilar and I later presented on a scholarly panel together about COLOR's work.[166] After organization leaders had read my work about their organizations, I was invited to join the boards of directors of CLRJ and ICAH and to make a presentation on civic engagement at the Leadership Development Institute in South Texas by the Latina Advocacy Network (LAN), sponsored by NLIRH. Over the course of this work I have formed warm friendships with some of these activists, who were generous with their time and insights (and even organizational swag).

All of these collaborations were part of my feminist praxis, and I provided feedback after the organizations' events and shared whatever critiques I had with them. Most of my feedback was about fine-tuning their work since for the most part I found myself with few substantive criticisms.

Overview of the Book

My overall argument in this book is the following: The organizations discussed here provide a compelling model for negotiating across difference during social activism. Further, in the current political era, in which the "war on women" and targeting of immigrants seems particularly egregious and there are widespread questions about whether "the resistance" can maintain its cohesion, the movement for reproductive justice offers a model for multiscalar politics in relation to opposing conservative agendas and the disparagement of specific social categories.

Chapter 1 explores the centrality of cultural politics, as reproductive justice organizations collaborate strategically with artists and researchers to inform specific campaigns. It discusses five initiatives that contest vilification of women of color and stereotypes about "the family" and offers alternative narratives and representations. I argue that through reframing, reproductive justice activists contest dominant thinking about women of color, serve as cultural translators of the reproductive justice framework, and promote the discourse about empowering women of color.

In chapter 2 I respond to Kimberlé Crenshaw's query, what are intersectionality's "ready-to-work skills?" by focusing on two campaigns run by reproductive justice activists. One is about the human right to health care in Texas that led eventually to the lawsuit *Whole Woman's Health v. Hellerstedt*, and the other is about the repeal of the Maximum Family Grant (MFG) rule in California. I argue that reproductive justice activists resist conservative forces using strengths-based messaging; cross-sector collaboration, including support for one another; and strategic use of storytelling in the context of safer spaces.

Chapter 3 focuses on youth mobilization by three different reproductive justice organizations that use the language of youth empowerment. I argue that increasingly storytelling is becoming a methodology within the movement for reproductive justice, and I illustrate how organizations train youth to use narratives to convey analyses of social problems and to garner support from policy makers and community members for specific policy changes. Youth's participation in reproductive justice youth programs helps them to navigate the transition to adulthood with the understanding that true empowerment addresses structural inequalities.

Chapter 4 explores the framing "from self-care to healing justice" by drawing on Gloria Anzaldúa's thinking about spiritual activism. I present four cases of self-care as well as public practices that help communities heal from historical trauma. I argue that the work of self-care and spiritual activism in communities of color contests the individualism embedded in neoliberal health-care systems and instead crafts the collective politics of healing justice.

The conclusion reflects on how the movement for reproductive justice addresses the increased polarization of politics around immigration and reproductive rights in the wake of the election of President Trump. I argue that women of color in the movement for reproductive justice craft a politics of inclusion that aims to empower those who are marginalized by intersecting systems of power. These activists insist that poor women of color have the human right to healthy lives and access to health care with dignity as well as the right to health itself.

1

Culture Shift Work

Let's commit to naming the risk instead of blaming young people for the violence they experience, or calling young people resilient without acknowledging we need culturally safe support.
—Alexa Lesperance, Native Youth Sexual Health Network

Through arts . . . we can become more in touch with our full humanity.
—INCITE! Women of Color Against Violence, SisterFire tour

The framing of contentious issues is a critical process by social movements and shapes how supporters and critics attribute meaning to their interventions.[1] Reproductive justice advocates are well aware of the need to frame issues from the perspective of women of color, as illustrated in the epigraphs. They are familiar with deficit thinking, influential views by political leaders and scholars that see social problems as originating in low-income people themselves. Deficit thinking includes concepts introduced by scholars, like "culture of poverty," "matriarchal Black family," or "urban underclass," all which view individual intelligence, behavior, decision-making, or cultural orientation by those with low incomes as predictors of poverty and poor health outcomes.[2] Even supposedly neutral frames that gloss over social inequalities, such as "colorblind," "not racism," or appeals to "individual responsibility" while ignoring structural impediments, are problematic for critical thinkers.[3] Deficit thinking also includes misleading stereotypes about women of color, such as "welfare queens," which circulated long before Ronald Reagan but continues despite the fact that during his administration 62 percent of recipients were white.[4] The notion of a "welfare queen" was a cover story for reducing government spending on social welfare programs while silencing the actual experiences of those who need support.[5] A more recent stereotype is immigrant mothers producing "anchor babies" to gain legal permanent residency through their US citizen children. Conservatives have proposed legislation that would deny the children of immigrants their US citizenship, which, the anthropologist Leo Chavez argues, views these women and their children's citizenship as undeserving.[6] According to the feminist historian Laura Briggs, these blaming discourses against women of color produce dual effects: "the illegitimacy of some families" and ongoing efforts to eliminate benefits to support them.[7] Indeed, the neoliberal notion that people with low incomes are irresponsible is widely accepted: in a poll conducted by the Pew Research Center, for example, 60 percent of respondents agreed that "most people who want to get ahead can make it if they are willing to work hard."[8] Health inequities often are linked to particular populations rather than cast as structural features of the US health-care system. Thus, when access to health care is limited or particular social categories experience health-care problems, attention is deflected away from structural causes.[9]

Mindful of the power of representation, reproductive justice activists view framing, which articulates dissent and presents new perspectives in ways that create shared identity, as critical for generating long-term change. Their framing takes on conservative ideologies such as "strong family values" or "children having children" and views social problems as based in structural inequalities that marginalize women of color. Reframing also entails seeing adversity in a positive light, according to Yamani Hernandez, former executive director of ICAH:

> I often tell the story of . . . when my parents separated before their long divorce. We lived without utilities for many, many months. My mother never phrased [that experience] to me as adversity. She gave us cool survival backpacks with flashlights and snacks and told us that we had been selected for the test of Jedi training and that we would *win*. I look back on that and I don't discount the pain and difficulty that she must have felt as a single parent with three children under 6 trying to make us feel secure. But seeing her resourcefulness and the magic of her reframing is training that stays with me as well.[10]

The meaning of resiliency to reproductive justice activists goes beyond people's ability to withstand or endure hardship and includes how they frame life challenges to incorporate people's creativity in coping with them. In this social movement that links intersectionality and human rights, reproductive justice activists insist on contesting hegemonic frames and offering representations and messages that link macro political and economic issues with the resilient lived experience of multiple generations of people of color, which they term "cultural shift work." Such reframing differs from the individualist notion of resiliency and has a long history in social movements.[11] Further, the movement for reproductive justice takes framing further by recognizing women's full selves with a balance between mind, body, and spirit (see chapter 4).

Scholars suggest that framing includes "ways of packaging and presenting ideas that generate shared beliefs, motivate collective action, and define appropriate strategies of action."[12] When used by social movements, framing encompasses four processes: frames define a social problem in relation to specific values, identify the causes of the problem, render moral judgments about the causal agents or forces, and identify remedies to address the problem as well as predict their likely effects.[13]

Culture shift work resonates with the conceptual work of scholars that illuminates how marginalized people survive institutional mistreatment and pejorative discourses by drawing on their cultural values and norms as well as their experience of lived resilience. For example, Gloria Anzaldúa calls our attention to "la facultad," the perceptual and interpersonal skills that allow border dwellers to assess uncertainties, power differentials within social relations, and tensions related to social meaning, as well as to negotiate them by drawing on their complex identities.[14] Inés Casillas and Jin Sook Lee argue that language other than English should be nurtured since it sustains the cultural heritage of youth of color and enables them to express their complex identities and social agency.[15] Lorena Garcia documents young Puerto Rican and Mexican heterosexual and lesbian women's strategies for safer sex and self-respect.[16] Norma González and her colleagues offer the concept "funds of knowledge," based on the premise, "People are competent, they have knowledge, and their life experiences have given them that knowledge."[17] Sofia Villenas reflects on Latina migrant mothers' narratives of dignity and moral education in rural North Carolina.[18] And Tara Yosso views "cultural capital" as incorporating marginalized people's aspirations and resiliency, recognition of family and kinship as including community members, ability to leverage social networks and community resources, ability to navigate through social institutions and communicate through multiple languages and expressive forms, and ability to use their knowledge and skills to challenge inequality.[19] These scholars emphasize how people of color find resiliency *despite* structural inequalities and pejorative discourses that objectify us. Reproductive justice scholar-activists frame how we conceptualize social inequalities and incorporate the dialectics related to historical memory, critical consciousness, fortitude, survival, and social transformation. The psychologist George Ayala and colleagues, who work with HIV-positive clients who are mainly Latinxs, illustrate how strengths-based cultural shift work frames people of color: "A strengths-based approach is crucial because it . . . values . . . individuals and communities as key social actors who not only face dilemmas, uncertainties, and responsibilities but also possess considerable agency, brilliance, and creativity."[20]

This chapter discusses the cultural politics constructed by activists in the movement for reproductive justice as well as their praxis in which they frame the family and women of color in public discourse. We explore how reproductive justice organizations engage in culture shift work, framing that uses a strengths-based approach that is organically constructed from their experience working in communities of color.[21] In everyday use, reproductive justice organizers refer to culture shift as "shifting the frame," "culture shift messaging," or "flipping the script." Further, cultural work is broader than framing. Reproductive justice organizations use cultural notions and the experiences of people of color with resiliency in their political praxis as well.

We will consider the multivocality of social movement discourse through five cases: (1) the theorizing of culture shift by the National Latina Institute for Reproductive Health, which launched a "Soy poderosa [I am a powerful woman] and my voice matters" campaign; (2) the "somos chingonas" (rough translation: "we're badass women") messaging of California Latinas for Reproductive Justice; (3) the critique of strong family values discourse and Strong Families Network led by Forward Together with organizational support by Strong Families New Mexico and Western States Center; (4) the critique of teen-pregnancy discourse and advocacy for young parents by CLRJ and Young Women United;

and (5) the Black Mamas Matter Alliance led by SisterSong. I argue that these organizations deploy framing that incorporates strength-based narratives to motivate collective action, to define appropriate strategies of action, and to shape dominant discourses about women of color.

Theorizing Culture Shift

NLIRH has conceptualized culture shift work as including four efforts aimed at transforming dominant cultural narratives (see figure 1.1).[22] Their representation resonates with the work of many reproductive justice advocates who work with other racial groups. Culture shift work includes cultivating women leaders and spokespersons who can articulate the reproductive justice approach to issues. Like NLIRH, other organizations, such as CLRJ, COLOR, Forward Together, ICAH, TWU, and YWU, have projects that train young women to become leaders and spokespersons for reproductive justice in relation to their respective communities. These young advocates become quite adept at articulating the specificities of a reproductive justice approach as well as local needs. Trainings that frame young women's experiences may be offered over a school term or during summers. Daylong workshops with other organizations, such as Advocates for Youth, enhance youths' skills in lobbying and storytelling and cultivate their identities as community leaders.

A second feature of culture shift work by reproductive justice organizations is that they conduct research, either reviews of scholarship or policies on key issues or primary research conducted through polls, surveys, interviews, or focus groups. Initially some activists in the movement resisted conducting research since they found that their own knowledge of women's lived experience was invaluable. However, over time, activists acknowledged that their communities are diverse and that research helps identify, recruit, and retain participants in the movement as well as identify new issues, as former Ford Foundation program officer Lourdes Rivera says: "You have to find the sweet spot so we don't lose people and we actually bring people along."[23] Since many of the executive directors have advanced degrees, they are trained in the use of research methods and use their findings to refine their advocacy work. YWU, for example, conducted focus groups

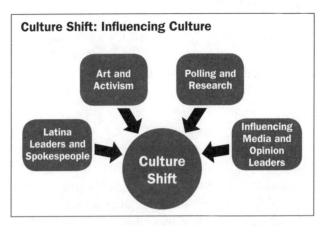

Figure 1.1. Culture shift: influencing culture, by the National Latina Institute for Reproductive Health (Used with permission by the National Latina Institute for Reproductive Health)

with mothers recovering from substance use. During the focus groups, women talked about their recovery, some for the first time, and their insights inform YWU's efforts to improve access to prenatal care and treatment for pregnant women in recovery.[24] According to former YWU executive director Tannia Esparza, "That is what started this campaign of ours: to really look at substance use and cycles of addiction, which here in New Mexico, it is very likely you will run into a family who has a family member or they themselves have been living through cycles of addiction. Instead of looking at the root causes of why our communities are coping with cycles of generational trauma in this way, what people do is they criminalize people."[25] The staff found that culture shift work was critical, according to Esparza: "In 2011 we passed a bill, Treatment Instead of Incarceration Bill. But with our very conservative governor it got vetoed. We decided, maybe policy isn't what we need to do, but what we need to do is change the hearts and minds of our community to really understand that cycles of addiction are really rooted in the cycles of criminalization that our families have been living through for years, for generations."[26] YWU's reframing was based on focus groups with mothers in recovery who acknowledged that their shame sometimes hindered their access to health care. By contesting societal stigma against families in which mothers are in recovery, YWU contributes to their social recognition and eventually their access to health care.

The third line of culture shift work is collaborating with artists and storytellers to create what NLIRH calls "culturally relevant and dynamic vehicles" for organizations' core reproductive justice messages.[27] Reproductive justice organizations commission artwork—by painters, graphic artists, poets, playwrights, photographers, or musicians—to be featured in their campaigns, or they invite artists to represent community histories or learn how to become working artists themselves.[28] SisterFire, a network of organizations led by women of color, formed a tour by artists who worked to highlight the importance of artistic expression and met with several RJ organizations. Increasingly reproductive justice organizations are making sure to include artists in their budgets instead of relying on artists' donated labor, and they are cultivating relationships with artists to help formulate their long-term strategies to shift dominant narratives.[29] Indeed, SisterSong initiated a program called Artists United for Reproductive Justice that aims to "raise new questions and conversations, inspire compassion, spark activism, and rally multitudes around a cause."[30]

As part of YWU's work to promote birth and parenting justice, for example, the organization held a public education campaign and five-week art and education workshop, "We Are More than Our Addiction," that included several posters, launched on Mother's Day 2014.[31] Esparza described the goals:

> To really talk about the ways that women and families are struggling with cycles of addiction and incarceration but also to talk about the strengths and resiliency that our communities bring: the way we provide our own healing when the state denies it to us. And so we worked alongside three New Mexico–based digital artists. . . . We were really proud to bring in the artists into the organizing to translate the messages that women and families were talking about through art on the sides of buses with the desert and a pregnant person holding her baby and struggling to keep herself and her family alive.

Esparza made a point of highlighting YWU's work with artists: "We really believe in resourcing our artists because the work that they do is not just to make us look pretty, but it is actually organizing work that needs to be valued. And so we were really proud to bring in the artists into the organizing to translate the messages that women and families were talking about."[32] In a presentation about YWU's work, Micaela Cadena, former YWU policy director, proudly pointed out, "We do research for ourselves, by ourselves."[33] Primary research is critical for tailoring campaigns by other reproductive justice organizations.

One of the reproductive justice movement's most important collaborations has been with Favianna Rodríguez, whose well-known artwork was birthed in immigrant activism. Her classic pieces "Migration Is Beautiful" and "Undocumented Unafraid" circulate widely. On her blog she depicts the butterfly as a metaphor for migrants, and a film clip characterizes her as an activist. She asserts through her artwork that "being undocumented is not a crime" and that "immigration is central to women's equality." More pointedly, Rodríguez argues, "the artist must fight for justice and peace," with an image that represents a woman of color.[34] Rodríguez's images are used by reproductive justice organizations across the country, particularly her "Yo Te Apoyo" (I support you), used by NLIRH's "soy poderosa and my voice matters" campaign (see plates 2 and 3). Indeed, Rodríguez's "Yo Te Apoyo" image echoes NLIRH's emphasis on racial diversity among Latinas in its prior logo, and she adds a woman (on the right) with gray hair that could be considered depicting an elderly woman.

Yo Te Apoyo is a campaign supporting women's right to regulate their fertility, including the right to have an abortion. The campaign includes a short video that represents the findings from NLIRH's survey on abortion. Then the video represents diverse people—women and men, whites and Latinas of different racial backgrounds—who state, "Yo te apoyo / I support you."[35] In 2017, NLIRH amplified its Yo Te Apoyo campaign by using Rodríguez's image in support of women's reproductive decision-making related to abortion.

Like some other activist artists, Rodríguez allows reproductive justice activists to use her images with their own political messages, a remarkable donation of artistic license. She has advised reproductive justice organizations about how to incorporate art into their advocacy work using strategic long-term planning. And she has conducted workshops with reproductive justice participants about how to become entrepreneurs and start their own businesses related to art. She has taken on the restrictions on women's access to reproductive health care directly with a poster titled "Stop the War on Women" that uses a reproductive justice framing of women's rights.[36]

Rodríguez also took part in a video that was part of the campaign, "1 in 3 women will have an abortion in her lifetime. These are Our Stories," sponsored by Advocates for Youth. Rodríguez is one of eleven prominent women featured in the "2016 1 in 3 Abortion Speakout." In the accompanying poster, she asserts, "There is No Shame in Having an Abortion. Come Out. Share Your Story. Break the Silence"; the poster circulates widely. On her website, Rodríguez explains that her abortion enabled her to accept her first prestigious art fellowship and that women should be open about enjoying sexuality and pursuing careers. Her "Sex Positivity" image, which she references during her abortion story, celebrates women's bodies and encourages viewers to "liberate" their sexuality.[37]

It is in Rodríguez's "Slut Series" (which she sometimes calls her "pussy powers" posters), where she boldly confronts the patriarchal politics of control over women's bodies, that we see her intersectional politics at work (see plate 4). Using depictions of women of color, she uses humor to critique the war on women with its derogatory language and threatens politicians that they will be voted out of office.

In an interview I conducted with Rodríguez about her "Slut Series" images, she pointed out, "When people look at it [Slut Series], they think, 'Oh, that's the missing link,' and they laugh and feel so good. It doesn't feel like a war [on women]. And that's exactly what I am trying to do. I am trying to frame our power and give people a stake that they can attach themselves to, in order for them to continue their work." The political messages in her art, including her Pussy Power Coloring Guides, critique the intrusiveness of politicians regulating women's intimate reproductive health decisions and contest the implicit racial demonization of women of color by assumptions that they are promiscuous. Thus, art can help framing by touching the heart or by making fun of the powerful. Rodríguez tweeted an image of the "I'm a Slut . . ." poster when the Trump administration announced its new policy allowing employers to opt out of paying for birth control if they have a religious or moral objection. (The Center for Reproductive Rights immediately filed a lawsuit challenging this policy, and it was blocked by the federal district court.)[38]

Finally, culture shift work by reproductive justice organizations includes cultivating relationships with traditional media and having a presence in social media in English and in other languages so as to reach broad and diverse audiences and to influence opinion leaders.[39] For example, in the midst of YWU's successful campaign against a proposed municipal ban on abortion, the organization formed a coalition that included faith-based activists and a range of others.[40] The group used photographs and memes on social media as well as radio ads from key leaders such as Dolores Huerta in its outreach efforts to the large numbers of Latinx voters. YWU's former executive director Tannia Esparza helped produce ads in Spanish for broadcast media, placing them on radio stations whose styles ranged from rock to country to *norteño* music, and she made presentations in Spanish on Univisión television news.[41] Another organization, SisterSong, started an RJ in the Media program that is working to bring the term "reproductive justice" "into its rightful place as a household term."[42] As we shall see in the cases to follow, multidimensional culture shift work entails creativity as well as long-term strategic planning.

Voicing Our Power: *Soy Poderosa*

As part of the National Latina Institute for Reproductive Health's strategic culture shift work, the organization has conducted a "soy poderosa and my voice matters" campaign for several years, highlighting it annually during early August. NLIRH defines its strengths-based approach this way: "A civic engagement campaign created to engage, organize, and lift the voices of the Latina community, regardless of immigration status and ability to vote, as we continue to mobilize a broad constituency in support of reproductive justice and work across movements to create sustainable change."[43] Diverse participants take their photos with a sign that says, "soy poderosa and my voice matters" and "I am powerful because"—and they fill in the blanks: "because I'm a human being," "porque soy feminista [because I'm a feminist]," "porque tengo una voz [because I have a voice]," and so on. The images of those who claim "soy poderosa" include women and men of diverse racial-ethnic backgrounds: Latinas, African Americans, and whites.

When NLIRH posts photographs of demonstrations or other events on social media where demonstrators are wearing tee-shirts with the organization's logo, often its supporters include young Latino men. These images disrupt our expectations about race and gender by having those who are not Latina post "soy poderosa" and leads this viewer at least to reflect on how and why those who are not Latinas post these photos. Are the women who appear to be Black or white actually Latinas? Does the man who appears white and posted "soy poderosa porque soy feminista" (I am a powerful woman because I'm a feminist) claim a feminine identity? Are those who are not Latina expressing their solidarity with NLIRH? I asked executive director Jessica González-Rojas about the diversity of participants represented in the organization's "soy poderosa" campaign. She smiled as she recalled, "For us it was about demonstrating support and being an ally to us. 'Soy poderosa' is a Latina claim, but it's part of our philosophy and values with a ton of alliances and collaboration and publishing work. So, engaging our partners in saying 'soy poderosa' was important." The "soy poderosa and my voice matters" campaign also illustrates intersectionality, according to González-Rojas: "Online women will say, 'I'm queer and I'm an activist and I'm an immigrant,' and like whoa, intersectionality! We try to really create the space to allow people to bring their whole selves to the movement. So that was really important." I asked a young man in South Texas how he felt wearing a "soy poderosa" tee-shirt, and he smiled and then shrugged and explained that the gender-bending language did not bother him because he was interested in supporting women.

The idea of "soy poderosa" came out of a survey that NLIRH conducted with the Reproductive Health and Technology Project on Latinxs' views on abortion. The organizations administered the survey to six hundred Latinx registered voters in twenty-five states, and half of the respondents used the Spanish version. The survey generated unexpected findings since the pollsters knew that the majority of Latinxs are Catholics and that the Catholic Church condemns abortion.[44] However, 68 percent of the survey participants agreed with the statement "Even though Church leaders take a position against abortion, when it comes to the law, I believe it should remain legal." Furthermore, 74 percent of the respondents agreed with the statement "A woman has a right to make her own personal, private decisions about abortion without politicians interfering."[45] Eighty-one percent agree that abortions should be covered by private or state-funded health insurance.[46] González-Rojas explained the significance of these findings: "From that poll we learned that you can't ask that four-way question; there's a standard way for asking: 'Do you think abortion should be legal all the time, legal most of the time, illegal sometimes, illegal always?' You'll get the 'illegal most of the time' when Latinos are asked that question that way. But when you say, 'No matter how you feel about the procedure, do you think women should make the decision for themselves?' You'll get like 70 percent of Latinos agree. So it's about language and framing." Later she emphasized that the survey was "a game changer": "The results were very complicated though and nuanced. And then about half the respondents were in Spanish, so it wasn't translated literally; it was 'what's the essence of the question?' and capturing that essence in Spanish, so it was a 'transcreation.'" As NLIRH researchers were analyzing the survey data, they categorized the respondents and began calling those in the category of being engaged and vocal as "las poderosas" and developed the campaign. González-Rojas stated, "We envision 'soy poderosa' as a civic engagement strategy: say, 'I am powerful and I vote. I am powerful and I support health care. I am powerful and I x, y, z.' So, the primary objective was to lift up our community by showing partners in cross-movement collaboration."

This research about abortion was instrumental in helping Young Women United and Strong Families New Mexico to lead the effort to defeat the proposed municipal ban on abortion in Albuquerque in 2013.[47] California Latinas for Reproductive Justice conducted similar research on abortion with 898 respondents. According to Ena Suseth Valladares, CLRJ's director of research: "We wanted to know what Latinos really think about abortion. We wanted to move away from the whole pro-choice/pro-life stance: Should it be restricted? Should it not be restricted? We wanted to ask in a completely different way, because the way that we understood it and the way that people talked about it was that it was a lot more complicated than just categorizing it as an either/or label. Also, we felt that pro-choice/pro-life was not something that was really translatable. I mean in Spanish what do you say?" CLRJ commissioned its survey with a research firm recommended by NLIRH and also had unexpected findings, according to Valladares: "We found that participants strongly believe that abortion should be an option for women; that tested really well. We also found that participants agreed that the information shouldn't be shaming or trying to change women's minds, so that was very heartening. We also found that over eight in ten participants strongly agree that every woman should have a right to decide for herself the number and spacing of her children." CLRJ uses these findings in its reproductive justice workshops and position papers.[48]

NLIRH sponsors Latina Advocacy Networks in Florida, New York, Texas, and Virginia with low-income Latinas, many of whom have limited opportunities for schooling. I witnessed how the organization promotes "soy poderosa" discourse during its leadership training in Texas. It makes the community meetings and trainings attractive and fun by offering food, playing games and holding raffles in which women win household items or notebooks, and playing popular music and showing film clips with political messages. Women who attend regularly receive a shirt that says "soy poderosa" on the front in royal blue and yellow colors with NLIRH's logo. When I was gifted one of the shirts, I felt welcomed into the fold. In addition, they normalize *poderosa* discourse when welcoming participants or asking how they are feeling; the response is always, "¡Poderosa!" When playing bingo, the winner yells out "poderosa" to signal that she has won. Women seem to delight in proclaiming that they are powerful, and several disclosed that coming to embrace their *poderosa* identity was a major departure from their previous experience. During the Leadership Training Institute, for example, Maria Bustamante felt compelled to share the reflections she wrote after learning about systemic causes of social problems: "As we empower ourselves through consciousness, we prepare ourselves with value and without fear. We continue the struggle, opening roads and transforming lives. In this great country that is formed by emigrants, we are part of this society. And we want the same rights to liberty and justice."

González-Rojas reflects on the overall importance of culture shift work: "I think that is the essence of power, knowing that you have a voice and you can use that voice in ways that could create change. Power is the use of your bodily tools, your autonomy, to be able to effect change in society and break down the structural barriers that prevent our community from being healthy."

Voicing Our Power: *Somos Chingonas*

CLRJ also engages in cultural shift work through its tag line, "somos chingonas," which can be found in its social marketing. The phrase originated after a presentation about its work, when one of its board members, Mily Treviño-Sauceda (a well-known activist with women farmworkers), remarked, '¡Ustedes son *chingonas!*' (y'all are badass women!), and it stuck. *Chingona* implicitly is sexually charged, since *chingar* literally means "to fuck," with problematic connotations of having dominance over those with whom one has sex. In *The Labyrinth of Solitude*, the Nobel Prize winner Octavio Paz rationalized misogynist treatment by colonized Mexican men over women by suggesting that *chingar* was culturally sanctioned. He also coined the epithet *Malinche*, critiquing the translator between the Spanish colonizers and indigenous peoples as a betrayer; the term is still used against women today and rationalizes mistreatment of women.[49]

Through the use of "chingona," CLRJ staff shift the frame from heteropatriarchal connotations, and "chingona" takes on three different meanings in the organization's work. "Somos chingonas" signifies an internal assessment, as executive director Laura Jimenez stated: "It is part of culture shift for us and within our own movement." On the one hand, women of color engage in a profound personal transformation as they come into reproductive justice organizing. Christina Lares, CLRJ's community engagement manager, clarified:

> When people get involved in movements, there's a place where you have to come to *within* and really find your own place in this work. A lot of times we have to heal ourselves and really address some of the issues that we have. And I think "chingonas" is the starting point for a lot of folks, of creating that power and then taking back of our stories and experiences and realizing we can change our realities, and we're not these stereotypes and these negative images that are portrayed in the media or are told to us by politicians. We're diverse, we're dynamic, we come from a history of struggle, and we have power. So, I think "chingonas" for a lot of folks, it jolts them, but that's who we are as an organization. We have those conversations, and I think a lot of folks, once they start to talk and learn and hear and heal, they really like to embrace that.

The cultural shift that women experience is reinforced by the ways in which the reproductive justice movement continually assesses its efficacy and resonance with the participants.

The second meaning is organizational, according to Laura Jimenez: "For me that ideology, 'somos chingonas,' is saying, 'We're not compromising here.'" In the long process of negotiating positions on proposed legislation with different coalitions, for example, often CLRJ activists have to explain their stances by pointing out that they would not choose between immigrant rights and women's rights since those categories overlap. This means they often have to educate, communicate, and negotiate with collaborators but also refuse to give up their core values. "Somos chingonas" articulates their intersectionality politics.

The third meaning of "somos chingonas" points to the hypervisibility and tokenism by women of color in institutional political venues. For example, in California, where fifteen million Latinxs made up 39 percent of the population in 2017,[50] there were only ten Latina state legislators.[51] For Myra Duran, formerly CLRJ's policy manager, the dearth of familiar faces can be daunting:

> For the longest time I was hard-pressed to find a lobbyist in Sacramento that was a woman and that was Latina. So, for me, "somos chingonas" is really about being unapologetic about who we are as Latinas, including how we look. Like for me, I'm all about disrupting professional attire in the capitol. I fucking hate that shit. So for me that brings up all that sentiment, especially for young Latinas that want to get into politics but they don't see themselves reflected in these places. And for me it's about being unapologetic and owning your voice, taking up space. We do badass work, but sometimes it's not reflected in or appreciated by mainstream organizations or mainstream movements. So it's trying to really flip the script on that.

In many ways, claiming "somos chingonas" also reflects a politics of integrity, in which the organization figures out its stance on an issue and is willing to accept the consequences for that, including being called obstructionist or other negative terms.

However, "chingonas" is a slang term that is more common in Mexican Spanish than in other countries in Latin America. Thus, "chingona" can reflect the dominance of Mexicans in California politics, with which some Latinxs do not relate. At a lobbying event, the group of five women I was with had a discussion of "somos chingonas," and a Puerto Rican woman said she preferred to use "jodona" (Caribbean Spanish with a rough translation of "badass woman"). When I mentioned this to the CLRJ staff, Lares smiled in acknowledgment and pointed out, "They find their own 'poderosa' or 'jodona,' 'peleonera [fighter],' 'ronca [bossy]'; whatever term they feel they can identify with, they can take that."

Other organizations have their own forms of empowering language. Eveline Shen, executive director of Forward Together, for example, signs her email with "In Power." COLOR calls its annual anniversary event that celebrates its founding *madrinas* (godmothers) "Viva la Diva." It also concludes its events by circling together and giving a group cheer: "¡Aaaay chingona!" (We're badass!). It also promotes COLORista discourse about young women's empowerment. The Strong Families Network extends strengths-based culture shift work toward the cultural politics related to families.

The Strong Families Network

Founded in 2005, participants are careful to say the Strong Families Network is not a coalition. It was initially called an "initiative," but eventually activists changed its name to a "network." In an interview, Shen characterized the Strong Families Initiative as incorporating the movement's three-pronged strategic approach: "Strong Families is a long-term initiative that is changing the ways we support a family, and for us a family is chosen or family of origin. And a strong family is one in which every member has the opportunity to thrive. So that means that we very much want to lift up the voices of those who can be more marginalized like women, girls, queer and trans folks. The core strategies that we use are movement building, policy change, and culture shift." According to González-Rojas, "Strong Families Initiative is a ten-year initiative to change the way people think about and feel and experience families."

The Strong Families Initiative was constructed organically out of EMERJ, Expanding the Movement for Empowerment and Reproductive Justice, led by Asian Communities for Reproductive Justice, which had been active since 1989.[52] Eveline Shen described the formation of Strong Families from EMERJ:

> Through EMERJ we brought groups that have never worked together and work in different states over an eighteen-month period. Then we realized that we wanted to figure out where we could really align ourselves around policy. For the most part, groups across the country are doing work around their communities, but we wanted to figure out what kind of united work we could do.
>
> We sat in a room for a few days in Oakland and mapped everything out, and what we came up with was the idea of families. Whether we were working on parental notification [of abortion], making sure that our youth have what they need, to banning of the shackling and taking advantage of women who are incarcerated and giving birth, to abortion access, to medication—everything. A lot that we worked on was tied to the notion that women are often the primary caretakers for the families. The connection that we have with each other—whether it is the chosen family or our family of origin—what gives us, as a human species, meaning to our lives. And so that is when the Strong Families Initiative was born, and we realized it's not just within reproductive justice; it's across the progressive movement. . . . So now Strong Families is the home for many organizations.

In 2018, there were over 220 partner organizations that had signed on as supporters of the Strong Families Network, which include those working on reproductive justice, immigrant rights, masculinity, tenants' rights, farmworkers' rights, and LGBTQ rights.[53] A few organizations collaborated on specific projects (see later in this chapter).

While Forward Together is the lead organization for Strong Families Network, anchor organizations include CLRJ in Los Angeles, COLOR in Denver, WSC in Portland, and Strong Families New Mexico and YWU in Albuquerque.

The Strong Families Network directly contests the conservative ideology of strong family values discourse. According to the sociologist Judith Stacey, strong family values discourse was promulgated by an "interlocking network of scholarly and policy institutions, think tanks, and commissions [that] began mobilizing during the late 1980s to forge a national consensus on family values that rapidly shaped the family ideology and politics of the Clinton administration and his New Democratic party."[54] Teen pregnancy in particular received extraordinary public attention, and often it was assumed pregnant teens were young women of color. The women's studies scholar Kimala Price clarifies, "By the early 1980s, the issue [teen pregnancy] entered the public consciousness and was placed on the national agenda along with other concerns such as crack-addicted mothers, drive-by shootings, and the failing educational system."[55] Prolife advocates viewed unplanned pregnancy as a lack of responsibility and control rather than contraceptive failure or lack of access to reproductive health care. By 2013, these supporters had formed the Traditional Values Coalition, which supports the "right to life" and "fidelity in marriage and abstinence before marriage," while opposing "homosexuality, bi-sexuality, transgenderism and other deviant sexual behaviors [sic]" as well as pornography and addictive behaviors.[56] These self-proclaimed warriors were "right-wing Republicans and/or fundamentalist Christians, overtly antifeminist, anti-homosexual, and politically reactionary."[57] The anthropologist Susan Greenbaum points out the political agenda of conservatives: "Family values, personal responsibility, the economic importance of marriage, the need to encourage work, and the diminution of the role of the welfare state, were prominent features of policy making and research."[58] This nostalgic ideology ignores structural and cultural changes going back to the 1950s, before the influences of the second-wave feminist and civil rights movements, which began transforming families in the United States.[59] The proponents of strong family discourse turn a blind eye to the multiple experiences of family life, and often their critiques of low-income families of color are expressed through coded language like "social decay" or "disorganization," ideas that circulate widely. Focus on the Family, for example, uses its nearly $90 million annual budget to deliver radio and other programs to an estimated audience of thirty-eight million listeners.[60]

The conservative views of families are belied by the twentieth-century discursive and material shifts that have led to the need for multiple contributors to household income. More than 50 percent of mothers with infants remain in the workforce, and 70 percent of US children live in households where all the adults are employed.[61] The decline in social welfare benefits to single parents, overwhelmingly women, led by "welfare reform" under the Clinton administration, means that more women are entering the labor market or returning to school, managing child care and other responsibilities with members of their support networks.[62] The marriage rate is the lowest ever, and the percentage of women who have children outside of wedlock has increased.[63] Further, increased immigration has led to families whose members have different legal statuses—US citizens, legal permanent residents, temporary protected status, or unauthorized. Immigrant families often maintain strong ties to their home countries and reconstitute intimacy through technology such as Skype or FaceTime that facilitates transnational communication.[64] And now that marriage equality is the law of the land, gay, lesbian, and gender-nonconforming families are gaining increased visibility as they juggle parenting, care for family members, and paid labor as they always have, though often through legal battles to have their families recognized.[65]

Reproductive justice advocates incorporate these many demographic, social, and legal changes into their representations of family and define their mission this way:

> Strong Families is a home for the four out of five people in the United States who do not live behind the proverbial picket fence—whose lives fall outside the outdated notion that a family consists of a mom at home and a dad at work. While that life has never been the reality for most of our families, too many of the policies that affect us are based on this fantasy. From a lack of affordable childcare and afterschool programs, to immigration policy and marriage equality, the way we make policy and allocate resources needs to catch up to the way we live.[66]

Highlighting family diversity and place, Strong Families New Mexico states, "We recognize that families come in all shapes, sizes, and ages; biological and chosen; living in one household, many households, or across national borders; documented, undocumented, or mixed status; with children or without. And we pursue both culture shift and policy change to ensure that all families have what they need to survive and thrive in New Mexico, the land of enchantment."[67]

The Strong Families Network has called for the right to comprehensive sex education and reproductive health care for adolescents, an exploration of sexual identities, recognition of diverse family formations among people of color, and a destigmatization and decriminalization of teenage parenthood. In an interview, Aimee Santos-Lyons, trainer and field coordinator for Western States Center, stated, "We brought people together to really challenge the discourse about strong family values directly: how do we build a *progressive* family values agenda? In that convening we developed guiding principles and a covenant among the organizations present to figure out how do we formulate our analysis and an agenda around this?"[68]

The Strong Families Network has three major goals: The first is to build movement infrastructure with a grassroots base of supporters through community organizing and developing organizational capacity. According to an interview with Adriann Barboa, executive director of Strong Families New Mexico, "The whole point of Strong Families is to see where there's a critical mass of folks already doing work that is aligned. If they need it, how do we connect them, but also how do we leverage some resources? And issues of power for coordination or facilitation or technical assistance? How do we bring resources to that critical mass already moving in a direction to really leverage it for the most power and most impact it can have?" One of Strong Families' reports, written with fourteen other organizations, fulfills this goal by presenting accessible information to help lesbians, gays, bisexuals, and trans people choose health-care plans.[69] Another pamphlet, a collaborative effort between the Strong Families Initiative, CLRJ, and NLIRH, provides information about how to vote in Spanish.[70] Second, Strong Families Network advocates policy changes that may be local, statewide, or national. At the national and state levels, they have been active in immigration reform and marriage equality, and at the local level, they were instrumental in helping defeat a proposed municipal ban on abortion after twenty weeks in Albuquerque.[71] A third key component of the Strong Families Network is a critique of the discourse that stigmatizes or marginalizes people of color, undertaken through cultural shift work. Cultural shift work can be seen in representations about families, in specific projects that advocate for particular marginalized groups and recognize that structural vulnerabilities place families at risk in relation to state policies that target, harass, jail, deport, or criminalize low-income people of color.[72]

Ongoing cultural shift work can be seen in the "Mama's Day Our Way" annual celebration of Mother's Day, launched prior to the Supreme Court's 2015 ruling in favor of marriage equality. Mama's Day Our Way includes a series of Mother's Day cards and artwork (see plate 5). These representations recognize the beauty and diversity of families of color and disrupt heteronormativity and dominant notions of masculinity by pointing out that men, including gay men, also nurture their children. There is also a "Papa's Day Our Way" project with artwork and cards representing diverse families. Mama's Day Our Way also includes political slogans—for example, "The flowers are lovely, but I'd prefer a revolution" and "Love makes a family"—and an online blog where anyone can post a photograph and narrative about their family, contesting the commercialization of Mother's Day and Father's Day. At the fundraiser at my house, Eveline Shen pointed out how heteronormative most Mother's Day greeting cards can be, which made her feel like her own family was not included and provided the impetus for honoring families that are diverse by structure, race, and identity. In 2016 Strong Families partnered with the immigrant rights organizations CultureStrike, Present. org, and NWDC (a grassroots undocumented-led movement) and sent Mother's Day cards to women in detention to help boost their morale after they staged a hunger strike to protest the conditions at detention centers.[73] The Mama's Day and Papa's Day cards have been downloaded in countries across the globe. Cristina Aguilar recalled that COLOR held a successful fundraiser using the Mother's Day cards: "People loved those cards! It's just incredible the way their imagery matches the communication and how much they resonated for our communities to actually see themselves."

The Strong Families Network is committed to creating the culture and conditions necessary for all families to thrive:

> We respect the decision of young people who make the choice to parent, or not to parent, and work collaboratively to change policies that inhibit young parents and families from succeeding. Strong Families knows that young parents have experience and expertise in identifying solutions to the challenges facing their families, which is why the leadership of current and past young parents is a necessary component of any change strategy we move. From advocating for legislation at the state level to addressing

problematic campaigns that shame young parents, the organizations and individuals involved in Strong Families [Initiative's] Young Parent Cohort are sharing and aligning their work to make culture and policy that shifts away from the culture of stigmatizing young parents.[74]

The reproductive justice movement's work of base building, policy change, and cultural shift about families came together in a recent election in Oregon. Western States Center had four organizations develop videos illustrating how families were being harmed by proposed ballot measures. According to Aimee Santos-Lyons, "These videos are very powerful with people telling their stories. One was saying her husband has been deported; she's now raising four children on her own, and she was pregnant when she was put in jail. She says, 'I understand why Strong Families is important. I understand why we need to be in solidarity with other organizations to build strong families. This election is going to be important because there are policies that matter.'" Strong Families New Mexico developed a Legislative Report Card that assessed eighteen pieces of legislation that would affect New Mexico families in 2014.[75] According to Adriann Barboa, executive director of Strong Families New Mexico, "For me it means not grading individual legislators; we didn't want to hurt relationships with legislators. We're pushing people to think about multiple issues at the same time—immigration, education, and environmental justice. The criteria are the heart of what we're trying to get at for community members and decision-makers. As we're building criteria, make sure are we including families of all formations, and ask, Will this harm other communities? Are we decreasing barriers? Yes, accountability but how we're measuring, not doing harm, and thinking positively." In Oregon and New Mexico, reproductive justice organizations saw framing the diverse needs of families as integral to their work advocating and monitoring policy changes. The Strong Families Network has produced numerous voting guides for different states.[76]

I was surprised when I first learned about the Strong Families Initiative, which tackles a discourse promulgated by powerful organizations. Yet Corrine Rivera-Fowler, former deputy director of COLOR, addressed my concerns: "Our opposition is really organized and really well funded, and we know that. But we have power and strength and muscle and might in our numbers. And it takes many years of organizing to change our public policies. But I know that we can do it together in unity." The notion of directly challenging powerful discourses also includes the cultural politics related to teen pregnancy prevention.

Contesting Teen Pregnancy Prevention

Cultural shift work critiques the discourse about teenage pregnancy that stigmatizes minors who bear children. Reproductive justice advocates believe that unintended pregnancy is the result of multiple structural inequalities that lead to lack of access to contraceptives or educational and employment opportunities that impede women's full autonomy. Further, reproductive justice proponents prefer to use the term "young parents" and highlight the strengths of families of color rather than blame women for making "poor decisions."[77] The need to frame teen pregnancy from the perspective of young women of color is clear, as Madeline Gomez and Sonya Rahders introduced a webinar titled "Shifting the Frame in Law & Policy from Preventing Teen Pregnancy to Supporting Young Parents":

> In recent years, pregnancy and birth rates among young people have declined, but young women of color still experience disproportionate rates of pregnancy and birth compared to their white peers. Additionally, young people that choose to parent are met with social and political stigma and policies that shame rather than support their families and choices. This session illuminates the need for a paradigm shift away from "teen pregnancy prevention" campaigns and toward dignity and respect for expectant and parenting youth, and identifies policies that can make this frame a political and social reality. Participants will leave with an understanding of the "young parents' dignity" frame, concrete tools and strategies for better messaging, and the ability to identify federal bills and that support young families.[78]

Tannia Esparza clarifies YWU's critiques of teen pregnancy prevention discourse: "We're really pushing against the teen pregnancy prevention model that tends to shame and stigmatize specifically young women of color for having children at a young age. That model is really utilizing young parents as scapegoats to avoid having to talk about larger systemic issues like poverty and lack of access to education."

In order to frame young parents with dignity, reproductive justice organizations take care to represent young parents at moments of accomplishment, such as being awarded their diplomas or completing certification for job training (see plate 6).[79] Further, in position papers RJ organizations cite research challenging the assumption that young parenthood inevitably leads to poverty, single parenthood, and isolation and instead point out that young parents are more likely to already be living in low-income communities and that their social networks provide resources and social support.[80] They also critique institutions such as prisons or the immigration system that separate families, including young parents. The Strong Families Network proponents advocate for policies that confer young people's rights such as access to health care or to an education. CLRJ has a ten-year "Justice for Young Families" project that critiques the discourse about the stigma of teen pregnancy (see plate 7).[81] According to executive director Laura Jimenez, prior to writing the position papers on young families, CLRJ staff members went through a self-reflexive discussion, as some of their families included young parents: "The staff realized, we are going to have to deal with this stuff, which means we are going to have to deal with our own stuff." The initiative asserts that adolescents who are parents should have the rights, recognition, and resources they need to thrive.[82]

Jessica González-Rojas explained the importance of contesting the pejorative framing of teen pregnancy:

> We fight against a lot of the teen pregnancy prevention rhetoric because it often doesn't include abortion and it often stops at the point when a woman becomes pregnant. Latinas have the highest teen birth rates in the country, and although it's going down a lot, it's still disproportionately higher, and their sexual behavior is not any different than young white teens. So it's not like they're having more sex; it's more that they don't have access to contraception and all those access issues. So we use a really different frame on our young parents, the perspective that they need support. You need to invest in them and engage them as leaders in the struggle.

Indeed, the pregnancy rate for Latinas who are fifteen to nineteen years old is about twice that of white women in the same age range.[83] However, the pregnancy rate for all teens has been dropping. In 2013 the teen

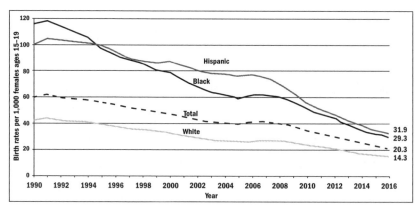

Figure 1.2. Birth rates per one thousand females, ages fifteen to nineteen, by race and Hispanic origin of mother, 1990–2016

pregnancy rate for all fifteen- to nineteen-year-olds was forty-three per one thousand women, which means that fewer than 5 percent of women in that age category became pregnant. In 2016, the US pregnancy rate among all fifteen- to nineteen-year-olds declined dramatically (see figure 1.2): "Although Hispanics still have a higher teen birth rate than their black and white peers, the rate has declined substantially in recent years. Since 2007, the teen birth rate among Hispanics has declined by 58 percent, compared with declines of 53 percent for blacks and 47 percent for whites."[84]

There has been an overall decline in sexual debut among youth, and the rate for Latina teen sexual debut is decreasing as well.[85] However, improvement in contraceptive use is the primary determinant of the decline in adolescent pregnancy and birth rates.[86] Clearly the discourse that women of color are having too many babies at a young age reflects the cultural politics that ignore the declining rates of teen pregnancy as well as the importance of addressing the structural issues that impede young women's access to contraception, education about preventing unwanted pregnancies, and jobs that provide resources that allow them to regulate their fertility.[87] Lauren Silver argues, "only when our analytical lens includes programmatic and institutional relationships can we fully understand the ways in which resiliency is not only individually located but also constructed within a social system."[88]

Young Women United developed a critique of deficit thinking that incorporated culture shift work in a recent report, "Dismantling Teen

Pregnancy Prevention." Micaela Cadena, Raquel Rivera, and their colleagues excoriate the discourse—and by implication the organizations that work on teen pregnancy prevention—and push for the human right to access health care.[89] Specifically, these activists critique the stigmatizing discourse about teen pregnancy that creates several myths. They marshal evidence against the myth that "teen parents are a drain on government resources and cost taxpayers a lot of money." Instead they argue that most of the estimates of the social costs attributed to young parents are connected to preexisting and systemic poverty. They critique the notion that "children of teen parents often have poor outcomes" by citing research demonstrating that having children at an early age has health benefits and that becoming a parent is often a time of turning toward more social and economic stability. In response to the stigmatizing discourse of "babies having babies," Cadena and colleagues point out that 73 percent of teenage mothers are over eighteen and thus legally adults in most states and that the adolescent birth rate has declined. They add, "We know that narratives that use young parents as scapegoats for alleged social ills deflect real accountability away from broad systemic issues plaguing our families."[90] Cadena and her colleagues conclude, "If we are committed to a bright future for all young people, then we must invest in honest dialog and real change, instead of perpetuating the misconception that teen pregnancy is a problem that must be prevented."[91] Former executive director Tannia Esparza pointed out, "It's not just about the policy, right? It is also about the culture shift and the hard work that we still have to do to make sure our communities are not being thrown under the bus. . . . We had to shape the narrative ourselves, but it was important to back it up with research." I first learned about this report through Twitter and then saw it posted on Facebook before receiving an email announcement about its release. Clearly the organization's audience includes young women who use social media.

YWU, in collaboration with other organizations in New Mexico, works on behalf of young parents' human right to an education, as seen in the organization's poster of a young parent in her everyday life (see plate 8). It also disseminates representations suggesting that young parents need recognition and social support, and it advocates for legislation that benefits all families. For example, YWU was able to secure legislation honoring teen parents. In 2012, YWU and Strong Families New

Mexico lobbied for passage of SM 25, which established a New Mexico Day in Recognition of Young Parents on August 25, the first legislation of its kind. A similar bill, "California Young Parents Day," was also passed in California in 2016 in a campaign led by CLRJ. YWU also helped gain passage of HB 300 (2013), which created a statewide excused-absence policy for pregnant and parenting students who need to take time to attend doctors' appointments for their children or themselves.[92] Further, its recommendations are based on primary research: YWU has conducted its own focus groups so as to understand the experiences and perceptions of young women, and its participants have engaged in self-reflection about their own experiences living and working in New Mexico communities. Its participants are Latina immigrants and US-born Hispanas, Native Americans, African Americans, and whites, heterosexual and non-gender-conforming. YWU has commissioned artwork by local artists, painters, photographers, and musicians to illustrate its campaigns. Tannia Esparza described YWU's strengths-based approach this way: "We are powerful, and the images that we want to put out are images of strength and resiliency."

By framing the needs of young families in relation to human rights, the movement for reproductive justice moves away from problematic blaming discourses and holds institutions accountable. In presenting the organization's work with young parents at a reproductive justice conference, YWU cultural strategy director Denicia Cadena pointed out, "We need to build the narrative before we can change policy." She elaborated further, "Young Parents Day wouldn't have happened if we hadn't organized young people and built relationships. We take a long-term approach, use graphic artists to change hearts and minds so people can feel what policy looks like. We built a frame that supports our families."[93] The importance of shifting the narrative about families of color is also seen in the Black Mamas Matter Alliance (BMMA), which advocates on behalf of Black women.

Black Mamas Matter

Initiated in 2013 and launched publicly in 2016, the Black Mamas Matter Alliance is a Black-women-led cross-sectoral collaboration formed to address the growing rates of Black women's maternal mortality and morbidity. This collaboration aims to stop the increasing numbers of Black women who are dying at a rate significantly higher than white women and other women because of pregnancy-related complications (see plate 9).[94] In New York City, Black women are twelve times more likely than white women to die because of pregnancy-related causes.[95] More worrisome, severe Black maternal morbidity affects approximately sixty thousand women per year in the United States, and that number has been increasing steadily.[96] These disproportionate rates of Black maternal mortality and morbidity occur across all educational levels and persist even after controlling for differences in socioeconomic status.[97]

The causes of maternal death in the United States are related to the social determinants of health, especially racial discrimination and poor treatment.[98] Where Black women live and receive health care significantly shapes their health outcomes and access to health care. Most Black women's deliveries (74 percent) occur in hospitals that are considered high and medium Black serving, many of which are located in the South. Black-serving hospitals provide lower quality of care and have higher severe maternal morbidity rates; these hospitals are also located in states that refused to expand Medicaid after passage of the ACA. In addition, the causes of Black women's mortality are complex and related to higher maternal age, obesity, rising caesarean delivery rates, and the increased number of pregnant women with preexisting chronic medical conditions. Black women have high rates of unintended pregnancy, more than twice the rate for white women—an indication of lack of access to contraception—and Black women have low rates of health insurance that would enable them to access health care.[99] Thus, any of women's preexisting conditions are exacerbated by the lack of access to quality health care.[100] Marsha Jones, executive director of the Afiya Center, summarized the "horrible conditions" of people living in poverty, also including a limited number of physicians who take Medicaid patients, higher unemployment rates, wage differentials, and segregated communities: "We see food deserts; these women are still eating from the corner stores. There is no store where you can get the best food possible. Are they really having those nutrition meetings? Is there any real full follow-through to make sure women have access to quality food care? And living in places where you have to travel on the bus for hours just to make your doctor's appointment. . . . We have legislators saying we are not going to expand Medicaid. Sixty days after the baby is born, they lose it [Medicaid]." In a live Facebook presentation that I happened to catch, Deneen Robinson, office manager of the Afiya Center, pointed out that all of these conditions are exacerbated by chronic stress that Black women face. "The stress of walking into a space where we're the only one. And then I decided I want to take on the stressful task of having a baby. The time of labor is its own stress."[101] Marsha Jones affirmed, "Every time you walk in the room, you expect to be on. And all the time you can't be on. . . . There's a lot of stress attached to being a Black woman."[102] The human rights scholar-activist Alicia Ely Yamin expresses the outrage that many of us feel about health disparities that produce maternal mortality: "it is primarily a social problem and a problem of political will at both the national and international levels . . . because [women] are discriminated against and excluded in their homes and communities and by health-care systems that do not prioritize their needs."[103] Clearly addressing these contributors to Black maternal mortality and morbidity requires a multifaceted approach.

According to the Black Mamas Matter Alliance, "We envision a world where Black mamas have the rights, respect, and resources to thrive before, during, and after pregnancy."[104] BMMA is led by Black researchers, doctors, midwives, doulas, and advocates, and its aims are fourfold: "1) Change policy: introduce and advance policy grounded in the human rights framework that address Black maternal health inequity and improve maternal health outcomes; 2) Cultivate research: leverage the talent and knowledge that exists in Black communities and cultivate innovative research methods to inform the policy agenda to improve Black maternal health; 3) Advance care for Black mamas: explore, introduce, and enhance holistic and comprehensive approaches to Black mamas' care; 4) Shift culture: redirect and reframe the conversation on Black maternal health and amplify the voices of Black mamas."[105] BMMA is staffed by SisterSong in Atlanta.

The BMMA initiative includes policy recommendations at the state level, acknowledging the ways in which different states have particular structural inequalities, racial groups, and political will.[106] BMMA's state policy framework provides a rationale for the focus on states: "When it comes to maternal health, states are strategically positioned to leverage regional knowledge about community needs and obstacles, build stakeholder networks, and implement targeted solutions. State leaders and lawmakers can take proactive measures to ensure that their states have effective health care systems to treat sickness and prevent disease and injury. They also have the power to design and implement other kinds of systems that create and promote health."[107] The standard of health that BMMA strives for is defined by the World Health Organization as "a state of complete physical, mental and social well-being and not merely the absence of disease or infirmity."[108] Different organizations are working on grassroots organizing in support of these policy changes and culture shifts. The Afiya Center, for example, based in Dallas, has been organizing Black women about their risk for maternal mortality, infant mortality, and HIV since its founding in 2010. Executive director Marsha Jones points out that Texas has the highest rate of Black infant mortality.[109] Like other partner organizations, the Afiya Center has organized workshops and used social media to educate Black women about their health risks, has issued a report, and is networking with other organizations.

While clearly this initiative includes policy work and grassroots organizing, it also highlights culture shift work. In a webinar, "Reproductive Justice and Black Women's Maternal Health," which launched BMMA to the public, SisterSong executive director Monica Simpson explained the organization's views on Black motherhood: "We wanted to make sure we include all working parents. 'Mama' is borrowed from Forward Together and includes cis women, gender-nonconforming and trans people— all that parent, that birth, that serve that role of mamahood."[110] Thus, this alliance's work echoes the culture shift work of the Strong Families Network, which is inclusive of gender-nonconforming people. Further, Simpson pointed out, "It's a strategy to actually shift perception, how people see and think, and in connection to those things that are heavier to talk about. . . . We need to really connect on a personal level and help people see issues from different perspectives. We can use strategies like art activism, like storytelling, to understanding the nuance. We are using it with a very broad scope." Then she quipped, "I could do culture shift work all day long!"

In 2018 Black Women for Wellness sponsored Black Maternal Health Week, in which the organization screened the documentary film *Death by Delivery* and sponsored presentations and discussions in Los Angeles.

The film includes footage of Monica Simpson, who calls the struggle for Black women's maternal health the "modern-day civil rights cause."[111] There is powerful footage of interviews with Black women who experienced childbirth as traumatizing. Katrina Anderson, formerly a human rights lawyer at the Center for Reproductive Rights, observes, "If the numbers were reversed and white women were dying at the rate that Black women are dying, there would be political will to address this problem. The US is the only country with an advanced economy where the maternal mortality rate has risen in the past decade. So we see this as not a problem of lack of resources but where resources are spent."[112] BMMA's work is gaining visibility as news outlets pick up the story.[113]

SisterSong is taking culture shift work a step forward. In 2017, it issued a call for artists to submit an image for its big conference, "Let's Talk about Sex," and started the Artists United for Reproductive Justice (AURJ) program: "Through AURJ, we are working to push communities beyond just telling stories and toward recalibrating reality through artistic mediums that allow for reclamation of space, representation, visuals, narrative, history, and community that is uncensored and fearless. We are also working to cultivate artistic leadership and strategy that can connect uncommon, idealistic, or even radical ideas with everyday life."[114] As BMMA moves toward implementing policy, conducting research, and engaging the other goals, clearly culture shift work is integral to this collaboration.

Conclusion

Reproductive justice advocates critique deficit thinking that blames subjects for their experiences of marginalization in relation to health, and they take a strengths-based approach. The reproductive justice organizations discussed here—Black Women for Wellness, California Latinas for Reproductive Justice, Forward Together, the National Latina Institute for Reproductive Health, SisterSong Women of Color Reproductive Justice Collective, Strong Families Network, Strong Families New Mexico, the Afiya Center, Western States Center, and Young Women United—and other reproductive justice organizations also engage in activist research. However, they also push our understanding of what activist research means. Their research enables them to better understand the nuances of women's experiences and to tailor interventions that garner trust and civic engagement with the aim of addressing structural inequalities and blaming discourses. These organizations use unexpected findings from their research and construct key frames—such as "soy poderosa," "somos chingonas," "strong families," "young parents," and "Black mamas matter"—that then inform their policy strategies.

By using the overall framing of human rights with intersectionality, reproductive justice organizations recognize both the diversity within communities of color and the historically specific struggles faced by particular social groups. They expect a standard of human dignity informed by human rights in which health care and the discourse about the struggles of women of color are culturally sensitive. Moreover, they offer a range of theories—concepts, metaphors, stories, models, and accounts—offering interpretive frames for making sense of evidence that is often ignored by political pundits, the public, and academic researchers. And they draw on the cultural practices in communities of color that allow for emotional expression. In this case, theory constructed by practitioners, designed, according to Faye Harrison, to "save our own lives," offers an innovative, multifaceted approach to framing.[115]

Further, the reproductive justice social movement illuminates its fluid engagement with multiple powerful forces. It illustrates the sociologist Marc Steinberg's point that "by artfully transforming the meaning of the discourses used to dominate them, challengers both provide their claims with credibility and cast doubt on the often assumed truths power holders voice through these words."[116] The artfulness of reproductive justice framing is particularly evident when representing the diversity of families in the United States. The intertextuality of discursive strategies is also striking: organizations use the slogans, images, research findings, and framing of sister reproductive justice campaigns and acknowledge one another's contributions. Reproductive justice advocates emphasize the diverse subjectivities, identities, emotions, and lived resiliency of women of color. More importantly, by recruiting women to engage in the internal work of contesting how they are represented by the dominant society, reproductive justice organizations work with women to find their "own place in this work" and begin the process of empowerment. By nurturing strengths-based approaches, reproductive justice activists contend that anyone can identify with powerful women.

2

Collaborating across Difference

If we are doing the work right, it shows us how to center access to ourselves first and then our communities and the oppressions that divide and connect us.
—Angela Moreno, board member of SisterSong

In 2014, Cecile Richards, then president of Planned Parenthood Federation of America, created uproar by reproductive justice activists when
the *New York Times* quoted her. She said, "I just think the 'pro-choice'
language doesn't really resonate particularly with a lot of young women
voters. We're really trying to focus on, what are the real things you're
going to lose? Sometimes that's rights. Sometimes that's economic or
access to health care for you or for your kids."[1] In this statement Richards ignored the long history in which women of color have contested
the term "pro-choice" and advocated for the human right to access
health care using the reproductive justice framework. Richards's comments sparked a national Twitter storm by those in the reproductive
justice movement who critiqued her statement. In addition, in a publicly circulated open letter cosigned by reproductive justice advocates
(including me), Monica Simpson, executive director of SisterSong, criticized Richards: "The recent exclusion of the long-term work of scores of
reproductive justice organizations, activists, and researchers that have
challenged the 'pro-choice' label for 20 years, seen recently in *The New
York Times* and *Huffington Post* articles, is not only disheartening but,
intentionally or not, continues the co-optation and erasure of the tremendously hard work done by Indigenous women and women of color
for decades."[2] I quote Richards's response at length for its complete con-
cession to all the letter's points:

We value your work deeply. We honor your past and present efforts to
broaden our collective efforts to address the multiple injustices that

women face. We appreciate that you push us to do this more, and to do it better. And we hear you when you say that we are not doing enough. Planned Parenthood has been proud to stand with our colleagues and partners who developed a reproductive justice framework that has contributed to important political and organizing victories—and has impacted millions of women's lives. The important fights that your letter outlined—from billboard campaigns to Medicaid expansion efforts to ballot initiatives—are battles that we have fought together, with and for women who need us to be strong, united, and focused on our common mission. I am eager to meet with leaders of national women of color–led RJ organizations to formulate shared strategies that honor all of our strengths. I'm also eager to talk to you about the events of the last few weeks, and what we can learn from this experience going forward. Thank you again for engaging in this dialogue openly and honestly. I can think of no better way to celebrate and honor the 20th anniversary of the RJ framework than to redouble our efforts to work together, and I look forward to continued conversation.[3]

Two months later, Monica Simpson and Cecile Richards issued a joint statement expressing their mutual support:

This summer, we found ourselves in a much needed, public conversation about the limitation of the pro-choice label, the important work of reproductive justice organizations, and the ways Planned Parenthood has fallen short in recognizing the contribution and framework of the reproductive justice movement. All of this led us to step back and think about how we could better work together.

A few weeks ago, we joined leaders from several reproductive justice organizations in Washington, D.C., and had a positive meeting about our desire to work more closely together to improve the lives of the communities we serve and advocate for daily. It was an honest conversation about some of the challenges in our working relationship, but more importantly, we agreed to an ongoing conversation and next steps to move our collective work forward.

We left our meeting hopeful and committed to building a stronger partnership, working together as we explore how intentional and mutually beneficial relationships translate into action. The people we serve need us to change our approach in order to secure reproductive health, rights, and most importantly justice. We jointly commit to being in better service to that goal and standing in community together.[4]

This new public expression of mutual respect with reproductive justice organizers helped Planned Parenthood weather the firestorm that erupted when a video that was edited to suggest the organization was selling fetal body parts surfaced a year later.[5] Several reproductive justice organizations issued their support of Planned Parenthood via social media and the press.[6]

We begin with this conflict and its resolution since it illustrates the challenges of collaborating on reproductive rights when using different approaches. Reproductive justice advocates have a history of confronting their silencing by mainstream feminist organizations, as we saw with the March for Women's Lives in 2004. In the years prior to and after this 2014 statement by Richards, many reproductive activists referred to mainstream feminists in frustration, often using the phrase the "big girls." I heard a number of stories in which women of color activists felt tokenized, and they strategized so as to be taken seriously as equal partners in organizing campaigns and receiving recognition for their work. However, many do not want those tensions aired publicly. With their human rights and intersectionality framework, RJ organizations desire and sometimes need to collaborate with feminist as well as other organizations, which means negotiating how collaboration occurs. I analyze the praxis by which participants in the reproductive justice movement deploy intersectionality strategically and concretely during collaboration with other social movement actors.

Scholarship using an intersectionality framework on women of color activism illuminates how participants negotiate dynamics of difference and sameness in relation to axes of power around race, class, sexuality, citizenship, or other power relations in local contexts. Chela Sandoval, for example, argues that women construct "differential consciousness" in which they express their material and psychic survival by negotiating across difference, highlighting their collaboration apart from hegemonic white feminism. She offers the concept "radical mestizaje," in which coalitions are built on the basis of "affinity and affection across lines of difference that intersect both in and outside of the body."[7] Cricket Keating suggests women construct "coalitional consciousness" by constructing practices oriented toward building and sustaining coalitions by creating narratives of identity and inclusion.[8] Elizabeth Cole and Zakiya Luna illustrate how women of color make coalitions work by actively constructing identities and negotiating shared values so as to deal with difference explicitly.[9] And Sonia Alvarez and her colleagues explore the many ways in which feminist discourses and practices travel through a "politics of translation" that is attentive to the production of situated knowledges in local sites.[10] Yet Kimberlé Crenshaw questions whether intersectionality has a "usable methodology" or "ready-to-work skills."[11] She advocates for the "need to *work* intersectionality and to develop methods that are both recognizable and insurgent within different disciplines."[12] Crenshaw is particularly interested in academics and activists "who use intersectionality to illuminate and address discriminatory situations that would otherwise escape articulation."[13]

This chapter examines how activists in the movement for reproductive justice work intersectionality by illuminating how discriminatory policies and negative discourses reinforce one another in denying women their human right to health care with dignity. I also address Shannon Speed and Jane Collier's call for analyses of the social life of rights that include "more detailed studies of human rights according to the actions and intentions of social actors, within wider historical constraints of institutionalized power."[14] I build on the theorizing about the politics of collaboration and examine two reproductive justice organizational processes that illustrate how their collaborative praxis incorporates intersectionality and human rights. I also discuss how reproductive justice advocates engage in the "politics of translation," in which feminist discourses and practices travel and become interpretive narratives that critique social inequalities in different contexts.[15]

As we see, the war on women takes on historically specific contours in states with a high percentage of immigrants where political, institutional, and social contexts—including employment, housing, and living conditions that include access to food and social services as well as their legal status—shape people's well-being.[16] In the first case, an effort in Texas by conservative state legislators to ban abortion led to debilitating barriers to accessing any health care for many low-income women. In the second case, in California, reproductive justice activists are training women who are often excluded from policy arenas and advocating for social welfare in ways that account for the complexities of women's lives. I argue that reproductive justice movement activists work intersectionality using particular methods—cross-sectoral collaboration, support for one another, storytelling in safe spaces, and a strengths-based approach. These practices concretize the praxis of intersectionality through what Kevin Duong calls "world-making"—creating a collective politicized identity that incorporates constituents across the political spectrum, including LGBTQ activists.[17] I begin by clarifying how cross-sectoral collaboration works in the movement overall, how reproductive justice organizations support one another, and how strengths-based storytelling is becoming a methodology, and then I present two cases in which storytelling was key.

Cross-Sectoral or Intersectional Collaboration

Reproductive justice activists often talk about working "across sectors" or doing "cross-sectoral work," which has two meanings.[18] "Cross-sectoral" refers to collaboration between social movements with different political goals and cultures. According to Adriann Barboa, executive director of Strong Families New Mexico, "Working across sectors sometimes means collaborating with those working on social justice—immigration, reproductive health and rights, or environmental justice, etc." These cross-sector collaborations are moments when social movements with different foci join forces. For example, SisterSong and Black Lives Matter, a racial justice movement, announced a new collaboration in a conference call in 2016. Alicia Garza, cofounder of Black Lives Matter, explained the rationale for joining forces: "We understand that conditions facing the black communities are multifaceted and complex. If we are able to make any successful interventions in those intersectional crises, we have to approach it in a more comprehensive position. . . . We understand that BLM and reproductive justice go hand in hand when women are losing their families, losing their children before they are becoming adults."[19] Cross-sectoral work, then, brings together social activists who initially were working separately.

Barboa clarified the second meaning of cross-sectoral organizing: "Sometimes 'cross-sectoral' means working with those who do service, policy advocacy, or organizing related to reproductive health." This view of "cross-sectoral" originated in the conceptual work by Asian Communities for Reproductive Justice and SisterSong in 2005 (discussed in the introduction):

> Although the frameworks [for reproductive health services, reproductive health policy, and reproductive justice] are distinct, together they provide a complementary and comprehensive solution. The Reproductive Health framework emphasizes the very necessary reproductive health services that women need. The Reproductive Rights framework is based on universal legal protections for women, and sees these protections as rights. Issues that were historically seen as private issues in the lives of women and girls have been made public and mainstream. And the Reproductive Justice framework stipulates that reproductive oppression is a result of the intersections of multiple oppressions and is inherently connected to the struggle for social justice and human rights.[20]

Barboa clarified the significance of this analysis: "For me that was a pivotal time in the movement when both these big orgs were saying . . . all of these pieces [reproductive health services, policy advocacy, and grassroots organizing] are needed and really lifting up this frame, that we do have a race, class, and gender analysis and this is by and for women of color."

The utility of cross-sectoral organizing became apparent when Forward Together first started organizing the Strong Families Initiative, according to Eveline Shen: "Many of these organizations don't normally talk to each other because of the way our movement is structured. The funding is very silent, so folks who work in environmental justice don't talk to any gender-based violence orgs, even though we are working with the same communities. We recognize that women and their families don't experience climate change on Monday and lack of child care on Tuesday. It's through our lived experiences. That's the power of intersectionality, recognizing that we are simultaneously facing these challenges and that we need solutions that address these and come up with solutions." Here Shen is illustrating how intersectionality highlights that low-income people of color experience multiple oppressions as well as that reproductive justice simultaneously addresses compound issues. This cross-sector collaboration created a powerful collective identity related to the purpose and goals of the Strong Families Initiative discussed earlier.

Reproductive justice activists often strategize about making a commitment to work with partners, since as Ena Suseth Valladares, research director at CLRJ, pointed out, "There are so many different issues that are intersectional with reproductive justice that we could be doing almost anything." Further, there is sometimes resistance to talking about sexuality, abortion, contraception, or other reproductive health issues by some social justice organizations. Laura Jimenez, executive director of CLRJ, pointed out that some collaborator organizations identified as Catholic or immigrant rights would caution CLRJ members not to discuss "controversial" issues: "They were telling us, 'We're not very sure about this,' 'This won't work,' or 'They won't continue the funding.'" Collaboration, then, must proceed with some delicacy and often begins by taking leadership about gender and women's issues, always calling out that some people are missing in the conversation. Liz Guerra, former outreach coordinator for the NLIRH, described the problem when collaborating with other social justice organizations:

> In the immigrant rights circles we're always asking, "Hey, what about Latinas? How about women?" In reproductive politics spaces it's like, "How about immigrant women? How about Latinas?" In the civil rights areas or LGBTQ spaces it's the undocumented folks, "How about Latinos?" To the mainstream LGBTQ organizations, which we learned can be very, very white and very, very male, we brought the T [trans]; they don't really want to talk about that. If you look a certain way, then it's okay. But if you're like a queer woman, or queer African American woman, a queer undocumented Latina, people don't see that; that's not comfortable for them. We're kind of adding that layer and adding that lens into spaces that, more often than not, forget about that.

Guerra pointed out that it is critical to include marginalized people who share some experiences yet have their own specific issues and identities. Myra Duran, then CLRJ's policy manager, recalled being pressured to choose between women's issues and immigrant issues and insisting, "We're not going to choose, and you have to do it all." Rocio Córdoba, cofounder and first executive director of CLRJ and, at the time of the interview, a program officer for the Ford Foundation, which funds youth, sexuality, and reproductive health and rights organizations, recalled that the inattention to intersectionality by other organizations was why they felt the need to form a reproductive justice organization to begin with: "Our goal [in 2004] was also to develop collaborations with the Latino civil rights groups and health groups, many of whom were not addressing gender or sexual reproductive health. It's been a very important role that groups like CLRJ in California and the National Latina Institute at the national level have played in having those conversations with our colleagues in the Latino civil rights groups." The inseparability of oppression means that activists should seek remedies that incorporate multiple issues and communities. When varied sectors—immigrant rights, faith-based organizations, queer rights, and so on—agree to collaborate on specific issues, they are agreeing to expand their politics to include issues that initially were not their primary focus.

In addition to helping to bridge issues and communities that were often seen as disparate, an intersectionality approach calls for including local participants who are often left out of organizations. Barboa recalled how she got involved in reproductive justice in New Mexico:

> Every single time in the beginning they talked about like, "Hey we don't have enough local people; we don't have enough moms; we don't have enough Black women; where's our Asian women?" . . . That was their goal: "How do we make this a powerful organization not by bringing the smartest most formally educated women but more like how do we make this the most representative of this community that we can?" So immediately it felt like, "Okay, I don't have to be anything else but myself." And immediately I wanted to build my leadership. And any of the women from here, the first folks that they were brought in, they were definitely, "How do we start building the leadership of the folks here?"

I heard this idea repeatedly in interviews with staff, that reproductive justice advocates call attention to all women, develop local leadership, and collaborate regardless of different religious backgrounds, race, sexual identities, educational levels, and so on.

Even within the movement, reproductive justice advocates saw strategic collaboration as requiring trust built over time. One executive

director discussed her deep frustration over having to continually educate allies about the importance of intersectionality and remind them
to make any proposed legislation inclusive of non-English-speakers: "I
often joke privately that someone should just pay us to sit in a room and
say, 'Is anyone else going to say, "We're thinking about the Latino community?" Is anyone else going to say, "We're thinking about linguistic
and cultural competency?" No? I'll say it!' We had an incident happen
this legislative session where our partners in the coalition *finally* heard
our asks and our calls to include cultural and linguistic competency in
a bill that we were running. We actually ask this in *every* bill!" These
activists are pushing for sensitivity to cultural and linguistic differences
and going beyond, addressing social inequities in a way that would be
beneficial for structurally vulnerable people.[21]

Successful collaboration also requires a willingness to negotiate regarding which organization will take the lead during particular campaigns. Shen explained,

> For us strategy is about, What do we want? Are we clear about that? And
> where are we going to look for it? Yes, we are going to be facing challenges
> along the way, and we will be attacked along the way; but we have to be able
> to have some clear guideline in terms of the vision we want. What is the
> change that we are seeking? Not just what we don't want. So being strategic
> is being able to (1) have a vision, (2) have a plan to get towards that vision,
> and (3) be able to figure out how and where are the opportunities we can
> leverage to help us get to that vision. . . . It's a very organic process because
> a lot of the work we do depends on the individuals in the organization.

Normally coalitions are based on shared goals, mutual trust, and clear
understanding of the terms of collaboration conducted by a chosen few
with little "horizontal exchange between participants."[22] However, coalitional work among reproductive justice activists requires a different,
strengths-based approach, as Shen clarified: "A lot of times coalitions get
really split up because they're focused on turf issues, or they're focused
on fighting for those crumbs. And what we are saying is, we are coming
from a place of assumption where there is more of a need for everyone.
Everyone has a role, everyone has strengths, but that doesn't mean that
everyone is a leader that is going to take point at the same time. What

it means is that we figure out together strategically who makes sense to lead at what time." Reproductive justice organizations have a history of "stepping up, stepping back"—deciding jointly when one organization will take the lead in a campaign and others will provide support, as described by Shen. Thus, coalitions with reproductive justice partners often entail intense collaboration. Rocio Córdoba recalled, "From the very beginning, CLRJ and the groups led by women of color that use the reproductive justice framework have been very collaborative with each other. Sometimes it's explicit, and sometimes it's really kind of supporting each other behind the scenes as well as up front; but that was always part of it. Always. It's always been a core component of the priority of the organizations to be collaborative, and that is a very strong value. And again, I am talking from when I was there [as executive director of CLRJ], and that's also my perception of it now." Certainly, personal tensions sometimes get in the way. For example, in a public forum on reproductive justice, one activist made a comment that was startling to me since it was so unusual: "Some of us don't like one another, but we focus on the work." However, the movement has a history of negotiating alliances, coalitions, and mutual support in which they work closely together.

Foundations have hosted convenings of reproductive justice organizations, especially in the early 2000s, when several organizations were newly formed. Córdoba, who is also chair of the Women of Color Working Group, which is funded by the Funders' Network and which includes about thirty place-based and national funders,[23] spoke at length about how funders support nonprofit organizations:

> We have some programs with grantees that are around bringing them in for capacity building, for example, for communications and social media. And we play a very hands-on role by bringing the groups that are going to provide the capacity building, developing a program together, inviting a cohort to be a part of that. And we're working very hands-on with everyone throughout the way. And we also do a lot of learning activities, analysis, and evaluation and some public events as well. We're organizing a number of different briefings around social media and innovative strategies that grantees are doing. We go to a lot of events—grantee conferences or other conferences—to go more deeply into these issues both with grantees as well as with other donors. . . . Our goal is to get grantee

organizations to the point where it's no longer thought of as something we do over here at the end—we do a press release and a tactic at the end—but to really integrate it into thinking, What and who is our target audience? What are the key messages that we're going to use in everything we do? How do we build that into our infrastructure in terms of staff or volunteers? How do we communicate what is most meaningful to us in terms of values and priorities across our programs? The notion of media outreach is only one tactic, but we're trying to provide that opportunity of integrating this into organizations. And the ones who have kind of gone through this process realize that it really helps them to be much more clear, much more focused in terms of all the work that they're already doing. It's not changing the work that they do; it's just helping them do the work more effectively and with greater impact.

Barboa, who was formerly the executive director of YWU, recalled the significance of these convenings:

> They [foundations] were instrumental in paying for these fabulous convenings every year that would bring together all the leaders of reproductive justice organizations they were funding. . . . At that point having those opportunities where the leaders, different women of color doing reproductive justice work in their communities, was just huge. Because then we could connect to each other, then we could say, "Oh, what I'm doing in Albuquerque is similar to what you're doing in Georgia, is similar to what you're trying to move in California or Colorado." As new young directors we really felt like we had resources, we weren't isolated, and that we could lead with that whole [intersectionality] frame, constantly talking about race, class, and gender.

SisterSong also held several conferences on the theme "Let's Talk about Sex," where organizations presented their work and socialized together. As reproductive justice activists learned about and from one another, they constructed a collective identity, often seen in posts on Facebook, Twitter, and Instagram. A common phrasing is "this is an RJ issue!" related to various struggles such as opposition to detention and deportations or to police violence toward African Americans or in support of raising minimum wages or of the right to clean water.

At other times reproductive justice organizations collaborate by coming together and sharing material resources during moments of crisis. For example, the Coalition for Choice launched a campaign against a proposed municipal ban on abortions after twenty weeks of pregnancy in Albuquerque; Young Women United and Strong Families New Mexico took leadership. At the press conference announcing the campaign, Respect ABQ Women, eighteen supporters, including a number of executive directors and staff from reproductive justice organizations from Oregon, California, Georgia, New York, and New Mexico, attended and spoke with reporters.[24] In other instances, research conducted by one organization was shared with others—for example, NILRH's poll on Latinxs' views on abortion was instrumental in crafting the successful campaign against the municipal ban on abortion in Albuquerque, which had large numbers of Latinx voters.[25]

Intersectional collaboration also means becoming proactive in sharing with one another as well as learning from one another. Angela Moreno, board member of SisterSong in Atlanta, pointed out,

> I think what connects us is not just the struggle that we share but also the struggles that we don't share and learning about each other's histories, which are always changing too. So it is a great place to critique and self-critique our organizations and our movement from the inside. We can have real talk with allies and sister organizations when you need to and then also produce an informed analysis about the world. So, campaigns and partnerships like Trust Black Women and Black Lives Matter and Black Women Equal Pay Day raise awareness and promote action around issues that we are required to address if we are really working for justice.

Thus, intersectional collaboration involves recognizing unique challenges faced by women of color who are different from one another. To address those differences, reproductive justice organizations create materials and host webinars to disseminate their framing of particular issues and share organizational research and toolkits to help others craft local tactics related to a range of issues such as Black maternal health, self-induced abortion, communicating about abortion to the Latinx community, or the rights of people with disabilities.[26]

In the course of collaborating on particular campaigns, getting to know one another at convenings, and sharing some hard-earned victories, these activists have established close friendships as well. Repeatedly I heard warm remarks about how collaboration among reproductive justice organizations was qualitatively different from that with other social justice organizations. For example, Cristina Aguilar recalled meeting up with Monica Simpson at a convening during a particularly challenging period: "I was with my movement sisters, my movement family, who gets it in a way that's different than other partners who are also working on multi-issues. But to be a reproductive justice organization that is led and serving and grounded in the reproductive justice movement and to have the connections that we have, it really is that reminder: what happens to some of us happens to all of us!" For reproductive justice organizations, mutual support goes far beyond the politics of solidarity that can be expressed publicly with little sustained effort. As Córdoba pointed out, "I think that power comes in the collaborations and partnerships that happen together. So, I'm very excited to see more and more organizations and individual activists who are really taking on this reproductive justice framework and taking on this work on behalf of their communities."

Thus, reproductive justice organizations' mutual support deepens the politics of solidarity and empathy by contributing materially over a sustained period of time. In this view, there is not necessarily reliance on the state as the provider of social justice, although often organizations target the state to be transparent, end discriminatory treatment, pass progressive legislation, and bring more resources to support policies on the books. In addition to efforts to shape state policies, they draw on indigenous human rights activists' view, according to Rosa Linda Fregoso, that rights are "lived and embodied practices, temporally and spatially enacted."[27] In this political imaginary, human rights are seen as *collective* rights and include the importance of mutual recognition, respect, recruiting local leaders, and negotiating the terms of their collaboration.

Increasingly social movements are using storytelling as a key tactic for influencing policy makers or shifting the frame in relation to dominant narratives.[28] Stories convey the nuanced meanings of intersecting systems of power in local contexts.[29] Storytellers speak truth to power through narratives about collective experiences of oppression and how individual transformation leads to collective struggles as well as convey women's agency, social support, and sense of community.[30] Life stories or *testimonios* also help people "think through expressions of difference or disagreements and incorporate various viewpoints" when articulating experiences of systemic violence and cultural ideologies that continually marginalize women.[31] The Latina Feminist Group (of which I am a member) argues, "through testimonio we learned to translate ourselves for one another," which enables us to negotiate nuanced understandings of differences and connections among us.[32] *Testimonios*, according to Rina Benmayor, evoke theorizing: "understanding oneself and one's experience in the context of one's own and other cultural communities."[33] She elaborates, "To testimoniar (testify) invokes an urgent voice of resistance to social injustices, an urgency to speak out, a collective interlocutor, and a collaborative process of production and interpretation."[34] *Testimoniando* or storytelling becomes a pedagogical and methodological approach to social justice by creating a sense of community and modes of analysis that are collaborative and attentive to myriad ways of knowing and learning.[35] *Testimonios* also contain political functions, according to Benmayor and her colleagues, by linking the "spoken word to social action and privileg[ing] the oral narrative of personal experience as a source of knowledge, empowerment, and political strategy for claiming rights and bringing about social change."[36] These reproductive justice organizations successfully organized Lois Weis and Michelle Fine's notion of "safe spaces," sites where youth and adults "engage a kind of critical consciousness, challenging hegemonic beliefs about them, their perceived inadequacies, pathologies, and 'lacks,' and restoring a sense of possibility for themselves and their peers, within and beyond narrow spaces of identity sustenance."[37]

Storytelling becomes an *effective* political tool, according to Francesca Polletta, when it evokes participation by listeners: "Narrative's power stems from its complexity, indeed, its ambiguity. More than other discursive forms, narrative demands an effort at interpretation."[38] Further, stories highlight affect in social movements, in which "emotions can be strategically used by activists and be the basis for strategic thought."[39] In the current neoliberal era, in which discourses commending market forces and individual responsibility are increasingly hegemonic, stories are widespread in popular culture. Polletta cautions us to carefully specify the historically specific conditions and how stories are told for political effects so we can assess their efficacy. As we see in the remainder of this chapter, reproductive justice activists strategically organize cross-sectoral collaboration along with strengths-based storytelling for women's collective rights.

Leadership Development in Texas

There have been chilling efforts to restrict women's access to reproductive health services in Texas. After passage of the ACA, Texas did not expand Medicaid.[40] Texas went further and does not allow legal permanent residents to enroll in the ACA even after completion of a waiting period.[41] The Center for Reproductive Rights and NLIRH estimate that this leaves two million people uninsured in Texas.[42] Further, in 2011 the Texas legislature cut state family planning funding by 66 percent and authorized the "affiliate rule," which barred health centers from receiving state funding if they were affiliated with facilities that provide abortions, in essence targeting Planned Parenthood. Two years later Texas passed one of the most restrictive abortion laws in the United States, House Bill 2, which required physicians performing abortions to have admitting privileges at a nearby hospital, banned most abortions after twenty weeks of pregnancy, and required that all abortion facilities meet the standards of an ambulatory surgical center. (This was legislation for which state senator Wendy Davis famously staged a filibuster in protest.) Texas laws require women seeking an abortion to undergo an ultrasound and counseling that includes detailed descriptions of the images and then wait twenty-four hours before receiving the procedure, and minors must have parental consent.[43] Clearly Texas has been a leader of "reproductive governance," using legislation and other inducements so as to restrict reproductive behaviors and practices, especially those related to abortion.[44]

Research on the aftermath of these policy changes in Texas indicates worrisome effects: by April 2014, almost half of the state's clinics that provide abortions had closed, and in 2017, 97 percent of Texas counties had no abortion clinic.[45] The admitting-privileges requirement of the Texas law "was almost certainly the main driver of the large number of clinic closures observed."[46] There was a relative increase of 27 percent of unintended pregnancy by women who underwent childbirth covered by Medicaid within eighteen months of the 2011 legislative changes.[47] Texas also experienced double the maternal mortality rate (per one hundred thousand live births) in 2011–12, "levels not seen in other U.S. states."[48] The barriers to accessing abortions were costly in multiple ways: women spent more time and money than initially anticipated when they obtained an abortion, which meant they received abortions later than initially planned, and often women had to drive an average one-way distance of eighty-five miles to obtain an abortion. Some women were unable to meet the increased costs and could not have abortions.[49] Since access to clinic-based care was restricted, more women living in South Texas attempted to end a pregnancy on their own.[50]

The four counties that make up the Rio Grande Valley near the Mexican border in South Texas are home to 275,000 women of reproductive age, about two-thirds of whom are estimated to be in need of subsidized contraceptive services.[51] Nine out of thirty-two state-funded family-planning clinics in South Texas closed, and those that remained open served 54 percent fewer clients.[52] According to Daniel Grossman and colleagues, "Both of the abortion clinics in the [Rio Grande] Valley closed in November 2013 because physicians were unable to obtain hospital privileges. The nearest clinic is in Corpus Christi, 150 miles away, and the nearest ASC [ambulatory surgical center] is in San Antonio, about 250 miles away, adding up to eight hours of travel time to the process of obtaining an abortion."[53] After reviewing these consequences of restricting access to abortion services, Grossman and his colleagues concluded that the Texas anti-abortion legislation constitutes a "public health threat."[54]

In this context, the Center for Reproductive Rights and NLIRH have been collaborating on the Nuestro Texas campaign. Since 2007 they had been researching the conditions in the US-Mexico border region, one of the poorest and unhealthiest regions in the United States. They conducted 188 interviews, documenting the poverty and poor access to health care for all but focusing on women in a region that is predominantly Latinx.[55] In relation to the restrictive legislation, they conclude, "The demand for services is now concentrated on fewer clinics, leading to delays of many months for appointments at one of the few clinics that continue to offer reduced-fee state services." Further, "the long delays are tantamount to a denial of reproductive health care because the window of opportunity to treat serious conditions such as breast, cervical, or uterine cancer may close by the time a woman finally sees a doctor."[56] Their research finds that some women attempt to purchase contraceptives or access health care in Mexico.[57] This is a dangerous prospect since they documented instances of women getting caught up in drug-cartel-related violence in northern Mexico, and the unauthorized take life-threatening journeys to return to the United States.[58] Other women have resorted to DIY (do-it-yourself) abortions with misoprostol purchased at local flea markets or in Mexico, a drug that in Texas is illegal to take at home.[59]

Part of the challenges of meeting low-income women's health-care needs is that so many live in colonias, unincorporated housing developments that often originate in promises to provide basic infrastructure like running water, sewage systems, paved roads, and utilities that developers fail to deliver. Colonias are located within one hundred kilometers of the US-Mexico border and can be found in California, Arizona, New Mexico, and Texas. There are about three thousand colonias with approximately four hundred thousand residents who are predominantly Mexican, including many immigrants, in South Texas. As part of the working poor, colonia residents live in trailers or dwellings they build themselves, often in phases. There are high unemployment rates in colonias, where approximately 80 percent of the residents are at or below the poverty level, and residents experience higher levels of chronic health problems.[60] The Rio Grande Valley has the nation's highest rates for cervical cancer and high rates of nutrition-related health outcomes such as diabetes, obesity, cardiovascular disease, and neural tube defects. There are high numbers of female-headed households, and a third of the residents do not have a high school education.[61] In Texas, Latinas have the highest rates of cervical cancer incidence and mortality compared to other women.[62] Poor access to health care is endemic, as there is little public transportation and colonia residents must travel long distances to access clinics that provide health care on sliding fees for those with low incomes.[63] According to Liz Guerra, "There are definitely huge amounts of class discrimination and class lines. Like, if you cross over one street, you go from shantytowns and colonias to these huge palaces, right? And most people don't know that colonias even exist." Despite the poor conditions and the racialization of whole communities, such that colonias are assumed to be sites of dirt and disease, residents demonstrate remarkable creativity and resiliency, using their social networks to go grocery shopping, for example, or share food with one another.[64] And with enough time, resources, and hard work, colonia residents can make their homes comfortable and well appointed, as I saw firsthand.

In this region, people with low incomes face other extraordinary conditions. There are an estimated 1.6 million undocumented immigrants in Texas,[65] with an increase in apprehensions, migrant deaths, and Border Patrol abuse of migrants.[66] Border Patrol officers have the legal authority to conduct searches and to inquire about one's legal status at checkpoints within one hundred miles of the US-Mexico border. Some of the checkpoints, such as the one in Edinburg, twenty miles north of the border, have multiagency initiatives in which local, state, and federal agencies collaborate and hold random checks.[67] Small offenses like driving infractions may lead to criminal arrests or even deportation because of immigration offenses.[68] Further, the National Guard has been stationed at the border since 2014.[69] While local civil rights organizations are monitoring this collaboration and residents post warnings about checkpoints on social media, these multiagency collaborations have led to people being extremely cautious when driving and carefully weighing when they need to drive outside their immediate neighborhoods or colonias to access health care. In this context, the undocumented often delay accessing health care except for emergency care. Indeed, Texas had the highest rate of uninsured nonelderly compared to other states during 2013–17, close to 25 percent.[70] However, lack of access to health care is not only related to legal status. As Katrina Anderson, formerly with the Center for Reproductive Rights said, "Geography has more to do with it and poverty level. 'Cause even the women who are insured can't afford the services. That was one of our findings: that many of the women are so underinsured that they can't even afford their copays."[71] In this borderland of poverty, race, and gender, citizenship becomes undermined.[72]

Given limited access to the Internet in colonias and fear of outsiders, the National Latina Institute used "old school" forms of communication—canvassing in neighborhoods, face-to-face meetings, and fliers—to recruit women. Lucy Ceballos-Félix, formerly a social worker in Mexico and now a naturalized US citizen, was field and advocacy manager of NLIRH's Texas Latina Advocacy Network. She told me that when she first began organizing in colonias in 2007, she borrowed an ice-cream truck and a loudspeaker to announce free popsicles and handed out fliers advertising a women's meeting. In addition, she would approach women at their homes and sometimes opened her conversation by admiring their images of the Virgen de Guadalupe or their flower gardens. Slowly she began recruiting women to join the network and meet in community centers or churches located in the colonias. Ceballos-Félix now coordinates thirty women's groups in four counties in South Texas with the help of a subcommittee of women who have completed LAN's leadership institute.[73] This means that she facilitates a meeting with a different group almost every day. The participants' ages vary tremendously. The majority are in their thirties and forties, although a few are older, up to the eighties. Also, women in their twenties are joining and bringing their children with them, so LAN activities include people of different generations. The process is to provide training to women who then graduate and become organizers to recruit new members, who attend monthly trainings and a leadership institute. The participants are gifted a NLIRH tee-shirt in royal blue and yellow that says, "soy poderosa." LAN has been holding Freirian type workshops in women's homes, patios, or parks.

After the restrictive legislation that closed clinics, the mobile bus that once visited colonias stopped coming, LAN began to bring *promotoras* (health outreach workers), like Paula Saldaña, who volunteered to train women to administer their own breast exams (see plate 10).[74] Ceballos-Félix recalled hearing about so many women's health challenges—for example, providers refusing to release test results until bills were paid—and having to learn how to counsel women who found lumps since they all knew gaining access to a clinic would take time.[75] These workshops utilized *conocimiento*, a process of gaining knowledge, awareness, and political consciousness based on the practice of storytelling, where self-awareness is rooted in a collective experience and leads to empathy and action for people in similar circumstances.[76] Indeed, *conocimiento* can initiate women's healing from the effects of oppression in their daily lives.[77] LAN trains women to see themselves as their own best advocates in the fight for the human right to health care and to embrace their *poderosa* identities.[78]

I was able to witness how women internalized their leadership training and NLIRH's "soy poderosa" discourse. The Center for Reproductive Rights and NLIRH sponsored "Nuestro Voz: Nuestra Salud, Nuestro Texas [Our Voice, Our Health, Our Texas]: A Women's Human Rights Hearing," which I attended in McAllen in 2015. The previous year, Ceballos-Félix had been invited to Geneva to testify at the United Nations Human Rights Committee during its periodic review of the United States' compliance with the International Covenant on Civil and Political Rights.[79] She told me that after her presentation, the attendees were shocked to hear about the conditions of poverty and denial of health care in the United States: "At first it was so quiet you could have heard a pin drop. Finally, someone said, 'This is happening in the United States? It sounds like Latin America!'" The Human Rights Committee, the Committee on the Elimination of Racial Discrimination, and the Human Rights Council issued strong recommendations urging the United States to eliminate discrimination in access to public health insurance for immigrants and to ensure timely and affordable access to health care for women regardless of immigration status.[80] The human rights hearings in McAllen were partly a public voicing of those conditions. The aim, according to Katrina Anderson, was "to give women in the Valley a voice because most that are directly impacted are unable to travel, to bring people who are actively engaged in the human rights movement to the Valley, and to expose this as an ongoing crisis in Texas."

The hearings were held on International Women's Day in 2015, and NLIRH called the event "Celebrating the International Day of Powerful Women." The event began with a rally held in Brownsville the day before near the US-Mexico border. The hearings themselves opened with music and printed lyrics from the song "Latinoamérica," by Calle Trece. This song provides a vision of the Americas without capitalist destruction and celebrates nature, indigeneity, and the racial diversity of people from the southern cone through the Caribbean.

After introductory remarks by executive director Jessica González-Rojas, the organizations provided an excellent training called "Human Rights 101." Besides being entirely in Spanish with simultaneous translation into English via headphones, it included moments for reflection.

The audience members were periodically asked to have conversations with someone sitting nearby about our reasons for attending or thoughts about the presentations. Mindful that human rights can be a problematic individualist framework, the training focused on social categories: immigrants and their families, African Americans, youth, and the LGBTQ community. The presentation was remarkable in that it illustrated Sally Engle Merry's point about the significance of vernacularizing human rights discourses in local terms.[81]

The hearings then provided a space where seventeen Latinas of working-class background read *testimonios* that had been written previously about their experiences trying to access reproductive health care in South Texas. Many used pseudonyms. We expect the desire for anonymity by the undocumented, but some citizens did not want their real names used either, suggesting that it is critical to historicize circumstances in which migrants and citizens are produced.[82] According to Ceballos-Félix, the women agreed to use pseudonyms in solidarity with those who were undocumented and fearful of using their real names in a public forum. The women gave some background information about themselves by indicating their country of birth or communities they lived in, along with biographical information—for example, "I'm a single mother," "I was born in El Salvador," "I am Mexican American and trying to complete college."[83] Their stories were heartbreaking. One woman told the story of a friend being diagnosed with late-stage cervical cancer, which could have been prevented if she had access to regular pap smears. With the closing of so many clinics in South Texas and her limited income, she could not afford the annual exam until it was too late. A college student who became pregnant decided to seek an abortion and had her partner's support. She had to travel hundreds of miles for a provider, which indicates that she is a citizen or legal resident, and was forced to view an ultrasound of her fetus and return the next day. She believed the staff was actively encouraging her to change her mind, yet she affirmed, "Getting that abortion was the best thing for me at the time." Another woman narrated her distress over her thirteen-year-old daughter's discharge from her breast and the physician's repeated denial that there was cause for alarm. When she finally got her daughter tested, they found tumors. The daughter is too young for the federally funded program for low-income breast cancer patients, and the family cannot afford the treatments. The stories were deeply moving—I don't think there was a dry eye in the room. Later Ceballos-Félix informed me that some women read another woman's story, and right up until they began the testimonies, they were unsure of the order of presentation. Yet the women seemed poised, and despite the pain expressed in these *testimonios*, they seemed proud as they told their stories. When I mentioned this to Katrina Anderson, she affirmed, "They don't necessarily want their real names or their status known, but they have no fear, in terms of speaking out."

After the *testimonios*, invited guests—including academic researchers, a state legislator who Skyped in, a physician, and leaders of Planned Parenthood and organizations working on immigrant rights or women's rights—were given time to respond to the women's stories.[84] The interlocutors expressed their shock at the women's treatment and promised to incorporate women's right to access health care into their future work. According to González-Rojas, the interlocutors were chosen strategically so as to expand their collaborators on the Nuestro Texas project.

The hearings ended with Ceballos-Félix telling us the story of how she got involved in working as a health advocate for low-income Latinas after migrating to the United States. She brought up her mother and school-age son and told us it was for her family that she did this work, so that women in their lives would not have to face these state-initiated barriers to accessing health care. Ceballos-Félix exhorted us to stand, hug the person next to us, and commit to working on behalf of our children. This produced a great deal of emotion in me, and I burst into tears as I considered the possibility of my family members facing these barriers to care. Ceballos-Félix then led us through some rousing cheers, and we left feeling inspired. The *testimonios* had successfully conveyed the range of structural problems women experienced accessing health care as well as their impressive resiliency, strength, and perseverance and was effective in mobilizing a sense of community by those who are committed to working for policy changes. I spoke with an organizer of the event afterward who said their follow-up work includes being proactive in trying to push legislation to restore funding that would open more clinics as well as to prevent other proposed legislation. She is based in Austin and has worked as a legislative aide for seventeen years, so she knows the players and how to navigate the legislative scene. She stated, "I think the *only* way to get policy makers to pay attention is through stories like these."

In the aftermath of the human rights hearings, the Center for Reproductive Rights and NLIRH continued the Nuestro Texas campaign and produced a report on the hearings. It includes photos of cross-generational bonding of Latina girls who are getting involved in the struggle with their mothers and other relatives. A photo posted on Facebook on International Women's Day the year after the hearings was captioned, "some of the leaders as we celebrate the international day of *powerful* women."[85]

I organized a focus group of eleven women who belonged to LAN, many of whom had participated in the human rights hearings. They informed me that these hearings were the first held in the state, and most of the women were very nervous about participating. One woman pointed out, "It's not easy to stand up and speak about something so intimate and so personal in front of strangers." Another woman who struggles with literacy and a minor speech impediment worried about speaking publicly. "Lucina," who read someone else's story because the writer was unable to attend, recalled how she was deeply moved: "I was crying because it was a very sad story, and I was seeing what this woman lived through. I was afraid that I would become tongue-tied, but I found my strength." One of the organizers found the hearings tremendously important, a culmination of their long-term work: "Women were able to overcome their fear, and they truly embraced a new way of seeing their lives. Some of the women had believed that there was no hope. But those hearings broke that fear; they broke those chains that prevented any hope."

The participants in LAN see themselves even stronger than before and embrace their *poderosa* consciousness:

For me *poderosa* means being united so as to have the strength. We critiqued the government and defended our rights.

For me, to be *poderosa* is to educate yourself about your rights and be able to share them with the community, focusing and empowering them. Because when you know your rights, you become powerful.

> For me it is a means of connecting to my dignity. It doesn't matter what I have suffered or my family has suffered or in my community.

> To be a *poderosa* means to have the ability to grow relationships, which are good. Because when one has good relations with people, they are going to help you and give you a hand to help you move forward so that you feel powerful.

One woman started acting goofy, and everyone laughed as she joked, "We are at the point where we feel super powerful. And sometimes I feel like Superman, and I twirl in my cape. And every year I expect to have strength because I am a *poderosa!*"

In the aftermath of the hearings, there have been some changes. There are more health-outreach programs for preventative services, and the Mexican consulate provides mobile clinics. However, with the delays to accessing care, by the time some women received diagnoses, their health conditions had advanced, and they required even more care. Further, with their lack of medical insurance, low incomes, and so many being undocumented, accessing health care remains difficult for many women. Nonetheless, the power of women telling their stories at the hearings has circulated widely: "When you're walking out on the street or when they see us in the van, people in the community say, 'There go the powerful women!'"

In the Nuestro Texas campaign we see the struggle by low-income women of color who now see themselves as strong and resilient despite their structural vulnerabilities. This is an intersectional praxis that is strategic, concretized, and flexible, using storytelling as a methodology by which women express their complex subjectivities—their national heritage, their roles within families, their aspirations—and their recognition that despite some common experiences, they are diverse. They also used transmedia organizing that ranged from the use of fliers to Facebook.[86] The National Latina Institute for Reproductive Health and the Center for Reproductive Rights use cross-sectoral work in which their coalition is not based on similar identities but in solidarity with other organizations working on behalf of women's human right to access health care.

Building Capacity in California

Since the founding of California Latinas for Reproductive Justice in 2004, the organization has engaged in a long-term effort to integrate its strengths in policy advocacy with culture shift work and grassroots organizing in which it offers community education about important issues. Initially founded by civil rights and immigrant rights activists, according to an interview with cofounder Rocio Córdoba, the organizers "recognized that there was a significant need for there to be a very strong Latina voice, in California in particular, that was more unified." Former senior director of community education and mobilization Gabriela Valle pointed out that in their experience working on immigrant rights, it was often CLRJ that took the lead on women's issues. According to Ena Suseth Valladares, director of research, CLRJ also wanted increased research on the conditions of Latinas. As part of its community education and mobilization work, it has held many daylong workshops around the state called "Latinas Empowered for Action," which train women about reproductive justice. I have attended thirteen of CLRJ's events, including multiple trainings about reproductive justice, storytelling, the legislative process, and policy advocacy, and organized two focus groups with the staff.

CLRJ's policy advocacy begins with systematic research. It organized focus groups and a survey about health-care access and found that women, especially the undocumented, needed more information about how to access reproductive health services. Young women were unaware they had the right to reproductive health care without parental consent. Many believed that physicians' perceptions of them impeded good communication.[87] They often felt disrespected by physicians for asking about contraception in particular. Further, legislation that mandates comprehensive sex education, a policy victory led by several social justice organizations, was not being implemented in all schools. Especially in California's Central Valley, youth received abstinence-only sex education, which has been found to be ineffective and "ethically problematic" for its coercive nature.[88]

Using this research and the organization's experience with popular education, one of CLRJ's efforts at tailoring its reproductive justice approach was the two-day El Instituto de Autonomía y Justicia (Institute of Autonomy and Justice), with all presentations in Spanish, which I attended in 2014. It was held at a public library in the predominantly low-income Black and Latinx South Los Angeles.[89] The participants were of varied national origins—mostly from Mexico but a few from El Salvador and Peru and some Latinas born in the United States. They had educational backgrounds that ranged from a few years of elementary school to college degrees, and their ages ranged from early twenties to sixty-three; a few were indigenous Mexicanas.

The two-day Instituto began with Gabriela Valle's presentation, which included an explanation of the reproductive justice approach, a critique of "pro-choice" politics, and an invitation to get involved in CLRJ's policy advocacy. There was also an in-depth presentation on women's reproductive anatomy by Mayra Lizzette Yñiguez, community engagement coordinator (see plate 11), in which we pinned names of genital and reproductive organs on large images. During the discussion about this presentation, some women disclosed that they had never received this education before and were shocked to see a vagina on the board. There were plenty of giggles and playful asides: One woman joked, "It's not a sin to talk about this, right?" Another fanned herself, indicating that she was embarrassed, and said, "Many adult words here." During the presentations, there were plenty of questions asking for clarification of particular issues and good rapport among the women. In between presentations we paired up to tell our stories to one another and to relate how the information was pertinent to our own lives.

On the second day of El Instituto, we shared our life stories, with reflections about what autonomy meant to us, in front of the entire group and practiced "compassionate listening" without questions or comments. Some of the women became quite emotional when sharing their stories about quotidian struggles—migrating to the United States, leaving relatives behind, finding work, taking care of their kin on either side of the border, or losing a parent—and several listeners teared up as they listened. Some disclosed they were undocumented, ineligible to access health care, which led to further reflection. One woman expressed her appreciation for the safe space provided by El Instituto and pointed out, "People are fearful when someone gives them new information about health, especially when they come from outside the community. They speak differently; they don't respect the community values. And people are afraid that it will cost too much." Another woman agreed, "We have to educate our community about what is available to them." The women's evaluations of El Instituto, to which I had access, included quite positive assessments: they felt a sense of solidarity with the others, and they expressed their compassion and empathy toward one another. Each woman had her photo taken while holding a Certificate of Participation, and several seemed quite proud of receiving one. We all had bonded with one another and left feeling inspired. Throughout El Instituto the three of us with advanced educational degrees always spoke in Spanish, honoring the goal of inclusivity, so that everyone could participate. Another CLRJ staff member did observations of another Instituto and pointed out, "Gaby [Valle] was able to really radicalize or change a lot of these women's thinking about certain issues." El Instituto is a microcosm of CLRJ's work, as it is enmeshed in a national network of organizations working on reproductive justice for transnational migrants.[90]

In 2016, CLRJ organized more focus groups and another community needs assessment. According to Ena Suseth Valladares, the goal was the following: "We were trying to figure out how our community needs assessment would be able to influence the policy priorities of the following year or subsequent years. How would that align with the work we were already doing?" During the needs assessment in low-income Latinx neighborhoods, the major issues identified by community members were reproductive and sexual health care, the environment, access to affordable child care, and mental health. These research findings then provide the basis for reports back to working-class Latinx communities about specific issues. According to Valladares, CLRJ's community education efforts that utilize results from the community needs assessments are multiple: "community forums, curriculum, *cafecitos*, or different issues that are specifically affecting our communities that we may not get to at a policy level." The latter point refers to activities like the multiple screenings of the award-winning documentary film *No Más Bebés*, about the sterilization of Mexican women that occurred at Los Angeles County USC Medical Center during the 1960s and 1970s. This film launches a discussion of the eugenic politics that enable sterilization to continue in some states. In California, legislation (SB 1135) signed by the governor in 2014 bans sterilization of women inmates after an audit found thirty-nine women had been sterilized without consent at eight different hospitals.[91] Virginia Espino, coproducer of *No Más Bebés*, is on CLRJ's board and brings women involved in the unsuccessful lawsuit *Madrigal v. USC* to speak at these events. In 2018, Los Angeles County formally apologized to the *Madrigal* plaintiffs, an emotional victory, but CLRJ would like some financial compensation to the sterilized women as well. CLRJ also holds workshops on issues such as the ACA and abortion and occasional celebratory events and fundraisers in Los Angeles, San Diego, and the Bay Area.

CLRJ's big policy win in 2016 was repeal of the Maximum Family Grant rule (SB 899), the seventh state to repeal family caps. The MFG rule was implemented in 1997 in response to the Personal Responsibility and Work Opportunity Reconciliation Act (PRWORA, 1996), commonly known as "welfare reform," which pushed women into the labor market as well as denied public services and benefits to all noncitizens.[92] PRWORA was "profoundly shaped by conservative family values and a belief that an unregulated ('free') market will produce a viable path to self support and individual/familial independence from the state—what is often termed neoliberalism."[93] Its proponents also held problematic assumptions that those who received social welfare were unworthy either for being lazy or irresponsible or for gaming the system as "welfare queens," notions contested by people with low incomes who attempt to gain recognition for being hard working and honoring heteronormative expectations about marriage.[94] In California, the MFG rule denied an increase in the maximum aid payment for a child born into the family of a CalWORKs recipient, based on the belief that women will have children so as to increase their income from the state, and it included exemptions if the pregnancy occurs because of rape, incest, or contraception failure.[95] There had been five attempts to pass bills limiting or eliminating California's Family Cap between 2007 and 2015. California was the only state to exempt children conceived because of contraceptive failure, and among MFG-impacted households, 57 to 60 percent were Latinx and 17 to 24 percent were African American.[96] SB 899 prohibits this cap as well as the conditioning of eligibility for CalWORKs aid on the basis of applicants' disclosure about how they became pregnant. Efforts to pass the bill had failed multiple times. Myra Duran, former CLRJ policy manager, pointed out, "This bill is the epitome of culture shift work aligned with policy work that needed to happen, especially since it would cost a lot of money if it would pass." CLRJ had to convince coalition members of the importance of reframing the issue, according to Duran:

> We wanted to go beyond the narrative and messaging around childhood poverty, which is super important, and California leads in the percentage of childhood poverty in the country. We also wanted to pair that with a narrative that was missing, which was the women. What happens with the mom when she actually is in a situation where she needs all these exemptions to qualify for extra aid? The exception to the rule was if your pregnancy was the result of rape or incest, the mother had to prove sexual assault, and if it was the result of failed contraception, then contraception [after birth of her child] had to be sterilization: IUD, Norplant—these really long-acting, irreversible contraceptives. . . . We had all agreed that we were going to say family caps are a form of eugenics because embedded in our state policies and rhetoric are efforts to control certain communities' reproductive health decisions.

Clearly this was another form of reproductive governance. Executive director Jimenez observed, "Basically they transformed the way the issue was talked about, switching to an issue of reproductive justice around the way money was being taken based on people's reproductive health decisions."

During the campaign, the coalition deployed canvassing tactics, storytelling, actions at legislative offices, and advocacy outlets in the media. Duran testified before a legislative committee, making the case that the rule was another form of eugenics, and she told the story of an African American woman: "She said, 'My daughter got lead poisoning, and there was no public housing. And it wasn't my plan to be on welfare, but I lost my job at Walmart when I got hurt. It wasn't my plan to get pregnant. It was not my plan to be poor, and I was for as long as I was, and the maximum family grant rule made it much more difficult to leave welfare and make it on my own.'" Duran concluded, "I want to make sure that when we're talking about policies, they're not abstract but there's a tangible action."[97] State senator Holly Mitchell, the bill's sponsor, was passionate about the issue, Duran recalled: "I think she really appreciated having women of color advocates standing beside her and pushing this idea." Valladares agreed: "Being able to work with someone like that is fantastic. She's the type of person that moves. She just makes things happen." This is the campaign that garnered the activism award for CLRJ from the Center for Reproductive Rights and Justice. As the lead on this successful multiyear campaign, Duran, a millennial, joked, "I feel like I could just retire now."

Building on these policy gains, CLRJ organized a 2017 policy advocacy event, "¡California Latinas Presente!" in the Bay Area, with a forty-five-minute YouTube webinar (in English or Spanish) that provided training about pending legislation, the legislative process, and how to lobby—how to introduce the rationale for specific bills, how to make the ask, and professional decorum. In preparation for this event, the community engagement coordinator had traveled twice to the Bay Area to meet with representatives of Mujeres Unidas Activas (Activist Women United) and Visión y Compromiso (Vision and Commitment), grassroots organizations that work with Spanish-speaking Latinas to collaborate with them about recruiting participants for lobbying.[98] The in-person training began with a reception and introduction; then we played bingo, designed to get us talking to everyone in the room; and then we were given lobbying assignments. All of this training was presented in Spanish and included celebrating our *chingona* identities.

I participated in lobbying two legislators. For the meeting with then Assembly member Tony Thurmon, I told the story of one of my former students who transitioned from female to male and why the Gender Recognition Act (SB 179) was critical, since it would facilitate the process of legally changing one's gender identity. When meeting with US Senator Diane Feinstein's staffer, I lobbied on behalf of the Women's Health Protection Act of 2019, which would supersede the various state bills aimed at impeding women's access to abortion. I spoke about how Texas's legislation has created significant barriers to accessing reproductive health in general with devastating effects that I discussed earlier. The staffer indicated that she would follow up and that Senator Feinstein would consider becoming a cosponsor of the bill; however, in fact Feinstein had already signed on as cosponsor.[99] It was very satisfying to me to be able to use research in support of a bill that would bring some remedy to women in many parts of the country, even if Feinstein was not always receptive to constituents' views.[100] CLRJ staff scheduled team visits with state and federal legislators in San Diego, Los Angeles, Fresno, and the Bay Area and organized a conference call to evaluate the effectiveness of the event.

All of this effort paid off. CLRJ had remarkable success with its 2017 policy platform: the governor signed eight out of ten of the bills for which the organization was advocating. Its policy platform included a range of issues:

> Timely access to quality mental health services for Medi-Cal recipients (AB 470); Strengthens support for domestic violence victims/survivors who are applicants or recipients of CalWORKS [social welfare] assistance (AB 557); Prevents private corporations from building new prisons / prevent the renewal of contracts for certain existing private prisons (SB 29); Expands parental leave to CA workers at companies with at least 20 employees (SB 63); provides a third gender option on the state driver's license, identification card, and birth certificate (SB 179); Lessens criminal penalties related to HIV that are higher than other communicable diseases (SB 239); Allows incarcerated persons to petition for a name or gender change under existing law (SB 310).[101]

I was pleased to see that the Gender Recognition Act had passed.

While CLRJ's staff are immensely proud of their accomplishments, they are continually looking forward. Community engagement manager Cristina Lares said, "We can't take on all the issues, so we definitely work in coalition with a lot of organizations to learn ourselves about these issues and what the needs are and really fine-tuning how we build leadership in the community so that folks can take action." While CLRJ members and followers are overwhelmingly of working-class or working-poor origins, CLRJ staff are well aware that they work with different constituencies, according to Lares: "Our base is very diverse and broad—older generation, very young folks, the young Latina professional audience, and folks on college campuses who are looking to plug in. We have a very mixed language use—Spanglish, Spanish and English, and Spanish speakers. So, we're still trying to figure out, How is the best way to reach out to the community? How should we work with different groups?" By continually analyzing the organization's research, working with allies, and designing programming tailored to its constituencies, CLRJ's long-term organizing has become more focused. According to Jimenez, "We're currently trying to figure out how to continue integrating voter-engagement work into our larger plan in the next iteration of the community-engagement work that we're doing."

CLRJ is a key collaborator on the Strong Families Network and continues to work with organizations devoted to immigrant rights. For example, the California Immigrant Policy Center coordinates an annual Immigrant Day, when community-based organizations bring their constituencies to lobby state officials about pending legislation, and for several years CLRJ participated. In preparation for these events, participants receive detailed training on the bills under consideration as well as best practices for effective lobbying. It was powerful seeing people "come out" as undocumented in front of legislators. I witnessed a woman tell her story as a single parent working as a domestic who was terrified of being deported and stranding her two pre-school-age daughters, who were sitting next to her, and she pleaded for passage of the Trust Act (AB 4), which eventually was signed into law a few years later.[102] As part of CLRJ's policy advocacy, the organization took a contingent of seventy of its supporters to Sacramento to lobby in an event called "¡RJ Ahora! Latina Leaders Speaking Story on Advocacy, Family & Reproductive Justice."

As part of a broad-based coalition working on behalf of immigrant integration called "One California," CLRJ has also contributed to California's becoming a leader of immigrant rights in the nation through passage of progressive legislation.[103] In the past three decades, California has made a remarkable pivot away from propositions that banned access to education and health services by unauthorized migrants except for emergency care (Proposition 187), instituted English as the official language (Proposition 63), and banned bilingual education (Proposition 227) and affirmative education (Proposition 209). Since 1987 the Latinx population has grown 40 percent, while Asian Americans became the fastest-growing racial group since 2000. More than one in four Californians is an immigrant, and there are an estimated 1.2–1.4 million undocumented migrants.[104] There is a powerful Latino Legislative Caucus, and Democrats have supermajorities in both houses of the legislature, which has led to the passage of legislation that benefits immigrants.[105]

For example, as of 2016, Health4All Kids allows undocumented children (under age nineteen) to enroll in Medi-Cal, and in 2017, the legislature passed SB 54, making California a sanctuary state that restricts state authorities from cooperating with federal immigration agents and limits agents from entering schools, churches, hospitals, or courthouses to detain undocumented immigrants.[106] While there is still a need for legislation that would provide health insurance to all undocumented residents, California is moving toward more inclusion of immigrants and policies that benefit low-income people. Alfonso Gonzales summarizes the activism that led to legislation that reflects the needs of more Californians: "We have witnessed the intensification of Latino migrant activism in many forms over the last several decades, from marches and voter registration drives to civil disobedience actions and the formation of coalitions with progressive allies in what has become a multiethnic and multisector migrant rights movement."[107] Reproductive justice advocates are integral to the political transformation occurring in California.

In sum, CLRJ provided more training to some women than they had ever had related to their bodies, sexuality, and the human right to access health care. Through interactive exercises and storytelling pedagogies, its trainings were accessible and encouraged self-reflexivity, community advocacy, and identifying as *chingonas*. CLRJ imparted new ideas about human rights while incorporating "existing cultural norms, values, and practices," especially those related to the value of family and community.[108] By presenting the information and holding discussions in Spanish, CLRJ sustains language and culture, which "are themselves forms of sustenance that nurture the identities of young people of color."[109] Through the use of intersectionality, CLRJ's trainings resonated with the challenges in women's daily lives yet presented a vision of collective resistance and change based on human rights discourse in the United States. Similar to the National Latina Institute, California Latinas for Reproductive Justice bridges the Latina experience as insiders who come from similar communities as their constituents, as well as people involved in the world of social activism around the globe.

Interestingly enough, NLIRH and CLRJ explored the possibility of collaborating by opening a new organizing effort in rural California. Some NLIRH staff flew to Los Angeles to discuss how it would work, and CLRJ staff raised several concerns. As the largest reproductive justice organization in the country, NLIRH has a decade more experience, about two-thirds more staff, and a considerably larger budget than CLRJ. After a frank conversation, the two organizations agreed they would not collaborate on this new initiative after all, yet they continue to work together on other projects. Specifically, CLRJ collaborates annually with the NLIRH and COLOR for a week of events, activism, and conversations dedicated to "securing reproductive justice for the nation's 26 million Latin@s, our families, and our communities."[110] And in their ability to have open conversations centered on their own needs and desires, NLIRH and CLRJ exemplify how they are able to mediate possible tensions between women of color–led organizations. Also, during the trainings provided at both of these institutes, the participants, many of whom were Catholics or Protestants, did not voice their opposition to abortion. It seemed as if they saw abortion as a legal right that when practiced by others did not infringe on their own spiritual beliefs.

Conclusion

Clearly there are some ready-to-work skills when using an intersectionality approach. The reproductive justice movement uses several processes—negotiating strategic intersectional collaboration, including which organizations will assume leadership in particular campaigns, framing issues on behalf of communities of color, and using strengths-based storytelling in safe spaces to convey women's structural vulnerability yet strength and resiliency—that are evidence of a distinctive approach to organizing. Members also have conversations about whether to collaborate at all and how to collaborate in ways that honors all allies' strengths and recognizes their vulnerabilities. We see these strategies at work in other reproductive justice campaigns. Reproductive justice organizations have a history of negotiating collaboration despite differences related to race, class, gender, sexuality, national origins, or citizenship, and they engage with the way "one form of power or exclusion is mutually constituted and managed through another."[111] These cases illustrate how reproductive justice advocates are making interventions in which intersectionality means intersecting forms of oppressions, intersecting issues for mobilization, and helping to craft politicized identities in which people share some experiences of marginalization yet belong to distinct communities with particular strengths and commitments. By selectively collaborating across sectors, learning from one another about the specific challenges within their respective communities, taking leadership or supporting others, and demonstrating their compassion for one another, they construct a praxis that navigates through tensions related to differential structural vulnerabilities and positions of strength.

These two "social lives" of human rights indicate the strategic use of specific tactics such as conducting research, grassroots organizing, and conscious-raising that, along with storytelling and coalition building, leads to a sense of efficacy that goes beyond women's individual problems and situates them in relation to broader changes occurring in either Texas or California. The work of NLIRH, the Center for Reproductive Rights, and CLRJ resonates with what Rosa Linda Fregoso calls a "pluriversal" view of human rights: "tied to a zone of human autonomy and agency" with a vision that "rights entail duties and obligations to something greater than the self and the state."[112] Indeed, reproductive justice organizations construct a new form of citizenship in which women learn their political rights as well as notions of social citizenship and cultural citizenship—the rights to civic engagement, to partake in social activities and express their own language publicly regardless of their structural vulnerabilities or marginalization.[113] This radical citizenship is complex, indicating multiple rights, obligations, contributions, and forms of belonging.

The evidence also suggests that NLIRH and CLRJ have worked as skilled translators by bringing structural violence to light, illuminating the experience of low-income women in human rights venues, legislatures, and other fora. These organizations engage in nuanced politics of translation so that low-income women see that they have the human right to health care and to raise their children in healthy environments yet still honor their own cultural values and social relations. Human rights campaigns often are directed at governments, and the Nuestro Texas and MFG campaigns critique Texas and California as perpetrating state violence. Simultaneously, NLIRH and CLRJ have been working with women who negotiate borderlands in their daily lives and struggle with quotidian issues like securing employment or housing for their families, avoiding apprehension and deportation, or making copayments for health care, if they qualify at all for medical insurance, and who have little time or resources to become activists. Yet regardless of their circumstances, low-income Latinas experience a consciousness-raising process based on the notion that their stories matter to policy makers, academics, other activists, and the public. Moreover, participating in activism was beneficial to the women. The social welfare theorist Loretta Pyles suggests that the capabilities that facilitate healing and transformation include mindfulness with compassion, curiosity alongside critical inquiry, and equanimity despite concerted effort.[114] While I have not seen or heard of a focus on equanimity, NLIRH's and CLRJ's training encourages developing mindfulness, compassion, curiosity, and critical inquiry. The women see themselves situated within a long-term struggle in which their participation is a step toward full human rights. Indeed, Sarah Combellick-Bidney argues that "stories . . . are critical interventions in the global debate on which rights count as universal rights and how they might be protected as such."[115]

Unlike the celebrity storytelling that is so prominent in public life today, these campaigns illuminate how deeply contextualized stories by low-income women of color critique structural inequalities and contest pejorative discourses. Indeed, Tannia Esparza, former executive director of YWU, reflected on the RJ movement's distinct views about storytelling:

> In policy spaces where strategies are made for movements, stories are often seen as just an additive to a campaign; they can be a media strategy. . . . What happens is most of the time people just want a sob story, like, "Hey, can you talk about that one time somebody did something horrible thing to you?" But we believe that the story *is* the expertise, and without them, then, there is no movement. . . . The people that are directly living through these issues are going to shape the strategy. . . . The storytelling is a methodology that comes from our community.

Sujatha Jesudason and Katrina Kimport suggest, "A reproductive justice framework demands a different methodology, one that explicitly attends to power," one in which "historically marginalized women speak for themselves at the nexus of multiple oppressions and in the context of their community lives."[116] These women's *testimonios* illustrate women's complex experiences, identities, and subjectivities as they confront the multiple dimensions of their subordination. They experience Gloria Anzaldúa's insight: "It is through narrative that you come to understand and know your self and make sense of the world. Through narrative you formulate your identities by unconsciously locating yourself in social narratives not of your own making."[117] These women's experiences with storytelling also confirm the notion that the embodiment involved in telling one's story—hearing one's own voice and those of others; witnessing another's emotions as he or she tells a story; experiencing the pain, sorrow, or joy in the story; seeing how the stories are treated by others—creates powerful bonds among storytellers.[118] The process of storytelling itself was compelling to movement actors by allowing them to build a collective identity as reproductive justice advocates: "Testimonio pedagogy asks the listeners for openness, respect, and self-reflexivity to forge connections between people who otherwise might never coalesce or build solidarity."[119]

In both of these storytelling campaigns, the reproductive justice organizers did not let the stories speak for themselves: they trained women how to be effective storytellers who linked their personal experiences to collective structural problems. They encouraged the listeners to interpret the stories for their policy implications, with high political stakes, as well as for the way women contend with social inequality. In both cases, the participants were diverse from one another and from the organizers who held advanced educational degrees. Their coalitional practice was based on a philosophy that values intersectionality and the human right to reproductive health care and that critiques the structural vulnerability enacted by the neoliberal state against low-income people. Simultaneously, these activists confirmed Zakiya Luna's observation that in claiming an authentic right to speak to and for marginalized communities, "representatives should have mutual relationships with the disadvantaged group, including mutual recognition of shared disadvantage and the role of representatives."[120] The movement for reproductive justices engages in a politics of translation that is complex, incorporating basebuilding, policy advocacy, and culture shift work.

By using a collectivist human rights framework, US-based reproductive justice groups establish productive working relationships with global human rights movements, which promote transnational partnerships and use narratives as key intervention tactics.[121] This framework is also useful for challenging US exceptionalism. Like all human rights activists, the Center for Reproductive Rights, the NLIRH, and CLRJ illustrate that similar to many nations in the Global South, access to health care and education in the United States is seriously limited for low-income women, particularly the undocumented.

By using intersectionality and human rights, the reproductive justice movement builds a broader vision that militates against state co-option. The state can only co-opt social movements or enact neoliberal incorporation when the most vulnerable are left out, that is, when some social categories are prioritized.[122] By insisting that *all* community members be included, these activists nurture a political commons that, according to Kevin Duong, articulates "an emergent normative vision of justice among allies and companions."[123] This form of world-making naturalizes that women are different from one another and that *everyone's* voice matters. These activists construct a methodology grounded organically in their experience in particular places with specific groups and thus *work* intersectionality with the radical idea that women of color have the collective human right to health care with dignity.

3

Youth Mobilization

When I came here, everybody seemed cool, and I wondered,
"Are you for real?"
—anonymous young woman

I had no idea that there could be such a place that was so
passionate about sexual education.
—anonymous young man

"Alysa," a seventeen-year-old high school junior, happened upon a youth group sponsored by the Colorado Organization for Latina Opportunity and Reproductive Rights. Prior to getting involved with COLOR, she recalled, "I was very shy and quiet, and I'm not a very open person, not so quick to get to know people." While in middle school, she had a relationship with a young woman and revealed this to her mother: "I told her, 'I don't know what's wrong with me, but I'm really in love with this girl. She was like, 'Okay, if that's what you want, I'm going to love you either way.'" Alysa explained, "You're just scared that people are just going to judge you," and disclosed that she had been bullied at school for the relationship: "People become more hateful and judgmental nowadays. So, you get this perspective of 'I should just keep to myself because no one is going to take the time to understand me. People are going to judge me. I'm going to get bullied. People will make fun of me, so I should just keep quiet, keep to myself.'" When she first got involved with COLOR, Alysa said, "I just thought it was about political stuff. When I came and I found out that it was about reproductive justice, I was like, 'Okay, so I'm not alone on some of the stuff I feel about reproductive justice, some of the health-care stuff. I should invest my time and see where it goes.'" She joined Latinas Increasing Political Strength (LIPS), COLOR's leadership institute designed to train Latinas ages sixteen to twenty-one in organizing and advocacy, including participating in demonstrations protesting a range of issues (see later in this chapter). When I met Alysa a year later during her senior year in 2013, she was deeply involved in COLOR's advocacy work and indeed was taking leadership in its lobbying efforts at the state legislature. During an interview, I asked if she felt COLOR had influenced how she thinks about herself and the work she wants to do, and she affirmed, "I learned not to be shy; it's okay to be outspoken—have this big voice and be loud about things that you're passionate about. Because other people are too, but other people don't have that force; they can't speak up for themselves." Alysa was planning on going to college and eventually working with youth and continuing to collaborate with organizations involved in youth advocacy: "Being in COLOR and being in LIPS and everything has really been inspirational. I've always wanted to advocate for stuff that I really care about, but I never had the confidence to really do it. And now I'm like, 'Hell yeah, we're going to do this!'" How did this formerly quiet, shy young woman become a confident, outspoken youth leader?

Part of the challenge of studying youth activism is that "youth" is a social construct whose meaning changes over time, and depending on context, who is considered a young person varies tremendously. The scholarship on youth recognizes that young people embody a liminal space. In the United States, we consider youth to be a time reserved for learning, developmental progress, play, and preparation for adulthood. We see youths as developmentally immature and in need of protection and thus place restrictions related to their legal rights (e.g., voting or in the criminal justice system) or ability to purchase controlled substances, and we also set standards of care for minors. Those youths who are undocumented experience an added dimension of liminality between belonging and exclusion and have fewer positive educational, economic, and mental health outcomes even after adjusting for indicators of ethnicity and class.[1] Further, there are gendered differences regarding when youth ends and adulthood begins. In poor communities within industrialized nations, young people often must begin to work and contribute economically as well as provide reproductive labor such as child care for their families' well-being at an early age.[2] Farmworker children, for example, make substantial contributions to their parents' wages.[3] In the Global South, in some rural indigenous communities, young people marry and start having children in their early teens.[4] Young men from poor communities begin their work histories earlier than young women do, which then facilitates transnational migration.[5] Migrants who settle in the United States bring these notions of youth and adulthood from their home countries and then must negotiate different expectations here.

The visibility of youth activism is only recently coming to light. Undocumented youths, especially those who received Deferred Action for Childhood Arrivals (DACA) by President Obama's executive order or who identify as DREAMERs have gained prominence for their leadership.[6] DACAmented youth and DREAMERs who push for immigration reform often live in mixed-status families, in which some kin are US citizens, and they have relatives in other countries. In mixed-status families, the legal privileges afforded to citizens or permanent residents but not the undocumented have significant material consequences with regard to access to health care or education and vulnerability to deportation.[7] Young Latinxs are more likely than other ethnoracial groups to remain uninsured despite passage of the ACA, and they are less likely to possess insurance through other sources, including their parents' insurance.[8] Often undocumented youths internalize their structural vulnerability, particularly when they do not discover they are unauthorized until adolescence.[9] According to members of the Students Informing Now Collective, undocumented youth often feel "social isolation, marginalization, stigma, fear, and shame" related to their unauthorized legal status, which limits their access to higher education and professional positions.[10] Yet young DREAMERs and DACAmented activists have promoted the framing of being "undocumented and unafraid," which profoundly influenced the immigrant rights and other social movements. Sometimes there is tension between the goals of immigrant rights organizations that want to highlight the experiences of a few undocumented immigrants and those of young DREAMERs who prefer their solidarity work to include all unauthorized migrants, especially the most vulnerable, such as queer migrants.[11]

Adolescence is a time particularly charged in relation to young people learning about and expressing their sexuality, especially for gender-nonconforming youths as well as gay, lesbian, bisexual, or questioning youths or those with nondominant sexualities.[12] Often young women's parents speak to them in opaque or coded language regarding sexuality, and they are subject to surveillance and control over their behavior, including by relatives living abroad.[13] When offered abstinence-only sex education in school settings, young women's and men's notions of desire are simply missing.[14] Abstinence-only sex education also carries implicit overtones about race and heteronormativity, according to the sociologist Jessica Fields, who critiques how these programs originated in notions of protecting young white women from the sexual aggressions of youth of color. Abstinence-only sex education also contains heteronormative notions that sexual activity outside of marriage is harmful physically and psychologically, and the least-advantaged students receive the most-restrictive sex educations. Fields concludes, "Adultism renders young people's sexual behaviors [as] indiscretions that challenge parental and familial authority, strain already depleted resources, and signal broad moral degeneration."[15]

So as to shift attention away from adult authority and toward youth agency, scholars have coined the term "youthscape," which views youth as actively producing meanings, narratives, cultural products, and social engagement in particular geographic sites and historical moments. Youthscape "revitalizes discussions about youth cultures and social movements while simultaneously theorizing the political and social uses of youth to maintain repressive systems of social control."[16] Scholars who analyze youth activism argue that youths understand a great deal of the power relations that shape their lives; teenage activists talk back forcefully and with great clarity about the social problems affecting their communities.[17] The sociologist Lorena Garcia demonstrates that young women confront racism, patriarchal and heterosexual privileges, and socioeconomic marginality and strategically engage in the politics of respectability.[18] That is, young Latinas are mindful of the stereotypes and expectations about their sexuality as well as the limited resources for navigating safer sexual practice and express their sexual agency by gaining knowledge and interpersonal skills as well as constructing meaning related to their own notions of sexual safety and pleasure. Scholars of youth participatory cultures encourage us to specify how different practices, tools, ideologies, and technologies contribute to youth participation and a sense of collective voice and efficacy through larger networks that work to bring about change.[19] I find the work on youth agency a helpful departure for analyzing how reproductive justice organizations offer knowledge and skills to youths using the framework of intersectionality and human rights.

Many reproductive justice organizations organize "youth empowerment" activities, often with storytelling projects. They work with youths ten to twenty-four years of age, mindful of the profound developmental differences within this age range, and some organizations include youths in decision-making roles.[20] Youth empowerment programs funded by foundations have led some of the youth-focused work; indeed, some reproductive justice organizations initially began as youth projects. Rocio Córdoba, formerly a program officer for the Ford Foundation who used to oversee funding programs on youth, sexuality, and reproductive health and rights programs, affirmed, "I'm very excited to see the work of organizations who are leading with young people and those who are working on behalf of young people and with young people as allies. The reproductive justice organizations have always had at the heart a new philosophy on leadership development and more decentralized notion of leadership."

What does "empowerment" mean for reproductive justice organizations that work with youths from low-income communities? Especially for young women who live in racially segregated cities, if they are not involved with DREAMERs or other organizations, they may have limited experience with activism. Also of interest are youth programs that use storytelling, an approach that could be problematic. Julia Paley warns that when activists use the language of empowerment through storytelling, there is a "paradox of participation" with a limited range of possibilities; that is, participants tell their stories, but the aftermath may not lead to structural change.[21] Further, Sujatha Fernandes suggests that during the current neoliberal era, storytelling has been reconfigured or "curated": in the current "culture of storytelling," subjects often are encouraged to present "carefully curated narratives with predetermined storylines as a tool of philanthropy, statecraft, and advocacy."[22] Indeed, often philanthropic organizations and foundations, corporations, and the US government use storytelling for their own purposes, as do celebrities and even former president Obama. Fernandes argues that storytelling is being reconfigured toward a market model that produces entrepreneurial, upwardly mobile subjects who "shift the focus away from structurally defined axes of oppression and help to defuse the confrontational politics of social movements."[23]

Given how encumbered notions of empowerment and storytelling could be, this chapter explores the following questions: Given that these organizations provide training to young women, are their stories curated in any sense? Are reproductive justice organizations promoting storytelling practices that emphasize individualism? Do young women, who are in the process of developing their own racial, ethnic, gender, and sexual identities, shift their subjectivities in relation to participating in reproductive justice campaigns? What does empowerment look like for youth participants?

I will discuss three examples of how reproductive justice organizations engage with youth and use the language of youth empowerment. I begin with the Oakland-based Forward Together, which works with predominantly Asian youth in its ambitious project on the limitations of sexual education in Oakland schools. I then move to discuss the Illinois Caucus for Adolescent Health's work predominantly with African American youth the summer I was in Chicago on behalf of repealing legislation requiring parental notification of abortion. The third case discusses COLOR's youth programs in Denver. Most of the youth working with these organizations come from low-income backgrounds, although a handful had parents who were professionals. However, all of these youth of color experience what Lois Weis and Michelle Fine call "circuits of dispossession" in their everyday lives. That is, they live in racially segregated cities in which public or private entities (think charter schools) deprive low-income communities of color of resources. In this context, institutions, such as schools, erode or even become punitive, subjecting youth of color to indignities and causing them to have few expectations for their success.[24]

I attempted to conduct research with rather than about youths, mindful of the power dynamics involved when youths are active in the research process, by using focus groups and open-ended interviews with youths.[25] I argue that these organizations increasingly use storytelling as a means of navigating difference within social categories and building solidarity as youths who are in a crucial phase in their lives. Further, by training youths to use research and craft narratives to convey analyses of social problems and to garner support from policy makers and com-

munity members for specific policy changes, the movement for reproductive justice deploys what Fernandes calls "deeply contextualized and
complex storytelling."[26]

Forward Together's "Sex Ed the City" Campaign

I conducted interviews with two members of Forward Together's staff
as well as did participant observation with its core group and conducted a focus group with seven seventeen-year-old Asian American
women. Executive director Eveline Shen pointed out that working with
young people "has been the anchor" of the organization's work, "ever
since the beginning." She presented an overview of the organization's
process of organizing youth: "It's providing leadership development
within your grassroots membership and providing resources. . . . We
brought in researchers who know how to work with young people and
do participatory research. We are also training them as organizers to
make change. The youth go and talk to city council members. They're
producing a video; they are talking about the impact of sex ed in young
people's lives. They are speaking, teaching, training other youth, advocating and lobbying. *They're* providing the leadership and the voice of
this campaign; and it's something that they directly wanted to do, and
it impacts them." Forward Together focuses on Asian, South Asian, and
Pacific Islanders, and when I did ethnographic research, the participants were Chinese, Cambodian, Indian, Laotian, Vietnamese, Filipino,
and Indonesian youths and youths with mixed heritage. Amanda Wake,
former youth organizing director, pointed out that these youths are not
necessarily immigrants themselves: "The majority of the youth have
very little physical connection with the homeland." However, Shen
clarified that Forward Together also works with Latinas and African Americans, so multiracial organizing "translates throughout all
the work" it does. "Identity is important, but we're not into identity
politics." Shen also clarified how Forward Together works through
the tensions related to multiple identities by its youth participants:
"'Women of color' is a starting point of inclusion from a bigger circle,
and also starting from the point for working with people who are ready,
which is also another key thing. People who are ready to see how their
issues are connected to other issues, how they are ready to connect to

other communities, they're ready to build relationships. That puts it out of who you are. We have explicit conversations about how we want to work on behalf of marginalized individuals, women, and families, and communities." Many of the youths' parents are immigrants, and Wake pointed out, "Our young people don't share a lot about their work with their parents. There's definitely like cultural and language barriers, like not knowing the words to even say 'reproductive justice' or even to say 'sex.' So, so we talk a lot about this language/cultural gap in communicating between generations. Our program isn't just about sex; it's also about other issues too."

Initially Forward Together's youth project was Sisters in Action for Reproductive Empowerment (SAFIRE), founded in the late 1990s. However, once Forward Together organized the Strong Families Initiative, according to Shen, "we realized that we needed to include young men. And it's been really amazing to have young men fighting for reproductive justice—like why didn't we think of it before!" Since there is little research that focuses on Asian men and that disaggregates the data by ethnicity, the staff conducted a focus group facilitated by a male staff member who works with young men. Wake confirmed this point: "There are a lot of issues that young Asian men are facing in their communities around masculinity: like defining masculinity for themselves, violence that they are seeing in their homes, in their communities, in their schools. They talked about being targets at school for bullying; they talk about Asian male masculinity that is asexualized at times, feminized at times, the model-minority stereotype, things like that that are really impacting their lives. These things are specifically happening to young Asian men in Oakland." The men's program was so successful that Forward Together was unable to accommodate all of those who applied. Forward Together also has a Core Leadership Program composed of fifteen young women and men who have completed SAFIRE or the men's group and are leading their campaigns, creating and then facilitating workshops on their work that they present to district administrators, teachers, school board members, health-center directors, and so on.

The youth participants at Forward Together engage in political education about reproductive justice, sexuality, gender, and systems of oppression related to racial or ethnic stereotypes. Depending on the time, the organization educates youths about other political issues like the Occupy movement or elections. According to Wake, "We did workshops with them on sex-ed issues. So, we did healthy relationships for a talk; we did a lot of talk about gender—gender as a choice, which does not have to be a binary; some people might identify as genderqueer; you get to choose your gender; there's a difference between gender and sex. We also talked about sexuality, all the different sexuality identities: What does that look like in your school? What does homophobia look like? How can you be an ally?" As youths learn this material, they begin to see themselves as part of broader social forces that affect youths of color.

Storytelling is an important part of youth training. Shen observed, "We tell our stories for different reasons: to help people understand the policy need or stories to legislators." Stories also enable political education, especially when provided by youth. Wake explained, "We also have queer students, so like giving them an opportunity to share their stories too. We had a LGBTQ panel of primarily Asian American young adults who came and talked about their identity, about coming out, about what they experienced on a daily basis." Forward Together uses storytelling, after the youths created a set of community agreements, which included, according to those in the focus group, "confidentiality, we leave drama at the door; this is a community safe space." They learn to negotiate different viewpoints: "If you don't totally agree with someone, you just say, 'I respect your idea and your thoughts, but I think that . . .' and go with your thoughts. So, it's not like putting someone else down; you're just saying your opinion while appreciating another person."

One of Forward Together's most well-known campaigns was its "Sex Ed the City: More than Just Protection," which it launched in 2011 as part of the Strong Families Initiative to address the ways in which sex education varied dramatically in different schools in California.[27] The organization brought in a consultant, Lailan Huen, who has expertise in conducting youth participatory action research (YPAR) projects, which engage young people as agents of change by conducting research in their own communities.[28] According to Wake, the YPAR process is the following: "First you come up with your research question and then figure out the methodology: Do you want to do a survey, a focus group, or oral histories? So, they picked a survey and some focus groups to get some more narrative responses." The research questions were, "What is the state of sex education in the Oakland Unified School District (OUSD)?

What do students want their sex education to look like?" Wake recalled, "They went through a *long* process of editing, because they came up with a ton of questions and they had to narrow them down." The youths aspired to meet the Sex Education Justice framework that had been created by reproductive justice organizations and that recommended the following goals: "Mandate comprehensive, culturally meaningful sexuality education curricula that honor all communities; Ensure language access for students with limited English proficiency and deaf students; Enforce compliance with state laws that require comprehensive, inclusive sex education; Reform parental opt-out laws to ensure student access to sexuality education; Promote school-based reproductive health clinics that provide students with information, services, and referrals for reproductive and sexual health."[29] The youths brainstormed about what Sex Education Justice is and learned California's sex-ed policy. In California, sex education must be medically accurate, science based, and age appropriate; contain thorough information about condoms and contraceptives; provide information about when, how, and why to delay sexual activity and teach healthy decision-making skills; be free of biases regarding gender, sexual orientation, race, and ethnicity; be accessible to English-language learners and students with disabilities.[30] Once these research instruments were ready, the youths administered them at six Oakland high schools and middle schools, taking care to include schools that were diverse by geography and by whether they were public or private and to administer them to different subject classes within schools.

The Let's Sex Ed the City campaign produced a report, "Let's Get It On: Oakland Youth's New Vision for Sex Ed," that showcased the YPAR project's findings. The research included 531 surveys and five focus groups with Oakland Unified School District high school and middle school students. The findings were remarkable: 62 percent of the respondents had spent no time on sex education during the previous school year, yet 75 percent believed that comprehensive sex education is important to their lives. Moreover, when asked with whom they feel comfortable talking about sex, 70 percent chose friends, 41 percent chose a health-care provider, 34 percent chose a parent or caregiver, 28 percent chose siblings, 18 percent chose teachers, and 11 percent chose nobody. Ninety-eight percent of the respondents believe they should have access to free contraception and a health center on campus. Along with excerpts from the focus groups, the report included a number of smart recommendations related to implementing current California sex education, changing the curriculum, hiring qualified teachers, reducing stigma, creating safer spaces and cultural competency, establishing health centers and resources for youth, and supporting community and school culture that is sensitive to youths' needs.[31] I attended the public launch of this project, "Oakland Speaks: Youth Share Their New Vision for Sexuality Education," in which youths made a presentation about some of their research findings that included professional graphics. They also enacted the need for comprehensive sex education through poetry, a game show, and skits—a memorable laugh line was, "Abstinence works!" Clearly, they had done good outreach since the event was quite successful, with excellent attendance by youths and adults such that there was standing room only in a room that held about one hundred seats. The audience was racially mixed—Asians, Blacks, Latinxs, whites, and mixed-race women and men. Free, delicious Thai food was offered as well.

After the youths had completed their report, ten of them took a trip to Washington, DC, and received training by Advocates for Youth, which has been working on the "Real Education for Healthy Youth Act." This act (H.R. 3602; S. 1653) would ensure that federal funding is allocated for comprehensive sexual health education that includes anatomy and physiology; growth and development; healthy relationships; prevention of unintended pregnancy and sexually transmitted infections; gender, gender identity, and sexual orientation; and protection from dating violence, sexual assault, bullying, and harassment. Further, the bill requires that sex education be evidence based, be medically accurate, provide age-appropriate information, and be inclusive of LGBT youth and survivors of sexual abuse and assault.[32] The youths lobbied Senators Diane Feinstein and Barbara Boxer and Representative Lee's offices. Initially there were no commitments to support the bill, but they were pleased that after their visit, Boxer's staff called to say that she was open to negotiating her support for the bill.[33]

Forward Together has strategically used social media as a means of recruiting and educating young people. According to Amanda Wake,

We have a blog that we're posting on almost every other day, our *Strong Families Blog*. We also are using Facebook and Twitter because that's where a lot of young people are, and then getting on other people's blogs too. And then we work sometimes with a social media strategist who helps us think about timing, messaging, and about the blogs that we want to build relationships with so that they're putting our stuff on their networks. Because some blogs have so much reach as far as how many people are reading them. And then sometimes like *Huffington Post* will pick up a blog or a framework that we're putting out there, which is great.

Like other reproductive justice organizations, Forward Together realizes that a savvy media strategy is key, according to Wake: "We recognize that policy shift and culture shift need to happen at the same time in order for actual institutional change to happen. Because you can rewrite a policy, but that doesn't mean that it's implemented. Or you can change culture, but that doesn't mean the policies and the laws are actually going to support that. So, they need to be happening in partnership with each other." Indeed, often other reproductive justice organizations deploy media strategies as an empowering tool with several benefits. Cristina Aguilar, former executive director of COLOR, noted, "We could project an image bigger that what we were; we could be small and mighty by using media tools." Moreover, young people are so attuned to the media that it has sparked new forms of activism.[34]

The focus group I conducted with Forward Together participants was fascinating because of the thoughtful, quiet strength that the young women conveyed. As an instructor accustomed to working with students eighteen and older, I was thrilled to hear seventeen-year-olds speak confidently about intersectionality and heteronormativity. One woman said, "I feel like we learn a lot here, and we can explain to people. Like someone was like, 'Sex and gender are the same thing,' and I said, 'It's not the same thing!' And I explained the difference." However, it was the process of negotiating difference among Asian Americans that was most revealing to me. They described the process of getting to know one another throughout their training by telling their life stories. One woman recalled, "We basically just talk about where we're born, the community where we live, what it's like. It really makes us realize how different we are even though we're not that different, but we have a lot of things that are really similar." Another pointed out, "I think while sharing our stories, we created a bond, and we get emotional. But then this space is safe.

Whatever is said here stays here. It's a story that you know not to spread it around, and you know you can trust them." They also found storytelling to be an effective way to lobby. One young woman opined, "Telling our story is really important 'cause we really want comprehensive sex ed, so it's vital to tell them. So they'd better listen. I think stories are really powerful, especially when they're coming from one person. Like, it sticks or something."

However, differences continued to be prominent in the youths' thinking. When I asked if the term "women of color" felt inclusive, I received mixed responses. One woman said, "I've never really thought of myself as a woman of color. I just thought of myself as Asian or Chinese." Another woman clarified, "Historically it's been used as a point to unify, not to separate, but still it depends on the context. And we talk about it as always being a choice. So, you have the self-determination. You have the power to decide how you identify. So, it's also totally okay when people feel comfortable or uncomfortable."

Forward Together planned ongoing work in the Oakland Unified School District on implementing more comprehensive sex education by working with administrators and teachers. According to Wake, this entails some culture shift work since California already has good sex-education policy, but it is not implemented in all schools. Forward Together planned on producing short films that can be used in classrooms or with youth organizations and that include lesson plans or dialogues for peer education, according to Wake: "We're also just thinking about other social media culture shift strategies that we can do, because to the youth, like, it's so natural. They're such consumers of culture all the time."

I conducted participant observation with the core group in 2013, which included eighteen youths (with two young men) and two staff members. During the course of an afternoon, we had several icebreakers that generated a lot of laughter. The youths reported back on a recent meeting with a school board member. They appreciated that they had rehearsed, so everyone knew what to say; the stories went well, and their training prior to the meeting helped: to make eye contact, have a strong voice, and use their "Forward Stance" to ground them (see chapter 4). One school board member apparently said something to the effect that comprehensive sexuality education was not a priority for him and that lots of school districts do not follow the law, so why should they require more work? It was hard not to feel discouraged. However, the youths moved on to discuss their process of sharing their personal stories about learning about sexuality and the need for comprehensive sex ed. When asked, "How did you feel about that experience?" several stated that it was good, that they drew closer and bonded as a group, that they appreciated the trust from one another, that sharing personal stories in which they felt vulnerable was hard but that they appreciated the support they received and that they are learning that sharing hard stories is part of the healing process.

Next the group worked on developing a strategy to increase knowledge and awareness of the participatory action research project and to recruit for a new core group. One of the facilitators encouraged them to reflect on the question, "What does our base mean?" After some discussion, she reminded them, "Our base is people in our community that support our campaign, who show up when we need them. We need to meet students where they are at and find simple, doable methods to meet our goals." The youths broke into small groups and brainstormed about possible next steps to educate the public about their report—one practiced a presentation to a school board member (with a "Forward Stance" practice beforehand), while the rest of us came up with ideas for sharing Forward Together's work on sex ed. I was impressed with the ideas they generated (see plate 12): organize a benefit concert with a booth with sex-ed information, a barbecue at a local park, a talent show, booths at street festivals, a picnic party, a smoothie party, a bake sale or ceramics party, a car wash, game shows, a flash mob downtown with skits, karaoke sessions, a 5k marathon, a tea party, or arts and crafts sessions at Forward Together's offices—and all of these should offer free food. They also suggested that having a guest speaker at local schools or playing sports would attract youths to attend. They suggested a bunch of activities to be held at local schools—classes with skills sharing; assemblies; lunchtime activities with food, games, or raffles; open mike related to the campaign; speakers at school clubs; or socials and classroom workshops through a play. Finally, the youths suggested producing an informational YouTube video or blog events. The facilitators wrote their ideas on a big piece of paper and promised they would discuss each one at their next meeting. Eventually they did produce a YouTube video with playful language—they made clear that the information would go beyond learning how to place a condom on a banana, with a joke that no bananas would be "abused"—presumably for demonstrating how to put a male condom on a penis.

A few years later at a reproductive justice youth-group meeting organized by CLRJ, I ran into one of the Forward Together focus-group participants, who was attending university in another city. As she updated me about her high school graduation and move to college, she was enthusiastic about having worked with Forward Together. She said, "They saved my life! . . . They're the reason I'm here." Clearly, like many others involved with Forward Together, she saw herself as working toward youth empowerment. Youths learned to conduct primary research, analyze and present the findings, make policy recommendations, lobby relevant authorities, and brainstorm how to disseminate the reproductive justice approach, all while claiming their particular identities and sense of efficacy by telling their life stories to one another and to authority figures.

ICAH's Work Contesting Parental Notification of Abortion

The Parental Notification of Abortion Act (PNA) was originally passed in Illinois in 1995 but was challenged many times in the courts. The Illinois Supreme Court ruled that the state would have to begin enforcing the law as of August 15, 2013. PNA requires physicians of females who are unemancipated or unmarried minors, seventeen years or younger, to notify an adult family member forty-eight hours before an abortion.[35] There are ways to get around this measure: a young woman can get a waiver if a judge rules that notification is against her best interest and the youth declares in writing that she is the victim of sexual abuse, neglect, or physical abuse by an adult family member.[36] In these instances, the attending physician must certify in the patient's medical record that s/he has received this written declaration by the minor. Any physician who willfully fails to provide notice before performing an abortion on a minor will be referred to the Illinois State Medical Disciplinary Board.[37]

Parental notification of abortion laws assume that notifying parents will garner parental support and are quite controversial. Supporters claim that allowing minors to get abortions without parental knowledge denies parents their basic rights. Supporters also believe that parental notification benefits minors by improving communication between parents and their children, promoting responsibility by teens to "think before they act," and ensuring that parents provide their children's full medical histories and protect young adolescents who are unable to make mature decisions, which leads to better medical care and ensures that parents are able to assist their daughters in responding to unplanned pregnancies. Supporters also argue that in the rare cases when parental involvement is not appropriate, the judicial-bypass provisions allow safe and effective means of protecting young women who wish to obtain abortions on their own.[38] Those who oppose parental notification of abortion in Illinois, including the American Civil Liberties Union, which sued to halt implementation of PNA, argued that the law is flawed because young women are capable of making informed medical decisions on their own.[39] Minors may consent to a range of sexual and reproductive health-care services related to contraception, sexually transmitted infections, prenatal care, adoptions, mental health, and alcohol- and drug-abuse treatment, and most states permit minor parents to make important decisions regarding their own children. However, a majority of states require parental involvement in a minor's decision to have an abortion.[40]

The evidence suggests that some teens are severely sanctioned when they seek an abortion. Many teens experience distress and intimidation by emancipation proceedings that would allow them to make their own decisions and have little recourse if an anti-abortion judge rules capriciously against them. The court bypass process is more likely to be used by older adolescents, those in higher socioeconomic brackets, and those who perceive that their parents hold positive attitudes toward abortion.[41] One study found that conflict between Black adolescents and their mothers might become exacerbated because mothers view teenage pregnancy as more socially acceptable than abortion.[42] Further, if minors are forced to involve their parents, many of them will not avail themselves of reproductive health services.[43] In the post-parental-notification phase, other states have seen dramatic drops in adolescent abortion rates, primarily because young women seek abortions in different states.[44] The mandate of parental consent appears to cause adolescents, especially older minors, who are less likely to communicate with their parents about their abortion, to delay abortion decisions, which may increase health risks.[45] Indeed, NARAL Pro-Choice America argues that mandatory parental-involvement laws actually threaten young women's health and safety by "increasing the possibility of illegal and self-induced abortion, family violence, suicide, later abortions, and unwanted childbirth."[46] The negative experience of young women who have to notify their parents about an abortion became clear to former executive director Yamani Hernandez when she began working at ICAH in 2011. Hernandez told a story that led her to critique the Parental Notification of Abortion Act:

> In our jobs program, it was pay day, and a young participant asked all of the young people that were in the program if she could pay them $10 each to kick her in the stomach so that she would miscarry . . . so that she wouldn't have to tell her parents that she needed an abortion. I understand that's a very violent story, and it's difficult to hear, but it's real. And it's something that is actually happening. That young person was so afraid to talk to her parents—she was willing to endure being violently beaten to avoid having a perfectly safe medical procedure.[47]

For those adolescents who feel they cannot obtain appropriate assistance from family members, parental notification of abortion laws may lead to increased family conflict.[48]

ICAH describes itself as "a network of empowered youth and allied adults who transform public consciousness and increase the capacity of family, school, and healthcare systems to support the sexual health, rights, and identities of youth."[49] Though ICAH was founded in 1977 as a teen-pregnancy-prevention program, it changed its name in 1991, embraced the reproductive justice framework in 2007, and began using "adult accomplice" rather than "adult ally" recently. ICAH periodically offers adult accomplice workshops in which youths make presentations to adults about ICAH's approach and specific projects, and the organization's staff also is young—most are twenty-four to thirty years old—and racially mixed.

ICAH is a youth-focused organization, according to Hernandez, which means that 90 percent of the decision-making is vetted by youth. ICAH intentionally recruits diverse youths ages sixteen to twenty-four. Since it was often young African American women who got involved in the programs, ICAH intentionally recruits other youths of color, gender-nonconforming youths, and young men. ICAH has a Youth Leadership Council, through which youth are trained in a weeklong institute. According to Nik Zaleski, then ICAH's youth education coordinator, "We make sure they have a ton of information and knowledge that makes them feel powerful enough to share their voices in the leadership spaces that they get put in. So it's like setting them up for success instead of tokenizing and just having them just be in the room because they're young people."[50] One of the consequences of the training was that the youths identify with the reproductive justice approach, according to Zaleski: "They're so diverse in terms of identity, but the training that they get in the beginning of the year I think actually really brings them onto a common page of compassion and core belief in the issues that we are working on together."

Zaleski approached the Youth Leadership Council with the idea of exploring how to support young people having conversations about sex with their families, and council members queried, "What do you mean by family?" Zaleski recalled, "Their definitions included what we defined as chosen family, which involved peers, partners, adult allies that people put in their lives strategically to fill in gaps that given families can't meet."[51] Zaleski and two others initiated a community-based participatory action research project with ICAH youths on the concepts of "family" and the role of family structures in supporting the sexual health, rights, and identities of youths, with the goal of identifying perceived barriers and benefits of starting family-supported conversations about sex and sexuality.[52] She recalled, "We wanted to legitimize this concept [chosen family] that seems really important to them."

Once the last court challenge allowed PNA to stand, according to Zaleski, "we jumped on it right away before it became an issue for the young people that we work with." During the summer of 2014, ICAH organized a MAKE/ART/SPACE public art program. I had interviewed Yamani Hernandez the previous fall, and she agreed that I could participate in the summer youth program. ICAH's press release explains the purpose of the summer program: "ICAH fully supports conversations between youth and their adult family members about sexuality. We also recognize that when this isn't safe for youth, they need the full range of confidential, safe, and legal reproductive options. Since forced notification mandates a conversation between youth and their given families about sex and reproductive services, we gathered both positive and negative experiences of talking to families about sexuality. The goal is to inspire a legislative repeal for the dangerous [PNA] law."[53]

Storytelling was at the heart of ICAH's MAKE/ART/SPACE public art program, where besides participant observation, I conducted a staff interview and a youth focus group. With the exception of a Latina, the rest of the youth in the summer program were Black. At the beginning of the program, Zaleski informed the participants, ages sixteen to twenty-four, that we would be working with the 178 stories ICAH had collected about the effects of PNA as well as with young people who were having sexuality-related conversations with their given families.[54] ICAH had excerpts of some of these stories printed on tee-shirts that youths wore to a rally in the capital and printed on postcards to send to legislators, voicing their desire for the repeal of PNA. The stories illustrated how youths experienced parental notification, and often there were dire consequences. For example, one story excerpt read, "My best friend got an abortion last year and the doctors told her mom and she got kicked out of the house (and no longer claimed her)." Another stated, "Just days after a young woman appeared for a judicial bypass hearing [that would have declared her legally emancipated] her parents received an anonymous letter from an anti-abortion group informing them of her hearing. The group saw the young woman in the court house." The stories were *testimonios* about how young women fared when parents were told about their efforts at autonomy, a form of speaking truth to power.

Zaleski informed the youth group, "We have been gathering stories from individuals around parental notification for the past year. We got to this point where we said, 'What are we going to do with all of these amazing stories?'"[55] She then problematized the process of storytelling:

Who cares about stories? They can be boring. But a picture speaks a thousand words. We can message about PNA all we want—why we should stop it, why it's a bad law. But until people hear from real people, they won't care. People react to negative stories rather than positive ones. But positive stories might be useful to show that people do talk to parents; everyone's experience will be different. Most young people seeking an abortion do seek some support from their given family, and when they don't, it's because it's not a good idea. So, when there is a mandate, it can be problematic. . . . Part of the work of the reproductive justice movement is taking the voices at the margins and putting them in the center. At ICAH we do it with youth. We focus on your voices, your experiences.

The guiding question for this project would be, What experiences do you have, positive or negative, talking with your given family about sex and sexuality? Zaleski informed the youths that they would use the stories that had been printed out to create artwork to illustrate how the mandate for parental notification affects young people. One eighteen-year-old woman in the workshop suggested that this process was "ekphrasis," a term she learned in an art history college course she took while in high school. Since none of us were familiar with this term, she explained the meaning: "When a piece of visual art has a poem or story to go along with it, it stays with you longer and can be taken a different way because some understand visual art better. So, more people can understand the art by using different logics."

After a discussion about the benefits and limitations of storytelling and ekphrasis, the youths spent the next few weeks creating art based on the story collection. One project involved creating flags, as illustrated in figure 3.1; another installation included windows painted with images of faces, another included painted shoes, and a third involved miniature terrariums, all with text that came from stories about PNA or that had messages related to the law that the youths made up themselves. For the shoe artwork, one-third of the shoes were painted yellow and two-thirds in black to resonate with the campaign "1 in 3 women will have an abortion in her lifetime," a storytelling project sponsored by Advocates for Youth that many reproductive justice organizations were supporting.[56]

During the many hours spent creating the art, we were asked to discuss issues like, Why are we making this art? Are families safe spaces? Why does PNA matter to you? We also did some role-playing about youth informing their parents about issues related to sexuality—being sexually active, coming out as gender nonconforming, or being pregnant. The role-playing generated some really thoughtful discussions. Zaleski has worked in a theater program with young girls. She disclosed, "I have theater tools that were helpful in getting people to explore deep conver-

Figure 3.1. Flags with story excerpt (Photo by Martin McKinney with University Church, Hyde Park)

sations in meaningful and complex ways." As the youths created art to illustrate the stories, they added context related to race, class, and gender, such as painting hair puffs on young women to represent stories told by African American girls. The youths also told stories about their daily lives to one another—going to high school as a young Black parent, dealing with immigrant parents, getting their hair straightened, and fending off stereotypes and prejudice about queer or racialized youth. For example, "Tyrone," a smart, self-reflexive young African American man, told us stories about how frustrating it was to have teachers and counselors assume that he was not interested in school or to be surveilled every time he went into a store. His examples elicited supportive comments and stories by the young women and me as we reflected on our own experiences with low expectations by school staff or racial profiling.

After weeks of making artwork, when everything was complete, ICAH organized a public display at University Church in Hyde Park and Hull House Museum at the University of Illinois Chicago campus.

At both events, the youths made presentations explaining the purpose of MAKE/ART/SPACE and invited the public to engage the youths and talk about the artwork. They were instructed to check in with members of the public and the press and ask them, "What are the questions this piece makes you ask?" They cooperated to set out the artwork, greeted people warmly, explained the artwork clearly and concisely, and had fun—there was a lot of youthful play and laughter, including voguing for our collective photo (see plate 13). I was impressed with the youths' poise and ability to articulate their views. Some of the youths' parents attended the events and told me they were proud of their children's artwork and participation in the summer program.

Zaleski sees ICAH's work on parental notification as an extension of its community-based participatory action research. She said, "The reason that we have such a problem with this legislation [PNA] is because it only sees given families as possible support systems for young people who might be navigating an abortion decision-making process. We learned in our research it is not always a safe space for young people to talk about complicated issues. So, we're connecting our parental notification action, which includes the summer program, to the lessons that we learned in this research." In reflecting on the process of collecting stories and embedding them in public art, Zaleski observed,

> Stories are powerful in helping young people connect to their experiences. But they're also helpful in doing the opposite, helping them form their own identities because it gives them power of authorship. There's an assertion process that happens. And young people being able to write themselves into existence, to tell their narratives in the way they want to tell them, it's kind of like the one thing they get to control. I think it is powerful in terms of connective, team-building, community-building stuff. But it's also really powerful for identity formation and in helping legitimize nondominant identities that we don't hear about so much in the cultural narrative in most of the stories that are crammed down the throats of the young people that we work with on a daily basis.

ICAH has plans for other venues to continue its work against PNA as well as plans to have more meaningful conversations about sex and sexuality more generally.

I conducted a focus group with the youths involved in the MAKE/ ART/SPACE summer program, and it was one of the best focus groups I have ever done. In response to my question, "What makes something youth-friendly?" the keywords the youth contributed were "no judgment, safe space, open arms, not oppressive, understanding, open ears, no age restrictions, just like wanting to be there, youth-friendly language, colors, food," and repeatedly, "respect." What they learned about reproductive justice was contextualized by their own experience. Those who had been youth educators about sexuality appreciated the attention to gender-nonconforming youths. One woman stated, "Reproductive justice affects everybody whether they own a uterus or not. And not everybody who owns a uterus identifies as female. So, I learned a lot about changing my language from reproductive justice at ICAH." Another woman agreed, "I learned a lot, even how you label people or categorize people; preferred gender pronoun, that's reproductive justice right there. And I learned how to do that properly, where you don't offend people. I learned to be respectful." In addition to understanding the approach of the reproductive justice movement, the youths learned a great deal about themselves:

I've learned that communication is key.

I have learned that when I'm taught something and introduced to it in-depth, like PNA, I can be more proactive. I learned about myself that I'm down for a good cause.

I learned that I'm a leader and an activist, 'cause usually when it comes to speaking or teaching or even leading something—like when we went to Springfield [to the capitol]—I felt like I could actually speak on things that I care about.

I learned that I am a leader, but I don't have to be in the front lines. I'm taking the role more of helping everybody that was new or just needed help in general. As I'm transitioning out of ICAH as a youth leader and Advisory Council member, I'm becoming an adult ally, and it feels awesome!

I really learned how to take what I learned here and put it outside to people that are close to me, to my really close friends or my family members.

I learned about how to speak and be more comfortable sharing information with people who don't know about it.

I think being at ICAH has helped me strengthen my ability to balance out a room. I feel like I'm a good listener, and I think that if need be, I can lead or take charge. I feel like I can do either. And I just feel like I've gotten so much better at that here.

What I've learned about myself was figuring out what I want to do for the rest of my life. Because ICAH has shaped me as a human person from the time I started and hopefully for the rest of my future.

In the time since the MAKE/ART/SPACE summer program, ICAH continues to organize and educate about parental notification of abortion, which remains the law in Illinois as of this writing. However, there were a number of changes that occurred in the youths involved with this reproductive justice organization. These sixteen- to twenty-four-year old youths were articulate and nuanced in the ways they analyzed parental notification of abortion as well as other issues such as sexual identity or the right to access health care. They also learned a great deal about themselves, their strengths, passions, and ability to continue organizing for social justice. Clearly these youths' involvement in ICAH's work on reproductive justice was transformative.

COLOR's Youth Programs

The Colorado Organization for Latina Opportunity and Reproductive Rights offers three programs for young women. Latinas of Vision (LOV) recruits middle and high school young Latinas "seeking to make change in their communities," while in Hermanitas (little sisters), thirteen- to fifteen-year-old women "learn about self-esteem, their bodies, as well as the natural changes and feelings that they are experiencing."[57] COLOR's Latinas Increasing Political Strength program has an annual leadership and mentorship institute designed by Latinas for Latinas who are sixteen to twenty-one years old: "LIPS mentors the next generation of Latina leaders to promote the advancement of the Latino community and advocate for reproductive justice issues."[58] As part of the organization's efforts to encourage intergenerational collaboration, COLOR also sponsors *cafecitos* in which parents and other family members are invited to learn about reproductive justice and other issues such as immigration in informal settings.[59] In Colorado, Latinxs make up 21 percent of the population, yet only eleven members of the legislature (out of one hundred legislators) were Latinx in the 2015–16 sessions. COLOR aimed to change this picture: "Our programs serve as entry points for young Latinas to become engaged with organizing and advocacy."[60] Over the course of five years, I conducted interviews with seven current or former staff members and youths and organized three focus groups with youths. I also conducted participant observation with the Hermanitas and LIPS programs as well as several other events, including two of COLOR's annual "Viva la Diva" anniversary celebrations, its twentieth-anniversary celebration, and three presentations by the former executive director and deputy director. There is a long history of advocacy on behalf of Latinxs in Colorado, much of it focusing on civil rights and immigrant rights going back to the Chicana/o Movement in the 1960s.[61] Since my family history is based in Colorado, I have a personal interest in understanding COLOR's Latinx advocacy.

The Hermanitas program of 2013 was supposed to start with a lesson on anatomy and physiology on a hot summer day. The workshop began with a memorable ice-breaker in which the two facilitators, Issamar Pichardo and Maribel Morales, entered the room wearing costumes of a vagina and penis (see plate 14). Their appearance sent all of us into gales of laughter. They explained that their purpose was to demystify the body and sexuality in general. After explaining that Pichardo's grandmother had made the costumes initially for a Pride parade, they then asked us to brainstorm about and write down all the slang terms we had ever heard for the penis and vagina while they changed back into normal clothes. They then wrote the terms on the board, to more gales of laughter. The terms we came up with, in English and Spanish, for vaginas included "vajay-jay, pussy, kuka, cookie, cunt, bump-uglies, love button, taco, and privates." For penises, the terms were "d, dick, the stick, wiwi, pito [whistle], disco stick, cock, pee pee, special place, and pajarito [little bird]." We then had a discussion about why these terms carry so much currency.

Over the course of several weeks, we had a number of assignments and even homework. Pichardo and Morales passed out images of female external anatomy, and we were asked to identify the external organs. We watched a clip from the film *Purity Ball*, which documents the father-daughter black-tie event held in Colorado Springs where fathers pledge to be examples of purity before God and daughters commit to live pure lives.[62] The young women wanted to see the entire film, and then we had a lively critique of the pledge to wait to have sex after marriage and of abstinence-only sex education. The young women shared their examples of what sex education looked like at their schools; some of them had abstinence-only sex ed. The facilitators informed us that in contrast, COLOR offers comprehensive sex education, which gives young women the option of having safe sex if they become sexually active. They suggested that we claim pride in our bodies and our sexuality and even give names to our vaginas. One of the facilitators informed us, "I named mine Plush Owl Spartacus," because she felt fierce and strong, which impressed all of us; and there was discussion about names the young women would choose for their vaginas. We were then given art materials and encouraged to draw images of our vaginas and what they would wear, and some young women added text to explain their views (see plate 15). One thirteen-year-old (who is dyslexic) articulated her strength and autonomy and drew a vagina flexing her biceps. She wrote, "My vagina would wear the same style as me. My vagina would be a shy portector [*sic*] of it's self and strong (stay away from me)." Another young woman drew a vagina with a happy face and wrote, "I am as comfortable as can be and don't care if people don't like me or think I'm useless to everyone else in this world. . . . I am me, so no one should bother to shut me up or anything." The Hermanitas program illustrated the research finding that artistic expression gives youths time for reflection and enables them to express complex ideas or emotions that may be challenging to put into words.[63]

Over the course of the next few weeks, these thirteen- to fifteen-year-olds learned about anatomy, self-image, how the media shapes our notions of beauty, preventative health including using condoms or dental dams to prevent sexually transmitted infections, eating well and exercising, and reproductive justice. The lessons also informed the young women about the ACA, for which COLOR was canvassing to encourage people to sign up, as well as gender roles, stereotypes, and sexual identities. There was no training related to storytelling; but the young women seemed to really enjoy the Hermanitas workshop, and there was plenty of informal storytelling and bonding with one another. Several women shared stories about their *quinceañera* (coming-of-age celebration at age fifteen) and showed us photographs. Morales informed me regarding her motivation for seeking an internship with COLOR: "I'm interested in saving young women from a lot of sorrow I went through." Pichardo said, "I think starting education at a young age can change everything— society, how it functions, how they [youths] think."

"Sandy" was fifteen years old when she participated in COLOR's other program, Latinas of Vision. She found the information provided— specifically related to anatomy, reproduction, contraception, and avoiding sexually transmitted infections—to be really helpful: "All my friends were going through having their first time [sexual debut] and not having the resources or info to be safe. One friend got pregnant her first time, and it was shocking. Later the school found out, and she was never told about any options. And the school told her parents, and they were really upset. She was so sad 'cause she's no longer having a *quince* [*quinceañera*]." Not long after joining LIPS, Sandy discovered she had a sexually transmitted infection and did not know what to do. "I was sick and having pain and a lot of discharge. So, when I went to COLOR, I told the coordinators what was happening and I didn't know what to do. They directed me to Planned Parenthood because it was supposed to be affordable depending on your income, and they checked me." She was grateful that COLOR had provided information and support so she could heal, and she continues to appreciate its material support— she takes free condoms from the huge bowl of condoms near the door and distributes them to her friends, and she advises them about sexual health. She now realizes that young women have the right to information, access to long-acting and reversible contraception, and support for accessing health care.

The Latinas Increasing Political Strength program provides training about multiple issues. Alysa, introduced at the beginning of the chapter, recalled the LIPS storytelling training: "We learned a lot about the media and how we are perceived and how music sometimes degrades women, and we had never really thought about that. . . . We learned a lot of views on history and about COLOR, what they did for all of our rights, for reproductive justice—the laws that are coming up, the laws that have already been passed. We got training to lobby when we go to DC and talk to our senators." Besides the story of being bullied as a bisexual, the other "heart-crushing" story Alysa told during the training was about her former boyfriend's father, who had been deported: "We were, like, crushed. That was, like, my family too; like, how are we supposed to get him back? You know, he supported the family, helped them. Now my ex had to be the man of the house; he had so many jobs to help his mom and sisters and his brothers. And then finally his dad came back, and we were all happy." I asked if it was hard to tell her stories, and she reflected:

> I think it is because it's not something that you talk about every day. It's not something that you just say or tell random people because you don't necessarily trust people. So, you have to go in there with all this confidence and look very strong when inside you're really scared to tell your story and how they're going to react to it. But when you hear other people's stories, you feel like, "Hey, I had the same experience." You feel you're not alone anymore. So, then you build up that confidence to be like, "Okay, I can do this. I got this!"

When I asked if it felt safe to tell her stories during the training, she affirmed, "Yes, I felt very safe and in this comfort zone. And these girls were just open off the bat. They didn't care; they were like, 'Oh, what's your name? How are you doing? Where do you go to school?' Open—open to talk, to be friendly, to be kind. So I was like, 'Okay, this is very comfortable for me. This works.' It was a really good program for me; I benefited a lot from it."

The phrase "I got this!" that Alysa used resonates with a COLOR campaign (that it translates into Spanish as "lo tengo bajo control"), which was in response to abstinence-only education and was led by youths to encourage youth empowerment: "'I Got This!' sends the message that whether young people practice abstinence or decide that they are ready for sex, they are armed with the skills necessary to make informed decisions about their education, bodies, birth control, STD and

STI and HIV prevention, healthy relationships, as well as where to access resources."[64] COLOR draws on the work of Dr. Karen Rayne and suggests that there are things youths should do before having sex and explains the rationale at length on its website: "Have an orgasm; Know the other person's sexual history; Know the other person's STD status, as well as your own; Talk about exactly what STD protection and birth control you will be using; Have your best friend's blessing; Meet your partner's parents; Be comfortable being naked in front of each other; Have condoms on hand; Make sure that your partner has done all of these things too."[65] Between 2008 and 2014, COLOR hosted the "I Got This Summit: Mind. Body. Spirit" (formerly the Latina Health Summit), a weekend of workshops designed to introduce youths to the reproductive justice approach. The last summit was an intersectional, intergenerational symposium where Monica Simpson (executive director of SisterSong) was the keynote speaker, using reproductive justice to mobilize around the 2014 election. Simpson opposed the constitutional amendment that would have included fetuses under the definition of "person" and "child" in the Colorado criminal code. This was the legislation for which I conducted two focus groups, which helped COLOR fine-tune its messaging and helped lead to the defeat of the amendment.

The spring following the Hermanitas program, I was able to join the preparatory workshop for COLOR's "Where's Our Sex Ed?" campaign, which would include a trip to Washington, DC, with the Latinas Increasing Political Strength participants. The governor had signed a bill authorizing comprehensive sex education, but there were no funds allocated to enable new sex-ed modules for youths or for teacher training.[66] The campaign included plans to network with organizations and families that supported increased funding, to create a media campaign, and to visit schools and target youths as young as fourth grade, including on social media. The facilitator advised us, "We need to create smart goals: specific objectives, measurable, attainable, realistic, and timely," and suggested we use the hashtag on Twitter #WHERESOURSEXED?

In an effort to concretize the leadership training, COLOR constructed an exercise using a fictional character, Chuchita Pérez, and told her story. Corrine Rivera-Fowler, then deputy director, explained the exercise:

Chuchita is experiencing many issues that are keeping her from making decisions and having a choice. She is a single mom and going to Metro State University, which is in downtown Denver, but she is only able to get child-care assistance for twenty-four months because of our child-care policy. So she will not be able to finish her degree; she will have to find a full-time job in order to afford child care. She rides the bus and the light rail to school and takes her daughter to child care, and transit is really becoming an issue in Denver. She has student loan debt heavily and is wrapping up, and she doesn't know how she can pay that debt. When she does get out of school, she gets a job that is paying $12 an hour, and the self-sufficiency rate in Denver is $18 an hour for a single person with a child. So she cannot afford housing in Denver. She doesn't qualify for Medicaid in our state, so she is going without health care. She accesses her reproductive health needs at Planned Parenthood, which is under attack, so now she is really worried about having reproductive-health-care services.

You can apply this story of Chuchita and her life to the public policies and to the barriers that exist in any community. The host of issues can be addressed through community organizing, public policy, advocacy, and activism. So this is the story that we tell to try make this real, to have a solid connect to this situation of Chuchita and the intersections of reproductive justice.[67]

Later Rivera-Fowler, who had completed her bachelor's degree several years prior, disclosed, "At one point I *was* Chuchita."

The "Where's Our Sex Ed?" campaign planned on setting up a Facebook page for Chuchita with the slogan, "What does she need to achieve total reproductive justice?" We were prepped about the coming trip to Washington, DC, including what to wear and how to meet security measures when entering Congress and visiting the White House. COLOR covered all the women's travel expenses, but the young women organized a fundraiser, selling delicious homemade enchilada dinners so they would have some money for incidentals.

The trip to Washington, DC, included eight young women along with COLOR's former field and advocacy manager Amber Garcia. The women brought along a doll they named Chuchita (see plate 16), which became a vehicle for expressing their feelings and thoughts about the trip, including for many their nervousness about flying for the first time. They frequently mused about what Chuchita would think of their activities. We participated in an excellent training by Diana Thu-Thao Rhodes, director of public policy at Advocates for Youth; the training began with a presentation about the importance of comprehensive sex education and then about how to lobby one's congressperson, informing us that we had the right to speak to our congressional representatives. We then met in pairs and practiced telling stories that we would share when lobbying. However, we were not told what to say, and there was no detailed agenda for our lobbying with one legislator and another's staffer. It was unclear exactly which stories would be shared during the lobbying—I actually felt a little stressed by this. But I recalled what Alysa had learned about storytelling during LIPS the previous year: "You have to be quick because they're not going to listen to your ten-minute spiel, so you have to say what you feel is right and try to get them to see things in different views. If you have a chance, be able to tell your story and experience that you've had." With Alysa's advice in mind, I tried to relax.

We took cabs to the congressional building and met with Representative Diana DeGette, whose congressional district includes Denver (see plate 17), and her staffer and I happened to ride in a cab with Ana Portillo and Chuchita. We did brief introductions in which the young women identified their neighborhoods in Denver, which is a signifier that most came from working-class and low-income families, and they explained their purpose. One young woman spontaneously began talking about why the need for well-funded sex education was crucial: "I have a personal story about how important this work is: My cousin got pregnant when she was fourteen, and she had to get an abortion. And then another cousin got pregnant. She got an abortion too, and my aunt was really upset. They should have had access to sex ed and to contraception." Other women shared brief stories, including their work with COLOR, and another one explained why they brought Chuchita, which signified the intersectional identities of young women in Colorado. Representative DeGette was warm and gracious and seemed really engaged with the young women. She took numerous photographs with them after the meeting, complimented them on their poise, and promised to look into funding comprehensive sex education.

After a tour of the White House and some souvenir shopping, we all took photos in front of a faux Oval Office and presidential lectern, with lots of laughing and comments about how we would each be a strong woman president. We then had a collective discussion over lunch in Chinatown, and the young women agreed that the trip was "amazing." I asked them to share what they learned on the trip, and here are some of their responses: "I flew for the first time!" "I learned how to hail a cab and ride the Metro." "I learned how to use chopsticks." "I love DC; I have a passion for it and enjoyed everything. I was glad that I was able to talk to Congress people." "I really liked our bonding." "The training by Advocates for Youth was really well done." "I really liked taking Chuchita everywhere." Clearly this trip was a once-in-a-lifetime experience for these young women.

Indeed, the experience of participating in LIPS can be empowering in different ways. For some young women the training and experience shifts the course of their lives, which becomes evident when they do presentations at graduation ceremonies. All of the young women talked about their increased confidence and self-esteem, and many of them wept. Here are some examples: "When I came into LIPS, I didn't know what 'policy' meant and was intimidated by elected officials. Now I know I have a voice. I want to continue being involved." "I can talk to my community and my friends, and I didn't think I mattered." "I'm really shy. I don't make friends easily. I feel like I met sisters I will be friends with for the rest of my life. I felt like we all were really doing something." One woman plans to attend George Washington University and work on policy with elected officials. All of them found a sisterhood that was not judgmental. Cristina Aguilar, former executive director, pointed out, "Through our important leadership pipeline, we're really trying to cultivate youth and create opportunities that are radical. It's completely radical, and I think it's a gift that we have the funding to do this work; there are supporters out there nationally, statewide, and locally." Young women may start off in Hermanitas but then move on and participate in other COLOR youth programs. Lourdes, for example, participated in LIPS after completing Hermanitas. I participated in a daylong lobbying event at the Colorado Capitol that COLOR cosponsored (where I was dubbed an honorary Coloradoan!) and witnessed Lourdes take the lead in lobbying with state officials. She was poised, articulate, and on point, and the adults in our group marveled at her skills at lobbying. Later she took a Youth-Adult Partnership training by the ICAH and presented at a workshop that provided training to adults about how to become a youth ally. Clearly participating in COLOR activities would have long-term consequences for Alysa, Sandy, Lourdes, and other young Latinas. They learned to understand their own experiences in relation to the broader social context and gained skills related to analysis, public speaking, lobbying, and expressing their own views.

Conclusion

Similar to the youths quoted in the epigraphs to this chapter, many of the youths involved in reproductive justice organizations arrive expecting to be treated paternalistically and instead find that staff are "cool"—they are passionate, treat them with respect, and see them as social justice activists.[68] In these three cases of grassroots organizing with youths, we see deep political socialization at work. Young people learn the tenets of reproductive justice: to express their respect for one another; to see how they are different from one another in relation to national origins, ethnicity, language, gender, or sexual identities and yet share common values related to the right to knowledge and access to health care; to understand that their voices matter; and to learn that they can become skilled organizers who strive for consequential evidence-based policy changes. While some of the youths may not embrace the term "women of color," they certainly understand and support the notions of intersectionality and human rights.

These cases also illuminate how policy advocacy, culture shift work, and grassroots organizing go hand in hand in the movement for reproductive justice, which does not engage in values-based rather than issue-based organizing but does both.[69] Forward Together, ICAH, and COLOR see youth as active agents who are skilled at taking leadership in storytelling as part of policy advocacy on important issues and incorporating notions of culture shift work. In their workshops and other fora, these organizations create learning environments in which students and facilitators listen to one another and affirm youths' sexual identities as well as the inequalities with which they contend. We see that these organizations do not limit young people's political participation to storytelling, nor are their stories confined to preordained scripts or formats. Instead, youths are central to constructing a more participatory culture that engages difference and uses multiple forms of communicating their values and critiques of structural vulnerability. These reproductive justice organizations and the youth participants engage in transmedia practices, telling their stories in various venues—directly to state officials, members of the public, and the press or through online blogs or social media—which may have significant repercussions, according to Henry Jenkins and his colleagues: "Multiple entry points allow donors, activists, partners, and audiences to have a comprehensive and coordinated experience of a complex issue, and co-creation allows increased engagement with an issue and greater movement toward action."[70] In the process of mobilizing young people, the movement for reproductive justice strives for a politics of inclusion in which young people's rights are honored and visible.

In many ways, storytelling is becoming a methodology for engaging difference. Similar to chapter 2, where we saw storytelling being used to build coalitions and work at the intersections of multiple oppressions, with youths, storytelling evokes mutual compassion and strategies for enacting change. In the exchange between listener and storyteller, "we . . . open doors into another's world, open hearts and minds and at times become invited participants—we are becoming emparejadas—aligned, next to each other, in solidarity."[71] Indeed, the youths' cultural wealth, what Tara Yosso views as "knowledge, skills, abilities and contacts . . . often unrecognized and unacknowledged," become the center of transformative teaching that leads to organizational strategy and education of one another.[72]

However, storytelling with youths is also transformative in a slightly different way. The young people in these organizations learned the invaluable lesson that they are becoming empowered by claiming their own identities, experiences, and perspectives as *youths*. These organizations use varied methods—participatory action research, self-reflexive writing and artwork, role-playing, ice-breakers, brainstorming, lobbying, and more—that encourage youths to be active participants rather than passive recipients of knowledge related to reproductive justice. As the youths develop their analyses of social inequalities, they see a range of ways to participate politically. Instead of offering neoliberal visions of individual responsibility, these youths come to realize that they are "not alone," that they are youths who are also members of other social categories that are marginalized by the state and social discourses. These experiences are consistent with the research that finds programs that provide youths with opportunities to learn and see their collective experiences of inequality lead to politicized identities and provide protection and resilience to marginalized youth.[73] The notion of empowerment that the youths learn is collective, in relation to the overlapping social categories in which they belong. Further, this consciousness about empowerment comes at an especially critical time, when so much of how their lives are structured is disempowering. Unlike some of the scholarship, especially about DREAMERs, that illustrates tensions between an organization's goals and those of the youth activists, here we see a resonance in which young women see their participation as based on respect and their unique perspectives.

Conducting research with young people was an interesting and enjoyable process for me. I came away from these organizations marveling at the initiative, maturity, and wisdom of these thirteen- to twenty-four-year-olds whom I came to know through participant observation, focus groups, and individual interviews. As an introverted person myself, it is hard to imagine my participation in organizations such as these when I was their age. All of these youths were remarkably respectful and accepting of my presence and occasionally let me know they appreciated my views. Even something as taken for granted as hailing a cab or eating Chinese food reminded me that these youths are young, having some experiences for the first time and learning about the world. They relished having new experiences beyond what they were learning in their reproductive justice workshops and found ways to play even as they learned about serious reproductive politics. The group from ICAH in particular was happy that I was writing a book that includes their work and even joked that they would become famous. While it is difficult to gauge the effects that these youth projects accomplished, since policy changes occur in phases over a long duration, I envision these politically conscious youths assuming leadership in the future.

The campaigns discussed here seem poignant when we recall that the United States has not signed on to the UN Convention on the Rights of the Child, which supports children's rights to express their views and be heard in policy matters.[74] Nonetheless, the young people involved in reproductive justice are prepared to take active roles during civic engagement about the right to bodily autonomy, knowledge about sexuality, sexual identity, safer sexual practices, and access to health care with dignity. In short, they are participating in transformative empowerment, which helps them navigate the transition to adulthood with the understanding that true empowerment addresses structural inequalities.

4

From Self-Care to Healing Justice

I do not separate the struggle from my spirituality.
—Beata Tsosie-Peña, Tewa Women United

Our organizations have to be built around health and wellness.
—Patrisse Khan-Cullors, Black Lives Matter

While conducting research on the movement for reproductive justice, I heard countless instances of burnout and stress, sometimes at great length, and will provide but one example: "We move back and forth between policy work, organizing, and doing research, but we're also still dealing with these issues ourselves: some of us are really struggling; and we are living in poverty, and we're holding up our families and trying to keep everything together. So it's hard to live and exist within this reality and also try to push it forward and imagine something better and greater and bring others along with us to that place. It's a lot of work, and it's a lot of responsibility." This reproductive justice activist eloquently illustrates the challenges of working in the nonprofit sector, where salaries and benefits are modest and the work unrelenting, and it is especially challenging when activists themselves are structurally vulnerable—such as being undocumented, as we saw with Lola, introduced at the beginning of the book; being a minor; or identifying as queer, as we saw earlier. Most of the activists in the movement for reproductive justice attributed their burnout not to intramovement tensions but to external ones related to social inequalities.[1]

As we have seen, participating in the movement for reproductive justice can be beneficial for the well-being of individuals and communities, as women gain a sense of political empowerment and organizations mobilize and win policy changes that ameliorate inequality and address dominant pejorative narratives. However, with the intense pace and stressful conditions, social activism may also engender exhaustion, emotional distress, trauma, or burnout for participants.[2]

In addition to contending with the many stresses from social activism, those who work in reproductive justice organizations are often among the first generation in their families to attend college, come from low-income or working-class families (some with limited English-language skills), and may have heavy family responsibilities. Some movement participants are not paid staff; these activists contend with their own struggles balancing work schedules and family responsibilities, so they often engage in a triple day that includes work, family, and activism. All of these women have a fierce passion for their communities and strong dedication to their work that leads them to put in long hours. Moreover, nonprofit organizations must meet funders' demands for deliverables, including detailed reports on their productivity so as to garner more funding, which leads some to feel they are constantly being surveilled as part of the nonprofit industrial complex.[3] Often activists feel that there is additional rigor for organizations staffed by people of color, which one executive director believed "added additional constraints and are part of the layered and complex institutional oppression that is rampant in funder spheres." And for reproductive justice organizations to ensure they continue their projects and initiate new campaigns, they must actively raise funds from multiple sources, which generates a tremendous amount of stress. In addition to political campaigns with fixed deadlines or major events that require extraordinarily long days, reproductive justice activists travel frequently to attend convenings, strategic meetings, conferences, trainings, lobbying events, and demonstrations, and some of them work in the evenings on a regular basis. There is also a social dimension in which women feel they should not reveal their personal vulnerabilities—whether emotional burnout or physical challenges—which might be used against them in the rough world of politics, where they must negotiate from positions of strength. Often they have to push for full inclusion of all people of color, people with disabilities, or queer folks repeatedly, and the active or even passive opposition by political allies leaves them feeling drained. When their own health issues are placed in the background, such pressures can become debilitating.

I became accustomed to hearing about staff departures from reproductive justice organizations, especially for those in leadership positions. During the five years I conducted my research, four out of the thirteen organizations studied lost their executive directors, and two of these lost two executive directors each. Other organizations lost high-profile staff members. Losing staff was not always entirely negative—some left for better opportunities with higher pay or more interesting responsibilities, to explore their desires for creative expression such as writing, or because of increased family responsibilities. However, several also left because of burnout, and the staff that remains must cope with the stress of their demanding work.[4] Burnout is so prevalent that funders have started provided training about how to counter the effects of stress on staff so they do not become demoralized and how to cultivate wellness within reproductive justice organizations.[5] Some organizations provide three-month sabbaticals or the option to work part-time, allowing staff a much-needed reprieve, and there are programs that pair up coaches with executive directors to help them debrief about ongoing job stress and strategize about how to cope with the demands of their work.

In addition to the stress and burnout associated with social activism, many reproductive justice activists see their work as motivated by a desire to express their spirituality.[6] Women's reproduction can be a space of vulnerability: when women seek to control their fertility, terminate pregnancies, express their sexuality, or consider whether they can raise healthy children, spiritual considerations are often at the fore. Intimate relationships can be fraught with interpersonal aggression—date rape, sexual abuse, physical violence, opposition to abortion, emotional manipulation, body shaming, infidelities, and so on—that shatters individuals' sense of their selves. When religious leaders perpetrate various forms of violence or abuse, women must find alternative means of seeking spiritual support. SisterSong organized a webinar on "faith and reproductive justice" that was marketed to RJ members and allies across the country. During the webinar, the Reverend Kentina Washington-Leapheart stated, "We are working to reclaim the narrative away from those folks of faith invested in white supremacist, straight, Christian perspective on faith."[7] Expressing one's spiritual beliefs during social activism allows women to begin healing from the multiple traumas they have experienced as low-income women of color who face multiple barriers to accessing health care and social equality.[8] During a focus group, a woman who works with the LAN in South Texas explained this perspective:

> The process of struggle is healing one's soul: while you are struggling, you are healing. This is what we have learned and believe. We are very affected by the laws, but at the same time we have healed tremendously. And it's important to examine the scars, the hurts, because they remind us that we are going to continue struggling and we will never stop. I think the program is essential for these women because it alleviates the pain, it heals, and women struggle for themselves. That is key for our success, and it is huge. And we *will* be successful.

The others nodded in agreement, and one of her colleagues stated, "Having a voice brings the power that carries women and transforms them. Gaining a voice is healing." These women's determination to achieve change is rooted in their spiritual beliefs in their collective rights to freedom, social justice, and liberty that go beyond their individual processes of healing and include transformation that affects everyone.

This chapter analyzes how women in the movement for reproductive justice use spiritual expressions as tools for healing from the traumas of colonialism, patriarchy, white supremacy, heteronormativity, and state violence to give deep meaning to their work and to address the burnout associated with social activism. I will examine how reproductive justice organizations incorporate spiritual practices that enable collective healing when their communities experience trauma.[9] Specifically, I query, How do reproductive justice activists engage in self-care to counter burnout? How do women of color in the movement for reproductive justice view spirituality and wellness? How do they incorporate spiritual practices into their activism? Overall, these questions allow me to explore, How are reproductive justice advocates offering alternatives to neoliberalism?

While not every reproductive justice organization incorporates spiritual practice directly into its work related to grassroots organizing, policy advocacy, and culture shift, all of them honor women's right to express their spiritual traditions. Conferences and webinars open with an acknowledgment of indigenous peoples on whose land the convening is taking place. Most reproductive justice participants are not faith-based activists, yet many draw on the religious training they received as children and their respective experiences with the Black church; liberation theology if raised Catholic; Eastern traditions of mindfulness, chanting, or structured bodily movement; or indigenous ancestral knowledge and ceremony. They also are shaped by the self-care practiced by the civil rights, feminist, or queer rights social movements.[10] Indeed, respected leaders who expressed their spiritual views alongside their political practice, such as Martin Luther King Jr., César Chávez, Dolores Huerta, and others, inspire them.

Reproductive justice activists engage in healing practices aware of the health disparities in which some have access not only to reproductive health care but also to quality food, air, space, and peace in their communities. Those with low incomes, however, often have limited access to any of these, and many, especially immigrants, may prefer their own cultural healing practices.[11] Some formerly alternative spiritual practices—such as yoga—have become commercialized and followed by millions of people worldwide.[12] And sites of spiritual practice—churches, temples, mosques, dharma communities, and the like—may be places of inequality where women of color and youth are silenced, marginalized, patronized, or abused.[13] Activists also see the irony that current Eastern spiritual practices that have been commercialized and popularized in the West, such as yoga or Buddhism, are threatened by the same colonial processes that now are the center of multimillion-dollar industries.[14] Nonetheless, despite the commercialization of Eastern spiritual practices, they continue to bring solace to many people, including me.

The self-care practiced by reproductive justice activists goes beyond the encouragement that is popular in neoliberal society today, where individuals are exhorted to cope with burnout by purchasing goods and services through global self-care industries. Instead, activists and scholars explore how self-care expresses Gloria Anzaldúa's notion of "spiritual activism."[15] Anzaldúa writes, "The work of *conocimiento*—consciousness work—connects the inner life of the mind and spirit to the outer worlds of action. In the struggle for social change I call this particular aspect of conocimiento spiritual activism."[16] Recall that *conocimiento* is a process of coming to political consciousness in which women see their own troubles in the context of structural inequalities and develop a sense of community with people in similar circumstances. Spiritual activism, then, goes beyond individual self-care by linking political consciousness to the right to express one's spiritual practices publicly, a form of cultural citizenship.[17] Women of color have been enacting spiritual activism by distinguishing spirituality from organized religion, which has played a role in dominating indigenous and other peoples through colonialism, violence, racism, homophobia, transphobia, patriarchy, and attempted destruction of non-Western spiritual practices.[18] Indeed, the feminist theorists Elisa Facio and Irene Lara suggest that "spirituality . . . plays a decolonizing role in creating meaning, inspiring action, and supporting healing and justice in our communities."[19] Like other scholars and spiritual practitioners, Facio and Lara critique the dichotomies of mind-body, spirit-body, spirituality-sexuality, masculine-feminine, or religious-secular. Instead, they offer a framework that emphasizes balancing the "bodymindspirits" of people and healing through the multiple ways in which corporal experience, cognition, and emotional, erotic, artistic, and spiritual expressions are interrelated and consequential.

Reproductive justice advocates also go beyond individualized notions of self-care by honoring their communities' spiritual expressions in relation to historical trauma and engaging in "healing justice." Initially formulated at the 2010 US Social Forum by activists, healing justice is a framework that "responds to and intervenes in generational trauma and violence and brings collective practices that can impact and transform the consequences of oppression on our bodies, hearts and minds."[20] Loretta Pyles sees healing justice as "a practice of attention and connection" that heals the sense of being fractured or disconnected "that may be a result of trauma or oppressive socio-cultural narratives and practices. . . . It is a practice that asks social practitioners of all kinds to cultivate the *conditions* that might allow them to feel more whole and connected to themselves, the world around them, and other human beings."[21] The construction of spiritually affirming conditions begins with being in relationship with and connected to others.

Reproductive justice activists take spiritual activism beyond intersubjectivity—the cognitive and affective experiences with others—and toward the power of more encompassing collective restoration through broader connections to all living things, the natural world, and spiritual beings.[22] Beyond helping participants deal with burnout or stress,

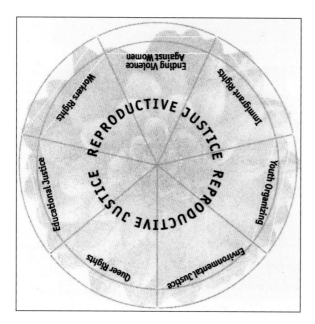

Plate 1. Intersectionality of reproductive justice with social justice issues (Used with permission by Forward Together)

Plate 2. National Latina Institute for Reproductive Health logo (Used with permission by National Latina Institute for Reproductive Health)

Plate 3. Favianna Rodríguez's "Yo Te Apoyo / I Support You" (Used with permission by Favianna Rodríguez)

Plate 4. Favianna Rodríguez's "Slut Series" posters (Used with permission by Favianna Rodríguez)

Plate 5. Mama's Day Our Way greeting cards by Strong Families Initiative (Used with permission by Forward Together)

Plate 6. Young parent with certificate of participation (Used with permission by California Latinas for Reproductive Justice)

Plate 7. "Age doesn't define a good parent" (Used with permission by California Latinas for Reproductive Justice)

Plate 8. "Young parents holding our families' future: education is a right" (Used with permission by Young Women United)

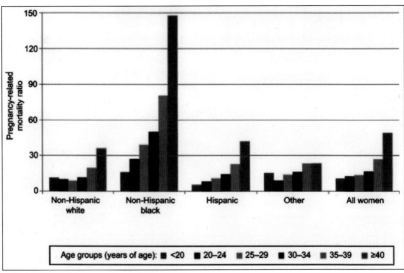

Plate 9. Pregnancy-related mortality ratios by age, race, and ethnicity: United States, 2006–2010

Plate 10. Paula Saldaña demonstrating a breast self-examination (Used with permission by Jennifer Whitney for the Center for Reproductive Rights)

Plate 11. Presentation at El Instituto by Mayra Lizzette Yñiguez (Photo by the author)

Plate 12. Forward Together youth facilitating workshop (Used with permission by Forward Together)

Plate 13. ICAH staff, youth, and the author (second from right) (Photo by Martin McKinney with University Church, Hyde Park)

Plate 14. COLOR staff members in costume (Photo by the author)

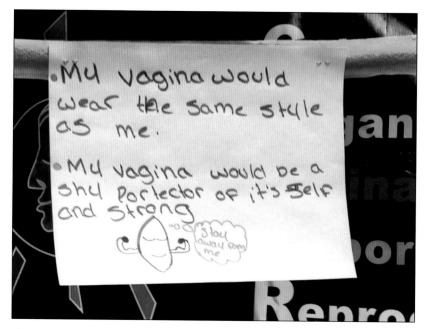

Plate 15. COLOR youth artwork (Photo by the author)

Plate 16. Ana Portillo holding Chuchita with Representative DeGette (Photo by the author)

Plate 17. Representative DeGette with young COLORistas (Photo by the author)

Plate 18. Centering-table honoring Mother Earth and the four directions (Photo by the author)

activists are concerned with sustaining positivity and an orientation toward wellness. Many of those involved in healing justice draw on the leadership of Native American activists who have long pushed for an incorporation of the importance of place-based activism, in which local notions of belonging and meaning are honored—whether in a city or rural site.[23] The justice studies scholar Corrine Sanchez, executive director of TWU, expressed the value of centering wellness and connections to place: "When we talk about the intersections of our lives that reproductive justice facilitates, it connects to every aspect in our mind, our heart, our spirit, and our connection to the earth. We also need to talk about what it means for us to grow healthy, loving, caring, children; what it means for us to as grow loving, caring, healthy adults."[24] Here Sanchez is drawing on indigenous notions of wellness, in which the four areas of the self—the physical, emotional, mental, and spiritual—are in balance and harmony.[25]

I will discuss four organizations' efforts to integrate reflection, corporality, and spirituality through healing justice on behalf of their communities. Pyles suggests that there are four different "genera" of healing justice practices—breath, meditation, movement, and reflective inquiry.[26] While these four organizations are practicing some of these forms of healing justice, especially reflective inquiry, their practice was constructed organically based on the particular constituencies and location of their work. Tewa Women United, located in the ancestral Tewa homelands of northern New Mexico, is a multicultural and multiracial organization founded and led by Native women that works at the intersections of reproductive justice and environmental justice.[27] TWU works toward community healing from the historical traumas experienced by Native Americans by crafting exercises in cultural memory. Based in Oakland, California, Forward Together envisions a nation where all families have rights, recognition, and resources.[28] It incorporates the Eastern structured movement and meditation traditions in the approach of Forward Stance to build strength by individuals and social movements. The Colorado Organization for Latina Opportunity and Reproductive Rights is a Denver-based, Latina-led, and Latina-serving grassroots organization that advocates for reproductive rights, health, and justice for Latinas, their families, and their allies.[29] COLOR aims to sustain a bilingual, bicultural, resilient, and appreciative work culture that resonates with its Latinx constituencies. Based in Albuquerque, New Mexico, Young Women United works with young women of color to advance reproductive justice through destigmatizing mental health and including LGBTQ youth of color, leading criminal justice reform while decriminalizing substance use and pregnancy, increasing access to reproductive health care to include a full range of birthing options, and building educational equity and support for expectant and parenting young people.[30] YWU engages multiple forms of spiritual practice linked to the erotic as articulated by women of color activists. I argue that the movement for reproductive justice provides alternatives to neoliberal self-care by incorporating spiritual activism as well as particular forms of collective healing justice by drawing on spiritual practices originating in communities of color.

Healing Multigenerational Trauma

Tewa Women United was initially formed as a support group, Women in Transition, for women from the eight northern pueblos of New Mexico who had recently separated from their husbands, suffered the loss of a loved one, or struggled with addiction or family violence. At first they met in women's homes and shared their experiences with one another, learning life skills and beginning a process of "cultural repatriation," according to executive director Corrine Sanchez: "In the protection of circle gatherings, women (re)called stories passed down by their grandmothers that spoke of women's sacredness, the power women possess, and their vital role in carrying on Tewa/Pueblo ways of being."[31] Sanchez's mother, elder Kathy Sanchez, TWU's environmental justice and health program manager, attended the early women's circles and stayed to see the development of the gatherings into a formal organization in 1989.[32]

In 2001, TWU formed a nonprofit concerned with the traumatic effects of the colonizer mentality, with its religious inquisition and militarization, which, as Kathy Sanchez said, "are symptoms of the colonial violence we found ourselves in."[33] Settler colonialism tried to eliminate Native peoples so as to usurp their lands but also debased the cultures of those who remained, which has had long-term consequences.[34] Most Native activists and scholars agree that sexual violence was a rare occurrence in Native communities prior to contact with Western systems. The coloniality of power is evident in the interpersonal violence perpetrated against women that continues today.[35] In the contemporary era, the Native American lawyer and gender studies scholar Sarah Deer points out, "Native women suffer the highest per capita rates of sexual violence in the United States." Moreover, "most perpetrators of rape against Native women are white," which makes prosecution challenging, since tribal law enforcement sometimes does not have jurisdiction or resources to prosecute perpetrators of sexual violence.[36] Deer critiques the effects of violence: "Sexual assault mimics the worst traits of colonization in its attack on the body, invasion of physical boundaries, and disregard for humanity. A survivor of sexual assault may experience many of the same symptoms—self-blame, loss of identity, and long-term depression and despair—as a people surviving colonization."[37] Further, sexual violence is a fundamental violation of the soul.[38] TWU joins other women of color who critique how intimate violence is linked to larger colonial and institutional forms of violence.[39] Corrine Sanchez states, "Today the challenges that our families and communities face are magnified, not only by historical trauma and institutionalized oppressions but by intergenerational and complex individual traumas, resulting in disproportionate levels of violence and abuse between men and women."[40]

TWU decided to organize and support those who are most vulnerable to colonial violence and trauma: women, girls, and Mother Earth, offering an alternative to the patriarchal structure of the cultural violence that is still upheld by racism, militarism, and consumerism, promoted by nearby Los Alamos Base. Specifically, TWU highlights healing the deeper soul woundings and traumas such New Mexico's high rates of alcoholism, substance abuse, suicide, and intimate partner and sexual violence against women and girls. TWU's approach is inclusive, according to Kathy Sanchez: "We say equality is the support of each other— men and women, inner [Native] communities and out [non-Native] communities—so all can recover."[41] TWU also focuses on the degradation of Mother Earth perpetrated by ill-advised use of water, nuclear experimentation (Los Alamos Lab is built on sacred land taken by the federal government through eminent domain), and the loss of indigenous knowledge related to sustaining life. Kathy Sanchez stated, "It is our responsibility, we believe, to maintain full awareness of this reality and, from our lineage of landedness, caring for holistic ecological system and uproot this culture of violence to grow a culture of peace."

TWU is different from other reproductive justice organizations in the sense that it developed a theory of practice to action. *Opide* (oh-peh-dee) is a braiding or weaving that utilizes intersectional analysis centered on the lived experience of Pueblo/Tewa women and the organization's values:[42] "Respect for self and others; Together we live these values; Loving, caring for each other; female/male energy—ancestral knowingness; Our Mother, Mother Earth, multi-versity; Letting go; Our breath, our prayer, commitment to live life with purpose and good intentions."[43] Corrine Sanchez explained how the metaphor of weaving came about: "The women in my family would gather and sit and braid each other's hair, and while you are combing each other's hair, you're praying; you are saying things that you want to pass on—beauty, light, values—and you are braiding it into a pattern."[44] Through dream-space, Kathy Sanchez envisioned TWU's logo, a butterfly that dissolves the binaries (male-female, Native-non-Native, etc.) that Tewa people navigate. "The Butterfly Model is based on the concept of 'two sides become one.' Thus, the image of the fluidity/movement of the butterfly wings, which to Tewa people signifies transformation, mobility, vulnerability, and power to impact the multi-verse because of and despite its delicacy. . . . The model continues to serve as the foundational philosophical model for TWU because it discusses our wholeness of being, using identity, language, and spirituality as a strength that leads to our mobility (fluidity) in changing and challenging times."[45] In addition, *Opide* weaves in principles of cultural sovereignty, which, according to the Native American scholars Wallace Coffey and Rebecca Tsosie, is a process of reclaiming sacred cultural legacy, including "our rights to language, religion, art, tradition, and the distinctive norms and customs that guide our societies and build community."[46] Coffey and Tsosie elaborate: "affirming tradition validates the importance of Native people's epistemologies, resists the dominant society's message that those beliefs and ways of knowing the world are 'pagan and uncivilized,' and evokes group autonomy, affirming the notion that the tribal community is the locus of cultural sovereignty."[47] Under the framework of cultural sovereignty, Native people engage in the process of reclaiming history by narrating from their own perspective, reclaiming sacred traditions, which are fluid and evolving, and reclaiming cultural identity centered on tribal wisdom, people's relationship to the land, and storytelling.[48] Coffey and Tsosie emphasize that stories "are the wealth of our people; they are what give life and continuity to our existence; they are what link us with our collective past, and our collective future."[49] Further, stories emphasize relations to the land, water, and nearby mountains, which are considered sacred, as well as to plants and animals, which are seen as relatives to indigenous people.[50]

TWU offers a number of programs, and I only mention a few that emphasize their spiritual practice. The Circle of Grandmothers project provides spiritual grounding and cultural guidance to TWU staff and the board and promotes intergenerational learning and sharing, especially related to trauma, as well as to traditional language, arts, and ceremony. TWU's Indigenous Women's Health program "utilizes an intersectional approach to reproductive justice" and "braids together gender justice, birth justice, environmental justice, economic justice, healthy sexuality and body sovereignty, advocacy and healing for survivors of sexual violence, to form a comprehensive approach to building beloved communities and ending violence against women, girls, and Mother Earth."[51] In an effort to counter the high rate of maternal mortality and postpartum depression, for over ten years TWU has offered free training for women who want to become doulas and agree to work in Native communities. In an interview, Corrine Sanchez clarified how TWU melds reproductive justice and environmental justice: "Intersectionality is also bringing in cultural pieces; for us it's always about the protection of our Mother Earth, always the giver of life and water, and then through that all of these other pieces that stem from how we fight for justice in our community. So it's not just talking about it but putting it to practice in our programs and how we involve our people. It is intergenerational; it's gender encompassing. We try and talk about those issues we are facing in our community." For example, TWU celebrates Mother's Day by acknowledging how Native women needed to reframe their struggles. Corrine Sanchez states, "A devastating reality, that 1 in 3 Native women will experience sexual assault/rape in their lifetime. Where there are over 5,600 missing and murdered Indigenous women. How have our communities gone from core values of centering women, respecting the bearer of generations and treating women/mothers as sacred, to unprecedented levels of violence perpetrated against our minds, hearts, bodies and spirits?"[52] TWU joins other Native women who see that the principal sources of strength for women survivors of violence are found within social relations and kinship circles.[53]

To help individuals reclaim their ancestral knowledge and cope with these horrific circumstances, TWU practices spiritual activism, as Kathy Sanchez has noted: "We're being supported by our circle of grandmothers. They're always our guidance to find out if we're implementing, if we're doing or we're thinking, especially with trauma-informed services: you're really overwhelmed—it's never ever been lessened. We're still finding ourselves doing the same struggles. It can become hardening. You can get angry, and you can get embittered unless you have your cleansings and recharge and [get] your connections back."[54] Thus, TWU explicitly incorporates practices of spiritual and collective healing: "Our mission was to provide safe spaces, courageous space for indigenous women to discover the strength within, the power we possess, the skills to make social change."[55] TWU has received recognition for its work centering on indigenous women's leadership.[56]

Kathy Sanchez and Beata Tsosie-Peña, environmental justice / environmental health coordinator of TWU, presented their work at the Summer Institute sponsored by Mujeres Activas en Letras y Cambio Social (Activist Women in Letters and Social Change), or MALCS, of which I am a member.[57] The panel began with an explanation of a "centering-table that brings our ancestral energies," which Sanchez and Peña constructed in the middle of the room with items signaling the four directions (see plate 18). The healer Elena Avila from New Mexico points out, "The altar [centering-table] of every curandero [healer] includes objects that represent the four elements: earth, water, air, and fire. These elements teach us lessons about how to release toxins and harmful emotions from our bodies, and how to purify and ground ourselves."[58] Sanchez and Tsosie-Peña's centering-table included corn, a sacred plant that symbolizes indigenous people's history as well as centers their political, social, cultural, and ceremonial practices and identity.[59] They also included locally grown sage, used in ceremonies for cleansing people's spirits and spaces. Two eagle feathers represent air or the wind and remind us that we sustain life through breathing. Kathy Sanchez explained,

We light a candle to light our energies into focus and then call our protector, so if we become vulnerable and want to share, that the space is sacred. And then we have the elements of our roots: sweet grass, sage, and other elements such as rock. Water is present in clay, so that we never forget our connections to Mother Earth and are rooted in the work that we do, that we have our soulfulness and relational connectivity to Mother Earth visible, especially when we're teaching young people. Because sometimes they don't say what is troubling their minds right away, and adults' tendency is to want to get them to therapy or counseling. But sometimes they can find a centering if they speak to water, to the trees, or animals. So that is what we want to instill, that the healing presence is here all around them.

Water is also considered sacred, as the Mohawk midwife and environmental researcher Katsi Cook explains: "the waters from the earth and the waters of our bodies are the same water."[60] All of these sacred items were placed on a beautiful, brightly colored weaving by members of their pueblo. Sanchez and Tsosie-Peña then staged a participatory exercise, Weaving Webs of Women's Wisdom, which explores, as Sanchez explained, "what it means to be as a network and a support for each other." We sat in a circle, introduced ourselves, and then, after winding a piece of yarn around our hand, tossed a ball of rainbow-colored yarn across the circle, introducing one another over and over. After tossing the yarn many times, we learned each other's names, and in the end, we created an intricate weaving that beautifully illustrated our connections to one another. Even though we were in a public setting, I was mindful that scholars have been criticized for writing about Native American spirituality,[61] so I requested and received permission to record the presentation and photograph the centering-table.

Then Sanchez and Tsosie-Peña showed excerpts from a powerful film depicting historical injustices toward Native peoples that included the conquest, violence, enslavement, brutality, enforced assimilation, language repression, and ongoing discrimination. They invited comments and questions from the audience, and we had a lively discussion about how Native American history is often excluded from school curricula so that Native people are unaware of their ancestors' experiences and others are oblivious of the historical origins of violence in Native American communities.

I was most interested in Sanchez and Tsosie-Peña's presentation of an exercise that they have used to help heal multigenerational trauma. Sanchez explained that the idea came to her in a dream: "I believe in dream-space," which to the Pueblo peoples of northern New Mexico is a way to pray through one's dreams so as to access spirit and find guidance.[62] She asked, "So how do we show the harm that's being done to our children and that generational trauma is not right?"[63] She dreamed of a bag hidden under her bed that held the physical manifestation of trauma wrought on their community over time. In her dream she took out the bag and found rocks that symbolize both violence and healing. Sanchez designed a practice in which seven generations of Native people come together, beginning with representatives of the first generation, who experienced the trauma of the conquest and violence inflicted on them. The facilitators add exponentially a multiplicity of three stones for each generation, and they discuss particular traumas. For example, great-grandmother was a child when the violence came, and "that's when genocide was happening." Yet she felt pressured not to talk about the horrors she had witnessed, which brought up so much sadness by those who survived, according to Sanchez. "So her pain, her sorrow, her peace offering is put in a bag because in that generation they were told, 'Don't say anything! They might find us' or 'We're protecting the women or the men who are going to be hurt.' So her soul was wounded; she couldn't cry in public; she couldn't say anything. The guilt, the anger, the shame—not being able to do anything, and the women would hold it inside of her when giving birth to the next generation."[64] This everywoman, great-grandmother, lived her life continuing the silence, which then led her to seem mysterious to her children, grandchildren, and great-grandchildren, who never understood the source of her sorrow and silence.

A bag with more rocks is then passed to the grandmother from the next generation, and so now the bag holds three times three rocks, symbolizing the pain and sorrow held internally. The facilitators explain the traumas that occurred in each subsequent generation—being sent away to "Indian schools," being punished for using their Native language, dire poverty especially during the Great Depression, feeling pressured to assimilate and not wear traditional clothing, and more.[65] Sanchez

FROM SELF-CARE TO HEALING JUSTICE | 155

said, "They took away our villages, our ability to farm; they think we're low. . . . And the pain is getting heavier, and people are getting dependent on painkillers, on drugs. But the pain is still silent. And the children are not being spoken to, and they're thinking, 'Why is my grandma talking to my uncle and they're not talking to me? Did I cause my grandma to cry every night?'" The witnesses realize how horrible such repression was for great-grandmother and the following generations and come to understand why open communication might be challenging and sometimes manifested in alcoholism, domestic violence, or retreating into isolation. By the seventh generation there are 2,187 rocks. As they lift the bags, youths feel firsthand how the pain of historical trauma accumulates, and they gain insight into the long-lasting effects of trauma. Sanchez explained how healing occurs:

> As we get to be conscious of these things, the healing happens on multiple levels of existence. As we heal, so do our ancestors. We heal them, and they come back and help us. And they can come back in many different forms to help us, and that is what we're trying to show here. Like, we're seeing they might come as a bird, a tree, another person. The presentation of harmony is talking about creating your relations, of *who* is my purpose in life, not what is my purpose in life but *who*. And that way the bird is coming, the *who* in the bird is going to be respectful; the *who* is singing beautiful songs. Thank you, birds, for being here; you are brightening my day. And if you get in that sort of relational thinking with trees, and all of these beautiful trees, please thank them for giving the winds and shade. Or if you just have laughter—the rhythm of the vines—all help us with healing. And so in order to bring full circle to that soul wounding, what we do is that we have the children form a circle, and when children open their bags, they end up dealing with what is in the generation that experienced it first. They do not have to carry guilt, anger, or shame. They release and help their parents. As parents heal, they help heal their parents, and so forth in backward unchaining.

Here Sanchez is illustrating a key point that the Native scholar Suzanne Crawford O'Brien clarifies: "For Native people the spiritual world is not transcendent, separate from the material and natural world, but intrinsically within it."[66] Sanchez concluded,

We help them [the youths] understand where this is coming from. And then the children are cared for in a beloved community, which may not be the immediate family. We have a program with food for the children. We want to feed them, and we want to get back to organic foods. And there's a basket of hope, a basket of seeds coming forward with the rocks also. So the children are silently watching but at the same time passing on a basket with seeds and water that feeds their spirits to survive. Anytime the soul wounding comes out, you ask for smudging, which is a way of cleansing away the negative thoughts. That is why all the elements are here.

Corrine Sanchez elaborated: "As we heal ourselves, we heal our ancestors and simultaneously transform the future for our children." The presentation about Trauma Healing Rocks was deeply moving and well received by the MALCS participants. As the panel ended, we were gifted pouches of locally grown lavender, shells, sand, and rocks assembled by Tewa grandmothers. I carry mine in my purse to remind me of this powerful exercise and my connection to Mother Earth.

Through the Trauma Healing Rocks exercise, TWU enables youth and their relatives to understand the source of trauma and enact spiritual practices that lead toward collective healing. The Trauma Healing Rocks exercise has been used in schools with adolescents and graphically illustrates the importance of reconnecting and beginning the healing of multiple generations through sharing knowledge through stories. Indeed, the stories revealed in the practice and then elaborated on during discussion and later in people's homes or classrooms function like *testimonios* and "help to connect generations of displaced and disenfranchised communities across time."[67] The Trauma Healing Rocks exercise illustrates what the religion historian Albert Raboteau calls the "sacramental" principle, in which "a spiritual world coinheres with this one" so that "material objects of ritual not only symbolize spiritual realities, but make them present."[68] The exercise is innovative since it is presented publicly by women and allows vulnerability, which is where healing happens. It is also a teaching tool for those who do not understand how colonization and genocide impacts the losses of identity. Kathy Sanchez stated, "This exercise is really focusing on those that were groomed to be oppressors as well as those that were oppressed. When presented to non-Natives, they were also crying; they don't know how to identify in the healing process. So this gives them the chance to heal as well. That is powerful and inclusive of them to witness their own healing."

TWU continues the work of spiritual activism for individuals and healing justice for the community by linking open conversations about Native American oppression with celebratory events. One example is its Española Healing Foods Oasis, which transformed a barren slope in downtown Española into a garden. TWU utilized dry-land farming techniques and permaculture principles such as harvesting rainwater and mycoremediation with mushrooms to remove chemicals from soil and heavy metals from water. The goal is to nurture seasonal vegetables, trees, medicinal herbs and plants, and grasses and wildflowers that will support a pollinator habitat. TWU also constructed accessible pathways and a beautiful setting of plants, rocks, and trees, all with donated labor and organic seeds planted by volunteers from multiple communities. The photos of TWU's annual amaranth harvest, with bright-red seeds packed with protein, were lovely, and TWU posted a video of a Guatemalan gardener illustrating how to make amaranth candy with local honey, an event TWU now offers annually.[69] The Española Healing Foods Oasis is part of TWU's environmental justice work, in which it attempts to counter the effects of global warming and honor multiple forms of sustainable agriculture. Beata Tsosie-Peña writes, "The Healing Food Oasis is part of our vision to end all forms of violence against women, girls, and our Mother Earth. It's facilitating our reconnection to the plants, water, air, and all the elements."[70] TWU envisions staging community events like poetry readings and ceremonies at the completed gardens.[71] The Healing Foods Oasis celebrates the affinity between people and place in which "ceremony is an expression of kinship grounded in a common spirit."[72]

The Trauma Healing Rocks exercise and Española Healing Food Oasis are powerful expressions of Tewa healing justice that take the tenet of critical inquiry to deeper complexity by providing historical context and terminologies of intergenerational trauma that are appreciated by diverse people. TWU offers an alternative to neoliberalism by venerating Pueblo cultural sovereignty. Further, its healing justice repertoire includes crafting women-designed and women-led practices, gestures of gratitude that express an indigenous worldview and affirm "relational-tivity"—relations between human communities and the plants, animals, landscape, and cosmos. TWU encourages social interactions and storytelling with others in similar circumstances and collectively honors traditional values and sacred practices.

Forward Stance

Within the movement for reproductive justice, Forward Stance is a prominent mind-body approach used by several organizations. Forward Stance is coordinated movement rooted in Eastern practices such as Tai Chi or Qigong, both sometimes called "meditation in motion," with their low-impact, slow-motion, flowing movements that invite conscious breathing and awareness of sensations as well as how energy moves in the cosmos.[73] When I attended the conference "Activists Mobilizing for Power," sponsored by Western States Center, a workshop leader taught us to use Forward Stance, in which the body moves in a flowing manner, similar to Qigong, but also includes rhythmic, loud vocalizations timed with pronounced movements. In the workshop discussion afterward, we agreed that Forward Stance engenders a sense of power and joy through collective movement.

According to Forward Together's executive director, Eveline Shen, the decision to use Forward Stance came out of reflection about the internal conflict and physical and mental exhaustion that several members of the staff were experiencing during a period of rapid organizational expansion. During that period, they also found themselves experiencing tension with their allies. Recall that Shen discussed how social justice organizations in Oakland and the Bay Area generally sometimes found themselves in competition with one another over funding: "Many of these organizations don't normally talk to each other because of the way our movement is structured. The funding is very silent, so folks who work in environmental justice don't talk to any gender-based violence orgs, even though we are working with the same communities." These material tensions were in addition to the ways in which this region has pronounced racial and class segregation. Some social justice organizations in the Bay Area work with specific racial groups, so collaboration entails negotiating across multiple differences. The staff decided to start talking circles with nonviolent communication practices and interviews with their allies to explore the causes and implications of these multiple tensions and to hear each other's perspectives. Shen also reached out to Norma Wong Roshi, a Zen priest, former state senator, and political strategist from Hawaii, who worked with the organization to design Forward Stance.

Ryuko (Norma) Wong Roshi views Forward Stance as a "mind-body approach [that] utilizes the physical *experience* to develop, explore, and demonstrate human actions."[74] Wong Roshi clarifies that Forward Stance is a "technology and not a practice"; that is, it is a "body of knowledge" she adapted through her work at the Institute of Zen Studies in San Francisco: "I developed it as a means to bring experiential learning to concepts of individual, organizational and societal change . . . that evolved over time in the work with ACRJ [Asian Communities for Reproductive Justice, which later became Forward Together] and the EMERJ [Expanding the Movement for Empowerment and Reproductive Justice] project."[75] Wong Roshi explains the rational for developing Forward Stance: "Social justice work is highly conceptual, but change cannot occur if it is just a state of mind. Change is inherently a state of *being* in movement of time and space. If we are trapped in the concepts of social change, how can we expect people to step forward to experience and embrace social change?"[76]

When I interviewed Shen, she demonstrated that Forward Stance begins by standing and placing one's body so that it is leaning forward, indicating a posture of awareness and readiness. She said,

If you lean back with 60 percent of your body weight on the balls of your feet, this is what we call "leaning back stance" or "defensive stance." . . . So then if you move to a 50-50 stance, you are more neutral. And then if you then lean forward so 60 percent of your weight is on the balls of your feet, and then you're looking at me but you're aware of 180 degrees, and you start to be aware of what's outside in terms of noises and what's going on. And then we do a lot of relaxation and focus on your breath, and a lot of time we are in our mind, and so we try and breathe low and slow. . . . And so we want to get organizations into a Forward Stance, where they are in a state of relaxed readiness, so even in the midst of chaos they are calm, they have a strategy, they want to move, they have a vision they want to move toward, they are aware of what's going in in front of them with the political climate with other organizations.

Forward Stance encourages practitioners to intentionally exhale longer than inhaling, which is calming and makes one feel more clarity and engenders trust. Forward Stance is integral to individual self-care, as Amanda Wake writes: "Forward Stance has shown me the power I have inside of me. Whenever I feel doubt or scared or unsure, I use Forward Stance to connect to my breath and broaden my awareness. It reminds me I can trust my gut."[77]

Many reproductive justice activists have been trained how to use Forward Stance. A film clip posted on Forward Together's website describes the approach:

> The visionary and innovative work of building a strong and vibrant Reproductive Justice Movement requires us to physically move people, move institutions, and change the way the world works. Too often in our work, we are "in our heads," focusing on conceptual ideas and frameworks while ignoring the physics of social change work. Forward Stance provides us with a powerful way to learn and gain new insight through physical movement and by reconnecting our bodies with our minds. Forward Together uses Forward Stance in all aspects of our work, and also trains allied organizations in the practice to support their movement-building efforts.[78]

The film includes images of a group of racially diverse people participating in Forward Stance; the people are smiling and seem peaceful as they move in unison. The narration begins with Aimee Santos Lyon of Western States Center, who describes the practice: "Forward Stance is able to bring movement into movement building, so helping us demonstrate a range of organizations' concepts and strategies like alignment, coordination, integration." Then Adriann Barboa from Strong Families New Mexico states, "Forward Stance has really been the way that we helped sustain an idea of health promotion and healing for all the work we do and how we take care of ourselves and our communities." Taj James from the Movement Strategy Center states, "The Forward Stance work really helped me and our team really find focus and find rhythm and figure out how to reshape our work in a way that we could have more impact. And our team has really grown and our work has really grown over the last couple of years." Eveline Shen concludes, "Forward

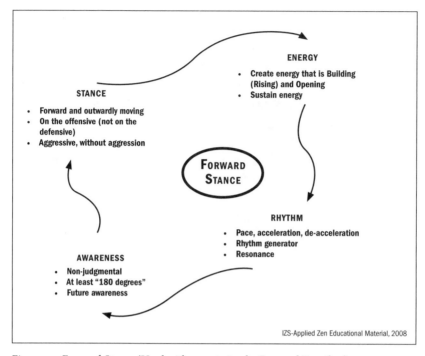

Figure 4.1. Forward Stance (Used with permission by Forward Together)

Stance is about cultivating energy in a very basic way by using breath, sound, and movement. And it is amazing to be in a room full of people when we are all acting and moving as one! Because if we can act and move as one when we're in the gym, we can act and move as one when we are spread out across the country through time and space." Participants perform choreographed movements of their bodies and shout out rhythmically in unison, "Hey! Hey! Hey!" Music plays and then fades away as the logo and website are displayed: "Forward Stance: Bringing Movement to Movement Building." The visual representation of Forward Stance is seen in figure 4.1, which includes an explanation of the practice that is posted online:

> Stance is how we move through the world. We can have a walking, standing, sitting and lying stance. When we are standing or sitting in Forward Stance, we have 60% of our body learning forward. This is a stance in which we are in a state of readiness and able to take action.

Energy gives life to stance. The energy of a forward stance is deep, strong, and rising and can be sustained over time and through challenging circumstances.

Rhythm is the pace of our actions. Individuals, organizations, and the world around us have an inherent rhythm and pace. In Forward Stance, we have an awareness of rhythm and we are intentional about our pace.

Awareness is a clear, broad sense of what is happening around us. Too often, we have tunnel vision—only seeing what is directly in front of us—the project we are working on, the action we are planning. The awareness of Forward Stance provides context and ability to see what is actually happening around us.

By refining our ability to look within we learn to hold and channel our power in specific ways that are relational to others, allowing us to see what is all around, rather than what is simply in our line of sight. Whether we are working on a challenging campaign with our allies or at an action demanding change from our opposition, Forward Stance provides tools that enable us to strategically and proactively move through difficult situations with clarity.[79]

This graphic, along with the accompanying explanation and film clip, makes Forward Stance accessible to those who have not had the opportunity to learn it during a training. Forward Stance incorporates corporality with mindfulness, an intentional "practice being present with and noticing what is happening in the moment."[80] Tai Chi and Qigong have beneficial effects on people's physical and mental health, in that structured movement of the body releases endorphins and creates euphoria.[81] Moreover, mindfulness has been shown to lead to increased body awareness through attention to physical sensations, changes in perspective of the self through self-compassion and acceptance, greater use of social support, less stress, and more direct action as well as direct health benefits.[82] Pyles asserts that "establishing healing justice as a practice necessitates the creation of a certain amount of structure," something clearly occurring with Forward Stance.[83]

The reproductive justice organization Forward Together has now integrated Forward Stance into weekly staff meetings and quarterly strategy sessions and conferences.[84] I observed the youths in the Core group at Forward Together practice using Forward Stance in preparation for a presentation to a school board member. The facilitator called out as they moved, "breathe, feet flat, hip distance apart, 180-degree awareness, relax." The youths shouted very deep, resonant, and powerful sounds with their coordinated movements. They seemed to enjoy the practice, and we could feel the vibrancy in the room. Eveline Shen assessed the utility of using Forward Stance: "It's really been transformational in terms of integrating this mind-body work. . . . We want to bring *all of us*, each of our selves, into the room and into our work. It can affect everything from sustainability to resiliency to agility to coordination that translates into more effective movement building work and social change." Some reproductive justice organizations practice Forward Stance regularly, and a number of leaders in the movement I interviewed had been trained in Forward Stance.

While Forward Stance uses breath, movement, and reflective inquiry, part of the genera central to healing justice, this approach is unique since it was constructed organically out of Forward Together's efforts to counter staff burnout and cross-sector tension. Forward Together's healing justice repertoire emphasizes the mind-body connection and group coordination by diverse social activists. The Forward Stance technology is an alternative to the commercialization of structured movement offered by a master with individual followers who pay for participating in the practice; instead it offers collective exercise in a group setting designed to ground and enhance social movements. With its broad dissemination to an array of organizations across the country, Forward Stance helps to sustain the movement for reproductive justice.

COLOR's Culture of Appreciation and Resiliency

COLOR has been working on changing its organizational culture for some time. This work was recognized when COLOR was invited to a Ford Foundation convening in 2013 to share some of its best practices with other organizations. In an interview, then executive director Lorena García pointed out, "What sets COLOR apart is our strong work in cultural competency. This means hiring staff whose skill sets include experience in the communities they are trying to organize, who understands their cultural background: What kind of families do Latinos have? How do disabled youth access comprehensive sex ed? COLOR tries to hire as diverse as possible, representing local populations so as to work effectively." Staff were encouraged to decorate their offices and the meeting room, so there was a festive air in the place. Some staff's work was conducted in Spanish as they organized in the Latinx community.

Like many social justice organizations, COLOR worked on constructing *acuerdos* (agreements) that they posted on a large poster board at work. In 2013 the agreements included, "Step up / step back; Respect time; 1 diva, 1 mic; Don't yuck my yum; Expect accountability. What's said here, stays here; what's learned here, leaves here." These agreements, which are used across movements as well, encouraged strategically taking leadership, honoring timelines and deadlines, enabling others to speak and express their preferences, and being prepared to explain one's work. These agreements provided some grounding for their work, especially during moments of crisis or intense activity. Over the years as I visited COLOR's office, I noticed that new items were added. In 2017, in response to a suggested prompt—"I feel appreciated when:"—staff brainstormed and updated their list of *acuerdos* to include, "My work is acknowledged; Use manners (thank you, excuse me); Ask for help, options; Team work / contributions; When people do their part so I can do my part; Team celebration, spending time together; Proper credit is given; When given feedback; Feelings/responsibilities taken into consideration; Experience/perspective is validated/acknowledged; Punctuality; Read / respond to emails (being responsive)." These agreements, which encourage transparency, would facilitate collaboration in any worksite.

Another deliberate practice was that everyone took turns facilitating staff meetings. During a staff meeting that I attended, there was a notable effort to make sure everyone was heard as they strategized to move forward with multiple projects. In 2013, COLOR was working a bill that would increase funding for comprehensive sex ed for Colorado youth, canvassing to enroll people in the ACA, attempting to end hospital discrimination based on nonmedical issues such as religion or legal status, and repealing the state Hyde Amendment, for which there was no funding to cover staffing. And as part of COLOR's ongoing work, periodically during times of transition the staff would intentionally have check-ins over their greatest successes. The staff would also have accountability sessions where they took turns reflecting on their strengths and areas where they could use support from others, which led to better collaboration with one another, and they would report to their immediate supervisors how they were improving their work. There was an altar in the office, and occasionally the staff would incorporate *limpias* (spiritual cleansings) by burning sage, *palo santo* (Peruvian tree bark), or other sacred plants.

When hired as deputy director in 2013, Cristina Aguilar was asked to focus on developing COLOR's organizational culture, which originated in the organization's history. Aguilar said, "It certainly was from the *madrinas'* [foremothers] original vision of saying that care for mind-body-spirit is a critical part of reproductive justice for COLOR." She elaborated:

> I think our founding mothers were very brilliant in how they formed COLOR [in 1998] by recognizing that it is as important to take care of ourselves in a traditional way. So that's why we fight for access for health care but also that so many Latinos really do have indigenous roots with other ways of healing. I believe that it is on some level about giving reverence to that and recognizing that we are a full person; our minds, our bodies, and our spirits need to be clear; and that autonomy over our body is important. But having healthy bodies also encompasses having a healthy spirit or soul or just an emotional sense of being able to take care of yourself in that way.

Here Aguilar resonates with practitioners and scholars who recognize the de-Indianization that occurred after colonization in which many Native Americans were detribalized and forced to assimilate into US society, and many Latinxs have lost the knowledge systems practiced by their indigenous ancestors.[85] Aguilar said that care for mind-body-spirit "always remained": "That part is really important. Even though we're about to be twenty years old, it has always been a cornerstone of our work. Certainly it's a passion I've brought to the work. I draw on my own practice in the LGBTQ community and work as a Reiki master healer and my own connections to spiritual work through my family."[86]

After Aguilar became executive director, the work context became even more stressful, and COLOR faced a number of challenges related to working in Denver. In 2015, there was a shooting at Planned Parenthood in nearby Colorado Springs (seventy miles away), which profoundly shook everyone since it targeted a close ally. Many of the staff had been in Colorado during the mass shooting in Columbine in 1999 (only sixteen miles away) and Aurora's mass shooting in a movie theater in 2012 (eleven miles away) that killed twelve people and injured seventy more. Then in 2016, the Denver police shot and killed a transgender youth, sixteen-year-old Jessie Hernández, who had participated in COLOR activities. In 2016, there was another shooting in Denver in which some of COLOR's collaborators, a youth member of Latinas Increasing Political Strength and a board member, were in the building where the shooting happened. Denver has one of the highest populations of Latinxs in the country, with Mexicans displaced from land grants in southern Colorado to more recent migrants from Latin America. There have been a number of detentions and deportations of immigrants, including the former spouse of one of the staff, which was particularly difficult on her and her child as well as the staff, and some COLOR participants lost family members to deportation. Aguilar recalled, "There was so much other state violence—there was Ferguson in 2014; there was Mike Brown—that was really impacting so many of our partners in the movement work. . . . And there were other violent things happening in abortion clinics as well. There's a hashtag from the Black Lives Matter movement, which is '#Ican'tbreathe,' and I think that was what was quite honestly being expressed by a lot of us."[87] Indeed, research demonstrates that police killings of unarmed Black Americans have adverse effects on the mental health of Black Americans overall.[88] Moreover, when people of color experience historical racially based trauma—such as genocide against Native Americans, slavery of African Americans, exclusion of Chinese migrants, Japanese American internment, mass deportations of Mexicans that included US citizens, and so on—the consequences are passed to subsequent generations.[89] Aguilar reflected, "There have been all these layers. . . . I'm grateful to be the person in this seat and in this role. But it's harder than I ever imagined."

In response to these collective historical and contemporary stressors, Aguilar decided to try and "cultivate the best work culture" that she could. She implemented mindfulness practices such as opening and ending strategic planning sessions with a breathing meditation session. She said, "Because it's always something I've believed in; it's equally important to have strong beginnings and endings and also to just ground ourselves, which is important culturally. . . . In many of our cultures there are these honoring practices, even if you just say, 'Provecho' [enjoy] before you start a meal, it's almost a blessing. It makes you take a breath and honor your space; you honor your food; you honor the people that you're with." She also had a masseuse come in and do some chair massages with the staff. Aguilar recalled, "Afterwards she told me that she really felt there was some collective trauma happening and that she felt it in our bodies. And it wasn't a surprise to me in many ways because of the very direct and indirect trauma that we have been experiencing in our movement and what we're exposed to—such as the things the staff hears in our *cafecitos*, in our comp-sex-ed work." Indeed, during *cafecitos* with parents and other adults, the staff often heard about state violence in which people were racially profiled, detained, or deported. And, as we saw earlier, during comprehensive sex education during the youth programs, young women sometimes disclosed experiences of sexual assault or abuse, sexually transmitted infections, domestic violence in their families, or bullying. Aguilar affirmed, "I had known for a while we needed to have some really good protections for boundaries and a sense of a place to get guidance. Like, what do we do with some of the exposure to trauma our staff was experiencing? There are traumatic things that have happened to me at the capitol behind closed doors too, so it's on all the staff levels." Aguilar planned a staff reset resilient retreat that would focus on responses to trauma exposure. She had a security system installed and created a security plan for the staff in case of an emergency. She worked toward providing an employee assistance program (initially pro bono but later a budget line item) and normalizing that the staff would benefit from using mental health services: "We're part of an organization committed to wellness and mental health, so we're trying to walk our talk." And in response to rapid growth, she developed a pipeline so staff would receive training and develop new skills that would leverage them into other positions in COLOR with more responsibilities and higher pay, encouraging a strong sense of remaining with the organization rather than seeking new opportunities elsewhere. COLOR staff also is trained in and occasionally uses Forward Stance. By engaging in self-care as an organization, COLOR staff would become better witnesses to the trauma in Colorado communities as well as become more effective advocates on behalf of those communities.

Then Aguilar was invited to a grantee convening sponsored by the Ms. Foundation that included workshops on burnout, resiliency, and executive transitions. The participants were trained in a Resiliency and Renewal Model by Strategies for Social Change that encouraged executive directors to move away from reacting to crises. Instead the model encourages long-term planning with anticipated times of rest, reflection, and renewal, including a celebration to mark the end of a project before slowly transitioning toward new ones. The Resiliency and Renewal Model advocates the principles of leadership development, which include advice to become "emotionally intelligent," foster a continuous learning organization, practice self-care that "strengthens our movements," and develop a leadership plan.[90] Aguilar recalled that after the explanation of the model, "In the room there was this collective exhale! It was amazing to me, and so telling, that we were all like, 'I've needed this model my whole activist life! And it's so simple!' So of everything that I took away from that training, I was just like, 'I'm folding this and putting it in my back pocket and bringing it back to COLOR!'" Aguilar incorporated the Resiliency and Renewal Model into the reset resilient retreat: "It was almost like braiding a trenza, trying to figure out, 'Okay, we have these pieces; we have this model. How do we start to bring it all in?'"

Over the course of two years, the staff collaborated to craft a shift toward a "resilient and appreciative work culture." Recall that they ended events by circling together and giving a group cheer, "¡Ay chingona! [We're badass!]," which built team spirit. They elaborated on the self-care messages quoted earlier. Staff meetings began with reading the organization's mission statement, and staff modeled best practices. For example, if the facilitator wanted everyone to share an insight, she would share first, which, according to Aguilar, "helps with trust and vulnerability." They ended meetings with an example of self-care and a brief story expressing their hope for the week, in which the latter was related to personal desires. Here the staff was engaging in what Pyles calls "conscious communication," a form of healing justice in which "communication tools and practices acknowledge differences with others while still maintaining connections to one another."[91] While conscious communication can be undermined by power differentials within an organization based on staff hierarchies, COLOR staff worked to focus on what they shared in common as Latinas, and over time they got to know one another well. They started a "building resiliency" practice in which staff would write poems or comments on postcards and place them in a big mason jar, Aguilar recalled: "They would write stuff like, 'I felt resilient when we all shared together,' or 'I felt resilient when doing a scavenger hunt in the mountains.'" Further, by occasionally reading notes from the past, the staff reminisced and bonded further. They would practice expressing appreciation or gratitude verbally to one another or in writing using colored paper and pens.[92] Aguilar reflected on the importance of all this mindful resilience and appreciation work: "It's almost been a lifeline. What better lifeline than the concept of resilience? And really that is what our work is about at its core too. That's really about having that resilience, and that really starts in ourselves. So, what is my responsibility as a leader in COLOR and a leader in community to really walk my own talk with resilience at the same time I'm trying to institutionalize practices within COLOR, create strategies and tactics in much the same way we do in campaigns? It almost became a campaign, a resilience campaign." These group activities in which the staff shared their emotions with one another—sadness, compassion, pride, or joy—led to greater staff morale, which was evident time after time when I attended COLOR events. And their vision of resilience was not about endurance but about expressing positivity.

COLOR has also incorporated its attention to mind-body-spirit in its work with young women. Like many other reproductive justice organizations, COLOR often hires young people to work in their youth programs. Aguilar pointed out,

> Especially in our work here in COLOR with women and with youth who have had trauma, and what that does to you on a mental, emotional level, on a spiritual level, as well as what it does physically to your body. I think having that holistic approach really honors every part of who we are. And it's not always popular, I think, to believe in that. I think saying it, "mind, body, spirit," can be so woo-woo kind of anymore. But I see it as honoring all of who you are and what you bring into a space, what really comes with you as a result of whatever your life experience has been: the good, the bad, the hard, the wonderful of it.

For young participants and young staff, paying attention to mind, body, and spirit may be relatively new experiences. Yet young women participants appreciate the holistic approach that COLOR cultivates. Sandy, the shy young activist quoted earlier, said, "I like the way COLOR talks about mind, body, and spirit. I think that should happen in any program you develop where mind, body, and spirit reside."

Through COLOR's holistic approach that pays attention to care for the staff through using mental health services, care for their bodies, and spiritual expressions, the organization is attempting to counter the effects of burnout and stress from the dominant society. Aguilar pointed out,

> Our work is so intense, and it's so personal for people—what we're trying to change, the opposition that we have. I really feel that we just put everything into our work. We're throwing our hearts out there on the table and our passion and all of our ferocity at times. We have to be taking care of ourselves too in order to negotiate the differences, to be able to sit at a table and have opposition or have things said that are deeply offensive or the silencing that often happens for our community and having to sit there and be strong and empowered and not coming from a place of exhaustion and anger. I think that trying to build an appreciative culture really is an antidote to that, really trying to support us internally so that we can be that much more effective externally.

Aguilar views COLOR's holistic work as helping young staff: "When we're hiring people right out of college, and they're just like so fired up and everything, but I think that you have to balance that. It's great to be fired up, it's important, but you can't do it to your own detriment. Adding in that self-care piece, adding in that appreciative piece, I think helps with balancing that piece." After Aguilar left the organization, where she had a number of high-profile accomplishments and received a major award for her activism, she saw her work to cultivate appreciation and resiliency at COLOR as her proudest achievement.

COLOR implements the healing justice tenets of breath, meditation, and reflective inquiry but goes far beyond those. COLOR is concretizing a holistic approach to self-care that counters state and interpersonal violence by making physical and mental health, spiritual and cultural affirmation, and staff development central to organizational wellness. In the process, COLOR disrupts the neoliberal emphasis on healing through individualized practices. The COLOR staff is building a repertoire of collaborative work strategies as well as a sense of egalitarian-ism and community spirit that enables them to continue their policy advocacy on behalf of Latinas and their allies. They are practicing Audre Lorde's famous dictum, "Caring for myself is not self-indulgence, it is self-preservation, and that is an act of political warfare."[93]

Young Women United Guided by Spirit

Young Women United sees spiritual activism as an integral part of its culture shift work, which, as mentioned earlier, is related to how to work with and represent women of color who are vulnerable, such as moth-ers with addictions or young parents. Former executive director Tannia Esparza disclosed that YWU's work goes beyond shifting the narra-tive about women of color and occasionally is "guided by spirit."[94] She explained that the organization sees spirituality as key to sustaining its organizing and culture shift work as well as maintaining staff morale.

The key to imbuing spirituality into YWU's work is its insistence on honoring the importance of place as well as the strength and resilience of people in New Mexico. This approach was especially evident in its successful Respect ABQ Women campaign, which defeated a proposed municipal ban on abortion after twenty weeks of pregnancy.[95] Esparza stated,

One of the first pieces of literature that came out of the campaign was a picture of real people that belong to our communities that were standing up for people to be able to make their own decisions about their bodies and their lives. And that to us is an image of strength and resiliency. We did a photo campaign around picturing people in their neighborhoods. In New Mexico, it's really important to people to have expressions of place, to claim, to reclaim their sense of land and of space for the genera-tions that have been here. I think that was so powerful because we just talked about the histories of the Barelas neighborhood and the other old neighborhoods in Albuquerque. The pride that people feel about their neighborhoods and communities is really huge for New Mexican families. And the fact that they were standing and identifying with their sense of place and also their values, I think that's what "strength-based" means for us.

Place is significant for those who work in New Mexico in part because of the unique history of the state. New Mexicans are proud of their state, the "Land of Enchantment," which has a complex history of conflict and cooperation between Native Americans and Hispanos (Mexicans of Spanish and Native American descent) going back to the conquest. These relations were complicated by the influx of Anglos who migrated to and settled in New Mexico in large numbers in the nineteenth century and became the largest and dominant racial group.

New Mexico's history, along with a desert mountainous landscape, shapes a distinctive style of architecture derived from Native American pueblos and Spanish use of adobe, as well as art, fashion, cuisine, and religious ceremonies, some of which have been performed since before the conquest.[96] Locals celebrate Native resistance to Spanish colonization and their unique heritage in New Mexico, "their sense of sociocultural distinctiveness."[97] Furthermore, there are twin settlement processes that make Albuquerque, the largest city in the state, distinct: there are twelve indigenous nations, mostly Pueblo, within a fifty-mile radius, which facilitates close relations between Native Americans living in cities and those on reservations, with implications for cultural, religious, political, and economic exchanges. Over thirty thousand Native Americans live in Albuquerque, and they have complex relationships with those from other indigenous nations who have distinct cultural expressions.[98] According to Micaela Cadena, YWU is sensitive that there are twenty-three Native American sovereign nations overall in the state of New Mexico, with distinct regional languages and cultural expressions.[99] Simultaneously, New Mexico has the largest land-based Mexican population in the United States.[100] Some Hispano neighborhoods were villages before being incorporated into the city of Albuquerque, so neighborhood identification is strong. Since the 1980s, there has been increased settlement by migrants from Latin America, especially from Mexico. Local activists sometimes use "Hispanas/os-Chicanas/os-Latinas/os" to signify their inclusiveness of those with multiple generations of history in the state, politicized Mexicans, and migrant newcomers. Or activists use "Hispanos" or Spanish terms such as *nuevomejicanos* or *manitas* for those of mixed Spanish and indigenous heritage with a long-term presence in the state. And more recently the term "Latinx" is being used to distinguish people of Spanish or Latin American heritage from Native Americans and whites. Adding to the complexity of identity politics, contemporary Hispanos have a history of colonization if they have indigenous heritage but also of being part of settler colonialism if they can trace their ancestry to the Spanish colonizers, which seems odd to those small land-grant owners struggling to retain their land.[101] Like the rest of the state, there are a number of people in recovery from substance abuse in Albuquerque, related to high unemployment and poverty.[102] According to Pyles, in a place-based view of the self favored by the healing justice approach, "context matters to not only one's identity, but it is intricately connected to other parts of the self, including the body, mind, community, and spirit."[103]

In addition to representing pride in place during the organization's work, Alicia Chávez, YWU's youth and community organizer, recalled that while running the Respect ABQ Women campaign, YWU staff took efforts to counteract their fatigue and stress: "There was a real spiritual aspect to the campaign as well. We did a lot of Forward Stance. We even did some sage smudging a few times," a sacred practice of burning sage to cleanse people and spaces.[104] YWU's spiritual practices include celebrating traditional events like Día de los Muertos (Day of the Dead), a joyous gathering of those who have lost family members, which includes food, beverages, and decorating gravesites and providing a pathway for spirits of the deceased to return and visit the living. Celebrated on November 1 in Mexico, Día de los Muertos is becoming integrated into university and school programs and celebrated publicly in the United States. During the Respect ABQ Women campaign, YWU joined a Día de los Muertos event by dressing up as *calacas* (skeletons often depicted by Mexican and Chicanx artists); the event had a huge turnout. Esparza composed and sang a song that honored women and then spoke about the importance of defeating a proposed municipal ban on abortion that would remove women's right to make their own reproductive health decisions. Esparza recalled, "We practice spirit, so we wanted to create a song through a different methodology that would resonate with our community. We wanted to offer this song because we wanted to ground ourselves in some of the traditions that serve as a context for reproductive justice but also the tools that our communities come with every day." Here Esparza is alluding to the belief that songs, chanting, mantras, or even speeches are considered a manifestation of divine breath and are spiritual practices.[105] Alicia Chávez elaborated on YWU's spiritual work: "[During the campaign] we brought our full selves into the work as much as possible." The notion of "bringing our full selves to the work" indicates that participants are mindful of the importance of integrating spirituality with bodily care and awareness as well as strategic planning and publicly claiming all of their identities. I often heard a variant of the phrase "we bring our full selves to the movement" from reproductive justice advocates. Pyles suggests that the healing justice framework views the self as having six dimensions—the body, emotions, thoughts, spirit, community, and the natural world.[106] For people in the movement for reproductive justice, the whole self also signifies the safety to claim all their identities related to place, sexuality, race, ethnicity, gender, documentation, ability, age, and so on. "Coming out" publicly as a queer woman or as an undocumented mother or as a New Mexico native was a way in which reproductive justice activists got in touch with their sense of authenticity and pride, a political stance long articulated by women of color.[107]

As part of YWU's spiritual work, the organization has sponsored Panocha Pláticas (rough translation: "pussy talks") for many years. *Panocha* is the Spanish word for brown sugar formed in the shape of a hard cone and is slang for the vagina or vulva. Panocha Pláticas are social gatherings to share stories related to sexuality, the body, and spirituality. In this work, YWU is honoring the thoughts of Audre Lorde, who famously stated, "The dichotomy between the spiritual and the political is also false, resulting from an incomplete attention to our erotic knowledge. The bridge which connects them is formed by the erotic— the sensual—those physical, emotional, and psychic expressions of what is deepest and strongest and richest within each of us, being shared: the passions of love, in its deepest meanings."[108] Adriann Barboa, former executive director of YWU and current executive director of Strong Families New Mexico, recalled,

> One of our old board members went to the SisterSong conference in Chicago [in 2007], and there were women from California [Sophia Arredondo, Jessica Far, Irene Lara, and Eneri Araz] who presented on the "Panocha Plática" booklet. They held a workshop that used that book; the whole format that we got for those Pláticas came out of that workshop.

And Mónica Trujillo, who was on the board at the time, asked them for permission, and they were like, "Yes, use it. That's why we're doing this! Share it and recopy it as much as you want." So that's how we started doing Panocha Pláticas. Mónica led it.

Sophia Arredondo, Jessica Far, Irene Lara, and Eneri Araz situate Panocha Pláticas in Chicana feminist writings and clarify, "Panocha conveys an embracing of our whole selves—bodymindspirit—in a way that the proper terms vagina and vulva do not."[109] They clarify the purpose of formulating Panocha Pláticas:

It is a revolutionary act to love and respect panochas such as our own. Having a panocha plática is a big "fuck you" to a society that has continually attempted to use and abuse our panochas, our bodies, our minds, and our spirits. We think about the unthinkable and we speak about the unspeakable. We challenge sexist mind sets that claim panochas are powerless objects. We challenge racist views that teach us darkness is something to be feared, controlled, tamed. We challenge classist views that claim our panochas reproduce like rabbits just to be part of a welfare system that doesn't care about our well-being. We challenge homophobic views that push our panochas into closets where we are supposed to wait until heterosexual marriage sets us free. We challenge patriarchal religions that silence our desires and conceptualize pregnancy as a one-woman act. We challenge able-bodied views that assume disabled women's panochas are incapable of sexuality. We challenge ageist views that insist wrinkles and sagging breasts need to be fixed. We challenge body image views that tell us that women aren't *beautiful*. We challenge rigid views of gender that restrict boys from wearing pink hot pants and crying, and girls from sporting buzz cuts and kicking ass. We are warriors, healers, curanderas, brujas, witches, alchemists, poets, lovers. As we challenge and transgress these views, we transform—through plática, in plática, from plática.[110]

The booklet suggests that Pláticas include more than chatting; they are forms of storytelling and self-representation: "These oral traditions persist in our songs, our call and responses, carvings on our ancient ruins, marks on our bodies, the art tattooed onto our flesh, the spoken word over bonfires honoring the full moon. These oral traditions are kept alive by our plática, by our panochas rejoicing in healing and collective memory."[111] The "Panocha Pláticas" booklet celebrates women's sexual pleasure and a range of body types by including poetry and images such as the goddess of fecundity and photographs of women's diverse expressions of sexuality.[112] One of the "Panocha Pláticas" authors, Irene Lara, further explains the power of the erotic: "This 'creative energy/power' can relate to spirit and spirituality, teaching, writing, parenting, and more."[113] Moreover, this reframing of sexuality and spirituality critiques the binary of virgin-whore, which is based in patriarchal, Eurocentric, and homophobic cultures. Instead, Lara suggests that erotic imagery "counters the body-loathing ideology that treats sexual desire as a human weakness in need of constant surveillance."[114]

Initially YWU's Panocha Pláticas were held in women's homes, and the participants would bring food and make a night of it in which women shared their pain and laughter. Barboa explained why YWU started sponsoring them beginning in 2008: "It was another way to engage. Since then, that has been one of the most popular ways that we bring in young adult women is having those Pláticas at somebody's house. We would cook a meal together and then have the last half focus on the Plática. But it started to get where folks weren't coming for the cooking part but coming for the Plática so we started getting [take-out] food for the Pláticas." Eventually YWU changed the name to Las Pláticas, "in order to better reflect and honor a broader range of bodies": "Las Pláticas are a safe space for women of color to come together to share and discuss sex, sexuality, women's empowerment, sisterhood, and our bodies. Open to all self-identified women of color and native women including queer and trans folks ages 18–100!"[115]

When I visited YWU in 2013, I saw of handful of staff practice Forward Stance as I pulled up for my first interviews with them. I also observed one of YWU's Sister Sharing Circles for self-identified women of color of any age interested in birth and parenting justice. This group was racially mixed—African Americans, Latinas, whites, and mixed-race women. After hearing about the purpose of the Plática, all of the women seemed intrigued by the possibility of a discussion about sexuality and spirituality and were enthusiastic about attending. YWU is creating its own version of a booklet based on Panocha Pláticas, and I saw a draft in the office when I visited. In this work, YWU is incorporating a sex-positive politics in which it balances the emphasis on women's rights to freedom from various forms of oppression with women's right to freedom of expression.[116] The "sex wars" debates of the 1980s and 1990s, sparked by feminists and queer theorists about the politics of sexuality, have shaped contemporary theoretical, social, and political demands for sex positivity that acknowledges women's sexual identities, desires, erotic diversity, and freedom from repressive norms. As the feminist theorist Elisa Glick argues, "both pro-sex and radical feminists reproduce the ideology of personal emancipation within contemporary capitalist society by making the liberation of sex a fundamental feminist goal." I take her point that "we cannot proclaim any cultural practices, sexual or otherwise, as resistant without examining how these practices function within the racist, imperialist, and capitalist social formations that structure contemporary society."[117]

YWU incorporates movement in its regular use of Forward Stance as well as ongoing reflective inquiry central to healing justice. However, its healing justice repertoire also includes cleanses, using songs to convey political messages, building altars, and hosting open discussions of women's erotic powers through Las Pláticas. Along with the organization's work of countering racialized-sexualized discourse about women of color and its successful efforts to change the material conditions of women through legislation and grassroots organizing, YWU's healing justice work is truly an alternative to individualized neoliberal modes of self-care. It honors Lara's assertion that by trusting the *conocimiento* of intuition and feelings alongside our ability to reason, "our questions aim to decolonize our bodymindspirits, decolonize knowledge, and contribute to a methodology of the decolonizing erotic spirit."[118]

Conclusion

All four reproductive justice organizations discussed in this chapter engage in forms of critical inquiry central to healing justice, which Pyles suggests also includes breath, meditation, and movement.[119] In the process of focusing on wellness and spirituality, these reproductive justice organizations solidify a sense of belonging in which participants believe their right to spiritual expression is honored alongside their political, social, and cultural citizenship. In the complex ways in which they craft healing justice, these reproductive justice organizations offer a practice of radical citizenship that includes collective well-being. Each organization's expression of spiritual activism is unique, yet overall they resonate with other work by women and people of color in the movement for reproductive justice who honor women's right to spiritual expression. These organizations practice spiritual activism and create healing justice shaped by their participants' cultural heritage as well as local and personal context.

Tewa Women United honors Native Americans' right to spiritual activism as well as encourages healing on behalf of Native Americans and others in its programs located in northern New Mexico. The organization built on the self-care by women and brought healing justice into TWU's organizational work. TWU's healing justice repertoire includes expressing indigenous notions of the self, in which the physical, emotional, mental, and spiritual are in balance and harmony. TWU members center their right to cultural sovereignty and honor their language, traditions, and Tewa worldview, in which the mountains, land, rivers, animals, birds, and plants are cherished kin, and TWU offers exercises to the public designed and led by women. TWU builds community through spiritual exercises that include storytelling and sharing ancestral knowledge across generations.

Forward Together draws on Eastern philosophy and Zen practices of meditation and structured movement by incorporating Forward Stance into its organizational work in Oakland. Forward Together's repertoire of healing justice includes the use of movement, breath, and self-awareness to foster coordination by diverse social movement activists and counter the economic competition and racial/class segregation of the Bay Area. Forward Stance is oriented toward participation by diverse communities so as to enhance cross-sector collaboration. Individuals within the organization may use Forward Stance to get in touch with their own sense of strength, but Forward Together trains others in the reproductive justice movement and thus encourages coordination and mindfulness by those who have different cultural heritages across the country.

The Colorado Organization for Latina Opportunity and Reproductive Rights cultivates an organizational culture based on self-care grounded in their *madrinas'* vision of caring for minds, bodies, and spirits and to communicate openly about their needs and desires. COLOR's work culture, based on resiliency and appreciation, goes far beyond corporate notions of encouraging more productivity and healing justice's attention to breath and meditation. COLOR incorporates indigenous and spiritual practices that promote the well-being of individuals and the collectivity. COLOR's healing justice repertoire includes practicing open appreciation, accountability, and exercises designed to recognize and sustain Latinx cultural resiliency at work and to encourage healing from state and interpersonal violence in Denver. Its healing justice work, which seeks a balance of mind-body-spirit in community, forms the bedrock of its political advocacy and intergenerational intersectional movement building.

Young Women United venerates the diversity of all women regardless of circumstances. Beyond critical inquiry and movement and breath expressed through Forward Stance, its healing justice repertoire includes a body- and sex-positive politics and deliberate methodology that goes beyond the cognitive to incorporate the erotic and spirituality. YWU deliberately created a cultural fusion of indigenous and other religious practices that includes setting up an altar at work, cleanses, artistic representation, and nurturing women's bodies and erotic powers. This approach counters the forms of interpersonal and state violence with which young women of color must contend in Albuquerque, as elsewhere. As an organization, YWU places its spiritual work front and center, and members claim their pride as New Mexicans of diverse racial and ethnic heritages.

The activists in these reproductive justice organizations view spirituality and wellness in holistic terms—bringing their "full selves" into the work—as well as understand the significance of place. A number of individuals in the movement for reproductive justice engage in self-care or spiritual expressions—for example, praying, chanting, meditation, yoga—on their own. In these four examples of healing justice, reproductive justice organizations enact Loretta Pyles's observation that healing justice "is both a paradigm and a set of practices that invites practitioners to heal themselves at the same time that they heal the world."[120] These four organizations are promoting collective well-being through their policy advocacy, grassroots organizing, and cultural shift work. They are disrupting neoliberalism through the ways that they encourage their participants to heal within a broader structural context connected to the struggle for sovereignty, decolonization, and the myriad ways racialized women struggle against state and interpersonal violence. Moreover, these organizations are going beyond the spiritual traditions within their respective cultural communities and actively crafting spiritual tools designed and led by women of color. That is, these organizations are engaging in cultural shift work in their respective communities and within the secular progressive movement by "coming out of the spiritual closet."[121] All reproductive justice organizations that are integrating self-care, spiritual activism, and healing justice are following Norma Wong Roshi's advice: "Self care is foundational to our power, our resilience, our creativity, our health and our collective impact."[122] By encouraging self-care and spiritual activism, reproductive justice organizations are countering the burnout engendered by social activism.

In addition, as in previous chapters, we see reproductive justice advocates using storytelling as a method for engaging participation in spiritual practices by their constituents and allies. They illustrate that storytelling, according to Dion Million, "is creating new language for communities to address the real multilayered facets of their histories and concerns by insisting on the inclusion of our lived experience, rich with emotional knowledges, of what pain and grief and hope meant or mean now in our pasts and futures."[123] Further, by using storytelling in their healing practices, these organizations are deploying what Delgado Bernal, Burciaga, and Flores Carmona call a "pedagogical tool that lends itself to a form of teaching and learning that bridges the mind, body, and spirit and [brings] political urgency to the fore."[124]

In the effort to place individual self-care and spiritual activism in a broader social context, reproductive justice organizations disrupt the individualism embedded in neoliberal health-care systems, where everyone is supposed to take responsibility for his or her own health and purchase health-care services. Healing justice is the antithesis to a neoliberal order "that is placing increasing value on outcomes, performance measures, and the bottom line."[125] Instead, women of color are encouraged to take pride in their cultural heritages, consciously linking their diverse spiritual traditions with political consciousness. And by incorporating self-care, spiritual activism, and healing justice practices, reproductive justice activism moves toward multiple forms of wellness, refines cross-sector solidarity, and solidifies a sense of radical citizenship in which women's whole selves are honored. If, as Gloria Anzaldúa asserts, "activism is engaging in healing work," the spiritual healer Elena Avila reminds us, "healing is a lifetime journey."[126]

Conclusion

Reproductive Justice Advocacy in the "Post-Truth" Era

Radical simply means "grasping things at the root."
—Angela Davis

Love is the energy that sustains us.
—Kathy Sanchez, Tewa Women United

The only viable alternative to a politics of division is a politics of solidarity and empathy.
—E. J. Dionne Jr., Norman J. Ornstein, and Thomas E. Mann

After the 2016 presidential election, state, interpersonal, and symbolic violence against immigrants, the poor, women, and people of color increased dramatically.[1] This political climate increased the stakes for social activism, as a reproductive justice leader disclosed when I asked how her organization was faring after the inauguration: "One of the things I saw really strongly post–Trump's election is that at the same time my peers are doing this work, they're also genuinely in an existential crisis right now. And taking care of ourselves is very secondary to what we're doing right now because we're privileged and we're supposed to be taking care of things and making things happen. At the same time, we're self-medicating and really just devastated and just kind of stumbling a little bit under the weight." This activist links the challenges of mounting reproductive justice policy advocacy, culture shift work, and grassroots organizing to the political firestorm led by a president who views race, class, gender, sexuality, and citizenship through a white-supremacist, nativist, and misogynist lens, which encourages his followers to express similar views openly.[2] How did reproductive justice advocates respond to the existential crisis created by a new political regime? If, as Laura Briggs argues, all politics become about reproductive politics, in the post-Obama era reproductive justice activists were confronting increased opposition to their work.[3] Further, with Trump's flouting of norms by open disparagement of Mexicans, Arabs, Muslims, Jews, and trans people and his derision of the injured, disabled, and women and his history of sexual assaults,[4] as well as his efforts to delegitimize the role of science, the press, Congress, and the judiciary, partisan politics based in different interpretations of the "truth" became even more pronounced.[5]

Even though the norms of political discourse seem to have shifted toward more acrimony, scholars suggest that political polarization actually has antecedents going back to the McCarthy era, debates about civil rights, and the Republican "revolution" that culminated in the refusal to even consider Obama's Supreme Court nominee and the party's continued resistance to the ACA.[6] While there were unique circumstances that led to Donald Trump's election,[7] scholars have argued persuasively that his rise was fueled by a number of structural political and economic changes in the United States that originated in the 1960s. These included the "Great U-Turn" in the economy, in which deindustrialization led to outsourcing and the growth of low-paying service-sectors jobs as well as increased women's employment and decreasing real wages, as well as structural male unemployment that undermines heteronormative expectations that men are leaders of familial economic stability.[8] Two Supreme Court rulings diminished full voter turnout, both eviscerating the Voting Rights Act (*Shelby County v. Holder*) by allowing states to pass legislation that effectively suppresses the vote by racial minorities, the young, and the poor, through partisan gerrymandering as well as through a ruling (*Citizens United v. Federal Election Commission*) that views political spending a form of protected speech under the First Amendment and allows corporations or unions to contribute lavishly to political campaigns.[9] Another significant influence paving the way for Trump's 2016 election was the media, in which ultraconservative moguls, cable news outlets, and radio stars inflame public opinion.[10] Finally, immigration increased after the 1965 immigration reform bill through displacement from Asia and Latin America, though the percentage of foreign-born people in the United States is not quite as high now as it was in the early twentieth century.[11]

In the context of growing racial and cultural diversity and increasing economic disparities—where people of color are seen as competing for jobs, housing, and social benefits like health care or education—many whites came to feel dispossessed. Among white working-class voters who had anxieties about feeling like a "stranger" in their "own country," 79 percent voted for Trump.[12] However, two-thirds of Trump voters were well off economically, and white women supported him in large numbers too, indicating that his support was not only based in white, working-class, male angst.[13] Many Trump supporters project their fears on immigrants instead of criticizing the restructuring of capitalism that leaves entire regions and social categories vulnerable. They refuse to acknowledge US complicity in other governments' processes that displace people and force them to migrate to the United States or to accept the evidence that there is no causal connection between immigration and increased crime in the United States.[14]

Thus, the historical shift ushered in by the Trump election actually had long antecedents. Genevieve Negrón-Gonzales suggests, "This moment is both new and distinct, yet also . . . bears a striking resemblance to some of the darkest moments in the annals of American history."[15] Jonathan Rosa and Yarimar Bonilla agree with this stance and caution against the characterization of Trump's election as exceptional, which effectively delinks contemporary tensions from colonial histories of power.[16] I follow Rosa and Bonilla's lead and address their query, "what populations and communities have long been imagining and enacting alternatives and how might we take our cue from them?"[17] In other words, how have reproductive justice activists sustained their organizing work in the "post-truth" era?

The new political regime pursued a neoliberal agenda that endeavored to impede women's right to reproductive health care and to restrict immigration. President Trump ordered defunding of Title X, the federal family-planning program, which would strip millions of federal dollars from reproductive health providers that perform abortions and abortion referrals.[18] He asked Congress to slash the budget and staff of the Department of Health and Human Services, failed to secure timely reauthorization for the Children's Health Insurance Program, and proposed cutting programs that support low-income families.[19] Federal officials did not enforce requirements for Medicaid coverage of abortion in the limited circumstances when it is legal because of rape or incest or because the life of the woman would be endangered.[20] The Trump administration issued an executive order allowing employers to opt out of paying for birth control if they had religious or moral objections, which was blocked by a federal district court.[21] The Department of Health and Human Services released a draft of a new "conscience protection rule" that would allow health-care practitioners to discriminate against LGBTQ people in health-care settings and refuse to provide treatment, referrals, or assistance with procedures if these activities would violate their stated religious or moral convictions.[22] In a move with international reach, Trump instituted the global gag rule, which barred US foreign-aid dollars from any group that provides or counsels women about abortion, has ties to groups that do so, or advocates for abortion rights.[23] His rule that forbids counseling on all reproductive options, including abortion, and referrals to doctors who perform abortions eventually led to Planned Parenthood deciding to withdraw from the federal family-planning program, effectively denying access to reproductive and other health care for millions of women.[24] Trump's appointment of more than eighty lower-court judges and two Supreme Court justices set the stage so that access to health insurance, the right to seek an abortion, and a host of other issues would probably be decided by conservative judiciary in the years to come. The Supreme Court's 2018 ruling that a California law requiring "crisis pregnancy centers" to provide abortion information violated the First Amendment was evidence that his Supreme Court appointees have pushed the court toward the right.[25] Inspired by the president's support, conservative networks proposed unprecedented assaults on women's rights to abortion in the states.[26] Clearly reproductive governance increased under Trump.

In addition, President Trump "pressed one of the most activist agendas on immigration of any chief executive in modern times" by framing immigration as a threat to national security, the economy, and the very identity of the United States as a "nation of immigrants."[27] During his first two years of office, he issued seven executive orders with policy changes based on notions of "deserving" and "underserving" immigrants, an idea that actually has shaped US immigration policy going back to the Reagan administration, which militarized the US-Mexico border. Trump's policies included banning travel for people from predominantly Muslim nations,[28] reducing refugee admissions to the lowest numbers since the statute guiding refugee resettlement was enacted in 1980,[29] ending Temporary Protected Status for four hundred thousand immigrants from ten countries, making it more difficult for immigrants to qualify for legal permanent residence or become citizens,[30] and preventing migrants from filing asylum applications unless they enter at an official border crossings and then "metering" their access to those crossings and forcing them to remain in Mexico.[31] Security vetting of those who are seeking to migrate legally to the United States increased with the addition of in-person interviews at consulates and the prioritization of high-skilled workers.[32] He also enhanced interior enforcement,[33] sent the National Guard to the US-Mexico border, and stopped prioritizing the deportation of immigrants with criminal records, deporting thousands of ordinary people.[34] Immigration and Customs Enforcement (ICE) began targeting sanctuary cities and deporting DACA recipients who have the right under Obama's executive order to remain in the United States, as well as deporting high-profile activists.[35] Under a "zero tolerance" immigration policy, the administration saw detention facilities, increasingly housing families and unaccompanied minors rather than adult men, as a means to deter immigration rather than to help those who are seeking asylum, which led to children's deaths and charges of neglect and abuse of minors and trans migrants held in detention.[36] In an effort to deter migrant families from trying to enter the country, Border Patrol separated thousands of children from their parents.[37] The Trump administration increased efforts to curb the effects of various state-level immigration enforcement, which led the US attorney general to file a lawsuit in 2018 against the state of California for its policies and practices protecting the rights of immigrants, which the majority of Californians support.[38] A federal district judge struck down plans to add a question on citizenship to the 2020 census, which critics alleged would lead to reduced participation by immigrants regardless of legal status. The president staged a historically long government shutdown and declared a national emergency on behalf of securing funding to build a wall on the southern border, even though "for the past 10 years the primary mode of entry for the undocumented population has been to overstay temporary visas."[39] Trump's aggressive enforcement ignored that the number of unauthorized people in the United States decreased by nearly four hundred thousand from 2016 to 2017, and though there has been a surge in unaccompanied minors, the number of people entering dropped to the lowest level in a decade.[40] Also, Trump issued a new standard for applicants seeking legal permanent residency in the United States that will make it more difficult for those who use public benefits such as Medicaid, food stamps, or housing assistance, effectively blocking immigrants living in poverty from having a chance at naturalization.[41] These shifts in federal policy and enforcement practice with the goal of decreasing immigrant admissions and expanding deportations constitute what Cecilia Menjívar and Leisy Abrego call "legal violence," in which convergence and implementation of immigration and criminal law with xenophobic discourse constitute forms of violence that create extraordinary vulnerability for immigrants.[42] Legal violence also has a long history but clearly increased dramatically during the Trump administration.[43]

The response to the new political regime began immediately after the 2016 election, as social activists around the world mobilized protests. The Women's March on the day after Trump's inauguration, organized by over seven hundred partner organizations, "has been heralded as the largest single-day synchronized global mass mobilization ever," with over five million people demonstrating in the streets in more than 673 marches around the globe.[44] However, the US Women's March displayed long-standing tensions among women activists, which makes unifying across differences delicate. Women of color challenged the organizing committee for lacking diversity and called for speakers who represented a broad range of communities. This stance produced backlash, and some white women either backed out or threatened to stay home; there were questions regarding whether the factions within the resistance could "hold together."[45] During the second and third iterations of the march, there were continued demands for inclusion of more diverse speakers representing the LGBTQ and trans communities, which led to more than one march in some cities. Regardless of internal schisms, protests against the Trump administration's policies are ongoing.

In addition, since the inauguration, more than six thousand organizations registered with Indivisible, an organization formed by former congressional staffers who published a postelection guide to congressional advocacy.[46] The 2018 March for Our Lives, sparked by the Parkland shooting and the historically high number of mass shootings, predominantly by white men, drew hundreds of thousands of supporters at more than eight hundred protests that took place in every state and on every continent except for Antarctica.[47] Discourse related to "resist," being "woke," or "the resistance" now circulates widely, "calling millions of Americans to a new sense of citizenship."[48] Commentators remark on the novelty of activism during the Trump era, in which people from the middle class—the chess moms and scientists—describe their activism as new. Indeed, some suggest that the ongoing agitation was key to the Republicans' inability to repeal the ACA in its entirety. However, the press and often organizers themselves frequently focus on the internal tensions between social activists rather than the long history of activist collaboration despite differences in political goals and constituencies.

From an RJ perspective, the increasingly hostile climate has made social activism even more complex. The holistic reproductive justice approach, with well-thought-out strategies for multiple forms of activism so as to bring reproductive justice for everyone, is more urgent than ever in light of intensified state violence. Further, the reproductive justice movement provides a model for how to respond to conservative, ideologically driven politics by organizing across differences within political constituencies. This book has shown the importance of recognizing social activism that has a history of negotiating across difference for insights on the way to sustain a social movement and for the way this approach can solidify the reproductive justice movement's distinct contributions.

Reproductive Justice Advocates Respond to the Trump Political Regime

Immediately after the 2016 presidential election, reproductive justice organizers, among many others, experienced a range of emotions—shock, anger, fear, despair, and a desire to connect with fellow activists—and many needed time to process their feelings. One advocate told me that she immediately checked in on social media: "I was trying to find any hope and any sense of survival." Organizations had to take time for reflection and to find resources to help their staff cope with their feelings about the election results. COLOR staff, for example, met and had some collective meditation before sharing their feelings and brainstorming about their next steps. Cristina Aguilar, then executive director of COLOR, recalled, "We talked about what our fears were, what it was bringing up. . . . We just all tried to share and express. And we did a group hug; we brought in the idea 'let's come together.' . . . It was pretty incredible to me that we were able to be present with each other and to really have a place to express and also be, really be nonjudgmental for whatever was being expressed. I feel like we came through much stronger than I think we might have, had we not been already trying to deepen our resilience." Other organizations reassessed their priorities. CoreAlign's director, Sujatha Jesudason, said, "Three weeks after the election . . . I started asking some hard questions about CoreAlign's work. What did we need to do differently to respond strategically and thoughtfully to this new reality? How could we do our best and bravest work in this moment?"[49] Reproductive justice advocates renewed their commitment to intersectionality, in which they advocate on behalf of marginalized people, and affirmed their decolonial human rights approach that included state accountability and more.

The movement also found itself responding to new concerns. As the Trump administration began implementing its policies targeting immigrants, women, and the poor, mental health concerns increased dramatically and became more visible in communities of color. Ena Suseth Valladares, research director for CLRJ, explained how staff learned about mental health through their focus groups and door-to-door canvassing after the Trump inauguration:

> The mental health issue was really around the stress and anxiety of everyone in the community, like little children, preschoolers, and the moms. We spent a long time processing and talking about how we needed to support young people because they were in tears and they were afraid, because maybe they were documented but their family members weren't. And how a lot of times when we think about mental health, we don't think about middle schoolers, high schoolers who have to carry the burden of their family. So, we had really interesting conversations around that, trying to figure out what to do.[50]

An immigrant Latina in another city, a US citizen known as an eloquent public speaker on behalf of reproductive justice, was now intimidated since she had a Spanish accent and was worried that would elicit threatening comments from the public.[51] Other immigrant activists found Trump's authoritarianism traumatizing since it reminded them of coups that took place in their countries of origin. These responses resonated with research that shows overwhelmingly negative responses to President Trump's policies by young Latinxs.[52] Scholars have found that anti-immigrant discrimination is related to illness for immigrants, and undocumented migrants have long experienced mental health symptoms such as depression, anxiety, or posttraumatic stress disorder especially in light of possible detention or deportation.[53] Since the unauthorized can only access emergency and prenatal care, and even hospitals open them to the risk of detention, many forgo seeking health care and are forced to take care of themselves.[54] Increasingly, reproductive justice advocates have found themselves exploring new resources, developing strategies to address the Trump regime, resisting feeling defensive, and remaining determined to continue their work.

Reproductive justice activists have repeatedly put out calls to action that link threats to reproductive rights, immigration, and more, and they have offered to be interviewed by the press so that their perspectives can circulate more broadly. Moreover, the increased danger has become palpable as interpersonal violence, name-calling, and the use of guns has escalated. Several organizations have installed security systems in their worksites. In a workshop at a reproductive justice conference, "This Is How We Do It: Taking the Fight to the Opposition," Pamela Merritt, cofounder and codirector of Reproaction, a direct-action group working to increase access to abortion and advance reproductive justice, stated, "Whenever you do a direct action, they will come after you—they will come for you in an organized, well-funded way. You need to expect the reaction."[55] In response to repeated verbal and online threats, Marsha Jones, executive director of the AFIYA Center in Texas, which works to reduce Black women's HIV/AIDS and maternal mortality, hired a bodyguard to protect her.[56]

Mainstream organizations such as NARAL Pro-Choice America and Planned Parenthood and foundations that fund nonprofits have stepped up their activities. Several reproductive justice organizations have had funders reach out to them precisely because they have histories of working with immigrants, low-income women, and youth of color. One executive director recalled, "We had some rapid-response funding that came through right away. It was pretty incredible to just look at my email and to see new funders say, 'What can we do? You're working with the Latinx community, the immigrant community that is so clearly under attack.' They wanted to help!" This preemptive stance had long been an approach by some funders, as the former Ford Foundation program officer Rocio Córdoba said: "We've been trying to support organizations that have a proactive vision and have developed a strong strategy and infrastructure that can both do the proactive work and be responsive to changing conditions, and that's really important to keep our movement going in the long term because it can't be all reaction all the time. The political challenges have been there for forty years. It's nothing new. I started this work in the early '90s, and there were all kinds of challenges then too." The new opportunities for designing campaigns and intensifying the organizations' work after the 2016 election, while gratifying, were also demanding. The need for self-care to help cope with this existential crisis increased at the same time that reproductive justice activists saw their work as intensifying. I heard a number of reproductive justice advocates voice their thoughts that despite their increased workloads and burnout, they felt a keener sense of the importance of their work and the privilege of working in the movement. After the initial process of feeling destabilized and in need of ongoing self-care, the reproductive justice movement formulated two types of responses.

One reproductive justice organization performed a radical pivot that included cutting programming and staff and redesigning their work. Sujatha Jesudason explained CoreAlign's new focus: "Over the next eight weeks [after a period of postelection reflection], this re-examination of our work in a new political context resulted in cutting 2/3 of our programming, radically redesigning the rest, and trimming our staff by 1/3 (four people) so that we could effectively meet this current moment." (CoreAlign offered a generous severance package to those who left the organization.) CoreAlign then focused solely on training three hundred to five hundred leaders a year in "innovation and speaking race to power" and brought in all staff to think strategically about best practices for accomplishing this goal.[57]

Most reproductive justice organizations instead doubled down on work that helps structurally vulnerable people to understand the many policy changes brought by the Trump administration. Within days of the election, SisterSong organized a webinar called "Elections 2016: What Do the Results Mean and What's Next for Reproductive Justice?," which featured speakers who detailed how they have been organizing to get out the vote as well as working with immigrants in ways that began long before the 2016 election. Later in 2017, SisterSong organized a webinar called "Immigration, Refugees and Reproductive Justice," which had speakers talk about their ongoing work on immigrant rights, including youth, and workers' rights; lawyers and activists from ally organizations explained Trump's February 23 executive order on immigration and how to inform their constituencies. SisterSong hosted another webinar after the 2018 elections as well.

Several reproductive justice organizations intensified their work, especially related to immigration and women's access to reproductive-health-care services. COLOR, for example, shifted from hosting *cafecitos* where people could come and learn about reproductive justice, immigrant rights, and the ACA in informal settings to offering "Know Your Rights" workshops, which brought in lawyers to explain how the un-documented could navigate the new anti-immigrant climate. COLOR is part of the #HERETOSTAY Network of immigrant rights activists. A flier, titled "Know Your Rights," that COLOR circulates includes the following points and a link to the National Immigration Law Center: "Everyone has certain basic rights, no matter who is president. You have the right to remain silent. You may refuse to speak to immigration officers. Carry a 'know-your-rights' card and any valid immigration documents you have. Show them if an immigration officer stops you. Do not open your door unless an ICE agent shows you a warrant signed by a judge. You have the right to speak to a lawyer. Before you sign anything, talk to a lawyer. Learn more about your rights and how to find legal help at: NILC.org/everyone-has-certain-basic-rights." Many organizations issued protests on social media about the separation of children from their parents while in detention, asserting, "immigration is a reproductive justice issue"; one posted an article that would help supporters engage in social action, while Reproaction sponsored a webinar in 2018 with that title.[58] In relation to women's access to reproductive health rights, many reproductive justice activists participated in demonstrations and Twitter storms in support of retaining the ACA and protesting the global gag rule and allowing employers to drop contraception coverage on moral grounds. Since most reproductive justice organizations are nonprofits, they are careful to remain nonpartisan when they critique political policies.

Knowing that Immigration and Customs Enforcement was arresting immigrants at courthouses, hospitals, and schools, reproductive justice organizations also were careful about where they held their events and how they advertised them. Some reproductive justice organizations have staff members that are currently or formerly undocumented, so they are particularly sensitive to the threat of deportation. Aguilar pointed out, "When we had Latino Advocacy Day this year, we were worried there could be ICE raids. So, we had to think that through and plan, and the same for our 'Know Your Rights' workshops. The reality of the fear has been the hardest."

Finally, reproductive justice organizations have found themselves increasing their coalition building, which means negotiating new collaborations and addressing sensitive issues related to diversity among their respective constituencies. In some instances, that means confronting allies who are hesitant to take political stances in relation to structurally vulnerable people such as the undocumented. Ena Suseth Valladares of CLRJ said, "We're really trying to have a response that's about calling out the injustices and then looking for ways to transform." Similarly, Aguilar recalled, "We started to call for more authentic intersectionality within our coalition space and really putting our challenge out to our partners: 'COLOR is going to be more focused on immigrant rights and justice work. Remember we've always focused on this, but it's going to elevate and we hope you'll join us, stand with us at press conferences, and send out calls to action to your lists.' We were really trying to make the case and do calls to action."[59] In addition, the delicate negotiations around intersectionality have become even more fraught in the climate of increased racial polarization. One reproductive justice organizer sadly pointed out, "Since Trump, there is more visibility of anti-Black racism in Latinx communities." Another activist pointed out, "We've been really working hard to try to dismantle white supremacy as it exists within our own progressive spaces and then moving beyond that and doing it in a way that is about calling on consensual allyship and calling on restorative justice practices." This renewed coalition building illustrates Benita

Roth's observation: "Intersectionality is already typical of the politics of many grass-roots feminist efforts. An intersectional feminist approach requires that we think of US feminist politics as a coalitional collective of diverse voices, where the 'strategic interests' . . . will only be created by having difficult discussions among coalitional partners."[60] Coalition building between feminists and those who work on behalf of women of color yet do not identify publicly as feminist took on more urgency.

Two years after Trump's 2016 election, I returned to the Rio Grande Valley in South Texas for additional research that included participant observation and a focus group. Years before Trump was elected, this region saw deployment of the National Guard and multiagency collaboration on immigrant detention, Border Patrol agents have been stationed outside reproductive-health clinics, and ICE officials have raided protest marches. I kept asking about whether things had changed with the new administration and was told repeatedly by women from the colonias a variant of one undocumented Latina's comment: "Things have changed a great deal, but we are not going to allow him to dominate us. We have rights here, and those are the ones that we are going to push for even though the president doesn't know our rights; he doesn't know that we are human beings. He is someone who—I don't know why he has such a twisted perception. So, we are showing him what it means to have rights!" Clearly, she had benefited from the trainings about "Know Your Rights" and other policy issues that she had attended. One of the organizers affirmed her stance and provided more context: "We're not saying that all of our fear is gone. The fear has to continue to exist because if we teach that fear doesn't exist, they are going to call us insensitive to their experiences. We have to gain the force, we have to express the power that we have to support them [low-income women] to practice it, but with the sense of love and with compassion and with humanity. And that is something we don't want to lose." Indeed, these activists take a long-term perspective on social activism. They offer a vision of dynamic social transformation that will continue indefinitely regardless of who holds formal power. When Paula Saldaña was asked about her hopes for the future, she said, "In my perfect valley there would be access to health services for everyone, including for immigrants. I would like immigration reform without barriers with a pathway to citizenship. Also, I would like that everyone has the opportunity to become well educated and that universities were not so expensive. I want the Valley to be prosperous and beautiful."[61] Lucy Ceballos-Félix stated, "I would like a future where there is real respect for human rights, where everyone has health, drivers' licenses, good jobs, and fair wages. I hope that someday we will have these in Texas. We have to continue struggling and educating our children and the coming generations so they continue our legacy. I truly believe that we will achieve this vision. Maybe it won't be during my generation but perhaps during my son's or my grandchildren's time. We will continue being united, continue the movement, and push forward the struggle."[62]

These women in South Texas, along with so many other reproductive justice activists around the country, understand their privilege as activists who know their rights, have critiques of discriminatory policies and pejorative representations, and have compassion for those women who are not able to join their activism. They would agree with elder Kathy Sanchez's statement, spoken after a presentation about Trauma Healing Rocks in 2018. When asked how she finds the wherewithal for activism after the Trump election, she pointed out that even in times of extreme hardship, when working on behalf of our communities, "love is the energy that sustains us."[63] In many ways, reproductive justice advocates find themselves reaching for reservoirs of compassion and strength in themselves and in their communities even as they remind us that "immigration is an RJ issue!" or that a host of other forms of inequalities are linked to women's right to access health care. As the stakes have grown higher, the need for large-scale agitation toward women's rights to reproductive health care, for many activists crystallized in the Women's Health Protection Act, which would overturn state-level obstacles to abortion and repeal other onerous provisions, as well as immigration reform, is becoming increasingly critical.

Empowering Women through Reproductive Justice Advocacy

Scholars theorizing about social activism call for analytical bridge-building that would put into conversation the scholarship on three different foci by social movements: the organization of protests, identity formation, or policy advocacy.[64] Activists in the movement for reproductive justice enact all three of these processes as well as contest dominant narratives about women of color and frame their lives in terms of strength and resiliency, so in many ways this social movement stands out from others.

Throughout the history of this movement, beginning in the late 1980s when women of color formulated the approach that led to organizations devoted to reproductive justice, the movement has prided itself on using the frameworks of intersectionality and human rights to advocate for women's rights to bear children, terminate their pregnancies, raise their children in safe and healthy environments, voice their own gender identity, and maintain bodily autonomy.[65] As we have seen, largely led by and working on behalf of women of color, the movement has done impressive work in contesting the pejorative representation of their constituencies, engaging in grassroots organizing, and pushing policies that address social inequalities caused by intersecting systems of power. Activists in the movement for reproductive justice have a long history of organizing efforts that highlight the specific experiences of different racial groups. Simultaneously they have been working in solidarity by consciously using the term "women of color" and forging coalitions grounded in historically specific issues and racial groups in particular locations. Reproductive justice organizations have been active long before Trump was elected and will continue their activism after he has left office.

During the Obama administration, reproductive justice organizations opposed unjust state policies (such as restricting access to abortion in Texas or the Maximum Family Grant rule in California) while sponsoring or supporting legislation that would bring some benefits to communities of color. Reproductive justice activists ran a host of local campaigns that critiqued racist and sexualized representations of women of color as well as offered images of strength and resiliency in which people of color are loving, nurturing, accomplished, or proud. They were instrumental in defeating a proposed municipal ban on late-term abortion in Albuquerque in 2013 and defeating the third proposed "personhood" constitutional amendment in Colorado in 2014, to name but two successful electoral campaigns. And reproductive justice advocates contributed briefs to the Supreme Court rulings affirming marriage equality (*Obergefell v. Hodges*, 2015) and striking down anti-abortion legislation in Texas (*Whole Woman's Health v. Hellerstedt*, 2016) after years of organizing. All these successful campaigns illustrate that empowerment is possible and deeply satisfying. In addition, from these concrete political gains, there are four implications of the reproductive justice movement's novel approach.

First, this movement vernacularizes intersectionality and human rights discourse through grassroots organizing with women in modest circumstances, ranging from adolescents to the elderly. Women are recruited and then led through a process of consciousness-raising and trainings on a wide range of issues that have far-reaching consequences. The organizations literally present the reproductive justice framework in women's preferred language, which means that women learn to center themselves and find their own transformation, identities, and healing by becoming activists. Reproductive justice organizations are sensitive to women's experiences being further contextualized by their race, sexual orientation, legal status, age, ethnicity, and place of residence. As we have seen with immigrant women in South Texas and Los Angeles, Native American women in northern New Mexico, and young women of color in Oakland, Denver, Chicago, and Albuquerque, when they took the time to truly get to know one another by creating safer spaces that enable women to tell their life stories, the process of empowerment began. The training they received did not curate their stories but instead encouraged them to reflect on their own lives, to place their individual struggles in a larger social and political context, and to voice their critiques of the inequalities they experienced in relation to their own structural vulnerabilities. They learned to trust one another by telling their life stories and sharing the work of reflecting on the reproductive oppression they have witnessed or experienced themselves. The trainings also provided an orientation toward thinking structurally and using the approach of intersectionality as a means of critiquing intersecting forms of domination as well as welcoming all vulnerable or marginalized people in their communities. Through trainings and self-reflexive workshops, women mobilize *poder* by learning skills—analysis, self-reflection, research, writing, public speaking, lobbying, organizing, facilitating meetings, questioning presenters—as well as gaining knowledge about a range of issues such as legal rights, reproductive anatomy, how to conduct their own breast examinations, how to cope with sexually transmitted infections, how to prevent pregnancy, and how to seek abortion services with support by reproductive justice organizations, finding and sharing resources in their communities, and so on. Women participants came to understand that the barriers to accessing health care that require them to drive long distances, endure inordinate waits to see a practitioner or insensitivity during examinations, or be excluded from health insurance if they are poor and/or undocumented are structurally based injustices. They also learned that they have the right to economic and social entitlements such as health information, examinations, and medical care at a reasonable cost; to health insurance despite their low incomes, place of residence, age, or legal status; and to make claims on the state to ensure the conditions in which they can exercise meaningful agency. This movement has built a repertoire of "ready to work skills" or a methodology that includes cross-sector coalition building, storytelling in safer spaces, and strengths-based messaging. These organizations also document social problems and use their findings for lawsuits with wide implications for changing legislation in local sites or garnering resources to support policies that are already in place.

Through grassroots organizing and the trainings, women come to see themselves in a new light. These activists marshal robust critiques of pejorative representations of communities of color and craft a variety of ways to illuminate and circulate a politics that focuses on the strength and resiliency, worldviews, cosmologies, and spiritual practices of communities of color. As participants are reminded of the beauty and positive values expressed in their communities, they enact the power of self-love. Women of color involved in the movement for reproductive justice embrace their identities as powerful women and express their identities in an array of vibrant terms—"badass," "chingonas," "poderosas," "strong families," and "young families." They also incorporate organizationally inspired phrases into their daily lexicons: "my voice matters"; "I got this!"; "Black Mamas Matter"; "Panocha Pláticas"; "this is an RJ issue!"; and "I bring my whole self into the movement."

Second, as activists began to integrate intersectionality and human rights frameworks, they also came to recognize other structurally vulnerable or marginalized people and developed some compassion for their circumstances as well as an understanding of how and why their activism might be constrained. Women participants began a process of working in solidarity on others' behalf as well as for their own needs. Thus, intersectionality becomes generalized, with a simultaneous inward and outward gaze, and leads women toward *collective* social action. This movement's approach to intersectionality also incorporates multigenerational activism, as the activists work with other social movements with their own long histories and as they enable youth along with older women to see themselves with common goals.

Third, by using a human rights framework, reproductive justice activists turn their gaze toward the perceptions of people from around the globe about the United States. By inviting scrutiny on social conditions in the United States, this movement disrupts US exceptionalism, the debilitating silencing that social problems mainly happen elsewhere. Indeed, in 2017, after hearing about the conditions in South Texas, the United Nations investigated extreme poverty, a term normally used in the context of the Global South, by touring the United States and exploring the question, "Can Americans enjoy fundamental human rights if they're unable to meet basic living standards?"[66] Reproductive justice organizations, then, become enmeshed in transnational networks of activists who present their work in high-profile venues such as the United Nations, and they are in communication with activists from around the world. Manisha Desai reflects on the implications of transnational organizing: "At its core, this logic is about a methodology and epistemology that values an open, democratic, nonhierarchical process; diversity and plurality of ideas and strategies about the matrix of domination; the network for alliances with other movements, and an understanding of power that operates not just in macro structures and institutions but also at micro and meso levels, within and between movements. In short, this new cultural logic is about a new way of doing politics."[67] This transnational human rights work increases the efficacy of reproductive justice organizations that stand in solidarity with struggles in faraway places.

Fourth, this reproductive justice approach enables advocates to go beyond making a claim on the state. These activists are expanding the notion that citizens should have access to quality care by advocating that noncitizen residents, including the undocumented, have access to health insurance and health care. This philosophical stance is the basis of ongoing political activism, as Yamin suggests: "A human rights framework must include those categories of people because they are *human beings*."[68] Moreover, their insistence on using intersectionality that honors women of color in all of their complexities establishes of mode of operation in which women's full selves—their bodies, identities, and spiritual beliefs and practices—are welcomed. Laura Pérez suggests that this type of organizing opens up a profound transformation in women participants: "coalition and solidarity toward lasting social justice and human well-being necessitate, as inevitable, profound personal as well as social transformation in a cycle of receptivity and deepening knowledge in which we open ourselves to the other as both other *and* self, as different yet same in our human, natural, and spiritual interconnectedness."[69] In short, reproductive justice activists practice what Rosa Linda Fregoso calls "decolonial thinking": "through partnerships with grassroots activists, working across multiple registers of gender and ethnicity, spirituality and race, decolonializing human rights unearths an understanding of rights as potentially liberating praxis rather than as a mode of governing through formal procedures enacted by states."[70]

This social movement's notion of citizenship, of belonging to the nation, is expansive, a radical vision of what constitutes citizenship. By insisting on using the broad social category "women of color," which includes women from quite diverse racial, ethnic, national, and class origins along with those who are cis gender or trans, underage, or living with disabilities or with an unauthorized or temporary legal status, the reproductive justice movement counters exclusionary politics. In addition, this movement welcomes fellow travelers—that is, those who support its central philosophy that women have the right to bear children, terminate their pregnancies, raise their children in healthy environments, express their gender identities, and maintain bodily autonomy— alongside its supporters' other beliefs. So, we see participants in this movement whose political philosophies vary from LGBTQ rights or environmental justice to immigrant rights or faith-based activism, to name a few. Perhaps most radical of all, this movement advocates beyond the right to access health care with dignity by advocating for the right to *health*, which is not guaranteed by human rights norms or practice.[71] By grounding their efforts with people with low incomes, this movement takes on struggles for a living wage or adequate state resources for the poor, with the right to open space, parks, and toxin-free environments as well as full access to clean air and water and quality food. This social movement offers multiple expressions of collective *politicized* identity by reproductive justice activists who contest historical structures and processes and advocate for empowerment for all, what Kevin Duong calls world-making, "which consists of the articulation of an emergent normative vision of justice among allies and companions . . . [for a] common cause."[72]

Through this history of intersectional activism, women of color have carefully negotiated collaboration with other sectors, focusing on specific issues and working with different constituencies, and thus have expanded our understanding of civic engagement. Thus, their history is exemplary and goes beyond the call by the political scientists E. J. Dionne Jr., Norman Ornstein, and Thomas Mann for expanding civic engagement: "a more active and intentional pursuit of political alliances that cross the traditional fault lines in our society is imperative."[73] The movement for reproductive justice has forged "differential consciousness" or "coalitional consciousness"—practices oriented toward building and sustaining coalitions and creating narratives of identity and inclusion—for over three decades.[74] Further, instead of emulating well-established organizations, the movement aims to sustain women of color organizations and believes other social movements should follow its lead. As SisterSong founder Loretta Ross pointed out, "We expect the mainstream to parallel us; we have a unifying framework for protecting all the aspects of women's lives, not just the reproductive rights."[75] And even though the Trump regime felt apocalyptic to these activists, they present a long-term vision of social activism that persists despite individual officeholders or regime changes.

Empowerment, then, began with consciousness-raising but encompasses the notion that women have the right to participate fully in civic engagement as well as the right to express their language and cultural values, norms, beliefs, and spiritual practices. Empowerment entails learning to negotiate difference by respecting others' identities, experiences, and points of view. It also includes the energy of coordinated movement, of fellow humans, and of nature and the cosmos and trust created within safer spaces. Empowerment also includes individual health—with balance in one's body, mind, and soul—as well as wellness in worksites, spaces of collaboration, and communities. Women expressed their notions of spiritual *poder*—the power of collective prayer, good deeds, mutual support, cocreating safer spaces, and respecting religious differences within their groups. And empowerment means that women gain knowledge about key issues; they develop confidence in their abilities to understand the roots of social problems and voice their critiques to those who hold institutional power; and they gain a sense of the importance of pursuing their civic engagement through multiple venues.

In sum, the movement for reproductive justice mobilizes different types of power. Through crafting progressive legislation and enforcing broadminded social policies, by critiquing derogatory representations of women of color and offering a discourse honoring the historical strength and resiliency of people of color, and through organizing activities that raise women's consciousness and offer educational resources to low-income communities, the movement for reproductive justice takes a multifaceted approach to social transformation, which has profound implications. The human rights scholar-activist Alicia Yamin reminds us, "When we begin to rethink power relations and to question the root causes for our own and others' suffering, it 'de-naturalizes' both the biological individualism of the medical and health fields and many of the societal arrangements that perpetuate poverty, inequality, and violations of human rights."[76] Thus, just as intersectionality interrogates multiple forms of inequalities, identifies intersecting issues for mobilization, and helps craft politicized identities in which people share some experiences of marginalization yet belong to distinct communities with particular strengths and commitments, so a human rights approach sees rights as interdependent and interrelated. The organizations working on reproductive justice also are part of broad coalitions intent on challenging conservative policies and cultural politics. Reproductive justice activists provide a model for multiscalar politics that is fluid in relation to shifting conservative agendas and vilification of specific social categories, and they offer concrete strategies for building collaborations with diverse participants. They remind us that it is "reasonable to fight for the impossible."[77]

This book's discussion of the movement for reproductive justice of course is incomplete; there is no way I can do justice to the many campaigns and organizations working on reproductive justice. The reproductive justice movement is dynamic, constantly identifying critical issues and planning new campaigns. Since I began my research, some organizations have updated their logos, while others embarked on coalitions with different partners. The work of framing continues with efforts to use more inclusive language such as "womanx" or "gender-affirming surgeries" to reach out to trans women or "chest milk" instead of "breast milk" for those trans men who want to give birth to and care for their own children. The importance of balancing mind-body-spirit and expressing women's full selves continues, as some organizations are organizing staff-appreciation activities or body work or are encouraging spiritual expressions at work. These activists engage in advocacy on behalf of communities of color, especially for women and girls, not by using the loaded term "feminism" but by using the term "women of color," which expresses their intersectional views that are less about identity politics and more about pursuing structural change and social justice. And as we have seen, this movement has profoundly shaped other social movements: "A key feature of women's movements in the contemporary era is their focus on coalition building and intersectionality."[78] Other organizations and social movements undoubtedly use some of the tactics discussed here—such as using primary and secondary research findings to build long-term strategies and policies, building coalitions for specific campaigns, reframing social problems to reflect their particular perspectives, and organizing diverse sectors within communities. Nonetheless, if participants take a long-term approach to organizing, take time to get to know one another and negotiate difference through storytelling, pay attention to participants' desires beyond the pressing problems of the day, and carefully engage in mindful collaboration and policy advocacy, this organizing model could work well in relation to other important issues.

The movement for reproductive justice is part of the long genealogy of radical women of color who work for social justice for all.

ACKNOWLEDGMENTS

This work has been blessed by the support and feedback of friends, colleagues, and activists whose suggestions made it much stronger. In the reproductive justice world, so many activists, advocates, practitioners, and community organizers have taken time out of their very busy schedules to share their experiences and have trusted me to convey their stories. In alphabetical order by organization and based on their affiliation at the time of our interviews/conversations, I thank Jan Robinson with Black Women for Wellness; D. Cole with Brown Boi Project; Marisol Franco, Rocio García, Laura Jiménez, Christina Jogoloff, Christina Lares, Carina Reyes, Ena Valladares, Gabriela Valle, and Mayra Lizzette Yñiguez with California Latinas for Reproductive Justice; Katrina Anderson from the Center for Reproductive Rights; Cristina Aguilar, Jacqueline Gallinar, Amber Garcia, Lorena Garcia, Georgina Millan, Jayce Montoya Price, Maribel Morales, Ryan Nickerson, Ana Ortega, Charlene Ortiz, Sofia Picatoste, Issamar Pichardo, Corrine Rivera-Fowler, and Alicia Ybarra with Colorado Organization for Latina Opportunity and Reproductive Rights; Eveline Shen and Amanda Wake with Forward Together; Jasmine Leyva with Fresno Barrios Unidos; Lara Brooks, Yamani Hernandez, Nik Zaleski, and the staff with the Illinois Caucus for Adolescent Health and especially the young people who participated in the MAKE/ART/SPACE public art project; Juana Rosa Cavero with the Reproductive Justice Coalition of Los Angeles; Miriam Yeung with National Asian Pacific American Women's Forum; Laura de Anda, Karina García, Jessica González-Rojas, Liz Guerra, and Diana Lugo-Martínez working with the National Latina Institute for Reproductive Health, especialmente todas las mujeres del Valle Rio Grande trabajando con NLIRH's Red de Abogacía para Latinas: Myra Blas, Lucila Ceballos, Lucy Ceballos-Félix, Cecilia De Angel, Dinorah Martínez, Paula Saldaña, Cupertina Uniendo, y las demás poderosas; Angela Moreno, board member of SisterSong Women of Color Reproductive Justice Collective; Adriann Barboa with Strong Families New Mexico; Corinne Sanchez, Kathy Sanchez, and Beata Tsosie-Peña from Tewa Women United; Cynthia Lin and Amy Santos-Lyons from Western States Center; and Charlene Bencomo, Denicia Cadena, Micaela Cadena, Alicia Chávez, Martha Cruz, Esperanza Dodge, Tannia Esparza, Paweena Prachanronarong, and Christian Redbird with Young Women United. Thanks to California Latinas for Reproductive Justice, Forward Together, National Latina Institute for Reproductive Health, Young Women United, and Martin McKinney, affiliated with University Church in Hyde Park, Chicago, and Jennifer Whitney from the Center for Reproductive Rights for permission to use their images. I am grateful for the insights provided by the young women and men with whom I conducted interviews or focus groups that were affiliated with the reproductive justice organizations I discuss here, who unfortunately must remain anonymous.

I also conducted interviews or had extended conversations with activists/advocates in social justice organizations that were close allies to people working on reproductive justice or with those working in reproductive health programs. Thanks to Aimee Thorne-Thomsen and Diana Rhodes from Advocates for Youth, Javier Benavides with the Center for Civic Policy, Yesenia Cervantes and her staff with the Educational Partnership Center, Lian Cheun of Khmer Girls in Action, Joan Lamunyon Sanford with New Mexico Religious Coalition for Reproductive Choice, Lupe Rodriguez with Planned Parenthood Mar Monte, Marsha Garcia with ProgressiveNowNM, Jennifer Ford with Respect ABQ Women, Fe Moncloa from the Santa Clara County Adolescent Pregnancy Prevention Network, Alison Hayes with the Santa Cruz County Health Department, Julie Brock for the Unitarian Church, and Leticia Mendoza with the YWCA Watsonville. I had the opportunity to interview some funders and appreciate that they took time from their busy schedules: Sarah Abelow with the Oberbrook Foundation and Rocio Córdoba and Lourdes Rivera from the Ford Foundation. Favianna Rodríguez graciously took time out of her busy schedule for an interview at her studio and also allowed me to use some of her artwork.

A number of colleagues helped me throughout this project. At the beginning of my project, Kim Lau sent me a list of contacts that was instrumental in jump-starting my research. I had extended conversations with several colleagues that were helpful in clarifying my ideas: Arlene Dávila, Virginia Espino, Sujatha Fernandes, Elena Gutiérrez, Ed Mc-Caughn, and Ana Ramos Zayas. Gabriel Escovedo and Inés Hernández-Ávila generously shared references on movement and spirituality, and Louise Lamphere provided key resources to contextualize scholarly engagement with Native American spiritual practices. I am grateful to my able research assistants, Nallely Ramírez, Marjory Ruiz, and Katherine Trejo, for help with transcriptions and other support, and they also helped me clarify my project in the initial phase, as did conversations with my graduate students: Kati Barahona-López, Ismael Illescas, and Nadia Zepeda. Thanks to my good friends and colleagues who gave me helpful feedback on my work in progress either as conference papers or drafts of chapters: Felicity Amaya, Cindy Cruz, Sylvanna Falcón, Iris Lopez, Steve McKay, Veronica Miranda, Jessica Taft, and Veronica Terriquez. Mil gracias to my fierce writing sisters, Nadine Suleiman Naber and Maylei Blackwell, for your super helpful, fine-grained critiques and advice!

My fellow Latinx anthropolocas/os were instrumental in the formulation of the *poder* analytic that informs this work at our seminar at the School for Advanced Research in Santa Fe. Thanks to the conveners, Alex Chávez and Gina Pérez, as well as to Ana Aparicio, Andrea Bolivar, Sherina Feliciano-Santos, Jonathan Rosa, Gilberto Rosas, Aimee Villar-real, and especially Santiago Guerra for your wonderfully helpful suggestions and fun collaboration.

Several activists from the reproductive justice world read drafts of my work, and their feedback was invaluable: My dear friend Cristina Aguilar commented on two chapters, and she helped to bring more nuance to my analysis. I appreciate the feedback from the activist-scholars Rocío García and Nik Zaleski and a conversation with Loretta Ross early in my research. Thanks to the staff of California Latinas for Reproductive Justice—Hatzy Carrillo, Lorena García Zermeño, Laura Jiménez, Jazmyn Marquez, Rochelle Martín, and Alexis Pérez—for a wonderfully helpful discussion of chapter 3. I very much appreciate the staff at Young Women United, including Charlene Bencomo, Denicia Cadena, Micaela Cadena, and Esperanza Dodge, who gave me feedback on chapter 2. Corrine Sanchez and Kathy Sanchez honored me by helping me to clarify their approach to healing justice.

My work benefited from comments from two anonymous reviewers for New York University Press, who were generous with their suggestions for improving how I historicize this social movement. Thanks to my editor at NYU Press, Jennifer Hammer, for her proactive vision and to copyeditor Andrew Katz, Alexia Traganas, Veronica Knutson, and the rest of the staff at NYU Press, who were always helpful.

I appreciate being able to join the Reproductive Justice Working Group affiliated with the Center for Reproductive Rights and Justice, University of California Berkeley School of Law, directed by Jill Adams. Thanks to Zakiya Luna, who facilitated the group and organized the miniconference "Conversations on Reproductive Justice" and generously shared some primary documents. To the group, I appreciate your feedback on my first effort to write about reproductive justice.

I am grateful for funding provided by the following agencies that made this research possible: the Committee on Research, the UC Santa Cruz Blum Center, the Social Sciences Division, the Edward A. Dickson Emeriti Professorship Award at the University of California, Santa Cruz, and the University of California Center for New Racial Studies.

Thanks to those who helped me keep some balance in mind, body, and spirit as I completed this book: Kesha Fikes, Jason Fouts, Jim Gallas, Joanne Gramo, and Susan Merritt. My loving family—Jim Jatczynski, Laura and Jon Schneider, and Anthony Zavella Gonzales—all listened to stories about my work and supported me in more ways than I can mention.

I will donate proceeds from the sale of this book to organizations working on reproductive justice.

APPENDIX

Reproductive Justice Organizations Consulted

1. Black Women for Wellness, founded in 1997 and located in Los Angeles, is "committed to the health and well-being of Black women and girls through health education, empowerment and advocacy."[1]
2. California Latinas for Reproductive Justice, founded in 2004 and based in Los Angeles, "is a statewide organization committed to honoring the experiences of Latinas to uphold our dignity, our bodies, sexuality, and families. We build Latinas' power and cultivate leadership through community education, policy advocacy, and community-informed research to achieve reproductive justice."[2]
3. The Colorado Organization for Latina Opportunity and Reproductive Rights, founded in 1998, is located in Denver. "COLOR is a sisterhood of Latinas dedicated to building a movement of Latinas, their families and allies through leadership development, organizing and advocacy to create opportunities and achieve reproductive justice."[3]
4. Forward Together, founded in 1989 and based in Oakland, "is a multiracial organization that works with community leaders and organizations to transform culture and policy to catalyze social change."[4]
5. The Illinois Caucus for Adolescent Health was founded in 1977, has its offices in Chicago, and "is a network of empowered youth and allied adults who transform public consciousness and increase the capacity of family, school and healthcare systems to support the sexual health, rights and identities of youth."[5]
6. The National Asian Pacific American Women's Forum was founded in 1995 and has headquarters in Brooklyn with chapters in the Northeast, the Midwest, and the South: "We are building a movement to advance social justice and human rights for AAPI women and girls in the United States."[6]
7. The National Latina Institute for Reproductive Health, founded in 2002, is located in New York City and Washington, DC, with

state initiatives in California, Wisconsin, and South Carolina and
Latina Advocacy Networks in Arizona, Florida, New York, Texas,
and Virginia. Its mission is to build "Latina power to guarantee
the fundamental human right to reproductive health, dignity and
justice": "We elevate Latina leaders, mobilize our families and communities, transform the cultural narrative, and catalyze change."[7]

8. The Los Angeles Coalition for Reproductive Justice, founded in
1980, is a "network of grassroots, community-based, women of
color organizations" that aims to "build leadership among women
of color, immigrant women and young women."[8]

9. The Strong Families Network is "a home for more than 200 organizations committed to ensuring that all families have the rights,
recognition and resources they need to thrive." Founded in 2005, it
is staffed by Forward Together.[9]

10. Strong Families New Mexico, founded in 2012 and based in Albuquerque, is "a state based program of Forward Together [that]
works to shift culture and create new policies that recognize the
many kinds of families" in New Mexico: "We are a network of over
20 partner organizations and individuals working in alignment to
build a better life for all our families and generations to come."[10]

11. Tewa Women United, founded in 1989, is based in Española, New
Mexico: "The mission of TWU is to provide safe spaces of indigenous women to uncover the power, strength and skills they possess
to become positive forces for social change in their families and
communities."[11]

12. Western States Center, founded in 1987, works in the Northwest
and is located in Portland, Oregon: "Our mission is to connect
and build the power of community organizations to challenge and
transform individuals, organizations and systems to achieve racial,
gender and economic justice."[12]

13. Young Women United, founded in 1999 and based in Albuquerque, "leads reproductive justice organizing and policy initiatives by
and for self-identified young women of color in New Mexico": "We
work to build communities where all people have access to the information, education, and resources needed to make real decisions
about their own bodies and lives."[13]

NOTES

PREFACE

1. Castañeda and Isgro 2013; Evans and Grant 2008; Ghodsee 2011; Ward and Wolf-Wendel 2012.
2. Moraga 2002a, 346.
3. Facio 2014.
4. Boston Women's Health Collective 1971.

INTRODUCTION

1. All translations are by the author unless indicated otherwise. All names initially presented in quotation marks are pseudonyms.
2. Blanca Borrego was detained and deported after seeking access to contraception while undocumented in Texas (Barajas 2015).
3. Structurally vulnerable people are positioned in ways that "impose physical/emotional suffering on specific population groups and individuals in patterns ways," and their vulnerability "is a product of class-based economic exploitation and cultural, gender/sexual, and racialized discrimination, as well as complementary processes of depreciated subjectivity formation" (Quesada, Hart, and Bourgois 2011, 340; also see Green 2011; Holmes 2011).
4. Prior to the formation of the movement for reproductive justice, other organizations, namely, the Committee to End Sterilization Abuse and the Committee for Abortion Rights and Against Sterilization Abuse, in the 1970s documented and litigated against sterilization abuse and advocated for addressing poverty and racism that impeded women's access to reproductive health services (Lopez 2008, xvii).
5. Bond Leonard 2017, 44.
6. Bond Leonard 2017, 41–42. WADRJ issued a statement, "Black Women on Health Care Reform," signed by 836 Black women, which insisted that the Clinton administration's efforts at health care reform include the needs of Black women and insisted on government support for "a full range of reproductive services for all women including abortion" as well as "universal coverage and equal access to health services"; "comprehensive coverage of diagnostic, treatment, preventative, long-term care, mental health services, prescription drugs and preexisting conditions"; and "protection from discrimination." For other works on the formation of the reproductive justice movement, see Cook and Dickens 2009; Herrero, Ander-

son, and Hooton 2017; Luna 2009, 2010, 2011; Luna and Luker 2013; Nelson 2003; Price 2010; Ross et al. 2001; Ross and Solinger 2017; Ross et al. 2017b; Silliman et al. 2004; West 2009.

7. Bond Leonard 2017, 48.
8. SisterSong Women of Color Reproductive Justice Collective, "What Is Reproductive Justice?," accessed August 4, 2019, www.sistersong.net.
9. Directed and produced by Rene Tajima-Peña and produced by Virginia Espino (Good Docs, 2015). Scholarly work on forced sterilization in mental and penal institutions and through coercion or the appropriation of women's reproduction is fueled by eugenics and is considered a form of torture that strips women of their dignity (Briggs 2002; Espino 2000; E. Gutiérrez 2008; Lopez 2008; A. Stern 2005; Vélez-Ibáñez 1980; Yamin 2016).
10. Center for Reproductive Rights, National Latina Institute for Reproductive Health, and SisterSong Women of Color Reproductive Justice Collective 2014, 7.
11. Roberts 1997.
12. Castro and Savage 2019; D'Gregorio 2010; Dixon 2015; Lopez 2008; Rebecca Martínez 2018.
13. Bridges 2011.
14. Gálvez 2011.
15. Paltrow and Flavin 2013.
16. Flavin 2009.
17. Denbow 2015.
18. Galameau 2013.
19. Brown Boi Project 2011, 2012; National Latina Institute for Reproductive Health 2011, 2013a.
20. Gurr 2014, 10. Bohren and colleagues (2015) analyzed sixty-five studies from thirty-four countries in which qualitative findings about mistreatment of women during delivery were organized under seven domains: physical abuse, sexual abuse, verbal abuse, stigma and discrimination, failure to meet professional standards of care, poor rapport between women and providers, and health system conditions and constraints.
21. Yamin 2016, 84.
22. Guttmacher Institute 2014c; Briggs 2017; Andaya 2019.
23. Ramírez and Morgan 2017.
24. Morgan and Roberts 2012, 243.
25. Jolly 2016; Luna and Luker 2013; Nelson 2003.
26. The right to bodily autonomy echoes the United Nations Committee on Economic, Social and Cultural Rights, which views the right to health as implying freedoms and entitlements, including "the right to control one's own body" and "the right to be free from torture, non-consensual medical treatment and experimentation" (quoted in Evans 2002, 205).
27. Byrant and Levi 2012; Byrant et al. 2014.
28. Lopez 2008, 143.

29. I arrived at this number through interviews with reproductive justice activists. Some RJ organizations have closed, one because it refused to conform to the nonprofit industrial complex that would compromise their work (Burrowes et al. 2007), while others are recently formed.

30. Increasingly, reproductive justice programs are affiliated with law schools or programs in social work, nursing, or religion, which expands the universe of fellow travelers. Two prominent reproductive justice law programs are the Center on Reproductive Rights and Justice affiliated with the University of California Berkeley Law School, which offers an informal working group on reproductive justice (Center on Reproductive Rights and Justice, accessed August 12, 2019, www.law.berkeley.edu), and the Women and the Law Program affiliated with American University Washington College of Law, which sponsors the Reproductive Justice Lawyering Webinar Series on reproductive justice (Women and the Law Program, accessed August 12, 2019, www.wcl.american.edu).

31. McCammon et al. 2017, 7.

32. Costanza-Chock 2014; for exceptions, see Hondagneu-Sotelo 2001; Milkman 2000; Milkman and Ott 2014; Pardo 1998; Peña 2007.

33. The 2013 demonstration, held in front of Congress, included one hundred women from around the country who demanded comprehensive immigration reform, including a path toward citizenship; protection from violence and workplace abuses; protection for the health and well-being of women and children, including access to medical insurance; and less border enforcement (Preston 2013).

34. Bookman and Morgen 1988, 4.

35. Bookman and Morgen 1988, 4.

36. Bookman and Morgen 1988, 4 (emphasis in the original).

37. Freire 1970, 126.

38. Gold and Nash 2012; Gold and Hasstedt 2016, 2017.

39. "As a result of these resources and strategies, noncitizen removals increased significantly, while apprehensions and overall deportations both remained far lower than the numbers seen under the Bush and Clinton administrations" (Chishti and Bolter 2017, 3).

40. Chishti and Bolter 2017, 4.

41. The Obama administration initially established violence against migrants as the crux of the migration crisis while erasing the role of the United States in supporting the very conditions that expel migrants from their home countries. Scholars argue the crisis actually is US intervention and long-term unwillingness to enforce human rights protections in Central America, supporting Mexican state agencies as well as economic development that increased militarization while elites benefited, and granting Central Americans Temporary Protected Status (which may last for years) rather than refugee status (Abrego 2018; Briggs 2016; Menjívar and Abrego 2012).

42. Briggs 2017, 13. Neoliberalism involves the deregulation of capitalist markets, privatization, and devolution and decentralization of social welfare policies and

values interventions by nongovernmental or faith-based organizations (Harvey 2005; Rubén Martínez 2016; Martínez and Rocco 2016; McGregor 2001). It contrasts with a Keynesian approach that views large-scale government spending and investment in human capital such as education and health care as leading to steady economic growth and stability.

43. Martínez and Rocco (2016, 6) remind us, "neoliberalism explicitly denies the structural features of society and opposes the pursuit of collective interests."

44. Ross et al. 2001, 81; Loretta Ross 2005; Price 2010, 48; Strickler and Simpson 2017. The initial Principles of Unity included committing to advocate for access to health care for communities of color, sharing information and materials, and coordinating with one another, and their organizational strategy was congruent with the decentralization efforts and flexible structures of other Black feminist organizations (Ransby 2000; Loretta Ross 2005, 351).

45. Moraga 2002b.

46. Pulido 2006, 4.

47. Williams 2012.

48. Pulido 2006, 4.

49. Robnett 2002.

50. Basu 2017b.

51. Blackwell 2015.

52. Walker 1983; Hernández cited in Blackwell 2018. Also see Hill Collins 1990; Pesquera and Segura 1993. Scholars find that young women often identify as feminist after taking Women's Studies courses or other interdisciplinary courses such as Ethnic Studies or American Studies (Aronson 2003; Hurtado 2003b) or after participating in social activism in their communities (Clay 2012).

53. Luana Ross 2009, 45, 50; Goeman and Denetdale 2009. Behar (1993) remarks on the "unnamed feminism" of an independent woman in Mexico, while Hurtado (2003a) uses "underground feminism" in relation to a working-class Mexican migrant woman's agency.

54. Million 2013, 58.

55. In an oral history, Loretta Ross recalled her own experience of sterilization abuse and an abortion, which shaped her efforts at organizing SisterSong. At SisterSong's first conference, the march's four sponsoring organizations—Planned Parenthood Federation of America, the National Organization for Women, NARAL/Pro-Choice America, and the Feminist Majority—were invited, which was historic and set the conditions for the participation of women of color, which included Ross agreeing to become codirector for women of color. "We came up with the name March for Women's Lives. . . . And we came up with the agreement that they would add women of color organizations to the steering committee, and two organizations chosen were the Black Women's Health Imperative . . . and the National Latina Institute for Reproductive Health. We also wanted them to put an Asian-Pacific-American group, National Asian Pacific American Women's Forum, on the steering committee, but they balked at that [because of the high cost of

subsidizing organizers' time]" (2005, 319–23). Eventually ACLU joined the steering committee as well.

56. Lopez 2008, 142.

57. Luna 2009, 2011. The National Organization for Women had organized successful marches on behalf of women's reproductive rights in 1986, 1989, and 1992 (Kauffman 2018, 48).

58. Luna 2011, 230; Petchesky 2000, 12.

59. The change in name came out of a retreat with twenty organization representatives. According to Eveline Shen, "While our local work is still very Asian based, the national work that we are doing with . . . Strong Families is very multiracial. Also because Strong Families is multisectoral but at the core is reproductive justice that we wanted a name that could reflect the entirety of what we were doing and where we want to grow."

60. Asian Communities for Reproductive Justice and SisterSong Women of Color Reproductive Health Collective 2005, 4.

61. Mingus 2010, 4; Jesudason and Kimport 2013. This definition also resonates with the World Health Organization's definition of health as "a state of complete physical, mental and social well being" (quoted in Evans 2002, 198).

62. M. Pérez (2015) clarifies the difference between reproductive health and reproductive justice: in the latter, "race matters; poverty does too; the most marginalized are at the center; RJ takes a holistic approach; a focus on the right to parent; building connections across movements."

63. While these nonprofits engage in policy advocacy, they are unlike second-generation NGOs that aim to become self-supporting or to provide services (Sampson 2003, 312).

64. Luna 2010, 555; Price 2010.

65. Asian Communities for Reproductive Justice and SisterSong Women of Color Reproductive Health Collective 2005, 7.

66. These women resonate with the work of the socialist feminists who formed the Committee for Reproductive Rights and Against Sterilization Abuse (CARASA) and Committee Against Sterilization Abuse (CESA) and who worked in coalition with other women of color (Nelson 2003). CESA was cofounded by Helen Rodríguez Trías, who won a Presidential Citizens Medal. These organizations emphasized social-historical bases of inequalities.

67. Forward Together's Strong Families Network 2017, 2.

68. SisterSong, email, October 26, 2017.

69. For a discussion of Nash's (2019, 6) point that there has been "rich engagement with intersectionality's multiple genealogies in both black feminist and women of color feminist traditions," see Anzaldúa 1987; Blackwell 2011; Combahee River Collective 1995; Crenshaw 1989, 1991; A. Davis 1981; Espinoza, Cotera, and Blackwell 2018; Alma García 1997; Hill Collins 1990; James and Sharpley-Whiting 2000; Lorde 1984; Moraga and Anzaldúa 1983. For citations about intersectionality's origins in theories of class conflict, lesbian feminism, and disability, see Lutz, Vivar and Supik 2011.

70. Blackwell 2015.

71. At the preparatory meeting prior to and then at the Beijing conference itself, women in Latin America organized a transnational network to contest their marginalization and honor local notions of feminist discourse and practice from the "bottom up" so as to gain political leverage (S. Alvarez 2000; Blackwell, forthcoming).

72. The UN World Conference against Racism helped establish international norms to which states can be held accountable, helped activists dialogue around shared oppressions in a global context, and crafted a perspective on racism as it intersects with multiple forms of inequalities (Blackwell and Naber 2002; Collins et al. 2010; Falcón 2016).

73. Those issues included civil rights, economic justice, educational access, ending violence against women, health, and immigrant and refugee rights. See NAPAWF, "History," accessed August 4, 2019, http://napawf.org.

74. Basu 2017a, 8.

75. Ross et al. 2001, 79.

76. Schwarzmantel 2015, 284.

77. Gramsci 1971, 324.

78. Moraga and Anzaldúa 1983; Blackwell 2015.

79. Santa Cruz Feminist of Color Collective 2014, 28 (emphasis mine).

80. Chavez 2004, 2008, 2017.

81. Gamson 1995.

82. Reichard 2015.

83. de Onís 2017.

84. Trujillo-Pagán 2018.

85. Vidal-Ortiz and Martínez 2018, 388.

86. Sanchez 2018, 11.

87. Ross et al. 2001, 80.

88. Price 2017, 2018.

89. Reed and Chowkwanyun 2011.

90. Blackwell 2010, 2015; Chun, Lipsitz, and Shin 2013; Sandoval 2000.

91. "Nepantla" is a Náhuatl term for in-between spaces. "Nepantleras" refers to women who move within and among multiple worlds and who have gone through a process of consciousness-raising that leads to activism (Anzaldúa 1987, 2015; Acosta 2013; Blackwell 2010).

92. On coalitional consciousness, see C. Keating 2005; Cole 2008; Cole and Luna 2010; Carastathis 2013; Sandoval 2000.

93. For examples, see Pallares 2015; Briggs 2017.

94. Marsha Jones, presentation at "Let's Talk about Sex" conference, sponsored by SisterSong, October 6, 2017, New Orleans, LA.

95. Crenshaw 1991, 1244–45; also see Crenshaw 1989. The notion that women of color should organize around their "triple jeopardy" related to the intersecting, simultaneous forms of oppression based on race, class, and gender was articulated in the 1970s (Blackwell 2015).

96. In 2013, two well-regarded journals, *Signs: Journal of Women in Culture and Society* and *Du Bois Review*, published special issues commemorating twenty-five years of "Intersectionality Studies" (Cho, Crenshaw, and McCall 2013; Carbado et al. 2013). In 2018, the American Studies Association held a panel called "Intersectionality at 30: States of Emergence" (accessed January 16, 2019, www.youtube.com).

97. Blackwell 2011; Blackwell and Naber 2002; Chun, Lipsitz, and Shin 2013; Falcón 2016; Nelson 2003; Thornton Dill and Zambrana 2009.

98. Lopez 1993, 2008.

99. May 2015, 34. Also see Grzanka 2014; Hill Collins and Bilge 2016.

100. May 2015, 77.

101. Bonilla-Silva 2003; Feagin 2013; Omi and Winant 2014.

102. Keynote talk presented at the Summer Institute, Mujeres Activas en Letras y Cambio Social, Northern New Mexico College, El Rito, NM, 2014.

103. Mignolo 2000, 2011.

104. Quijano 2000, 533.

105. Lugones 2010. Also see Briggs 2002; Grosfoguel and Georas 2000; R. Gutiérrez 1991, 2010; Smith 2006.

106. Cusicanqui 2012, 106.

107. L. Pérez 2010, 122.

108. Rosa and Bonilla 2017, 202; Blackwell 2017.

109. Choo and Marx Ferree (2010, 136) offer a helpful typology for thinking about how to use intersectionality theory by distinguishing between groups, processes, and systems. In contrast to the group-centered approach I take here, a process-centered approach explores how major institutions have interconnected processes that contribute toward inequality, and a system-centered approach focuses on interactive, historically codetermining social processes of inequality.

110. Sometimes called a "womanist" approach since may women activists do not explicitly identify with feminist politics, women of color activists often seen their work as benefiting women and men as well as youth and elders (Blackwell 2011; A. Davis 2012; Robnett 1997; B. Roth 2017; Stephen 2007).

111. Davis, Kalb and Kaufman 2014, 2.

112. Franklin Roosevelt argued that every American deserves equality of opportunity, jobs for those who can work, security for those who need it, the ending of special privilege for a few, the preservation of civil liberties for all, and the benefits of scientific progress and rising standard of living. These rights stemmed from four freedoms: of speech and expression, to worship as one pleases, and freedom from want and from fear (Davis, Kalb and Kaufman 2014, 81–82).

113. Jamar 1994, 4; Toebes 1999, 663; World Health Organization 2012; Yamin 2016, 53.

114. Center for Reproductive Rights and National Latina Institute for Reproductive Health 2013, 39.

115. Yamin 2016, 76–77.

116. Kinney 2001, 1465–66; Toebes 1999, 664.

117. Yamin 2016, 79.
118. The principles of the human right to health include "Universality—Health care goods and services must be available to everyone, without exception; Equity—Health care resources, goods, and services must be distributed and accessed based on need, not privilege; Participation—People have the right to participate in how decisions are made regarding their right to health, including government policies and resource distribution; Accountability—Governments must create mechanisms of accountability to enforce the right to health, including monitoring and evaluation of policies; Transparency—People should have access to information and be able to understand how and by whom, decisions about their health care are made; Non-Discrimination—The right to health should be ensured without discrimination of any kind, including purposeful discrimination and policies and practices with a discriminatory effect." Center for Reproductive Rights and National Latina Institute for Reproductive Health 2015b, 29 (citing National Economic and Social Rights Initiative, "What Are the Basic Principles of the Human Rights Framework?," Vermont Workers' Center, "Human Rights Principles for Healthcare"). Also see Center for Reproductive Rights and National Latina Institute for Reproductive Health 2013, 39; National Economic and Social Rights Initiative 2008; Yamin 2016.
119. L. Brown 2003, 52.
120. Wooden 2016, 1.
121. The United States has not signed on to several international human rights agreements, and the human rights approach has been criticized as normative for advocating an individualist model for social change (Falcón 2009; Goodale 2006a, 2006b; Lodhia and Falcón 2002; Thomas 2000).
122. Farmer 2005.
123. Petchesky 2000, 12.
124. Nagengast and Turner 1997; Goodale 2006a; Speed 2006.
125. Goodale 2006a, 4.
126. McLagan 2006, 191.
127. Collier and Ong 2005, 4. For discussions of the anthropology of human rights, see Cowan 2006; Goodale 2006a, 2006b; Merry 2006; Nagengast and Turner 1997; Speed 2006; Turner 1997.
128. Dutt 1998, 231 (emphasis in the original).
129. Nelson 2015, 9; Lopez 2008.
130. Petchesky 2000, 12.
131. Yamin 2016, chap. 5.
132. Ross et al. 2001, 86.
133. May 2015, 41; Million 2013; Spade 2013.
134. Million 2013.
135. In 2013, there were five thousand indigenous communities with 375 million people living in indigenous communities, which make the lack of definition of "indigenous" problematic (Champagne 2013, 13).

136. See Blackwell, Briggs, and Chiu 2015 for a discussion of the inherently transnational nature of collaboration between Native American and indigenous activists even when dominant nation-states do not recognize their national autonomy.
137. Evans 2002; Farmer 2005.
138. Obama 2016, E2.
139. Burke and Simmons 2014; Jones and Sonfield 2016. Waiver-modified Medicaid-expansion programs include personal responsibility requirements such as increased cost sharing and behavioral incentive programs designed to make consumers more involved with and aware of their own health care and its associated costs; such requirements blame those who are unable to fulfill them for their own health problems (Bell et al. 2017).
140. Urban Indian Health Institute 2016, 17.
141. Passel, Cohn, and Rohal, 2014, 7; Castañeda et al. 2015; Horton 2016. As of this writing, a federal judge ruled the Affordable Care Act unconstitutional, and the Supreme Court is likely to weigh in while twenty-seven million Americans remain uninsured (Henry J. Kaiser Foundation 2018).
142. S. Alvarez 2009; Smith 2008; INCITE! Women of Color Against Violence 2007.
143. Chidi Anselm Odinkalu, quoted in Farmer 2005, 1; also see Petchesky 2000.
144. Evans 2002, 206.
145. Dutt 1998, 230.
146. Merry 2006, 42.
147. Friedman, Gostin, and Buse 2013.
148. Fregoso 2014, 574.
149. de la Cadena 2010.
150. Cultural citizenship refers to the right to be different and to belong in a participatory democratic sense, as well as to express one's cultural expressions and language publicly (Rosaldo 1994, 1997). Also see Benmayor, Torruellas, and Juarbe 1997; Caldwell et al. 2009; Flores and Benmayor 1997.
151. Center for Reproductive Rights and National Latina Institute for Reproductive Health 2013; Center for Reproductive Rights, National Latina Institute for Reproductive Health, and SisterSong Women of Color Reproductive Justice Collective 2014; Falcón 2009; Gurr 2012; Smith 2008; Zavella 2016.
152. Ross et al. 2017a, 14.
153. Speed 2006, 71; also see Craven and Davis 2013; Desai 2013.
154. Desai 2013, 92.
155. Marcus 1995, 2011.
156. Statement made at the "Power Manifesto: Black Women for Wellness Annual Reproductive Justice Conference," Los Angeles, October 19, 2017.
157. Speed 2006, 74; Hale 2001, 2006; Fassin 2017.
158. Craven and Davis 2013; Juris and Khasnabish 2013; Lamphere 2018.
159. Falzon 2009, 16.
160. My research assistants and I produced literal transcriptions of interviews and focus groups. I was unable to send transcriptions for review to a few interview-

ees either because I was unable to locate them after they moved or because their interviews were lost when my pen that produces audio recordings malfunctioned.

161. Boellstorff et al. 2012; Schrooten 2012.

162. The Internet, and social media in particular, offers a means to analyze communication, global networks, and social constructions (Markham 2004; Baker 2013). Hine (2015, 43) suggests, "the Internet has become much more routinely a place to express an embodied self rather than a place to leave the body behind."

163. Similarly, Luna (2011, 226) found that virtually all of the fifty-five reproductive justice activists she interviewed had completed at least a college degree.

164. To name a few, Cristina Aguilar, executive director of COLOR, is a 2015 recipient of the prestigious Livingston Fellowship Program sponsored by the Bonfils-Stanton Foundation (posted on Facebook, June 10, 2015). In November 2015 both COLOR and Cristina Aguilar received a prestigious Civil Rights Award. Denicia Cadena of Young Women United was honored at the Ms. Foundation's gala event, "A Salute to Women of Vision," on May 1, 2014 (accessed July 12, 2014, http://forwomen.org). Tannia Esparza, executive director of Young Women United, received the 2017 Gloria Award by the Ms. Foundation for Women (accessed July 30, 2017, http://womenofvision.auction-bid.org). SisterSong Women of Color Collective for Reproductive Justice honored Laura Jimenez for her leadership in 2017.

165. National Network of Abortion Funds was voted Among Leading Reproductive Justice Organizations for 2010–13 by Philanthropedia, a resource for funders. The site features more than eleven thousand reviews from fourteen hundred experts who are interviewed and surveyed. The site also features rankings based on a combination of in-depth surveys and conversations with experts, including academics, funders, grant makers, policy makers, and consultants. Philanthropedia recently recognized Forward Together and National Latina Institute for Reproductive Health as among twenty-five high-impact nonprofits working in reproductive justice (posted on Facebook on October 4, 2013). The National Latina Institute for Reproductive Health was honored by the Department of Health and Human Services as a "Champion for Coverage" in 2013.

166. Patricia Zavella and Cristina Aguilar, "Antiabortion Collaboration and the Movement for Reproductive Justice," paper presented at the "Emerging Contestations of Abortion Rights: New Hierarchies, Political Strategies, and Discourses at the Intersection of Rights, Health, and Law" panel, European Association of Social Anthropologists, July 2016, Milan, Italy.

CHAPTER 1. CULTURE SHIFT WORK

1. Blackwell 2011.

2. Lewis 1966; Moynihan 1965; W. Wilson 1987, 1993. For critiques of these concepts, see Greenbaum 2015; Katz 1993; Leacock 1971; Lopez 2008; Moore and Pinderhughes 1993; Reed 1992; Small, Harding, and Lamont 2010; Zavella 2011.

3. For critiques of the frames that silence the experience of women of color, see Hill Collins (1990), Ioanide (2015). Bonilla Silva (2003) critiques the frame of "colorblindness," in which we have moved "beyond" race, while Lentin (2018) argues that "not racism" is a form of racist violence.

4. Briggs 2017, 48, 12; Greenbaum 2015; Hill Collins 1990. A related invention, the "crack mother" / "crack baby," circulated to justify harsh penalties for substance-abusing mothers, with the implicit notion that they were mainly women of color. In fact, "the use of AFDC, cocaine, and alcohol are all more common among white mothers" (Briggs 2017, 135).

5. Lubiano 1992; Briggs 2017.

6. Chavez 2017.

7. Briggs 2017, 13.

8. Pew Research Center, "Most See Inequality Growing, but Partisans Differ over Solutions" (2014), cited in Bridges 2017, 43.

9. Briggs and Hallin 2016.

10. Greenlee 2015, 6. Hernandez later became executive director of National Network of Abortion Funds.

11. For a critique of the individualist perspective on resiliency with evidence that parents, kin networks, and communities provide protective mechanisms as well, see Jarrett 1997. McCaughan (2012) and Chaves (2015) document how artists express collective notions of resiliency and belonging.

12. Merry 2006, 41.

13. Entman 1993.

14. Anzaldúa 1987.

15. Casillas and Lee 2017.

16. L. Garcia 2012.

17. González, Moll, and Amanti 2005, x.

18. Villenas 2001.

19. Yosso 2005.

20. Ayala, Cortez and Hebert 2010, 152.

21. The scholarship on strengths-based therapeutic approaches examines interventions that consider the environmental context and builds on strengths by families and individuals for coping with social problems such as domestic violence and lack of health-care access (Powell et al. 1997). Those who support this approach often attempt to help families remain united despite internal tensions by building on their love, values, and commitment to one another. Perreira, Chapman, and Stein (2006), for example, highlight the resiliency of immigrant parents in overcoming new challenges as parents. Sometimes strengths-based advocates use strident language such as "children at risk," aiming to "inspire a culture of possibility" (accessed March 3, 2016, http://childrenatrisk.org). Community-oriented strengths-based approaches, on the other hand, incorporate a Freirian process of developing a critical consciousness as well as raising capacity through "empowerment techniques" for women of color. This sounds like an improvement over the individualist interventions. Yet these scholars advocate efficacy through "personally mastering a new activity, seeing a similar person master the activity, being

told one is capable of mastering the activity, and experiencing manageable levels of anxiety while attempting the new activity" (Gutiérrez and Lewis 1999, 9). This community oriented strengths-based approach implicitly advocates that structurally vulnerable subjects take their critical consciousness and change themselves in the company of others rather than address structural inequalities.

22. National Latina Institute for Reproductive Health 2013c, 6.

23. For discussions of the use of political narratives see Thomsen 2013, 2015.

24. Women in prison have limited access to reproductive health care, especially abortion and safe childbirth, and are subject to complete control over their bodies, making prison an important site for reproductive justice activism (R. Roth 2017).

25. For analyses of drug addiction in New Mexico, see M. Trujillo 2009; Angela Garcia 2010.

26. Tannia Esparza, presentation at the "Reproductive Justice in the Southwest" panel, Mujeres Activas en Letras y Cambio Social Summer Institute, August 1, 2015, Albuquerque, NM.

27. National Latina Institute for Reproductive Health 2013c, 6.

28. Solinger 2017.

29. Scholars have documented the importance of popular culture for fomenting political engagement (Dávila 2012; Dorsey 2004; McCaughan 2012; Zavella 2011, 2012).

30. SisterSong, "Artists United for Reproductive Justice," accessed August 5, 2019, www.sistersong.net.

31. Young Women United, accessed October 10, 2016, http://youngwomenunited.org.

32. Esparza, presentation at the "Reproductive Justice in the Southwest" panel.

33. Micaela Cadena, presentation at the "The Movement for Reproductive Justice in the Southwest" panel, Mujeres Activas en Letras y Cambio Social Summer Institute, August 2, 2018, El Paso, TX.

34. Favianna Rodríguez, home page, accessed October 10, 2016, http://favianna.tumblr.com.

35. National Latina Institute for Reproductive Health, "Yo Te Apoyo, I Support You," accessed August 12, 2019, www.latinainstitute.org.

36. The full text reads, "All women have value independent of their relationship to a man and deserve the respect of society. We support the right of women to fight exploitation and poverty. We believe women have the right to control their own bodies. We support a woman's right to have children and to not have children, to resist and denounce rape and incest, to marry whom they want to or not to marry." Favianna Rodríguez's blog, accessed October 24, 2016, http://blog.timesunion.com.

37. Favianna Rodríguez, "My Abortion Story," Favianna Rodríguez's blog, October 10, 2014, http://favianna.typepad.com.

38. Pear 2017.

39. National Latina Institute for Reproductive Health 2013c.

40. The Coalition for Choice steering committee included representatives from the American Civil Liberties Union of New Mexico, New Mexico Religious Coali-

tion for Reproductive Choice, Planned Parenthood of New Mexico, Southwest Women's Law Center, Southwestern Women's Options, Strong Families New Mexico, and Young Women United.

41. Zavella 2017.
42. SisterSong, "RJ in the Media," accessed August 12, 2019, www.sistersong.net.
43. National Latina Institute for Reproductive Health, accessed July 2, 2016, http://latinainstitute.org.
44. Fifty-five percent of Latinos belong to the Roman Catholic Church, but that percentage is declining; and 24 percent are former Catholics. "Latinos who have left the Catholic Church are especially likely to say that an important reason was that they stopped believing in its teachings: 63% of former Catholics who are now unaffiliated and 57% of former Catholics who are now Protestants give this reason for having left the church" (Pew Research Center 2014, 14).
45. Lake Research Partners 2011.
46. National Latina Institute for Reproductive Health 2019.
47. Center for Reproductive Rights and National Latina Institute for Reproductive Health 2013, 2015a, 2015b; Zavella 2017.
48. California Latinas for Reproductive Justice 2006, 2012a, 2012b, 2014.
49. Paz 1961. However, women of color have recuperated *la Malinche* as a complex woman attempting to protect herself and her children and have roundly critiqued the silencing of women and sexuality generally in history through heteronormative patriarchal discourse. Indeed Emma Pérez (1999, xvii) calls for a decolonial imaginary in which scholars and activists "shift meanings and read against the grain" regarding the "pitfalls of coloniality." Also see Del Castillo 1977; Alarcón 1989.
50. López and Stepler 2016, 1.
51. Of a legislature with forty senators and eighty assembly members, the ten Latina legislators are all assembly members. California Latino Legislative Caucus, accessed October 4, 2017, http://latinocaucus.legislature.ca.gov.
52. Strong Families Initiative, "Winning Reproductive Justice," 2008, http://strong-familiesmovement.org.
53. Eveline Shen, email to author, January 23, 2018.
54. Stacey 1997, 454; Stacey 1996; also see Kornacki 2018.
55. Price 2011, 284.
56. Traditional Values Coalition, accessed November 17, 2013, www.traditionalvalues.org. Since then, the Traditional Values Coalition has broadened its scope: "The TVC has served as a leading voice in the halls of Congress for the Bible-based traditional values that . . . include: promoting religious liberty and a free society; uncovering wasteful spending in Washington; championing Judeo-Christian values in the public square; protecting traditional marriage and family as the cornerstone of society; securing the Constitution against the growing threat of Islam and Shariah law; defending human life from its earliest moments to natural death; and ensuring the economic security of future generations of Americans as a moral

issue." Traditional Values Coalition, accessed October 14, 2016, www.traditional-values.org. Also see Price 2011.

57. Stacey 1997, 454; Fox Harding 1999.

58. Greenbaum 2015, 16.

59. Those social forces included redefinitions of marriage based on love and legitimate children and access to contraception, education, and employment for women (Coontz 1992, 2005).

60. Stewart 2012.

61. Coontz 2005, 264–65; Coontz 1992; Briggs 2017, 7.

62. Fujiwara 2008; Marchevsky and Theoharis 2006; Reese 2005.

63. Ventura 2009.

64. Abrego 2014; Chavez 2017; Dreby 2010, 2015; Enriquez 2015; Schmalzbaur 2008; Zavella 2011.

65. Acosta 2013; Bernstein and Reimann 2001; Briggs 2017, chap. 5; Craven 2019; Lewin 1993; Moore 2011; Weston 1991.

66. Forward Together, "Strong Families Network," accessed July 30, 2017, http://forwardtogether.org.

67. Strong Families New Mexico Working Group 2014, 1.

68. Also see Western States Center 2006.

69. Strong Families et al., n.d.

70. Strong Families, California Latinas for Reproductive Justice, and National Latina Institute for Reproductive Health, n.d.

71. Zavella 2017.

72. SisterSong Women of Color Reproductive Justice Collective launched a campaign against shackling, "using any physical restraint of mechanical device to control the movement of a prisoner's body or limbs, including handcuffs, leg shackles, and belly chains," which is allowed in thirty states. SisterSong, email, March 19, 2018. In response, North Carolina changed its shackling policy (Blythe and Warren-Hicks 2018).

73. Vasquez 2016.

74. Strong Families, accessed June 27, 2014, http://strongfamiliesmovement.org.

75. Strong Families New Mexico Working Group 2014.

76. Forward Together, "Strong Families Network," accessed August 5, 2019, http://forwardtogether.org.

77. California Latinas for Reproductive Justice 2014; Gomez and Rahders 2016. Potter et al. (2019) argue that with the goal of reducing unintended pregnancy, we should not treat abortion as a failure but rather as a reproductive option to which all women should have access. This would shift the responsibility for achieving greater reproductive autonomy from women and onto the systems responsible for providing their reproductive health care.

78. The webinar was offered on June 20, 2016, www.wcl.american.edu.

79. Cadena et al. 2016; California Latinas for Reproductive Justice 2012b, 2014; Franco 2012; National Latina Institute for Reproductive Health 2015; Valladares 2016.

80. Cadena et al. 2016. Also see Briggs 2017; Eichelberger 2014.
81. Valladares 2009, 2010; Valladares and Franco 2010; California Latinas for Reproductive Justice 2014.
82. Franco 2012.
83. Kost and Maddow-Zimet 2016, 12.
84. Martin et al. 2018, 3.
85. While strong family expectations regarding educational attainment, parental messages objecting to premarital sex and pregnancy, resistance to the influence of peers and partners, and a greater sense of personal control over sexual behaviors were all positively associated with delay of sexual initiation, the latter was the strongest factor influencing delay, suggesting that "participants' own beliefs regarding timing of first sexual intercourse may outweigh the influence of family, friends, and partners" (Gilliam et al. 2007, 500).
86. Boonstra 2014; Lindberg, Santelli, and Desai 2016.
87. Only about 3 percent of those who received Aid to Families with Dependent Children were teen mothers, and "they were mostly white mothers and their children who had left an abusive relationship or gotten divorced." On average, recipients received welfare payments for only two years (Briggs 2017, 56, 65).
88. Silver 2010, 10.
89. Cadena et al. 2016.
90. Cadena et al. 2016, 12.
91. Cadena et al. 2016, 12.
92. Young Women United, accessed July 21, 2017, http://youngwomenunited.org.
93. Denicia Cadena, presentation at "Let's Talk about Sex" conference, sponsored by SisterSong, October 6, 2017, New Orleans, LA.
94. Creanga et al. 2015, 9. Maternal mortality includes pregnancy-related deaths that occur during pregnancy or within the following year due to pregnancy complications (Herrero, Anderson, and Hooton 2017), while severe maternal morbidity is a life-threatening diagnosis in which women may undergo a life-saving procedure during their delivery hospitalization (Howell et al. 2016).
95. Deborah Kaplan, Assistant Commissioner, Department of Health, quoted in *Death by Delivery* (accessed April 13, 2018, http://fusion.tv).
96. Howell et al 2016, e1. American Indian and Alaska Native women also have high maternal mortality rates; they are four and a half times more likely than non-Hispanic white women to experience maternal death (Urban Indian Health Institute 2016, 37). According to the World Health Organization, the United States is one of only thirteen countries worldwide with a rising maternal morality and is the only country with an advanced economy where maternal morality is getting worse.
97. Singh 2010, 1, cited in Herrero, Anderson, and Hooton 2017.
98. The World Health Organization defines social determinants as the conditions in which people are "born, grow, live, work, and age," which shape their health status (quoted in Yamin 2016, 76).

99. Guttmacher Institute 2016, 1; Centers for Disease Control and Prevention, "Summary Health Statistics: National Health Interview Survey," 2015, www.cdc.gov.
100. Black women, including professionals, also have higher rates of premature birth and low-birth-weight infants than do other women, which Dana-Ain Davis (2019) argues is produced by a long history of medical racism.
101. Deneen Robinson, Facebook presentation, October 24, 2017.
102. Robinson, Facebook presentation.
103. Yamin 2016, 7.
104. Black Mamas Matter Alliance, "About BMMA," accessed August 5, 2019, http://blackmamasmatter.org.
105. "Black Mamas Matter: Reproductive Justice and Black Women's Maternal Health," webinar sponsored by the Black Mamas Matter Steering Committee, August 22, 2017.
106. The Black Women Birthing Justice produced a report utilizing a human rights framework in California, where "Black women are three to four times as likely than white women to die of pregnancy-related causes," using interviews with one hundred Black women (Oparah et al. 2016, 1). The report offers policy recommendations as well.
107. Black Mamas Matter Alliance 2016, 29.
108. Quoted in Herrero, Anderson, and Hooton 2017, 1.
109. See Briggs 2017, chap. 4, for a discussion of the structural contributors to Black infant mortality.
110. "Black Mamas Matter: Reproductive Justice and Black Women's Maternal Health," webinar sponsored by the Black Mamas Matter Steering Committee, August 22, 2017.
111. *Death by Delivery*, produced and directed by Lyttanya Shannon, featuring Nelafar Hedayat, is available online (accessed April 13, 2018, http://fusion.tv).
112. Quoted in *Death by Delivery*.
113. Crear-Perry 2018; Gay 2018; Villarosa 2018.
114. SisterSong, flier sent through email, August 7, 2017.
115. Harrison 2017, 30–31.
116. Steinberg 2002, 224.

CHAPTER 2. COLLABORATING ACROSS DIFFERENCE
1. Calmes 2014.
2. Simpson 2014. For another reflection on tension between reproductive justice advocates and mainstream white feminists, see Howell 2007.
3. Richards 2014.
4. Simpson and Richards 2014.
5. Calmes 2015.
6. González-Rojas 2015; Hasstedt 2017.
7. Sandoval 2000, 170.
8. C. Keating 2005.

9. Cole and Luna 2010.
10. Alvarez et al. 2014.
11. Crenshaw 2011, 223.
12. Crenshaw 2011, 231 (emphasis in the original). Crenshaw has been credited with formulating the concept "intersectionality," which ignores the way this term grew organically out of organizing by Black women, Chicanas, and other women of color prior to Crenshaw's early publications (1989, 1991), including by Hill Collins (1986) and Moraga and Anzaldúa (1983). Blackwell (2011) traces Chicana feminist thought and activism to the mid-1960s; and Taylor (2017) cites the Combahee River Collective statement's notion of "interlocking oppression" in 1977.
13. Crenshaw 2011, 223.
14. Speed and Collier 2000, 879; also see R. Wilson 2006.
15. Alvarez et al. 2014.
16. Castañeda et al. (2015) suggest a social determinants approach to health that emphasizes structural rather than individual decision-making.
17. Duong (2012, 381) uses "world" to signify beyond "public," "community," or "group" and to examine "the struggle to create a commonality."
18. Price (2018, 581) argues that "political intersectionality" is the appropriate term for "cross-movement coalition building and identity politics." However, I never heard any reproductive justice activist use this phrase. Movement leaders distance themselves from engaging in identity politics.
19. "Leaders from the Reproductive Justice and Black Lives Matter Movements Talk about Black Women's Health," conference call moderated by Regina Mahone (Managing Editor, RH Reality Check), featuring Monica Raye Simpson (Executive Director, SisterSong, the National Women of Color Reproductive Justice Collective Director, Trust Black Women Partnership), Alicia Garza (Cofounder, Black Lives Matter), and La'Tasha D. Mayes (Founder and Executive Director, New Voices for Reproductive Justice), February 9, 2016.
20. Asian Communities for Reproductive Justice and SisterSong Women of Color Reproductive Health Collective 2005, 1.
21. Hester (2015) presents a critique of cultural competency models that may improve social services but do not intervene in social and health inequities.
22. Fox 2002, 351.
23. The Funders' Network's mission is "to inspire, strengthen and expand funding and philanthropic leadership to help create environmentally sustainable, socially equitable and economically prosperous regions and communities." Funders' Network, "Mission & Strategy," 2017, www.fundersnetwork.org.
24. Young Women United, Facebook post, August 21, 2013.
25. Zavella 2017.
26. Center for Reproductive Rights 2015; Center for Reproductive Rights and Sister-Song Women of Color Reproductive Justice Collective 2017; Guttmacher Institute 2014a; Strong Families Network 2017.
27. Fregoso 2014, 574.

28. S. Fernandes 2017.
29. Stories can be a form of resistance to assimilation (Hurtig 2005) or of selectively socializing youth about sexuality, where silences are significant as well (Zavella 1997, 2003).
30. Arias 2001; Beverly 1989; Cruz-Malavé 2017; Gugelberger 1996; Menchú 1984; Stephen 2013.
31. Latina Feminist Group 2001, 11.
32. Latina Feminist Group 2001, 11.
33. Benmayor 2012, 509.
34. Benmayor 2012, 510.
35. Delgado Bernal, Burciaga, and Flores Carmona 2012.
36. Benmayor, Torruellas, and Juarbe 1997, 153.
37. Weis and Fine 2000, 3.
38. Polletta 2006, viii.
39. Goodwin, Jasper, and Polletta 2001, 9; also see Gould 2009.
40. Commonwealth Fund, "Status of Medicaid Expansion and Work Requirement Waiver," July 31, 2019, www.commonwealthfund.org.
41. Center for Reproductive Rights, National Latina Institute for Reproductive Health, and SisterSong Women of Color Reproductive Justice Collective 2014, 7. Overall, low-income people of color, including immigrants, gained health insurance within one year of passage of the ACA, except in states that chose not to expand Medicaid (Tavernise and Gebeloff 2016).
42. Center for Reproductive Rights and National Latina Institute for Reproductive Health 2013.
43. A mixed-methods study of the impact of viewing an ultrasound prior to an abortion found that "the majority of women were certain of their abortion decision and the law did not change their decision" (Upadhyay et al. 2017, 2). Fifty-one percent of abortion patients in the United States reported that they had used a contraceptive method in the month they became pregnant (R. Jones 2018).
44. Morgan and Roberts 2012, 243.
45. NARAL Pro-Choice America 2017, 69.
46. Grossman, Baum, et al. 2014, 500.
47. Stevenson et al. 2016.
48. While researchers cannot attribute this increase to any particular cause, this increase in maternal deaths in Texas is unprecedented (MacDorman et al. 2016).
49. Baum et al. 2016; Fuentes et al. 2016; Gerdts et al. 2016.
50. In a survey with 318 women seeking abortion in six cities, 7 percent of all women and 12 percent of those living near the Mexican border reported attempting self-induced abortions (Grossman, White, et al. 2014, 73; Grossman, White, et al. 2015). Self-abortion methods include medications, malta beverage, herbs, physical manipulation, and misoprostol, which is widespread available in Latin America and the Caribbean (Grossman, Holt, et al. 2010; Texas Policy Evaluation Project 2015).
51. Grossman, White, et al. 2014, 74.

52. White et al. 2016.
53. Grossman, White, et al. 2014, 74. As the Supreme Court made clear in the 1992 decision in *Planned Parenthood v. Casey*, which affirmed the landmark 1973 *Roe v. Wade* decision, "These matters, involving the most intimate and personal choices a person may make in a lifetime, choices central to personal dignity and autonomy, are central to the liberty protected by the 14th Amendment" (Center for Reproductive Rights 2016).
54. Grossman, White, et al. 2014, 73–74; White et al. 2016. Grossman, White, and colleagues (2014) found that 7 percent of women reported taking something on their own in order to try to end their current pregnancy before going to an abortion clinic. This proportion was even higher, about 12 percent, among women at clinics near the Mexican border. Misoprostol is a safe and effective regimen and is recommended by the World Health Organization in settings without access to mifepristone. However, if women do not have accurate information, they may use ineffective dosages, or if the abortion fails, they may not realize until they have a later-term pregnancy, for which access to abortion services is limited. Women in other states faced similar structural barriers once restricted access to abortion legislation passed (Roberts et al. 2015), and increasingly fewer physicians are trained to provide abortions, even though most intend to administer them (Romero et al. 2015).
55. According to the US Census Bureau, "Hispanics" make up 86 percent of Cameron County, 90 percent of Hidalgo County, 97 percent of Starr County, and 86 percent of Willacy County. US Census Bureau, "QuickFacts: United States," accessed October 7, 2016, http://quickfacts.census.gov.
56. Center for Reproductive Rights and National Latina Institute for Reproductive Health 2013, 7.
57. Also see O'Leary and Simmons 2017.
58. In 2018 the State Department issued a travel advisory to Mexico, especially the northern states, because of increased dangers, which has affected businesses on both sides of the border.
59. Adams and Mikesell 2017; Center for Reproductive Rights, National Latina Institute for Reproductive Health, and SisterSong Women of Color Reproductive Justice Collective 2014; "Self-Induced Abortion: Emerging Trends and Opportunities," conference call organized by the Self-Induced Abortion Legal Team, March 14, 2016. Taking mifepristone and misoprostol at home to terminate a pregnancy is illegal in nineteen states. Research finds that medical abortions using these drugs, monitored via telemedicine, are not any less safe than when the drugs are taken after an in-person visit (Grossman and Grindlay 2017).
60. Research shows that 78 percent of colonia residents experience food insecurity, particularly limited access to fresh produce, leaving them with anxiety about the limited amount or poor quality of food for their families (Center for Reproductive Health and National Latina Institute for Reproductive Health 2013, 2015a, 2015b; Dean et al. 2012; Hill 2003; Mier et al. 2008; Sharkey, Dean, and Johnson 2011).

61. Day 2004.
62. National Latina Institute for Reproductive Health 2013b.
63. Núñez-Mchiri 2012, 115; Núñez-Mchiri 2009.
64. Abarca 2006; R. Pérez 2014.
65. Passel, Cohn, and Rohal 2014.
66. Isacson and Meyer 2013; Dorsey and Díaz-Barriga 2015.
67. These collaborations fall under the Agreements of Cooperation in Communities to Enhance Safety and Security established by the 1996 Illegal Immigration Reform and Immigrant Responsibility Act, which gives local law enforcement agencies the power to enforce immigration law (Alvord, Menjívar, and Gómez Cervantes 2018).
68. "In 2017 alone, ICE deported an estimated 2,800 residents from the Rio Grande Valley" (Human Impact Partners and La Unión del Pueblo Entero 2018, 1; Lee 2013).
69. Fernandez 2018.
70. Henry J. Kaiser Family Foundation 2018, 15.
71. Prior to passage of the ACA, Latinas who did not have health insurance, particularly predominantly Spanish speakers, were significantly less likely to have reproductive health examinations such as mammograms (Lapeyrouse et al. 2016).
72. Miguel Díaz-Barriga and Margaret Dorsey (2019) document how structural violence in the US-Mexico borderlands targets US citizens as well as immigrants and is contested by local officials and residents.
73. Additional staff includes a field coordinator, an education manager, and a senior trainer from New York City.
74. Paula Saldaña received the American Public Health Association's Outstanding Community Health Worker Award in 2016. National Latina Institute for Reproductive Health, "Paula Saldana," accessed February 20, 2019, http://latinainstitute.org.
75. NLIRH has posted a number of Texas women's stories about barriers to accessing health care. Nuestro Texas, "About the Women of the Rio Grande Valley," accessed August 5, 2019, www.nuestrotexas.org.
76. According to Anzaldúa (2015, 40), *conocimiento* (or love) involves a seven-stage process of coming to awareness that begins with a jolt of understanding in relation to gender, family, and religion and leads to Nepantla, a liminal space of openness to new perspectives that often leads to activism.
77. Pyles 2018, 55.
78. Center for Reproductive and National Latina Institute for Reproductive Health 2013, 10.
79. Félix 2014.
80. Center for Reproductive Rights and National Latina Institute for Reproductive Health 2015b, 10. The Center for Reproductive Rights has been directly involved in the UN Committee to Eliminate Racial Discrimination (CERD), including writing a "Shadow Report" that contested the US government's report on its compliance with CERD mandates (Falcón 2009).

81. Garcia and Tomlinson 2015; Merry 2006.

82. Luibhéid 2013.

83. In addition to the women directly affected by human rights violations, three others presented testimony: Lisa Fuentes, Senior Project Manager, who has studied the impact of abortion restriction and the loss of family-planning funding in the Rio Grande Valley; Kathryn Hearn, Director of Community Services with Access Esperanza, a family-planning clinic that lost significant funding in 2011; and Andrea Ferrigno, Vice President of Whole Woman's Health (Center for Reproductive Rights and National Latina Institute for Reproductive Health 2015b, 14).

84. The invited guests were Alicia Yamin (Policy Director of the Francois-Xavier Bagnoud Center for Health and Human Rights and Director, JD/MPH program, Harvard School of Public Health), Catherine Albisa (Executive Director, National Economic & Social Rights Initiative in New York City), Cynthia Soohoo (Director, International Women's Human Rights Clinic, City University of New York Law School), Edward Zuroweste (Chief Medical Officer, Migrant Clinicians Network; Assistant Professor of Medicine, Johns Hopkins School of Medicine), Marielena Hincapié (Executive Director, National Immigration Law Center in Los Angeles), Regina Tamés Noriega (Executive Director, Grupo de Información en Reproducción Elegida in Mexico City), and Sera Bonds (Founder/CEO, Circle of Health International in Austin).

85. Texas Latina Advocacy Network, Facebook post, March 22, 2016.

86. Costanza-Chock 2014.

87. These women's perceptions echo those found by scholars' research with physicians, who often have stereotypical perceptions of Latinas or lesbians that shape their medical practice (Chavez, Hubbell, et al. 1995; Martinez, Chavez, and Hubbell 1997; Stevens 1999).

88. After reviewing abstinence-only-until-marriage (AOUM) educational programs, the Society for Adolescent Medicine critiques them, since they provide incomplete and medically inaccurate and stigmatizing information and often discriminate against gay, lesbian, bisexual, transgender, and questioning youth. They conclude, "AOUM programs have little demonstrated efficacy in helping adolescents to delay intercourse, while prompting health endangering gender stereotypes and marginalizing sexual minority youth" (Santelli et al. 2017, 278; also see Santelli and Ott 2006).

89. The strategy of holding the Instituto in the Vermont Slausen neighborhood in South Los Angeles made it accessible to low-income women. The median household income is $31,236, which is low for the city and county; 60 percent have less than high school education; the average household size is 3.5 people, which is high for the city and the county; and 62 percent of residents rent rather than own their homes. Los Angeles Times, accessed November 3, 2018, http://maps.latimes. com. For a full discussion of El Instituto, see Zavella 2016.

90. CLRJ, "Collaborations," accessed August 6, 2019, www.californialatinas.org.

91. "California Passes Law Banning Sterilization of Inmates," *Legal Monitor World-wide*, August 21, 2014.

92. The denied benefits included Supplemental Social Security, Temporary Aid to Needy Families, social services block grants, Medicaid, and Food Stamps (Greenbaum 2015; Marchevsky and Theoharis 2006; Reese 2005). The overarching goal was "privatization and cuts / cost containment of massive entitlement programs" (Morgen, Acker, and Weigt 2010, 7).

93. Morgen, Acker, and Weigt 2010, 6. In California, adults qualify for cash aid for a maximum of forty-eight months through California Work Opportunity and Responsibility to Kids (CalWORKs); however, children may continue to receive cash aid for a longer period. California Department of Social Services, "Benefits & Services," accessed August 6, 2019, www.cdss.ca.gov.

94. Quesada 2011; Roschelle 2013.

95. Twenty-four states implemented the family cap after passage of the Personal Responsibility and Work Opportunity Reconciliation Act. Several human rights covenants and conventions view the family cap as a direct violation of women's reproductive rights (Romero and Agénor 2017).

96. Center on Reproductive Rights and Justice 2016, 14.

97. Myra Duran, presentation at the conference "CRRJ@5: Unrivaled + Undaunted," University of California, Berkeley, October 27, 2017.

98. Mujeres Unidas y Activas' mission is to promote personal transformation and build community power for social and economic justice. Visión y Compromiso is committed to community well-being and dignity by supporting *promotoras* (community health workers).

99. GovTrack, "S. 1645—116th Congress: Women's Health Protection Act of 2019," accessed May 23, 2019, www.govtrack.us.

100. Renfro 2019.

101. CLRJ, email, October 20, 2017.

102. California Trust Act (AB 4) went into effect in 2014. It was designed to encourage reporting crimes to local police without recrimination by ICE, since it limits cruel and costly immigration hold requests in local jails. California Legislative Information, "AB-4 State Government: Federal Immigration Policy Enforcement," accessed August 6, 2019, https://leginfo.legislature.ca.gov.

103. In 2013, "The Year of the Immigrant," according to the California Immigrant Policy Center, Governor Jerry Brown signed eight bills related to immigrant rights. These included the Trust Act (AB 4), which prohibits local law enforcement officials from detaining people with minor offenses for Immigration and Customs Enforcement; AB 60, which allows the undocumented to apply for driver licenses; AB 534, which prohibits extortion by threatening to call ICE; and AB 1024, which allows people here without documentation to become licensed as lawyers (McGreevy 2013). Governor Brown also signed AB 154, which authorizes nurse practitioners, certified nurse midwives, and physician assistants to perform first-trimester abortions, making California a leader in expanding reproductive

health care for women. This is a bill for which CLRJ had lobbied and that has had a positive impact on patient care (Battistelli, Magnusson, and Biggs 2018).

104. National Academies of Sciences, Engineering, and Medicine 2018, 15, 24.
105. Nagourney 2018. In 2018, the Latino Legislative Caucus was composed of twenty-nine members (seven senators, twenty-two Assembly members) and five auxiliary members (constitutional officers). California Latino Legislative Caucus, "Member Directory," accessed August 6, 2019, https://latinocaucus.legislature.ca.gov.
106. Arango 2018.
107. Gonzales 2014, ix.
108. Merry 2006, 39.
109. Casillas and Lee 2017, 54.
110. CLRJ, email, August 7, 2014.
111. Blackwell 2013, 131.
112. Fregoso 2014, 586.
113. Del Castillo 2002; Flores and Benmayor 1997; Caldwell et al. 2009.
114. Pyles 2018, 55.
115. Combellick-Bidney 2017, 818.
116. Jesudason and Kimport 2013, 213, 215.
117. Anzaldúa 2015, 6.
118. Benmayor 2012.
119. Delgado Bernal, Burciaga, and Flores Carmona 2012, 369.
120. Luna 2017, 437.
121. Combellick-Bidney 2017.
122. Blackwell 2013.
123. Duong 2012, 382.

CHAPTER 3. YOUTH MOBILIZATION

1. Negrón-Gonzales 2014. The Adolescent Family Life Act (AFLA), passed in 1981 during the Reagan administration, provided funding for the creation of "teen chastity" programs designed to curb the teen pregnancy "epidemic." Abstinence-only sex-education programs designed under the AFLA came to replace comprehensive sex education in many public schools across the nation, stimulated in part by over $1 billion in financial incentives by the Clinton and George W. Bush administrations (Price 2011).
2. Orellana 2001, 2009; Orellana, Dorner, and Pulido 2003.
3. Cooper et al. 2001.
4. Gálvez 2011; Hester 2013; París-Pombo 2008.
5. Ojeda de la Peña 2007.
6. Negrón-Gonzales 2013, 2014; Nicholls 2013; Soto 2018; Terriquez 2015.
7. Enriquez 2015; Gomberg-Muñoz 2017; C. Rodriguez 2016; Terriquez and Joseph 2016; Zavella 2011, chap. 4.
8. Terriquez and Joseph 2016.
9. Enriquez 2015; R. Gonzales 2016; Pila 2016; S.I.N. Collective 2007.

10. S.I.N. Collective 2007, 85.
11. Nicholls 2013; Terriquez 2015.
12. Bond, Hefner, and Drogos 2009; Moncloa, Wilkinson-Lee, and Russell 2010.
13. Zavella 1997, 2003; Castañeda and Zavella 2003; Zavella and Castañeda 2005.
14. Fine 1993; Fine and Weis 1998; Fine and McClelland 2006.
15. Fields 2008, 19. Abstinence-only sex-educational norms were codified in PRWORA in 1996 as a means of restricting poor women's sexual behavior.
16. Maira and Soep 2004, xviii.
17. Gordon and Taft 2011; Taft and Gordon 2013; Taft 2011.
18. L. Garcia 2009, 2012.
19. Jenkins et al. 2016, 41.
20. YouthNet, Family Health International, and Advocates for Youth 2005, 1.
21. Paley 2001.
22. S. Fernandes 2017, 2.
23. S. Fernandes 2017, 3.
24. Weis and Fine 2012; Clay 2012; V. Rios 2008, 2011.
25. Cooper et al. 2004; Hunleth 2011.
26. S. Fernandes 2017, 3.
27. Schwartz and Brindis 2011.
28. Quijada, Cahill, and Bradley (2013, 216) suggest that the participatory action research process offers a type of "radical inclusion" that "starts with informed understanding of personal experiences by those being legislated upon and then moves toward social analysis, critical inquiry, and reform."
29. SURGE: Mobilizing Communities for Reproductive Justice, "Promoting Sex Education Justice," accessed January 27, 2018, http://surgereproductivejustice.org.
30. Forward Together Youth 2012, 7.
31. Forward Together Youth 2012.
32. Advocates for Youth 2017. Rep. Barbara Lee (D-CA) introduced the Real Education for Healthy Youth Act in the House of Representatives on July 28, 2017, and it was introduced in the Senate by Sen. Cory Booker (D-NJ) on July 27, 2017. Human Rights Campaign, "Real Education for Healthy Youth Act," December 21, 2018, www.hrc.org.
33. These bills were referred to the Subcommittee on Health (US Congress, "H.R.3602—Real Education for Healthy Youth Act of 2017," August 4, 2017, www.congress.gov). Meanwhile, the California Comprehensive Sexual Health and HIV/AIDS Prevention Education Act and the California Healthy Youth Act (2016) require California students in grades seven to twelve to receive comprehensive sexual-education classes unless explicitly excused by their parents. The new curriculum includes instruction about preventing HIV and unintended pregnancy along with the knowledge and skills to develop healthy attitudes concerning adolescent growth and development, body image, gender, sexual orientation, relationships, marriage, and family; to promote understanding of sexuality as a normal part of human development; and to have healthy, positive, and safe rela-

tionships and behaviors. California Department of Education, "Comprehensive Sexual health & HIV/AIDS Instruction," March 12, 2019, www.cde.ca.gov.

34. Jenkins et al. 2016.

35. An adult family member is "a person over 21 years of age who is the parent, grandparent, step-parent living in the household, or legal guardian." Illinois General Assembly, "Parental Notice of Abortion Act of 1995" (750 ILCS 70, 1995). The US Supreme Court ruled in 1981 that states have the right to require parental notification of an unmarried minor woman's abortion (Clary 1982). The notice must be given in person, by telephone, or by certified mail, and parents must sign a form acknowledging that they have been notified, which becomes a permanent part of the female's medical record.

36. Parental notification laws are unlike laws that require parental consent, which the Supreme Court ruled are constitutional so long as they include a judicial-bypass procedure to accommodate those young women who cannot involve their parents (NARAL Pro-Choice America 2014).

37. NARAL Pro-Choice America 2014.

38. Collett 2001.

39. Major medical groups oppose parental-involvement legislation related to abortion, including the American Medical Association, the American Academy of Pediatrics, the American Public Health Association, the Society for Adolescent Medicine, the American Medical Women's Association, the American College of Physicians, and the American Psychological Association (NARAL Pro-Choice America 2014, 2–3).

40. Twenty-one states require parental consent to abortion; eleven states require parental notification only; five states require both parental consent and notification; and eight states require the parental consent documentation to be notarized. Guttmacher Institute, "Parental Involvement in Minors' Abortions," January 1, 2018, www.guttmacher.org.

41. Blum, Resnick, and Stark 1987; Clary 1982.

42. Griffin-Carlson and Schwanenflugel 1998.

43. Guttmacher Institute 2014c.

44. Cartoof and Klerman 1986.

45. Griffin-Carlson and Schwanenflugel 1998; Joyce, Kaestner, and Colman 2006.

46. NARAL Pro-Choice America 2014, 2. There is evidence that mandatory parental notification for adolescents to obtain prescribed contraceptives would impede their use of sexual-health-care services, potentially increasing teen pregnancies and the spread of sexually transmitted infections (Reddy, Fleming, and Swain 2002).

47. Fortino 2014.

48. Joyce, Kaestner, and Colman 2006.

49. ICAH, home page, accessed August 7, 2019, www.icah.org.

50. ICAH has produced a number of reports and educational materials, including a book on sex education (2015); many of these materials are available on its website.

51. For scholarship on chosen families, see Weston 1991; Bernstein and Reimann 2001; Moore 2011; Acosta 2013.

52. Zaleski, Martin, and Messinger 2015.

53. ICAH, "Press Release: Youth-Led Public Art Installation Highlights Need for Family Conversations," accessed July 28, 2014, www.icah.org.

54. ICAH had collected the stories at several events throughout the year and planned to systematically analyze the stories so as to inform its programming and messaging once the story-collection process was completed.

55. Woznak 2014.

56. See 1 in 3 Campaign, "These Are OUR Stories," accessed September 1, 2018, www.1in3campaign.org. This campaign has published books and booklets with stories and featured them on its website, including some in languages other than English. More recently, Advocates for Youth has adopted new research that finds that one in four women have at least one abortion by age forty-five. Between 2008 and 2014, the abortion rate declined 25 percent, from 19.4 to 14.6 per one thousand women aged fifteen to forty-four. The abortion rate for adolescents aged fifteen to nineteen declined 46 percent, the largest decline of any group. Changes in contraceptive use were probably the reason for the drop in abortion. However, abortion increasingly is concentrated among low-income women (Jones and Jerman 2017).

57. COLOR, "Hermanitas," accessed October 10, 2016, www.colorlatina.org. COLOR no longer has an Hermanitas program.

58. COLOR, "LIPS (Latinas Increasing Political Strength) Leadership Institute & Mentorship Program" accessed January 15, 2018, www.colorlatina.org. The LIPS program started in 2009.

59. COLOR, "Intergenerational Programs," accessed August 7, 2019, www.colorlatina.org.

60. COLOR, "Hermanitas," accessed January 15, 2018, www.colorlatina.org.

61. Martinez 2010a, 2010b.

62. Generations of Light, home page, accessed January 23, 2018, www.generationsoflight.com.

63. Hunleth 2011, 86.

64. COLOR, accessed February 13, 2018, www.colorlatina.org.

65. COLOR, accessed February 13, 2018, www.colorlatina.org.

66. HB1081, passed in 2013, was created to strengthen existing guidelines and help youths make informed decisions about their health and relationships. The law outlined age-appropriate education, with K–3 grade levels learning about hygiene and older grade levels studying sex education. The bill passed over objections by Republicans and after debate about the limitations of abstinence-only sex ed (McGraw 2013).

67. Corrine Rivera-Fowler, presentation at "The Movement for Reproductive Justice in the Southwest" plenary panel at the meetings of Mujeres Activas en Letras y Cambio Social, August 1, 2015, Albuquerque, NM.

68. Weis and Fine 2000.
69. S. Fernandes 2017.
70. Transmedia Activism website, quoted in Jenkins et al. 2016, 25.
71. Delgado Bernal, Burciaga, and Flores Carmona, 2012, 368.
72. Yosso 2005, 69.
73. Wexler, DiFluvio, and Burke 2009; Zimmerman 2013.
74. Jenkins et al. 2016, 29. The United States signed the Convention on the Rights of the Child in 1995 but has not ratified it because some states wish to continue executing minors, which the Supreme Court has held is constitutional. Humanium, "Children of United States of America," accessed August 8, 2019, www.humanium. org.

CHAPTER 4. FROM SELF-CARE TO HEALING JUSTICE

1. See Gorski, Lopresti-Goodman, and Rising 2018 for a discussion of differences between sources of burnout that come from within the movement and those external to the movement and how they affect the ways that activists cope.
2. According to Loretta Pyles (2018, 26), the experience of burnout is a "prolonged psychological response to chronic workplace stressors that includes three dimensions: emotional exhaustion, depersonalization or cynicism, and diminished personal accomplishment." Also see Cahuas 2018.
3. INCITE! 2007.
4. US-based employment policies are particularly miserly compared to other countries (e.g., scant vacation leave or parental leave), and there are norms that workers are expected to put in long hours, which leads to what Hochschild and Machung (2012) call "competing urgencies": tensions balancing work and family life.
5. Increasingly, employers are also using a variety of strategies to foster mindfulness for easing anxiety and facilitating better workplace productivity and creativity (Gelles 2016) and even tracking employees with penalties for not meeting proscribed health goals (Fitbit Health Solutions, "For Employers," accessed August 8, 2019, http://healthsolutions.fitbit.com).
6. Spirituality, according to Alejandra Elenes (2014, 43), is "a way of understanding someone's (or a community's) position in the world by trying to make sense of unfair economic conditions and gender inequality, and to do something about it."
7. Kentina Washington-Leapheart, "Faith and Reproductive Justice" webinar sponsored by SisterSong, December 12, 2018.
8. Pyles (2018, 134) defines healing as "part of the path of individual and collective liberation from oppression, wherein liberation is a sense of feeling safe and at home in one's person."
9. The indigenous scholar Dian Million (2013, 2) views trauma as "a violence that overwhelms, wounding individual (and collective) psyche, sometimes suspending access to memory. The victims of traumatic events suffer recurrent wounding if their memory/pain is not discharged."

10. A. Brown 2017, 2019; Brown Boi Project 2011, 2012; Chen et al. 2016; williams, Owens, and Syedullah 2016.

11. Bade (2004), París Pombo (2008), and Hester (2013) document the many ways that indigenous migrants in the United States avoid using conventional models of health and insist on working within their own epistemologies for healing, including for mental health conditions.

12. There are three hundred million yoga practitioners worldwide, including thirty-six million Americans. The Good Body, "Yoga Statistics: Staggering Growth Shows Increasing Popularity," November 16, 2018, www.thegoodbody.com.

13. williams, Owens, and Syedullah 2016.

14. David Forbes (2019) critiques "McMindfulness," which shores up the privatized self as a strategy to cope with our stressful society by emphasizing self-responsibility and self-promotion through corporatization and repackaging.

15. Anzaldúa 2000, 178. According to Leela Fernandes (2003, 10) spirituality includes "practices of compassion, love, ethics and truth defined in non-religious terms" as well as "mystical reinterpretations of existing religious traditions."

16. Anzaldúa 2000, 178.

17. Blackwell 2009; Benmayor, Torruellas, and Juarbe 1997; Caldwell et al. 2009; Flores and Benmayor 1997; Rosaldo 1994.

18. Brown Boi Project 2011, 2012; L. Fernandes 2003; Lorde 1984; Moraga and Anzaldúa 1983.

19. Facio and Lara, 2014, 3; also see Anzaldúa 2000, 178; Anzaldúa 2015; Facio 2014; A. Keating 2008.

20. Quoted in Pyles 2018, xviii–xix. Also see Astraea Lesbian Foundation for Justice 2019.

21. Pyles 2018, xix (emphasis mine).

22. Pyles 2018, chap. 9.

23. Harcourt and Escobar 2005. Restorative justice was formulated by indigenous activists to call for a process of working with perpetrators of interpersonal violence who contribute directly to community healing (Cheon and Regehr 2007; Kurki 2000; Sawatsky 2007; Stubbs 2009).

24. Presentation at "The Movement for Reproductive Justice in the Southwest" panel, Summer Institute, sponsored by Mujeres Activas en Letras y Cambio Social, Albuquerque, NM, August 1, 2015.

25. Linklater 2014.

26. Pyles 2018, chap. 7.

27. TWU, home page, accessed August 8, 2019, http://tewawomenunited.org.

28. Forward Together, home page, accessed August 8, 2019, http://forwardtogether.org.

29. COLOR, home page, accessed August 8, 2019, www.colorlatina.org.

30. YWU, home page accessed August 8, 2019, http://youngwomenunited.org.

31. Sanchez 2016, 52.

32. Kathy Sanchez is a potter whose great-grandmother was María Montoya Martínez, whose exquisite black pottery and recognition of the communal technique for producing it are world-renowned (Marriott 1948).

33. Kathy Sanchez, "Trauma Rocks" (presentation at Santa Fe Community College, NM, March 8, 2018), accessed June 18, 2018, http://tewawomenunited.org. Sanchez also credits Eduardo and Bonnie Duran, whose book *Native American Postcolonial Psychology* (1995) influenced TWU's thinking about including trauma-informed services in its work. TWU's postcolonial paradigm includes the effects of genocide when diagnosing Native people and views traditional knowledge from differing cosmologies as liberating and healing and as needing to be integrated into therapeutic interventions.

34. Pulido 2018. For a history of US legislation that forbade the practice of Native American religious practices until the passage of the American Indian Religious Freedom Act in 1978 and the many ways Native peoples resisted and undermined settler colonialism, see Treuer 2019.

35. A National Institute of Justice study finds that more than four in five American Indian and Alaska Native women and men have experienced violence in their lifetime, and more than one in three have experienced violence in the past year (Rosay 2016).

36. Deer 2009, 150. The 2013 revised Violence Against Women Act (VAWA) empowered tribal courts to charge and prosecute non-Natives who assaulted Native women on Native land (Treuer 2019). VAWA expired temporarily during the government shutdown of 2018–19.

37. Deer 2009, 150.

38. Deer 2009, 160; Million 2013, 53.

39. Blackwell 2017; Deer 2009; INCITE! 2006; Million 2013.

40. Sanchez 2016, 60.

41. Quoted in Zimmerman et al. 2010, 23.

42. Sanchez 2016.

43. TWU, "About Tewa Women United," accessed August 8, 2019, http://tewawomenunited.org; Moss 2019.

44. Presentation at "The Movement for Reproductive Justice in the Southwest" panel, Summer Institute, sponsored by Mujeres Activas en Letras y Cambio Social, Albuquerque, NM, August 1, 2015.

45. TWU, "About Tewa Women United," accessed August 8, 2019, http://tewawomenunited.org.

46. Coffey and Tsosie 2001, 196.

47. Coffey and Tsosie 2001, 199.

48. Lata Mani (2009, 67) reminds us that the sacred and traditions are fluid and responsive to social intervention: "Despite the fact that traditions are most often spoken of as if they were timeless, changeless, naturally occurring phenomena, they are historically variable, socially constructed, cultural specific forms."

49. Coffey and Tsosie 2001, 203.

50. Coffey and Tsosie 2001, 203.

51. TWU, home page, accessed June 14, 2018, http://tewawomenunited.org.

52. TWU, "The Strength of Our Mothers," May 9, 2018, http://tewawomenunited.org.

53. Deer 2009.
54. Kathy Sanchez, presentation at Santa Fe Community College, March 8, 2018.
55. TWU, "About Tewa Women United," accessed August 12, 2019, http://tewawom-enunited.org.
56. S. Graham 2018.
57. "Preserving Indigenous Cultures of Peace: Tewa Women United's Environmental Health and Reproductive Justice Program," Northern New Mexico College, El Rito, NM, July 31, 2014.
58. Avila 1999, 138.
59. Rodríguez et al. 2014.
60. Quoted in Sanchez 2016, 62.
61. Debenport 2015; S. Rodríguez 1994.
62. Zimmerman et al. 2010, 22.
63. Kathy Sanchez, presentation at Santa Fe Community College, March 8, 2018.
64. The indigenous writer Gloria Bird suggests, related to issues of silencing or shame, "it is most damaging that we are not allowed to express our anger" (quoted in Million 2013, 67).
65. Million (2013) presents a scathing critique of the role of Indian schools in surveilling and controlling indigenous notions of sexuality and sexual identities through Christianity and "civilizing" practices.
66. Crawford-O'Brien 2014, 117; also see Kelley et al. 2018.
67. Delgado Bernal, Burciaga, and Flores Carmona 2012, 364.
68. Quoted in Crawford-O'Brien 2014, 117.
69. Alicia Inez Guzmán, "New Mexico's Community Garden Revolution," New Mexico Tourism Department, March 2019, http://newmexico.org.
70. TWU, "Española Healing Foods Oasis," May 23, 2017, http://tewawomenunited.org.
71. Alicia Inez Guzmán, "New Mexico's Community Garden Revolution," March 2019, http://newmexico.org.
72. Crawford-O'Brien 2014, 117.
73. Pyles 2018, 152.
74. Quoted in Villanueva 2010 (emphasis in the original).
75. Villanueva 2010.
76. Villanueva 2010.
77. Villanueva 2010.
78. All quotations are from the short film clip "Forward Stance Is Now 'Courageous Practice,'" Forward Together, accessed August 13, 2019, http://forwardtogether.org.
79. Forward Together, "Four Core Elements of Forward Stance," accessed November 11, 2016, http://forwardtogether.org.
80. Pyles 2018, 55.
81. Yang et al. 2015; Wang et al. 2016; Pyles 2018, 152.
82. Wu and Buchanan 2019; Pyles (2018, 48, 73) summarizes the research on the health benefits of mindfulness, which include positive effects on brain function,

immune activity, chronic pain, stress, disordered eating, and cancer. Briody et al. (2018) illustrate how deploying rituals enables communitas and collaborative work strategies to become self-reinforcing and to endure over the long term.

83. Pyles 2018, 78.

84. Kristen Zimmerman, "Forward Together Breaks through with Bold Vision," *Let's Talk: At the Heart of Movement Building* (blog), April 5, 2016, http://letstalkmovementbuilding.org.

85. R. Gutiérrez 1991. Many of the essays in Facio and Lara 2014 explore women's process of reclaiming their indigenous roots and embracing alternative spiritual practices.

86. Reiki is a Japanese tradition of energy healing with one's hands.

87. The chant "hands up, don't shoot" circulated after the shooting of Michael Brown in Fergason, and the #Ican'tbreathe hashtag is from the Eric Gardner case, in which the police choked an African American to death for selling loose cigerettes.

88. Bor et al. 2018.

89. Harrell 2000.

90. E. Rios 2015, 4.

91. Pyles 2018, 120.

92. Self-reflexive writing has been found to be an effective self-care strategy for practitioners in the helping professions (Pyles 2018, 154).

93. Lorde 2017, 130.

94. Tannia Esparza, presentation at the "Beyond the State: Inciting Transformative Possibilities" conference, sponsored by INCITE! Color of Violence 4, March 27, 2015, Chicago, IL.

95. Zavella 2017.

96. The official state Zia symbol was appropriated from the Zia Pueblo. The United Nations considers intellectual and cultural property rights as human rights (Villela 2016).

97. P. Gonzales 2007, 4–5; M. Trujillo 2009.

98. Carpio 2011.

99. Micaela Cadena, presentation at "The Movement for Reproductive Justice in the Southwest" panel, Mujeres Activas en Letras y Cambio Social Summer Institute, August 2, 2018, El Paso, TX.

100. Pulido 2018, 316.

101. Pulido 2018. Cortera and Saldaña-Portillo (2015, 562) argue that Mexican Americans experience "mestizo mourning," in which they "mourn the loss of historically filial relationships with indigenous peoples forged over centuries of interaction, intermarriage, collaboration, and alliance."

102. Angela Garcia 2010; M. Trujillo 2009.

103. Pyles 2018, 52.

104. Sage burning has been found to actually disinfect the air and to make the environment cleaner (Nautiyal et al. 2007).

105. Pyles 2018, 146.

106. In chapter 3, Pyles 2018 presents a history of the Cartesian paradigm that splits the mind from the body as well as creates oppositions between rationality and irrationality, and sacred and profane.
107. Acosta 2013; Blackwell 2018; Brown Boi Project 2011; Combahee River Collective 1995; A. Davis 2012; Hill Collins 1990; Moraga and Anzaldúa 1983; Negrón-Gonzales 2014; S.I.N. Collective 2007; C. Trujillo 1991.
108. Lorde 1978, 56.
109. Arredondo et al. 2007, 3. The booklet contains a series of questions designed to enable women to reflect on their own experiences related to sexuality and their body, including establishing a healthy relationship with one's own *panocha*, as well as references to writings by women of color. It is available online: http://djqueenb.wordpress.com (accessed September 12, 2018).
110. Arredondo et al. 2007, 5.
111. Arredondo et al. 2007, 5.
112. One of the images in the booklet is a black-and-white photograph by Laura Aguilar, whose provocative body of work included photographing her own body in desert settings, contesting the expected anguish over her obesity and lesbian identity, and instead claiming her fluid subjectivity through representation (A. Jones 1998). The booklet also includes the provocative cover of *Living Chicana Theory*, with a painting of a Latina wearing black lingerie holding a *calaca* by the neck and an open pomegranate, sitting with her legs open to the viewer (C. Trujillo 1998).
113. Lara 2014, 114.
114. Lara 2014, 114.
115. YWU, "Las Pláticas," accessed September 12, 2018, http://youngwomenunited.org.
116. Fahs 2014; Rose 2003.
117. Glick 2000, 22, 41. Glick argues that the movement for sexual liberation actually began in the 1950s.
118. Lara 2014, 130.
119. Pyles 2018, chap. 7.
120. Pyles 2018, 9.
121. Zimmerman et al. 2010.
122. Quoted in Rios 2015, 13.
123. Million 2013, 57.
124. Delgado Bernal, Burciaga, and Flores Carmona 2012, 367.
125. Pyles 2018, 12; Cahuas 2018.
126. Anzaldúa 2015, 90; Avila 1999, 272.

CONCLUSION

1. The Southern Poverty Law Center found in the first thirty-four days after the 2016 election there were 1,094 bias incidents around the nation; 37 percent of them directly referenced president-elect Trump, his campaign slogans, or his remarks about sexual assault, and there was more violence in cities that hosted Trump rallies (Chokshi 2018; Eligon 2018; Potok 2017).

2. By the end of Trump's first year in office, federal agencies were banned from using the words "vulnerable," "entitlement," "diversity," "transgender," "fetus," "evidence-based," and "science-based" (Sun and Eilperin 2017).

3. Like reproductive justice activists, Briggs (2017) argues that social welfare, immigration, policing, abortion, schools, stagnant wages, poverty, child care, and so on are examples of reproductive politics.

4. Trump's Islamophobia, seen in his critique of Obama's middle name and questions about his citizenship, stem from a racialization that constructs Muslims as terrorists and in which state surveillance, media manipulation, and counterintelligence, which intensified after 9/11, shape ongoing everyday racist expressions (Naber 2008; Naber and Rana 2019; Curtis 2013). A leaked Department of Homeland Security report concluded that the Muslim ban order "would do virtually nothing to protect Americans from terrorism, and some government officials saw it as enlarging the danger by playing into the hands of ISIS propagandists" (Dionne, Ornstein, and Mann 2017, 124).

5. Donald Trump's repeated lying led the *Washington Post* to track his false or misleading statements (Kessler, Rizzo, and Kelly 2019), The *New York Times* to list all the people, places, and things the president insulted on Twitter by year, and the *Atlantic* to compile a "Cheat Sheet" of the sexual misconduct allegations against him. The *Washington Post*, accessed December 31, 2018, www.washingtonpost.com. In 2018 alone, the president insulted more than two hundred people (Quealy 2018; Graham 2017).

6. Kornacki 2018; Kruse and Zelizer 2019; Riotta 2017.

7. Analysts point to FBI director James Comey's announcement about investigating Hillary Clinton's emails close to the election, diminished voter turnout in key states because of voter suppression, ethical misconduct by the Trump campaign, and Russian interference to account for Trump's unexpected win through the Electoral College despite losing the popular vote (Comey 2018; Dionne, Ornstein, and Mann 2017; Isikoff and Corn 2018; Woodward 2018).

8. Green 2011; Harvey 2005; Rubén Martínez 2016; Martínez and Rocco 2016. Casselman demonstrated that the slower a county's job growth since 2007, the more voters shifted toward Trump (cited in Dionne, Ornstein, and Mann 2017, 167).

9. The Electoral College system also is at fault since it actually increases the electoral power of people living in sparsely populated states (Dionne, Ornstein, and Mann 2017, 28–30).

10. Kruse and Zelizer 2019.

11. National Academies of Sciences, Engineering, and Medicine 2018.

12. Dionne, Ornstein, and Mann 2017, 161; also see Hochschild 2016.

13. Dionne, Ornstein, and Mann 2017, 25.

14. Martinez and Valenzuela 2006; Aldeman et al. 2016.

15. Negrón-Gonzales 2017, 420.

16. Rosa and Bonilla 2017.

17. Rosa and Bonilla 2017.

18. The $286 million initiative provides funding to a range of services, including family counseling, preventive health screenings for breast and cervical cancers, contraceptives, and treatment for sexually transmitted infections, and serves millions of low-income patients (Del Real and Pear 2019).

19. Solomon and Maxwell 2018.

20. Pear 2019. The Hyde Amendment, which prohibits use of federal funds for abortions except when the pregnancy is caused by rape or sex abuse or endangers the woman's life, is likely to be challenged in the Supreme Court under Trump. The US abortion rate is at historic lows because of aggressive restrictions in the states (Dreweke 2017; Guttmacher Institute 2014b).

21. Pear 2017. In a review of scientific evidence regarding the use of contraception, Dr. Aaron Carroll (2017, A18) critiques the Trump policy and concludes, "There is ample evidence that contraception works, that reducing its expense leads to more women who use it appropriately, and that using it doesn't lead to riskier sexual behavior."

22. The deliberately vague language could apply to everyone from receptionists refusing to book appointments to scrub nurses refusing to assist with emergency surgery. Trump also rescinded a 2014 executive order issued by Barack Obama that strengthened the oversight of nondiscrimination protections regarding sexual orientation and gender identity for federal contractors, and he banned transgender people from serving in the military.

23. An anti-abortion group, the Center for Family and Human Rights (C-Fam), is a powerful behind-the-scenes influence on the Trump administration, which has shifted the international debate. Specifically, "gender" (seen as code for LGBTQ), "reproductive and sexual health," and "abortion rights" were deleted from an international agreement and replaced by "maternal health" (Borger and Ford 2019). The Global Health, Empowerment, and Rights Act, introduced in the US Senate and House of Representatives in 2019, aims to permanently repeal the global gag rule.

24. Planned Parenthood's decision meant it lost $60 million annually from Title X funds (Belluck 2019).

25. Liptak 2018.

26. Nash et al. 2019; Dias, Tavernise, and Blinder 2019.

27. Pierce and Selee 2017, 1.

28. There were three efforts to ban migrants from predominantly Muslim countries. The final version of the travel ban, issued on September 24, 2017, blocked visitors from eight designated countries (Chad, Iran, Libya, North Korea, Somalia, Syria, Venezuela, and Yemen, though Chad was removed from the list in April 2018). It also set up a waiver process, whereby otherwise-blocked foreign nationals could enter the United States if they established that denying their entry would cause undue hardship, that their entry would not pose a national-security or public-safety threat, and that it would be in the US national interest. "The result of these policies has been to reduce the number of visas issued by barring certain

immigrants and visitors from entering the United States, lengthening the application process for those seeking admission, or providing more opportunities for consular officers to use their discretion to deny visas" (Chishti and Bolter 2019, 2).

29. Pierce and Selee 2017, 1.

30. Temporary Protected Status beneficiaries receive provisional protection against removal and permission to work in the United States with possibilities for renewals (Pierce and Selee 2017, 6). Trump's policies revoked the visas of over one hundred thousand people (Dionne, Ornstein, and Mann 2017, 88), and the backlog for those seeking a court date to adjudicate their asylum claims has grown by more than 293,000 cases (Lu and Watkins 2019). However, the Supreme Court ruled that one provision of legislation mandating the deportation of immigrants who commit certain types of crimes is so vague that it is unconstitutional.

31. Most of these policy changes were challenged in court (Medina 2018). A federal judge blocked the administration's whole-scale detention of asylum seekers, which often leads them to abandon their claims and choose deportation instead (Lu and Watkins 2019; Chishti, Pierce, and Jacks 2018).

32. The expanded vetting includes filling out a supplemental questionnaire and providing fifteen years of travel and employment histories and residential addresses. Extensions and renewals of visas now receive closer scrutiny (Pierce and Selee 2017).

33. Pierce and Selee 2017, 3. The president revitalized the Agreements of Cooperation in Communities to Enhance Safety and Security (Section 287(g)), established under the 1996 Illegal Immigration Reform and Immigrant Responsibility Act (Alvord, Menjívar, and Gómez Cervantes 2018).

34. Reuters 2019. In 2016, more than 90 percent of those who were removed from the US interior had been convicted of what the Department of Homeland Security defines as serious crimes (Chishti and Bolter 2017). Under the Trump administration, there are more than twenty categories of "aggravated felony" for immigrants, "many of which are not classified as felonies for citizens" (Alvord, Menjívar, and Gómez Cervantes 2018, 2).

35. Dickerson 2018. The United States Court of Appeals for the Ninth Circuit upheld an injunction against the Trump administration's termination of the DACA program. The plight of DACA recipients was wending its way through the courts as of this writing. Alejandra Pablos, a reproductive justice leader, was detained (Alvarez 2017; Ortiz 2017; Rubin and St. John 2017; Salazar 2018).

36. Chapin 2018; Fernandez, Dickerson, and Villegas 2019.

37. As of December 2018, 2,737 children who were separated from their parents were required to be reunified by a federal court order issued in June 2018. However, thousands had already been separated from their parents prior to the court order. The *New York Times* counted an additional seven hundred migrant children and infants separated from their families, so the total number is unknown (Jordan 2019). Parents who paid to have their children smuggled into the United States were identified for removal (Pierce and Selee 2017, 4).

38. Sacchetti 2017; Ulloa 2017; Ulloa and Dillon 2018.
39. Warren 2019, 1.
40. Chishti, Pierce, and Telus 2019; Passel and Cohn 2018; Warren 2019.
41. Hauslohner et al. 2019.
42. Menjívar and Abrego 2012; Abrego et al. 2017.
43. Key legislation that advanced legal violence includes the 1986 Immigration Reform and Control Act (passed during the Reagan administration), which increased border enforcement, employer sanctions for those hiring the unauthorized (rarely enforced), and a legalization program that affected mainly men. The 1996 Illegal Immigration Reform and Immigrant Responsibility Act (passed during the Clinton administration) removed many basic legal rights previously given to migrants and asylum seekers and accelerated proceedings for exclusion and deportation by eliminating the right of appeal and judicial review of decisions made by one Immigration and Naturalization Service agent. Further, the law significantly expanded the list of crimes defined as "aggravated felonies," including retroactive ones that made legal permanent residents as well as undocumented migrants deportable, made asylum procedures more difficult, and in numerous other ways stipulated new grounds for exclusion and deportation (Alvord, Menjívar, and Gómez Cervantes 2018; Zavella 2011).
44. Tambe 2017, 223. Kauffman (2018, 95) points out the value of mass demonstrations: "Protests can shift the terms of public debate or expand the sense of what's politically possible. They can motivate people on the sidelines to step up and take action. They can put an issue on the agenda, or increase the urgency with which it is addressed. They introduce friction where injustice depends on the illusion of harmony. The work that protests do often can't be seen in the moment. Their effects tend to be subtle, dispersed, and catalytic."
45. Hess 2017.
46. Kauffman 2018.
47. The United States has the highest rate of gun violence of any developed nation, the rate is increasing, and the majority of shooters have been white men (Blair and Schweit 2014, Morris and Guardian US Interactive Team 2018). March for Our Lives issued a gun-reform agenda (March for Our Lives, "A Peace Plan for a Safer America," accessed August 21, 2019, https://marchforourlives.com).
48. Dionne, Ornstein, and Mann 2017, 3.
49. Dionne, Ornstein, and Mann 2017, 3.
50. The immigrant rights organization United We Dream offers a range of resources, including a Mental Health Toolkit designed to help migrants and their advocates. United We Dream, "Mental Health Toolkit," accessed August 12, 2019, http://unitedwedream.org.
51. One year after Trump's election, 40 percent of Latinxs experienced a discriminatory incident, including being called offensive names, being criticized for speaking Spanish in public, and being told go back to your home country (even though only 49 percent of adult Latinxs are foreign-born) (Lopez et al. 2018).

52. A survey with 562 Latinx adolescents in Southern California found that 96 percent of respondents were critical of the president's approach (Wray-Lake et al. 2018, 192), while young voters overwhelmingly oppose the president's policies (Levin 2019).

53. Alvord, Menjívar, and Gómez Cervantes 2018; Castañeda et al. 2015; Chavez, Campos, et al. 2019; Harthorn and Oaks 2003; Talavera, Núñez-Mchiri, and Heyman 2010.

54. Savransky 2017; for discussions of self-care see: Menjívar 2002; Ransford, Carrillo, and Rivera 2010; Waldstein 2010.

55. Pamela Merritt, presentation at "Let's Talk about Sex" conference, sponsored by SisterSong, October 6, 2017, New Orleans, LA.

56. Marsha Jones, presentation at "Let's Talk about Sex" conference.

57. Jesudason 2017. In a blog post, she offered guidance to activists about how to respond to the Trump regime.

58. The webinar was held on June 27, 2018.

59. COLOR had long been a supporter of the well-known labor and immigrant activist Jeanette Vizguerra (2017), who spent two-years in sanctuary in a First Unitarian Church basement before her release and was named one of *Time* magazine's one hundred most influential people in 2017.

60. B. Roth 2017, 259.

61. National Latina Institute for Reproductive Health 2019, 5.

62. National Latina Institute for Reproductive Health 2019, 5.

63. Kathy Sanchez, presentation at Santa Fe Community College, March 8, 2018.

64. Meyer 2002.

65. Women of color were part of organizing the women's health movement long before some of these organizations were founded in the 1980s and before the term "reproductive justice" was coined in 1994.

66. Pilkington 2017.

67. Desai 2013, 93; also see Falcón and Nash 2015.

68. Yamin 2016, 106 (emphasis in the original).

69. L. Pérez 2010, 143.

70. Fregoso 2014, 586.

71. The right to health "requires that healthcare goods, services and facilities be available in adequate numbers; financially and geographically accessible, as well as accessible on the basis of non-discrimination; acceptable that is, respectful of the culture of individuals, minorities, peoples and communities and sensitive to gender and lifecycle requirements and of good quality" (Committee on Economic, Social and Cultural Rights, General Comment number 14, quoted in Chapman 2016, 2–3).

72. Duong 2002, 382.

73. Dionne, Ornstein, and Mann 2017, xxviii. The authors see civic engagement as "demonstrating and attending town meetings to organizing a precinct, registering voters, working on campaigns, running for office, and voting" (7).

74. Sandoval 2000; C. Keating 2005; Cole and Luna 2010. SisterSong opened its doors in 1997 but closed temporarily, so it celebrates its twenty years of continuous history. Other high-profile reproductive justice organizations such as the Illinois Caucus for Adolescent Health, Forward Together, and Tewa Women United have over thirty years of continuous organizational history.
75. Loretta Ross 2005, 342.
76. Yamin 2016, 6.
77. Negrón-Gonzales 2017, 424.
78. Basu 2017a, 7.

APPENDIX

1. Black Women for Wellness, home page, accessed August 12, 2019, www.bwwla.org.
2. CLRJ, home page, accessed August 12, 2019, www.californialatinas.org.
3. COLOR, home page, accessed February 5, 2019, www.colorlatina.org.
4. Forward Together, home page, accessed February 5, 2019, http://forwardtogether.org.
5. ICAH, home page, accessed August 12, 2019, www.icah.org.
6. NAPAWF, home page, accessed February 5, 2019, http://napawf.org.
7. NLIRH, "Who We Are," accessed August 12, 2019, http://latinainstitute.org.
8. Los Angeles Coalition for Reproductive Justice, "About," accessed August 12, 2019, www.facebook.com.
9. Strong Families Network, home page, accessed August 12, 2019, http://forwardtogether.org.
10. Strong Families New Mexico, home page, accessed February 5, 2019, http://strongfamiliesmovement.org.
11. TWU, home page, accessed February 5, 2019, http://tewawomenunited.org.
12. WSC, home page, accessed February 5, 2019, www.westernstatescenter.org.
13. YWU, home page, accessed February 5, 2019, http://youngwomenunited.org.

REFERENCES

Abarca, Meredith E. 2006. *Voices in the Kitchen: Views of Food and the World from Working-Class Mexican and Mexican American Women.* College Station: Texas A&M University Press.

Abrego, Leisy J. 2014. *Sacrificing Families: Navigating Laws, Labor, and Love across Borders.* Stanford, CA: Stanford University Press.

———. 2018. "Central American Refugees Reveal the Crisis of the State." In *The Oxford Handbook of Migration Crises,* edited by Cecilia Menjívar, Marie Ruiz, and Immanuel Ness. Oxford Handbooks Online. Oxford: Oxford University Press.

Abrego, Leisy J., Mat Coleman, Daniel E. Martínez, Cecilia Menjívar, and Jeremy Slack. 2017. "Making Immigrants into Criminals: Legal Processes of Criminalization in the Post-IIRIRA Era." *Journal on Migration and Human Security* 5 (3): 694–715.

Acosta, Katie L. 2013. *Amigas y Amantes: Sexually Nonconforming Latinas Negotiate Family.* New Brunswick, NJ: Rutgers University Press.

Adams, Jill E., and Melissa Mikesell. 2017. "Primer on Self-Induced Abortion." Berkeley, CA: Center on Reproductive Rights and Justice.

Advocates for Youth. 2017. "The Real Education for Healthy Youth Act." Washington, DC: Advocates for Youth.

Alarcón, Norma. 1989. "Traddutora, Traditora: A Paradigmatic Figure of Chicana Feminism." *Cultural Critique* 13:57–87.

Aldeman, Robert, Lesley Williams, Gail Markle, Saskia Weiss, and Charles Jaret. 2016. "Urban Crime Rates and the Changing Face of Immigration: Evidence across Four Decades." *Journal of Ethnicity in Criminal Justice* 15 (1): 52–77.

Alvarez, Priscilla. 2017. "Trump Cracks Down on Sanctuary Cities." *Atlantic,* January 25.

Alvarez, Sonia E. 2000. "Translating the Global Effects of Transnational Organizing on Local Feminist Discourses and Practices in Latin America." *Meridians* 1 (1): 29–67.

———. 2009. "Beyond NGO-ization? Reflections from Latin America." *Development* 52: 175–84.

Alvarez, Sonia E., Claudia de Lima Costa, Verónica Feliu, Rebecca J. Hester, Norma Klahn, and Millie Thayer, eds. 2014. *Translocalities/Translocalidades: Feminist Politics of Translation in the Latin/a Américas.* Durham, NC: Duke University Press.

Alvord, Daniel R., Cecilia Menjívar, and Andrea Gómez Cervantes. 2018. "The Legal Violence in the 2017 Executive Orders: The Expansion of Immigrant Criminalization in Kansas." *Social Currents* 5 (5): 411–20.

Andaya, Elise. 2019. "'I'm Building a Wall around My Uterus': Abortion Politics and the Politics of Othering in Trump's America." *Cultural Anthropology* 34 (1): 10–17.

Anzaldúa, Gloria. 1987. *Borderlands / La Frontera: The New Mestiza*. San Francisco: Spinsters / Aunt Lute.

———. 2000. *Interviews/Entrevistas*. Edited by AnaLouise Keating. New York: Routledge.

———. 2015. *Light in the Dark / Luz en lo Oscuro: Rewriting Identity, Spirituality, Reality*. Edited by AnaLouise Keating. Durham, NC: Duke University Press.

Arango, Tim. 2018. "One America Fights Another as Rift Widens: California Pushes Back against White House." *New York Times*, January 7.

Arias, Arturo. 2001. *The Rigoberta Menchú Controversy*. Minneapolis: University of Minnesota Press.

Aronson, Pamela. 2003. "Feminists or 'Postfeminists'? Young Women's Attitudes toward Feminism and Gender Relations." *Gender & Society* 17 (6): 903–22.

Arredondo, Sophia, Jessica Far, Irene Lara, and Eneri Arauz. 2007. "Panocha Pláticas: A Guide to Healing Sex & Sexuality in Community." Booklet presented at the SisterSong conference "Let's Talk about Sex," Chicago, IL.

Asian Communities for Reproductive Justice and SisterSong Women of Color Reproductive Health Collective. 2005. "A New Vision for Advancing Our Movement for Reproductive Health, Reproductive Rights and Reproductive Justice." Oakland, CA: Asian Communities for Reproductive Justice.

Astraea Lesbian Foundation for Justice. 2019. *Healing Justice: Building Power, Transforming Movements*. New York: Astraea Lesbian Foundation for Justice.

Avila, Elena, with Joy Parker. 1999. *Woman Who Glows in the Dark: A Curandera Reveals Traditional Aztec Secrets of Physical and Spiritual Health*. New York: Jeremy P. Tarcher / Putnam.

Ayala, George, Jaime Cortez, and Patrick "Pato" Hebert. 2010. "Where There's Querer: Knowledge Production and the Praxis of HIV Prevention." In *Latina/o Sexualities: Probing Powers, Passions, Practices, and Policies*, edited by Marysol Asencio, 150–72. New Brunswick, NJ: Rutgers University Press.

Bade, Bonnie. 2004. "Alive and Well: Generating Alternatives to Biomedical Health Care by Mixtec Migrant Families in California." In *Indigenous Mexican Migrants in the United States*, edited by Jonathan Fox and Gaspar Rivera-Salgado, 205–48. La Jolla: Center for US-Mexican Studies, Center for Comparative Immigration Studies, University of California–San Diego.

Baker, Sally. 2013. "Conceptualising the Use of Facebook in Ethnographic Research: As Tool, as Data, and as Context." *Ethnography and Education* 8 (2): 131–45.

Barajas, Michael. 2015. "Woman Arrested at Gynecologist Appointment Could Face Deportation." *HoustonPress*, September 11.

Basu, Amrita. 2017a. Introduction to *Women's Movements in the Global Era: The Power of Local Feminisms*, 2nd ed., 1–34. Boulder, CO: Westview.

———, ed. 2017b. *Women's Movements in the Global Era: The Power of Local Feminisms*. 2nd ed. Boulder, CO: Westview.

Battistelli, Molly Frances, Sara Magnusson, and M. Antonia Biggs. 2018. "Expanding the Abortion Provider Workforce: A Qualitative Study of Organizations Implementing a New California Policy." *Perspectives on Sexual and Reproductive Health* 50 (1): 33–39.

Baum, Sarah E., Kari White, Kristine Hopkins, Joseph E. Potter, and Daniel Grossman. 2016. "Women's Experience Obtaining Abortion Care in Texas after Implementation of Restrictive Abortion Laws: A Qualitative Study." *PLoS One* 11 (10): 1–14.

Behar, Ruth. 1993. *Translated Woman: Crossing the Border with Esperanza's Story.* Boston: Beacon.

Bell, Hannah S., Anna C. Martínez-Hume, Allison M. Baker, Kristan Elwell, Isabel Montemayor, and Linda M. Hunt. 2017. "Medicaid Reform, Responsibilization Policies, and the Synergism of Barriers to Low-Income Health Seeking." *Human Organization* 76 (3): 275–86.

Belluck, Pam. 2019. "Planned Parenthood Refuses Federal Funds over Abortion Restrictions." *New York Times,* August 19.

Benmayor, Rina. 2012. "Digital Testimonio as a Signature Pedagogy for Latin@ Studies." *Equity & Excellence in Education* 45 (3): 507–24.

Benmayor, Rina, Rosa M. Torruellas, and Ana L. Juarbe. 1997. "Claiming Cultural Citizenship in East Harlem: 'Si Esto Puede Ayudar a la Comunidad Mía . . .'" In *Latino Cultural Citizenship: Claiming Identity, Space, and Rights,* edited by William V. Flores and Rina Benmayor, 152–209. Boston: Beacon.

Bernstein, Mary, and Renate Reimann, eds. 2001. *Queer Families, Queer Politics: Challenging Culture and the State.* New York: Columbia University Press.

Beverly, John. 1989. "The Margin and the Center: On Testimonio (Testimonial Narrative)." *MFS: Modern Fiction Studies* 35 (1): 11–28.

Black Mamas Matter Alliance. 2016. "A State Policy Framework for the Right to Safe and Respectful Maternal Health Care." In *A Toolkit for Advancing the Human Right to Safe and Respectful Maternal Health Care,* 28–65. New York: Black Mamas Matter Alliance and Center for Reproductive Rights.

Blackwell, Maylei. 2009. "Zones of Autonomy: Gendered Cultural Citizenship and Indigenous Women's Organizing in Mexico." In *Gendered Citizenships: Transnational Perspectives on Knowledge Production, Political Activism, and Culture,* edited by Kia Lilly Caldwell, Kathleen Coll, Tracy Fisher, Renya K. Ramirez, and Lok Siu, 39–54. New York: Palgrave.

———. 2010. "Lideres Campesinas: Nepantla Strategies and Grassroots Organizing at the Intersection of Gender and Globalization." *Aztlán: A Journal of Chicano Studies* 35 (1): 13–47.

———. 2011. *¡Chicana Power! Contested Histories of Feminism in the Chicano Movement.* Austin: University of Texas Press.

———. 2013. "Gender, Activism, and the Border." *Aztlán: A Journal of Chicano Studies* 38 (1): 127–39.

———. 2015. "Triple Jeopardy: The Third World Women's Alliance and the Transnational Roots of Women of Color Feminism." In *Provocations: A Transnational*

Reader in the History of Feminist Thought, edited by Susan Bordo, Cristina Alcade, and Ellen Rosenmen, 280–87. Berkeley: University of California Press.

———. 2017. "Geographies of Indigeneity: Indigenous Migrant Women's Organizing and Translocal Politics of Place." *Latino Studies* 15:156–81.

———. 2018. "Women Who Make Their Own Worlds: The Life and Work of Ester Hernández." In *Chicana Movidas: New Narratives of Activism and Feminism in the Movement Era*, edited by Dionne Espinoza, María Eugenia Cotera, and Maylei Blackwell, 138–58. Austin: University of Texas Press.

———. Forthcoming. *Scales of Resistance: The Practice of Indigenous Autonomy in the Age of Neoliberalism*. Durham, NC: Duke University Press.

Blackwell, Maylei, Laura Briggs, and Minnie Chiu. 2015. "Transnational Feminisms: A Roundtable Dialogue." *Frontiers: A Journal of Women Studies* 36 (3): 1–24.

Blackwell, Maylei, and Nadine Naber. 2002. "Intersectionality in an Era of Globalization: The Implications of the UN World Conference against Racism for Transnational Feminist Practices—a Conference Report." *Meridians: feminism, race, transnationalism* 2 (2): 237–48.

Blair, J. Pete, and Katherine W. Schweit. 2014. "A Study of Active Shooter Incidents in the United States between 2000 and 2013." Washington, DC: Texas State University and Federal Bureau of Investigations, US Department of Justice.

Blum, Robert William, Michael D. Resnick, and Trisha A. Stark. 1987. "The Impact of a Parental Notification Law on Adolescent Abortion Decision-Making." *American Journal of Public Health* 77 (5): 619–20.

Blythe, Anne, and Colin Warren-Hicks. 2018. "NC Prisons Reconsider Whether to Strap Pregnant Inmates to Their Beds during Childbirth." *Raleigh News & Observer*, February 17.

Boellstorff, Tom, Bonnie Nardi, Celia Pearce, and T. L. Taylor. 2012. *Ethnography and Virtual Worlds: A Handbook of Method*. Princeton, NJ: Princeton University Press.

Bohren, Meghan A., Joshua P. Vogel, Eric C. Hunter, Olha Lutsiv, Joao Paulo Souza, Carolina Aguiar, Fernando Saraiva Coneglian, Alex Luíz Araújo Diniz, Ozge Tunçalp, Dena Javadi, Olufemi T. Oladapo, Rajat Khosta, Michelle J. Hindin, and A. Metin Gulmezoglu. 2015. "The Mistreatment of Women During Childbirth in Health Facilities Globally: A Mixed-Methods Systematic Review." *PLOS Medicine*, June 30.

Bond, Bradley J., Veronica Hefner, and Kristin L. Drogos. 2009. "Information-Seeking Practices During the Sexual Development of Lesbian, Gay, and Bisexual Individuals: The Influence and Effects of Coming Out in a Mediated Environment." *Sexuality & Culture* 13:32–50.

Bond Leonard, Toni M. 2017. "Laying the Foundations for a Reproductive Justice Movement." In *Radical Reproductive Justice: Foundations, Theory, Practice, Critique*, edited by Loretta J. Ross, Lynn Roberts, Erika Derkas, Whitney Peoples, and Pamela Bridgewater Toure, 39–49. New York: Feminist Press at the City University of New York.

Bonilla-Silva, Eduardo. 2003. *Racism without Racists: Color-Blind Racism and the Persistence of Racial Inequality in America*. Lanham, MD: Rowman and Littlefield.

Bookman, Ann, and Sandra Morgen. 1988. Introduction to *Women and the Politics of Empowerment*, edited by Ann Bookman and Sandra Morgen, 3–29. Philadelphia: Temple University Press.

Boonstra, Heather D. 2014. "What Is Behind the Declines in Teen Pregnancy Rates?" *Guttmacher Policy Review* 17 (3): 15–21.

Bor, Jacob, Atheendar S. Venkataramani, David R. Williams, and Alexander C. Tsai. 2018. "Police Killings and Their Spillover Effects on the Mental Health of Black Americans: A Population-Based, Quasi-Experimental Study." *Lancet* 392 (10144): 302–10.

Borger, Julian, and Liz Ford. 2019. "How a Rightwing Group Accessed the White House to Spread Its Anti-Abortion Agenda." *The Guardian*, May 16.

Boston Women's Health Collective. 1971. *Our Bodies, Ourselves*. Boston: New England Free Press.

Bridges, Khiara M. 2011. *Reproducing Race: An Ethnography of Pregnancy as a Site of Racialization*. Berkeley: University of California Press.

———. 2017. *The Poverty of Privacy Rights*. Stanford, CA: Stanford University Press.

Briggs, Charles L., and Daniel C. Hallin. 2016. *Making Health Public: How News Coverage Is Remaking Media, Medicine, and Contemporary Life*. London: Routledge.

Briggs, Laura. 2002. *Reproducing Empire: Race, Sex, Science, and U.S. Imperialism in Puerto Rico*. Berkeley: University of California Press.

———. 2016. "Central American Child Migration: Militarization and Tourism." *American Quarterly* 68 (3): 573–82.

———. 2017. *How All Politics Became Reproductive Politics: From Welfare Reform to Foreclosure to Trump*. Berkeley: University of California Press.

Briody, Elizabeth K., Edward J. Berger, Elizabeth Wirtz, Anthony Ramos, Gireesh Guruprasad, and Edward F. Morrison. 2018. "Ritual as Work Strategy: A Window into Organizational Culture." *Human Organization* 77 (3): 189–201.

Brown, Adrienne Maree. 2017. *Emergent Strategy: Shaping Change, Changing Worlds*. Chico, CA: AK Press.

———. 2019. *Pleasure Activism: The Politics of Feeling Good*. Chico, CA: AK Press.

Brown, Lawrence D. 2003. "Comparing Health Systems in Four Countries: Lessons for the United States." *American Journal of Public Health* 93 (1): 52–56.

Brown Boi Project. 2011. "Freeing Ourselves: A Guide to Health and Self Love." Oakland, CA: Brown Boi Project.

———. 2012. "Toward Healthy and Whole: Rethinking Gender and Transformation for Bois of Color." Oakland, CA: Brown Boi Project.

Burke, Amy, and Adelle Simmons. 2014. "Increased Coverage of Preventative Services with Zero Cost Sharing under the Affordable Care Act." Washington, DC: Department of Health and Human Services.

Burrowes, Nicole, Morgan Cousins, Paula X. Rojas, and Ije Ude. 2007. "On Our Own Terms: Ten Years of Radical Community Building with Sista II Sista." In *The Revolution Will Not Be Funded: Beyond the Non-profit Industrial Complex*, edited by INCITE! Women of Color Against Violence, 227–34. Cambridge, MA: South End.

Byrant, Amy G., and Erika E. Levi. 2012. "Abortion Misinformation from Crisis Pregnancy Centers in North Carolina." *Contraception* 86:752–56.

Byrant, Amy G., Subasri Narasimhan, Katelyn Bryant-Comstock, and Erika E. Levi. 2014. "Crisis Pregnancy Center Websites: Information, Misinformation and Disinformation." *Contraception* 90:601–5.

Cadena, Micaela, Raquel Z. Rivera, with Tannia Esparza and Denicia Cadena. 2016. "Dismantling Teen Pregnancy Prevention." Albuquerque, NM: Young Women United.

Cahuas, Madelaine Cristina. 2018. "Burned, Broke, and Brilliant: Latinx Community Workers' Experiences across the Greater Toronto Area's Non-profit Sector." *Antipode* 51 (1): 66–86.

Caldwell, Kia Lilly, Kathleen Coll, Tracy Fisher, Renya K. Ramirez, and Lok Siu, eds. 2009. *Gendered Citizenships: Transnational Perspectives on Knowledge Production, Political Activism, and Culture*. New York: Palgrave Macmillan.

California Latinas for Reproductive Justice. 2006. "Promoting a New Policy Framework for Latinas' Reproductive Health, Rights and Justice." Los Angeles: California Latinas for Reproductive Justice.

———. 2012a. "Latinas/os and the 'A Word': What Latinas/os Really Think about Abortion." Los Angeles: California Latinas for Reproductive Justice.

———. 2012b. "Strengthening Latina/o Young Families and Communities." Los Angeles: California Latinas for Reproductive Justice.

———. 2014. "Justice for Young Families: Principles & Praxis." Los Angeles: California Latinas for Reproductive Justice.

Calmes, Jackie. 2014. "Advocates Shun 'Pro-Choice' to Expand Message." *New York Times*, July 29.

———. 2015. "Video Accuses Planned Parenthood of Crime." *New York Times*, July 15.

Carastathis, Anna. 2013. "Identity Categories as Potential Coalitions." *Signs: Journal of Women in Culture and Society* 38 (4): 941–65.

Carbado, Devon W., Kimberlé Williams Crenshaw, Vickie M. Mays, and Barbara Tomlinson. 2013. "Intersectionality: Mapping the Movements of a Theory." *Du Bois Review* 10 (2): 303–12.

Carpio, Myla Vicenti. 2011. *Indigenous Albuquerque*. Lubbock: Texas Tech University Press.

Carroll, Aaron E. 2017. "Calling on Dubious Science to Disrupt Birth Control Coverage." *New York Times*, October 11.

Cartoof, Virginia G., and Lorraine V. Klerman. 1986. "Parental Consent for Abortion: Impact of the Massachusetts Law." *American Journal of Public Health* 76 (4): 397–400.

Casillas, Dolores Inés, and Jin Sook Lee. 2017. "Language and Culture as Sustenance." In *Culturally Sustaining Pedagogies: Teaching and Learning for Justice in a Changing World*, edited by Django Paris and H. Samy Alim, 43–59. New York: Teachers College Press.

Castañeda, Heide, Seth M. Holmes, Daniel S. Madrigal, Maria-Elena DeTrinidad Young, Naomi Beyeler, and James Quesada. 2015. "Immigration as a Social Determinant of Health." *Annual Review of Public Health* 36:375–92.

Castañeda, Mari, and Kirsten Isgro, eds. 2013. *Mothers in Academia*. New York: Columbia University Press.

Castañeda, Xóchitl, and Patricia Zavella. 2003. "Changing Constructions of Sexuality and Risk: Migrant Mexican Women Farmworkers in California." *Journal of Latin American Anthropology* 8 (2): 126–51.

Castro, Arachu, and Virginia Savage. 2019. "Obstetric Violence as Reproductive Governance in the Dominican Republic." *Medical Anthropology* 38 (2): 123–36.

Center for Reproductive Rights. 2015. "Shifting the Frame on Disability Rights for the U.S. Reproductive Rights Movement." New York: Center for Reproductive Rights.

———. 2016. "Whole Woman's Health v. Hellerstedt." New York: Center for Reproductive Rights.

Center for Reproductive Rights and National Latina Institute for Reproductive Health. 2013. "Nuestra Voz, Nuestra Salud, Nuestro Texas: The Fight for Women's Reproductive Health in the Rio Grande Valley." New York: Center for Reproductive Rights and National Latina Institute for Reproductive Health.

———. 2015a. "Nuestro Texas: A Reproductive Justice Agenda for Latinas." New York: Center for Reproductive Rights and National Latina Institute for Reproductive Health.

———. 2015b. "Somos Poderosas! A Human Rights Hearing in the Rio Grande Valley." New York: Center for Reproductive Rights and National Latina Institute for Reproductive Health.

Center for Reproductive Rights, National Latina Institute for Reproductive Health, and SisterSong Women of Color Reproductive Justice Collective. 2014. "Reproductive Injustice: Racial and Gender Discrimination in U.S. Health Care, a Shadow Report for the UN Committee on the Elimination of Racial Discrimination." New York: Center for Reproductive Rights.

Center for Reproductive Rights and SisterSong Women of Color Reproductive Justice Collective. 2017. "Black Mamas Matter: A Toolkit for Advancing the Human Right to Safe and Respectful Maternal Health Care." New York and Atlanta: Center for Reproductive Rights and SisterSong Women of Color Reproductive Justice Collective.

Center on Reproductive Rights and Justice. 2016. "Bringing Families out of 'Cap'tivity: The Path toward Abolishing Welfare Family Caps." Berkeley, CA: Center on Reproductive Rights and Justice.

Champagne, Duane. 2013. "UNDRIP (United Nations Declaration on the Rights of Indigenous Peoples): Human, Civil, and Indigenous Rights." *Wicazo Sa Review*, Spring, 9–22.

Chapin, Angelina. 2018. "Drinking Toilet Water, Widespread Abuse: Report Detail 'Torture' for Child Detainees." *HuffPost*, July 18.

Chapman, Audrey R. 2016. "The Contributions of Human Rights to Universal Health Coverage." *Health and Human Rights Journal* 18 (2): 1–5.

Chaves, Angeles Montalvo. 2015. "'Free Means Libre': Racialization of Arts in Madrid and Latin American Resilience through Performance." *Transforming Anthropology* 23 (1): 14–26.

Chavez, Leo R. 2004. "A Glass Half Empty: Latina Reproduction and Public Discourse." *Human Organization* 63 (2): 173–88.

———. 2008. *The Latino Threat: Constructing Immigrants, Citizens, and the Nation.* Stanford, CA: Stanford University Press.

———. 2017. *Anchor Babies and the Challenge of Birthright Citizenship.* Stanford, CA: Stanford University Press.

Chavez, Leo R., Belinda Campos, Karina Corona, Daina Sanchez, and Catherine Belyeu Ruiz. 2019. "Words Hurt: Political Rhetoric, Emotions/Affect, and Psychological Well-Being among Mexican-Origin Youth." *Social Science and Medicine* 228:240–51.

Chavez, Leo R., F. Allan Hubbell, Juliet McMullin, Rebecca G. Martinez, and Shiraz I. Mishra. 1995. "Structure and Meaning in Models of Breast and Cervical Cancer Risk Factors: A Comparison of Perceptions among Latinas, Anglo Women, and Physicians." *Medical Anthropological Quarterly* 9 (1): 40–75.

Chen, Ching-In, Jai Dulani, Leah Lakshmi Piepzna-Samarasinha, and Andrea Smith. 2016. *The Revolution Starts at Home: Confronting Intimate Violence within Activist Communities.* Chico, CA: AK.

Cheon, Aileen, and Cheryl Regehr. 2007. "Restorative Justice Models in Cases of Intimate Partner Violence: Reviewing the Evidence." *Victims & Offenders: An International Journal of Evidence-Based Research, Policy, and Practice* 1 (4): 369–94.

Chishti, Muzaffar, and Jessica Bolter. 2017. "The Obama Record on Deportations: Deporter in Chief or Not?" Washington, DC: Migration Policy Institute.

———. 2019. "The Travel Ban at Two: Rocky Implementation Settles into Deeper Impacts." Washington, DC: Migration Policy Institute.

Chishti, Muzaffar, Sarah Pierce, and Hannah Jacks. 2018. "Trump Administration's Unprecedented Actions on Asylum at the Southern Border Hit Legal Roadblock." Washington, DC: Migration Policy Institute.

Chishti, Muzaffar, Sarah Pierce, and Herrica Telus. 2019. "Spike in Unaccompanied Child Arrivals at U.S.-Mexico Border Proves Enduring Challenge; Citizenship Question on 2020 Census in Doubt." Washington DC: Migration Policy Institute.

Cho, Sumi, Kimberlé Williams Crenshaw, and Leslie McCall. 2013. "Toward a Field of Intersectionality Studies: Theory, Applications, and Praxis." *Signs: Journal of Women in Culture and Society* 38 (4): 785–810.

Chokshi, Niraj. 2018. "Violence Increased When Cities Hosted Trump Rallies." *New York Times*, March 17.

Choo, Hae Yeon, and Myra Marx Ferree. 2010. "Practicing Intersectionality in Sociological Research: A Critical Analysis of Inclusions, Interactions, and Institutions in the Study of Inequalities." *Sociological Theory* 28 (2): 129–49.

Chun, Jenifer Jihye, George Lipsitz, and Young Shin. 2013. "Intersectionality as a Social Movement Strategy: Asian Immigrant Women Advocates." *Signs: Journal of Women in Culture and Society* 38:785–810.

Clary, Freddie. 1982. "Minor Women Obtaining Abortions: A Study of Parental Notification in a Metropolitan Area." *American Journal of Public Health* 72 (3): 283–85.

Clay, Andreana. 2012. *The Hip-Hop Generation Fights Back: Youth, Activism, and Post–Civil Rights Politics.* New York: NYU Press.

Coffey, Wallace, and Rebecca A. Tsosie. 2001. "Rethinking the Tribal Sovereignty Doctrine: Cultural Sovereignty and the Collective Future of Indian Nations." *Stanford Law & Policy Review* 12 (2): 191–221.

Cole, Elizabeth R. 2008. "Coalitions as a Model for Intersectionality: From Practice to Theory." *Sex Roles* 59:443–53.

Cole, Elizabeth R., and Zakiya T. Luna. 2010. "Making Coalitions Work: Reflections from the Margins of US Feminism." *Feminist Studies* 36 (1): 71–98.

Collett, Teresa Stanton. 2001. "Issue in Vermont Law: Protecting Our Daughters: The Need for the Vermont Parental Notification Law." *Vermont Law Review* 26 (101): 1–31.

Collier, Stephen, and Aihwa Ong. 2005. "Global Assemblages, Anthropological Problems." In *Global Assemblages: Technology, Politics, and Ethics as Anthropological Problems*, edited Aihwa Ong and Stephen Collier, 3–21. Malden, MA: Blackwell.

Collins, Dana, Sylvanna Falcón, Sharmila Lodhia, and Molly Talcott. 2010. "New Directions in Feminism and Human Rights." *International Feminist Journal of Politics* 12 (3–4): 298–318.

Combahee River Collective. 1995. "A Black Feminist Statement." In *Words of Fire: An Anthology of African-American Feminist Thought*, edited by Beverly Guy-Sheftall, 232–40. New York: New Press.

Combellick-Bidney, Sarah. 2017. "Reproductive Rights as Human Rights: Stories from Advocates in Brazil, India and South Africa." *International Journal of Human Rights* 21 (7): 800–22.

Comey, James. 2018. *A Higher Loyalty: Truth, Lies, and Leadership.* New York: Flatiron Books.

Cook, Rebecca J., and Bernard M. Dickens. 2009. "From Reproductive Choice to Reproductive Justice." *International Journal of Gynecology & Obstetrics* 106 (2): 106–9.

Coontz, Stephanie. 1992. *The Way We Never Were: American Families and the Nostalgia Trap.* New York: Basic Books.

———. 2005. *Marriage, a History: How Love Conquered Marriage.* New York: Penguin Books.

Cooper, Sharon P., Elizabeth Heitman, Erin E. Fox, Beth Quill, Paula Knudson, Sheila H. Zahm, Nancy MacNaughton, and Roberta Ryder. 2004. "Ethical Issues in Conducting Migrant Farmworker Studies." *Journal of Immigrant Health* 6 (1): 29–39.

Cortera, María Eugenia, and María Josefina Saldaña-Portillo. 2015. "Indigenous but Not Indian? Chicana/os and the Politics of Indigeneity." In *The World of Indigenous North America*, edited by Robert Warrior, 549–67. New York: Routledge.

Costanza-Chock, Sasha. 2014. *Out of the Shadows, into the Streets! Transmedia Organizing and the Immigrant Rights Movement*. Cambridge, MA: MIT Press.

Cowan, Jane K. 2006. "Culture and Rights after Culture and Rights." *American Anthropologist* 108 (1): 9–24.

Craven, Christa. 2019. *Reproductive Losses: Challenges to LGBTQ Family-Making*. New York: Routledge.

Craven, Christa, and Dána-Ain Davis, eds. 2013. *Feminist Activist Ethnography: Counterpoints to Neoliberalism in North America*. Lanham, MD: Lexington Books.

Crawford-O'Brien, Suzanne. 2014. "Salmon as Sacrament: First Salmon Ceremonies in the Pacific Northwest." In *Religion, Food, and Eating in North America*, edited by Benjamin E. Zeller, Marie W. Dallam, Reid L. Neilson, and Nora L. Rubel, 114–33. New York: Columbia University Press.

Creanga, Andrea A., Cynthia J. Berg, Carla Syverson, Kristi Seed, F. Carol Bruce, and William M. Callaghan. 2015. "Pregnancy-Related Mortality Ratios by Age and Race and Ethnicity, 2006–2010." *Obstetrics & Gynecology* 125 (1): 5–12.

Crear-Perry, Joia. 2018. "Race Isn't a Risk Factor in Maternal Health. Racism Is." *Rewire.News*, April 11.

Crenshaw, Kimberlé. 1989. "Demarginalizing the Intersection of Race and Sex: A Black Feminist Critique of Antidiscrimination Doctrine, Feminist Theory and Antiracist Politics." *University of Chicago Legal Forum* 1989:139–67.

———. 1991. "Mapping the Margins: Intersectionality, Identity Politics and Violence against Women of Color." *Stanford Law Review* 43:1241–99.

———. 2011. "Postscript." In *Framing Intersectionality: Debates on a Multi-faceted Concept in Gender Studies*, edited by Helma Lutz, Maria Teresa Herrera Vivar, and Linda Supik, 221–33. Farnham, UK: Ashgate.

Cruz-Malavé, Arnaldo. 2017. "Testimonio." In *Keywords for Latina/o Studies*, edited by Deborah R. Vargas, Nancy Raquel Mirabal, and Lawrence La Fountain-Stokes, 228–31. New York: NYU Press.

Curtis, Edward E. 2013. "The Black Muslim Scare of the Twentieth Century: The History of State Islamophobia and Its Post-9/11 Variations." In *Islamophobia in America: The Anatomy of Intolerance*, edited by Carl W. Ernst, 75–106. New York: Palgrave Macmillan.

Cusicanqui, Silvia Rivera. 2012. "Ch'ixinakax Utxiwa: A Reflection on the Practices and Discourses of Decolonization." *South Atlantic Quarterly* 111 (1): 95–109.

Dávila, Arlene. 2012. *Culture Works: Space, Value, and Mobility across the Neoliberal Americas*. New York: NYU Press.

Davis, Angela. 1981. *Women, Race & Class*. New York: Random House.

———. 2012. *The Meaning of Freedom: And Other Difficult Dialogues*. San Francisco: City Lights.

Davis, Dana-Ain. 2019. *Reproductive Injustice: Racism, Pregnancy, and Premature Birth*. New York: NYU Press.

Davis, Martha F., Joanna Kalb, and Risa E. Kaufman. 2014. *Human Rights Advocacy in the United States*. St. Paul, MN: West.

Day, R. Sue. 2004. *Nourishing the Future: The Case for Community-Based Nutrition Research in the Lower Rio Grande Valley.* Houston: University of Texas School of Public Health at Houston.

Dean, Wesley R., Joseph R. Sharkey, Cassandra M. Johnson, and Julie St. John. 2012. "Cultural Repertoires and Food-Related Household Technology within Colonia Households under Conditions of Material Hardship." *International Journal for Equity in Health* 11 (25): 1–13.

Debenport, Erin. 2015. *Fixing the Books: Secrecy, Literacy, and Perfectibility in Indigenous New Mexico.* Santa Fe, NM: School for Advanced Research.

Deer, Sarah. 2009. "Decolonizing Rape Law: A Native Feminist Synthesis of Safety and Sovereignty." *Wicazo Sa Review* 24 (2): 149–67.

de la Cadena, Marisol. 2010. "Indigenous Cosmopolitics in the Andes: Conceptual Reflections Beyond 'Politics.'" *Cultural Anthropology* 25 (2): 334–70.

Del Castillo, Adelaida R. 1977. "Malintzin Tenepal: A Preliminary Look into a New Perspective." *Encuentro Femenil* 1 (2): 58–77.

———. 2002. "Illegal Status and Social Citizenship: Thoughts on Mexicans in a Postnational World." *Aztlán: A Journal of Chicano Studies* 27 (2): 11–32.

Delgado Bernal, Dolores, Rebeca Burciaga, and Judith Flores Carmona. 2012. "Chicana/Latina Testimonios: Mapping the Methodological, Pedagogical, and Political." *Equity & Excellence in Education* 45 (3): 363–72.

Del Real, Jose A., and Robert Pear. 2019. "California Sues over Muzzle on Abortions." *New York Times*, March 4.

Denbow, Jennifer M. 2015. *Governed through Choice: Autonomy, Technology, and the Politics of Reproduction.* New York: NYU Press.

de Onís, Catalina. 2017. "What's in an 'X'? An Exchange about the Politics of 'Latinx.'" *Chiricú Journal: Latina/o Literatures, Arts, and Cultures* 1 (2): 78–91.

Desai Manisha. 2013. "The Possibilities and Perils for Scholar-Activists and Activist-Scholars: Reflections on the Feminist Dialogues." In *Insurgent Encounters: Transnational Activism, Ethnography, and the Political,* edited by Jeffrey S. Juris and Alex Khasnabish, 89–107. Durham, NC: Duke University Press.

D'Gregorio, Rogelio Pérez. 2010. "Obstetric Violence: A New Legal Term Introduced in Venezuela." *International Journal of Gynecology and Obstetrics* 111:201–2.

Dias, Elizabeth, Sabrina Tavernise, and Alan Blinder. 2019. "Beneath Anti-Abortion 'Wave,' Undercurrents of Activist Networks." *New York Times*, May 19.

Díaz-Barriga, Miguel, and Margaret E. Dorsey. 2019. *Militarization on the Edge: Necrocitizenship and the U.S. Border Wall.* Durham, NC: Duke University Press.

Dickerson, Caitlin. 2018. "Appeals Court Decision Keeps 'Dreamers' Safe from Being Deported." *New York Times*, November 8.

Dionne, E. J., Jr., Norman J. Ornstein, and Thomas E. Mann. 2017. *One Nation after Trump: A Guide for the Perplexed, the Disillusioned, the Desperate, and the Not-Yet Deported.* New York: St. Martin's.

Dixon, Lydia Zacher. 2015. "Obstetrics in a Time of Violence: Mexican Midwives Critique Routine Hospital Practices." *Medical Anthropological Quarterly* 29 (4): 437–54.

Dorsey, Margaret E. 2004. "The Role of Music in Materializing Politics." *PoLAR* 27 (2): 61–94.

Dorsey, Margaret E., and Miguel Díaz-Barriga. 2015. "The Constitution Free Zone in the United States: Law and Life in a State of Carcelment." *PoLAR: Political and Legal Anthropology Review* 38 (2): 204–25.

Dreby, Joanna. 2010. *Divided by Borders: Mexican Migrants and Their Children.* Berkeley: University of California Press.

———. 2015. *Everyday Illegal: When Policies Undermine Immigrant Families.* Berkeley: University of California Press.

Dreweke, Joerg. 2017. "U.S. Abortion Rate Reaches Record Low amidst Looming Onslaught against Reproductive Health and Rights." *Guttmacher Policy Review* 20:15–19.

Duong, Kevin. 2012. "What Does Queer Theory Teach Us About Intersectionality?" *Politics & Gender* 8 (3): 370–86.

Duran, Eduardo, and Bonnie Duran. 1995. *Native American Postcolonial Psychology.* Albany: State University of New York Press.

Dutt, Malika. 1998. "Reclaiming a Human Rights Culture: Feminism of Difference and Alliance." In *Talking Visions: Multicultural Feminism in a Transnational Age*, edited by Ella Shohat, 225–46. New York: New Museum of Contemporary Art.

Eichelberger, Erika. 2014. "10 Poverty Myths, Busted: No, Single Moms Aren't the Problem. And Neither Are Absentee Dads." *Mother Jones*, March 25.

Elenes, C. Alejandra. 2014. "Spiritual Roots of Chicana Feminist Borderland Pedagogies: A Spiritual Journey with Tonantzin/Guadalupe." In *Fleshing the Spirit: Spirituality and Activism in Chicana, Latina, and Indigenous Women's Lives*, edited by Elisa Facio and Irene Lara, 43–58. Tucson: University of Arizona Press.

Eligon, John. 2018. "Hate Crimes in U.S. Increase for the Third Year in a Row, the F.B.I. Reports." *New York Times*, November 14.

Enriquez, Laura E. 2015. "Multigenerational Punishment: Shared Experiences of Undocumented Immigration Status." *Journal of Marriage & Family* 77 (4): 939–53.

Entman, Robert M. 1993. "Framing: Toward Clarification of a Fractured Paradigm." *Journal of Communication* 43 (4): 51–58.

Espino, Virginia 2000. "'Woman Sterilized as Gives Birth': Forced Sterilization and Chicana Resistance in the 1970s." In *Las Obreras: Chicana Politics of Work and Family*, edited by Vicki L. Ruiz, 65–81. Los Angeles: UCLA Chicano Studies Research Center.

Espinoza, Dionne, María Eugenia Cotera, and Maylei Blackwell, eds. 2018. *Chicana Movidas: New Narratives of Activism and Feminism in the Movement Era.* Austin: University of Texas Press.

Evans, Elrena, and Caroline Grant, eds. 2008. *Mama, PhD: Women Write about Motherhood and Academic Life.* New Brunswick, NJ: Rutgers University Press.

Evans, Tony. 2002. "A Human Right to Health?" *Third World Quarterly* 23 (2): 197–215.

Facio, Elisa. 2014. "Spirit Journey: 'Home' as a Site for Healing and Transformation." In *Fleshing the Spirit: Spirituality and Activism in Chicana, Latina, and Indigenous*

Women's Lives, edited by Elisa Facio and Irene Lara, 59–72. Tucson: University of Arizona Press.

Facio, Elisa, and Irene Lara. 2014. "Introduction: Fleshing the Spirit, Spiriting the Flesh." In *Fleshing the Spirit: Spirituality and Activism in Chicana, Latina, and Indigenous Women's Lives*, edited by Elisa Facio and Irene Lara, 3–18. Tucson: University of Arizona Press.

Fahs, Breanne. 2014. "'Freedom To' and 'Freedom From': A New Vision for Sex-Positive Politics." *Sexualities* 17 (3): 267–90.

Falcón, Sylvanna M. 2009. "Invoking Human Rights and Transnational Activism in Struggles for Racial Justice at Home: Anti-racist Activists and the Committee to Eliminate Racial Discrimination." *Societies without Borders* 4:295–316.

———. 2016. *Power Interrupted: Antiracist and Feminist Activism inside the United Nations*. Seattle: University of Washington Press.

Falcón, Sylvanna M., and Jennifer C. Nash. 2015. "Shifting Analytics and Linking Theories: A Conversation about the 'Meaning-Making' of Intersectionality and Transnational Feminism." *Women's Studies International Forum* 50:1–10.

Falzon, Mark-Anthony. 2009. Introduction to *Multi-Sited Ethnography: Theory, Praxis and Locality in Contemporary Research*, edited by Mark-Anthony Falzon, 1–23. Aldershot, UK: Ashgate.

Farmer, Paul. 2005. *Pathologies of Power: Health, Human Rights, and the New War on the Poor*. Berkeley: University of California Press.

Fassin, Didier, ed. 2017. *If Truth Be Told: The Politics of Public Ethnography*. Durham, NC: Duke University Press.

Feagin, Joe R. 2013. *Systemic Racism: A Theory of Oppression*. London: Routledge.

Félix, Lucy. 2014. "Why My Fight for Latina Health Took Me All the Way to the UN." Commentary, National Latina Institute for Reproductive Health, March 31.

Fernandes, Leela. 2003. *Transforming Feminist Practice: Non-violence, Social Justice, and the Possibilities of a Spiritualized Feminism*. San Francisco: Aunt Lute.

Fernandes, Sujatha. 2017. *Curated Stories: The Uses and Misuses of Storytelling*. New York: Oxford University Press.

Fernandez, Manny. 2018. "Guardsmen, Seen and Unseen, Watch the Border." *New York Times*, April 12.

Fernandez, Manny, Caitlin Dickerson, and Paulina Villegas. 2019. "A Gamble Fails, Overcrowding Migrant Shelters." *New York Times*, January 5.

Fields, Jessica. 2008. *Risky Lessons: Sex Education and Social Inequality*. New Brunswick, NJ: Rutgers University Press.

Fine, Michelle. 1993. "Sexuality, Schooling and Adolescent Females: The Missing Discourse of Desire." In *Beyond Silenced Voices: Class, Race, and Gender in United States Schools*, edited by Lois Weis and Michelle Fine, 75–99. Albany: State University of New York Press.

Fine, Michelle, and Sara McClelland. 2006. "Sexuality Education and Desire: Still Missing after All These Years." *Harvard Educational Review* 76 (3): 297–338.

Fine, Michelle, and Lois Weis. 1998. *The Unknown City: Voices of Poor and Working Class Young Adults*. Boston: Beacon.

Flavin, Jeanne. 2009. *Our Bodies, Our Crimes: The Policing of Women's Reproduction in America*. New York: NYU Press.

Flores, William V., and Rina Benmayor, eds. 1997. *Latino Cultural Citizenship: Claiming Identity, Space, and Rights*. Boston: Beacon.

Forbes, David. 2019. *Mindfulness and Its Discontents: Education, Self, and Social Transformation*. New York: Fernwood.

Fortino, Ellyn. 2014. "Reproductive Rights Advocates Demand Repeal of Illinois' Abortion Notification Law." *Progress Illinois*, April 3.

Forward Together's Strong Families Network. 2017. "Reproductive Justice Reference Guide for Latinx Media." Oakland, CA: Forward Together's Strong Families Network.

Forward Together Youth. 2012. "Let's Get It On: Oakland Youth's New Vision for Sex Ed." Oakland, CA: Forward Together.

Fox, Jonathan. 2002. "Lessons from Mexico-U.S. Civil Society Coalitions." In *Cross-Border Dialogues: U.S.-Mexico Social Movement Networking*, edited by David Brooks and Jonathan Fox, 341–419. San Diego: Center for US-Mexican Studies, University of California.

Fox Harding, Lorraine. 1999. "'Family Values' and Conservative Government Policy: 1979–97." In *Changing Family Values*, edited by Gill Jagger and Caroline Wright, 119–35. New York: Routledge.

Franco, Marisol. 2012. "Supporting Latina/o Youth: Strengthening Latina/o Young Families and Communities." Los Angeles: California Latinas for Reproductive Justice.

Fregoso, Rosa Linda. 2014. "For a Pluriversal Declaration of Human Rights." *American Quarterly* 66 (3): 583–608.

Freire, Paolo, with Myra Bergman Ramos. 1970. *Pedagogy of the Oppressed*. New York: Continuum.

Friedman, Eric A., Lawrence O. Gostin, and Kent Buse. 2013. "Advancing the Right to Health through Global Organizations: The Potential Role of a Framework Convention on Global Health." *Health and Human Rights* 15 (1): 71–86.

Fuentes, Liza, Sharon Lebenkoff, Kari White, Caitlin Gerdts, Kristine Hopkis, Joseph E. Potter, and Daniel Grossman. 2016. "Women's Experiences Seeking Abortion Care Shortly after the Closure of Clinics Due to a Restrictive Law in Texas." *Contraception* 93 (4): 292–97.

Fujiwara, Lynn. 2008. *Mothers without Citizenship: Asian Immigrant Families and the Consequences of Welfare Reform*. Minneapolis: University of Minnesota Press.

Galameau, Charlene. 2013. "Farm Labor, Reproductive Justice: Migrant Women Farmworkers in the US." *Health and Human Rights* 15 (1): 144–60.

Gálvez, Alyshia. 2011. *Patient Citizens, Immigrant Mothers: Mexican Women, Public Prenatal Care, and the Birth-Weight Paradox*. New Brunswick, NJ: Rutgers University Press.

Gamson, Joshua. 1995. "Must Identity Movements Self-Destruct? A Queer Dilemma." *Social Problems* 42 (3): 390–407.

García, Alma, ed. 1997. *Chicana Feminist Thought: The Basic Historical Writings*. New York: Routledge.

Garcia, Angela. 2010. *The Pastoral Clinic: Addiction and Dispossession along the Rio Grande*. Berkeley: University of California Press.

Garcia, Karina A., and Yolande M. S. Tomlinson. 2015. "Introducción a los Derechos Humanos." New York and Atlanta: National Latina Institute for Reproductive Health and US Human Rights Network.

Garcia, Lorena. 2009. "'Now Why Do You Want to Know about That?': Heteronormativity, Sexism, and Racism in the Sexual (Mis)Education of Latina Youth." *Gender & Society* 23 (4): 520–41.

———. 2012. *Respect Yourself, Protect Yourself: Latina Girls and Sexual Identity*. New York: NYU Press.

Gay, Elizabeth Dawes. 2018. "Black Maternal Health Week May Be Over, but We're Just Getting Started." *Rewire.News*, April 17.

Gelles, David. 2016. *Mindful Work: How Meditation Is Changing Business from the Inside Out*. New York: Houghton Mifflin Harcourt.

Gerdts, Caitlin, Liza Fuentes, Daniel Grossman, Kari White, Brianna Keefe-Oates, Sarah E. Baum, Kristine Hopkins, Chandler W. Stolp, and Joseph E. Potter. 2016. "Impact of Clinic Closures on Women Obtaining Abortion Services after Implementation of a Restrictive Law in Texas." *American Journal of Public Health* 106 (5): 857–64.

Ghodsee, Kristen. 2011. *Professor Mommy: Finding Work-Family Balance in Academia*. Lanham, MD: Rowman and Littlefield.

Gilliam, Melissa L., Amy Berlin, Mike Kozloski, Maida Hernandez, and Maureen Grundy. 2007. "Interpersonal and Personal Factors Influencing Sexual Debut among Mexican-American Youth Women in the United States." *Journal of Adolescent Health* 41:495–503.

Glick, Elisa. 2000. "Sex Positive: Feminism, Queer Theory, and the Politics of Transgression." *Feminist Review* 64 (Spring): 19–45.

Goeman, Mishuana, and Jennifer Nez Denetdale. 2009. "Native Feminisms: Legacies, Interventions, and Indigenous Sovereignties." *Wicazo Sa Review* 24 (2): 9–13.

Gold, Rachel Benson, and Kinsey Hasstedt. 2016. "Lessons from Texas: Widespread Consequences of Assaults on Abortion Access." *American Journal of Public Health* 106 (6): 970–71.

———. 2017. "Flouting the Facts: State Abortion Restrictions Flying in the Face of Science." *Guttmacher Policy Review* 20:53–59.

Gold, Rachel Benson, and Elizabeth Nash. 2012. "Troubling Trend: More States Hostile to Abortion Rights as Middle Ground Shrinks." *Guttmacher Policy Review* 15 (1): 14–19.

Gomberg-Muñoz, Ruth. 2017. *Becoming Legal: Immigration Law and Mixed-Status Families*. New York: Oxford University Press.

Gomez, Madeline, and Sonya Rahders. 2016. "Shifting the Frame in Law and Policy from Preventing Teen Pregnancy to Supporting Young Parents." In *Reproductive Justice Lawyering: A CLE Webinar Series*. Washington, DC: American University, Washington College of Law, Women and the Law Program, Law Students for Reproductive Justice, June 20.

Gonzales, Alfonso. 2014. *Reform without Justice: Latino Migrant Politics and the Homeland Security State*. New York: Oxford University Press.

Gonzales, Phillip B. 2007. "Introduction: Place and Nuevomexicano Culture." In *Expressing New Mexico: Nuevomexicano Creativity, Ritual, and Memory*, 3–21. Tucson: University of Arizona Press.

Gonzales, Roberto G. 2016. *Lives in Limbo: Undocumented and Coming of Age in America*. Berkeley: University of California Press.

González, Norma, Luis C. Moll, and Cathy Amanti. 2005. Preface to *Funds of Knowledge: Theorizing Practices in Households, Communities, and Classrooms*, edited by Norma González, Luis C. Moll, and Cathy Amanti, ix–xii. New York: Routledge.

González-Rojas, Jessica. 2015. "Attacks on Planned Parenthood Are Not About One Organization." *Truthout*, August 11.

Goodale, Mark. 2006a. "Introduction to 'Anthropology and Human Rights in a New Key.'" *American Anthropologist* 108 (1): 1–8.

———. 2006b. "Toward a Critical Anthropology of Human Rights." *Current Anthropology* 47 (3): 485–511.

Goodwin, Jeff, James M. Jasper, and Francesca Polletta. 2001. "Introduction: Why Emotions Matter." In *Passionate Politics: Emotions and Social Movements*, edited by Jeff Goodwin, James M. Jasper, and Francesca Polletta, 1–24. Chicago: University of Chicago Press.

Gordon, Hava, and Jessica K. Taft. 2011. "Rethinking Youth Political Socialization: Teenage Activists Talk Back." *Youth and Society* 43 (4): 1449–527.

Gorski, Paul, Stacy Lopresti-Goodman, and Dallas Rising. 2018. "'Nobody's Paying Me to Cry': The Causes of Activist Burnout in the United States Animal Rights Activists." *Social Movement Studies* 18 (3): 364–80.

Gould, Deborah B. 2009. *Moving Politics: Emotion and Act Up's Fight against AIDS*. Chicago: University of Chicago Press.

Graham, David A. 2017. "The Many Scandals of Donald Trump: A Cheat Sheet." *Atlantic*, January 23.

Graham, Sarah Halasz. 2018. "Tewa Women United Awarded $900,000 Grant." *Santa Fe New Mexican*, June 16.

Gramsci, Antonio. 1971. *Selections from the Prison Notebooks*. Translated by Quintin Hoare and Geoffrey Nowell Smith. New York: International.

Green, Linda. 2011. "The Nobodies: Neoliberalism, Violence, and Migration." *Medical Anthropology: Cross-Cultural Studies in Health and Illness* 30 (4): 366–85.

Greenbaum, Susan D. 2015. *Blaming the Poor: The Long Shadow of the Moynihan Report on Cruel Images about Poverty*. New Brunswick, NJ: Rutgers University Press.

Greenlee, Cynthia R. 2015. "Fighting for Access and Justice: A Q&A with the Incoming Executive Director of the National Network of Abortion Funds." *RH Reality Check: Reproductive & Sexual Health and Justice News, Analysis & Commentary*, May 1.

Griffin-Carlson, Mary S., and Paula J. Schwanenflugel. 1998. "Adolescent Abortion and Parental Notification: Evidence for the Importance of Family Functioning on the Perceived Quality of Parental Involvement in U.S. Families." *Journal of Child Psychology and Psychiatry* 39 (4): 543–53.

Grosfoguel, Ramón, and Chloé S. Georas. 2000. "'Coloniality of Power' and Racial Dynamics: Notes toward a Reinterpretation of Latino Caribbeans in New York City." *Identities: Global Studies in Power & Culture* 7 (11): 85–125.

Grossman, Daniel, Sarah Baum, Liza Fuentes, Kari White, Kristine Hopkins, Amanda Stevenson, and Joseph E. Potter. 2014. "Change in Abortion Services after Implementation of a Restrictive Law in Texas." *Contraception* 90:496–501.

Grossman, Daniel, and Kate Grindlay. 2017. "Safety of Medical Abortion Provided through Telemedicine Compared with In Person." *Obstetrics & Gynecology* 130 (4): 778–82.

Grossman, Daniel, Kelsey Holt, Melanie Peña, Diana Lara, Maggie Veatch, Denisse Córdoba, Marji Gold, Beverly Winikoff, and Kelly Blanchard. 2010. "Self-Induction of Abortion among Women in the United States." *Reproductive Health Matters* 18 (36): 136–46.

Grossman, Daniel, Kari White, Liza Fuentes, D. Hopkins, Amanda Stevenson, S. Yeatman, and Joseph E. Potter. 2015. "Knowledge, Opinion and Experience Related to Abortion Self-Induction in Texas." Texas Policy Evaluation Project Research Brief.

Grossman, Daniel, Kari White, Kristine Hopkins, and Joseph E. Potter. 2014. "The Public Health Threat of Anti-Abortion Legislation." *Contraception* 89:73–74.

Grzanka, Patrick R., ed. 2014. *Intersectionality: A Foundations and Frontiers Reader*. Boulder, CO: Westview.

Gugelberger, Georg M., ed. 1996. *The Real Thing: Testimonial Discourse Latin America*. Durham, NC: Duke University Press.

Gurr, Barbara. 2012. "The Failures and Possibilities of a Human Rights Approach to Secure Native American Women's Reproductive Justice." *Sociologists without Borders* 7 (1): 1–28.

———. 2014. *Reproductive Justice: The Politics of Health Care for Native American Women*. New Brunswick, NJ: Rutgers University Press.

Gutiérrez, Elena R. 2008. *Fertile Matters: The Politics of Mexican-Origin Women's Reproduction*. Austin: University of Texas Press.

Gutiérrez, Lorraine M., and Edith A. Lewis. 1999. *Empowering Women of Color*. New York: Columbia University Press.

Gutiérrez, Ramón A. 1991. *When Jesus Came, the Corn Mothers Went Away: Marriage, Sexuality, and Power in New Mexico, 1500–1846*. Stanford, CA: Stanford University Press.

———. 2010. "A History of Latina/o Sexualities." In *Latina/o Sexualities: Probing Powers, Passions, Practices, and Policies*, edited by Marysol Asencio, 13–37. New Brunswick, NJ: Rutgers University Press.

Guttmacher Institute. 2014a. "Facts on Induced Abortion in the United States." New York: Guttmacher Institute.

———. 2014b."More State Abortion Restrictions Were Enacted in 2011–2013 than in the Entire Previous Decade." New York: Guttmacher Institute.

———. 2014c. "State Policies in Brief as of July 1, 2014: An Overview of Minors' Consent Law." New York: Guttmacher Institute.

———. 2016. "Unintended Pregnancy in the United States." New York: Guttmacher Institute.

Hale, Charles R. 2001. "What Is Activist Research?" *Social Science Research Council* 2 (1–2): 13–15.

———. 2006. "Activist Research v. Cultural Critique: Indigenous Land Rights and the Contradictions of Politically Engaged Anthropology." *Cultural Anthropology* 21 (1): 96–120.

Harcourt, Wendy, and Arturo Escobar, eds. 2005. *Women and the Politics of Place.* Bloomfield, CT: Kumarian.

Harrell, Shelly P. 2000. "A Multidimensional Conceptualization of Racism-Related Stress: Implications for the Well-Being of People of Color." *American Journal of Orthopsychiatry* 70 (1): 42–57.

Harrison, Faye V. 2017. "Engaging Theory in the New Millennium." In *The Routledge Companion to Contemporary Anthropology*, edited by Simon Coleman, Susan B. Hyatt, and Ann Kingsolver, 27–56. New York: Routledge.

Harthorn, Barbara Herr, and Laury Oaks, eds. 2003. *Risk, Culture, and Health Inequality: Shifting Perceptions of Danger and Blame.* Westport, CT: Praeger.

Harvey, David. 2005. *A Brief History of Neoliberalism.* New York: Oxford University Press.

Hasstedt, Kinsey. 2017. "Understanding Planned Parenthood's Critical Role in the Nation's Family Planning Safety Net." *Guttmacher Policy Review* 20:12–14.

Hauslohner, Abigail, Nick Miroff, Maria Sacchetti, and Tracy Jan. 2019. "Trump Officials Move to Deny Green Cards, Path to Citizenship for Poor Immigrants." *Washington Post*, August 12.

Henry J. Kaiser Foundation. 2018. "Key Facts about the Uninsured Population." Menlo Park, CA: Henry J. Kaiser Foundation.

Herrero, Pilar, Katrina Anderson, and Angela Hooton. 2017. "Black Mamas Alliance Toolkit." New York: Center for Reproductive Rights.

Hess, Amanda. 2017. "Forces in Opposition." *New York Times Magazine*, February 7, 35–43.

Hester, Rebecca J. 2013. "Bodies in Translation: Health Promotion in Indigenous Mexican Migrant Communities in California." In *Translocalities/Translocalidades: Feminist Politics of Translation in the Latin/a Américas*, edited by Sonia E. Alvarez, Claudia de Lima Costa, Verónica Feliú, Rebecca J. Hester, Norma Klahn, Millie Thayer, and Cruz C. Bueno, 168–88. Durham, NC: Duke University Press.

———. 2015. "Cultural Competency Training and Indigenous Cultural Politics in California." *Latino Studies* 13 (3): 316–38.

Hill, Sarah. 2003. "Metaphoric Enrichment and Material Poverty: The Making of 'Colonias.'" In *Ethnography at the Border*, edited by Pablo Vila, 141–65. Minneapolis: University of Minnesota Press.

Hill Collins, Patricia 1986. "The Emerging Theory and Pedagogy of Black Women's Studies." *Feminist Issues* 6 (1): 3–17.

———. 1990. *Black Feminist Thought: Knowledge, Consciousness, and the Politics of Empowerment.* Boston: Unwin Hyman.

Hill Collins, Patricia, and Sirma Bilge. 2016. *Intersectionality.* Malden, MA: Polity.

Hine, Christine. 2015. *Ethnography for the Internet: Embedded, Embodied and Everyday.* London: Bloomsbury Academic.

Hochschild, Arlie Russell. 2016. *Strangers in Their Own Land: Anger and Mourning on the American Right.* New York: New Press.

Hochschild, Arlie Russell, and Anne Machung. 2012. *The Second Shift: Working Families and the Revolution at Home.* New York: Penguin Books.

Holmes, Seth M. 2011. "Structural Vulnerability and Hierarchies of Ethnicity and Citizenship on the Farm." *Medical Anthropology: Cross-Cultural Studies in Health and Illness* 30 (4): 425–49.

Hondagneu-Sotelo, Pierrette. 2001. *Doméstica: Immigrant Workers Cleaning and Caring in the Shadows of Affluence.* Berkeley: University of California Press.

Horton, Sarah Bronwen. 2016. *They Leave Their Kidneys in the Fields: Illness, Injury, and Illegality among U.S. Farmworkers.* Berkeley: University of California Press.

Howell, Elizabeth, Natalia Egorova, Amy Balbierz, Jennifer Zeitlin, and Paul L. Hebert. 2016. "Black-White Differences in Severe Maternal Morbidity and the Site of Care." *American Journal of Obstetrics & Gynecology* 214:122.e1–7.

Howell, Marcela. 2007. "Walk in My Shoes: A Black Activist's Guide to Surviving the Women's Movement." Washington, DC: Advocates for Youth.

Human Impact Partners and La Unión del Pueblo Entero. 2018. "The Effects of Forced Family Separation in the Rio Grande Valley: A Family Unity, Family Health Research Update." Oakland, CA: Human Impact Partners and La Unión del Pueblo Entero.

Hunleth, Jean. 2011. "Beyond On or With: Questioning Power Dynamics and Knowledge Production in 'Child-Oriented' Research Methodology." *Childhood* 18 (1): 81–93.

Hurtado, Aída. 2003a. "Underground Feminisms: Inocencia's Story." In *Chicana Feminisms: A Critical Reader*, edited by Gabriela Arredondo, Aída Hurtado, Norma Klahn, Olga Nájera Ramírez and Patricia Zavella, 260–90. Durham, NC: Duke University Press.

———. 2003b. *Voicing Chicana Feminisms: Young Women Speak out on Sexuality and Identity.* New York: NYU Press.

Hurtig, Janise. 2005. "Resisting Assimilation: Mexican Immigrant Mothers Writing Together." In *Latino Language and Literacy in Ethnolinguistic Chicago*, edited by Marcia Farr, 247–75. Mahwah, NJ: Lawrence Erlbaum.

Illinois Caucus for Adolescent Health. 2015. *Sex Ed Saves: Amplifying Youth Voice through Sex-Positive Education.* Chicago: Bookbaby.

INCITE! Women of Color Against Violence, ed. 2006. *The Color of Violence: The INCITE! Anthology.* Cambridge, MA: South End.

———. 2007. *The Revolution Will Not Be Funded: Beyond the Non-Profit Industrial Complex.* Cambridge, MA: South End.

Ioanide, Paula. 2015. *The Emotional Politics of Racism: How Feelings Trump Facts in an Era of Colorblindness.* Stanford, CA: Stanford University Press.

Isacson, Adam, and Maureen Meyer. 2013. "Border Security and Migration: A Report from South Texas." Washington, DC: Washington Office on Latin America.

Isikoff, Michael, and David Corn. 2018. *Russian Roulette: The Inside Story of Putin's War on America and the Election of Donald Trump.* New York: Hachette.

Jamar, Steven D. 1994. "The International Human Right to Health." *Southern University Law Review* 22:1–53.

James, Joy, and T. Denean Sharpley-Whiting, eds. 2000. *The Black Feminist Reader.* Oxford, UK: Blackwell.

Jarrett, Robin L. 1997. "Resilience among Low-Income African American Youth: An Ethnographic Perspective." *Ethos* 25 (2): 218–29.

Jenkins, Henry, Sangita Shresthova, Liana Gamber-Thompson, Neta Kligler-Vilenchik, and Arely M. Zimmerman. 2016. *By Any Media Necessary: The New Youth Activism.* New York: NYU Press.

Jesudason, Sujatha, 2017. "Co-creating Our Future Together." *CoreAlign Blog*, February 24.

Jesudason, Sujatha, and Katrina Kimport. 2013. "Decentering the Individual and Centering Community." *Frontiers: A Journal of Women Studies* 34 (3): 213–25.

Jolly, Jallicia. 2016. "On Forbidden Wombs and Transnational Reproductive Justice." *Meridians: Feminism, Race, Transnationalism* 15 (1): 166–88.

Jones, Amelia. 1998. "Bodies and Subjects in the Technologized Self-Portrait: The Work of Laura Aguilar." *Aztlán: A Journal of Chicano Studies* 23 (2): 203–19.

Jones, Rachel K. 2018. "Reported Contraceptive Use in the Month of Becoming Pregnant among U.S. Abortion Patients in 2000 and 2014." *Contraception* 97 (4): 309–12.

Jones, Rachel K., and Jenna Jerman. 2017. "Population Group Abortion Rates and Lifetime Incidence of Abortion: United States, 2008–2014." *American Journal of Public Health* 107 (12): 1904–9.

Jones, Rachel K., and Adam Sonfield. 2016. "Health Insurance Coverage among Women of Reproductive Age before and after Implementation of the Affordable Care Act." *Contraception* 93:386–91.

Jordan, Miriam. 2019. "Many Families Split at Border Went Untallied: Report Says Thousands More Children Taken." *New York Times*, January 18.

Joyce, Theodore, Robert Kaestner, and Silvie Colman. 2006. "Changes in Abortions and Births and the Texas Parental Notification Law." *New England Journal of Medicine* 354 (10): 1031–38.

Juris, Jeffrey S., and Alex Khasnabish, eds. 2013. *Insurgent Encounters: Transnational Activism, Ethnography, and the Political.* Durham, NC: Duke University Press.

Katz, Michael B., ed. 1993. *The "Underclass" Debate: Views from History*. Philadelphia: Temple University Press.

Kauffman, L. A. 2018. *How to Read a Protest*. Oakland: University of California Press.

Keating, AnaLouise. 2008. "'I'm a Citizen of the Universe': Gloria Anzaldúa's Spiritual Activism as Catalyst for Social Change." *Frontiers: A Journal of Women Studies* 1–2 (Spring–Summer): 53–69.

Keating, Cricket. 2005. "Building Coalitional Consciousness." *NWSA Journal* 17 (2): 86–103.

Kelley, Allyson, Clayton Small, Maha Charani Small, Hawkeye Montileaux, and Shawnee White. 2018. "Defining Cultural Resilience to Strengthen Native Youth: A Brief Report from the Intergenerational Connection Project." *Practicing Anthropology* 40 (4): 5–9.

Kessler, Glenn, Salvador Rizzo, and Meg Kelly. 2019. "President Trump Has Made 12,019 False or Misleading Claims over 928 Days." *Washington Post*, August 12.

Kinney, Eleanor D. 2001. "The International Human Right to Health: What Does This Mean for Our Nation and World?" *Indiana Law Journal* 34:1457–75.

Kornacki, Steve. 2018. *The Red and the Blue: The 1990s and the Birth of Political Tribalism*. New York: HarperCollins.

Kost, Kathryn, and Isaac Maddow-Zimet. 2016. "U.S. Teenage Pregnancies, Births and Abortions, 2011: National Trends by Age, Race and Ethnicity." New York: Guttmacher Institute.

Kruse, Kevin M., and Julian E. Zelizer. 2019. *Fault Lines: A History of the United States since 1974*. New York: Norton.

Kurki, Leena. 2000. "Restorative and Community Justice in the United States." *Crime and Justice* 27:235–303.

Lake Research Partners. 2011. "Poll: Latino Voters Hold Compassionate Views on Abortion." Washington, DC: Lake Research Partners.

Lamphere, Louise. 2018. "The Transformation of Ethnography: From Malinowski's Tent to the Practice of Collaborative/Activist Anthropology." *Human Organization* 77 (1): 64–76.

Lapeyrouse, Lisa M., Patricia Y. Miranda, Osvaldo F. Morera, Josiah McC. Heyman, and Hector G. Balcazar. 2016. "Healthcare Use and Mammography among Latinas with and without Health Insurance near the US-Mexico Border." *Journal of Racial and Ethnic Health Disparities* 4 (2): 282–87.

Lara, Irene. 2014. "Sensing the Serpent in the Mother, *Dando a Luz la Madre Serpiente*: Chicana Spirituality, Sexuality, and Mamihood." In *Fleshing the Spirit: Spirituality and Activism in Chicana, Latina, and Indigenous Women's Lives*, edited by Elisa Facio and Irene Lara, 113–34. Tucson: University of Arizona Press.

Latina Feminist Group. 2001. *Telling to Live: Latina Feminist Testimonios*. Durham, NC: Duke University Press.

Leacock, Eleanor, ed. 1971. *The Culture of Poverty: A Critique*. New York: Simon and Schuster.

Lee, Esther Yu-Hsi. 2013. "Spate of South Texas Police Checkpoints Incite Fear among Immigrants." *ThinkProgress*, September 27.

Lentin, Alana. 2018. "Beyond Denial: 'No Racism' as Racist Violence." *Continuum: Journal of Media & Cultural Studies* 32 (4): 400–414.

Levin, Dan. 2019. "Young Voters, Even Republicans, Are Drifting to the Left on Social Issues." *New York Times*, January 24.

Lewin, Ellen. 1993. *Lesbian Mothers: Accounts of Gender in American Culture*. Ithaca, NY: Cornell University Press.

Lewis, Oscar. 1966. "The Culture of Poverty." *Scientific American* 215:19–25.

Lindberg, Laura, John Santelli, and Sheila Desai. 2016. "Understanding the Decline in Adolescent Fertility in the United States, 2007–2012." *Journal of Adolescent Health* 59 (5): 577–83.

Linklater, Renee. 2014. *Decolonizing Trauma Work: Indigenous Stories and Strategies*. Halifax, NS: Fernwood.

Liptak, Adam. 2018. "Anti-Abortion Health Clinics Win First Amendment Ruling." *New York Times*, June 26.

Lodhia, Sharmila, and Sylvanna M. Falcón. 2002. "Demanding the Right to Live without Violence: Reflections on Color of Violence II." *Meridians: Feminism, Race, Transnationalism* 3 (1): 265–73.

López, Gustavo, and Renee Stepler. 2016. "Latinos in the 2016 Election: California." Washington, DC: Pew Research Center.

Lopez, Iris. 1993. "Agency and Constraint: Sterilization and Reproductive Freedom among Puerto Rican Women in New York City." *Urban Anthropology and Studies of Cultural Systems and World Economic Development* 22 (3): 299–323.

———. 2008. *Matters of Choice: Puerto Rican Women's Struggle for Reproductive Freedom*. New Brunswick, NJ: Rutgers University Press.

Lopez, Mark Hugo, Ana Gonzalez-Barrera, Jens Manuel Krogstad, and Jessica Pumphrey. 2018. "More Latinos Have Serious Concerns about Their Place in America under Trump." Washington DC: Pew Research Center.

Lorde, Audre. 1978. *Uses of the Erotic: The Erotic as Power*. Brooklyn, NY: Out and Out Books.

———. 1984. *Sister Outsider: Essays and Speeches by Audre Lorde*. Berkeley, CA: Crossing.

———. 2017. *A Burst of Light and Other Essays*. Ithaca, NY: Ixia.

Lu, Denise, and Derek Watkins. 2019. "Big Barrier Facing Migrants: A Court Backlog." *New York Times*, January 25.

Lubiano, Wahneema. 1992. "Black Ladies, Welfare Queens, and State Minstrels: Ideological War by Narrative Means," in *Race-ing Justice, En-gendering Power: Essays on Anita Hill, Clarence Thomas, and the Construction of Social Reality*, edited by Toni Morrison, 323–63. New York: Pantheon.

Lugones, María. 2010. "Toward a Decolonial Feminism." *Hypatia* 25 (4).

Luibhéid, Eithne. 2013. *Pregnant on Arrival: Making the Illegal Immigrant*. Minneapolis: University of Minnesota Press.

Luna, Zakiya T. 2009. "From Rights to Justice: Women of Color Changing the Face of US Reproductive Rights Organizing." *Societies Without Borders* 4:343–65.

———. 2010. "Marching toward Reproductive Justice: Coalitional (Re)Framing of the March for Women's Lives." *Sociological Inquiry* 80 (4): 554–78.

———. 2011. "'The Phrase of the Day': Examining Contexts and Co-Optation of Reproductive Justice Activism in the Women's Movement." In *Critical Aspects of Gender in Conflict Resolution, Peacebuilding, and Social Movements*, edited by Anna Christine Snyder and Stephanie Phetsamay Stobbe, 219–46. Bingley, UK: Emerald.

———. 2017. "Who Speaks for Whom? (Mis)Representation and Authenticity in Social Movements." *Mobilization: An International Journal* 22 (4): 435–50.

Luna, Zakiya T., and Kristin Luker. 2013. "Reproductive Justice." *Annual Review of Law and Social Science* 9:327–52.

Lutz, Helma, Maria Teresa Herrera Vivar, and Linda Supik, eds. 2011. *Framing Intersectionality: Debates on a Multi-Faceted Concept in Gender Studies*. Farnham, UK: Ashgate.

MacDorman, Marian, Eugene Declercq, Howard Cabral, and Christine Morton. 2016. "Recent Increases in the U.S. Maternal Mortality Rate: Disentangling Trends from Measurement Issues." *Obstetrics & Gynecology* 128 (3): 1–9.

Maira, Sunaina, and Elisabeth Soep. 2004. Introduction to *Youthscapes: The Popular, the National, the Global*, edited by Sunaina Maira and Elisabeth Soep, xv–xxxv. Philadelphia: University of Pennsylvania Press.

Mani, Lata. 2009. *SacredSecular: Contemplative Cultural Critique*. New York: Routledge.

Marchevsky, Alejandra, and Jeanne Theoharis. 2006. *Not Working: Latina Immigrants, Low-Wage Jobs, and the Failure of Welfare Reform*. New York: NYU Press.

Marcus, George E. 1995. "Ethnography in/of the World System: The Emergence of Multi-Sited Ethnography." *Annual Review of Anthropology* 24:95–117.

———. 2011. "Multi-Sited Ethnography: Five or Six Things I Know about It Now." In *Multi-Sited Ethnography: Problems and Possibilities in the Translocation of Research Methods*, edited by Simon Coleman and Pauline von Hellermann, 16–32. New York: Routledge.

Markham, Annette N. 2004. "Internet Communication as a Tool for Qualitative Research." In *Qualitative Research: Theory, Method and Practice*, edited by David Silverman, 95–124. London: Sage.

Marriott, Alice. 1948. *María: The Potter of San Ildefonso*. Norman: University of Oklahoma Press.

Martin, Joyce A., Brady E. Hamilton, Michelle J. K. Osterman, Anne K. Driscoll, and Patrick Drake. 2018. "Births: Final Data for 2016." *National Vital Statistics Reports* 67 (8).

Martinez, Lisa M. 2010a. "Mobilization Matters: Moving Immigrant and Latina Women into the Public Sphere." In *Contours of Citizenship: Women, Diversity and Practices of Citizenship*, edited by Margaret Abraham, Esther Ngan-ling Chow, Laura Maratou-Alipranti, and Evangelia Tastsoglou, 127–45. New York: Taylor and Francis.

———. 2010b. "Politicizing the Family: How Grassroots Organizations Mobilize Latinos for Political Action in Colorado." *Latino Studies* 8 (4): 463–84.

Martinez, Ramiro, Jr., and Abel Valenzuela Jr. 2006. *Immigration and Crime: Ethnicity, Race, and Violence*. New York: NYU Press.

Martínez, Rebecca G. 2018. *Women out of Control: The Cultural Politics of Cervical Cancer in Venezuela*. Stanford, CA: Stanford University Press.

Martinez, Rebecca G., Leo R. Chavez, and F. Allan Hubbell. 1997. "Purity and Passion: Risk and Morality in Latina Immigrants' and Physicians' Beliefs about Cervical Cancer." *Medical Anthropology* 17:337–62.

Martínez, Rubén O. 2016. "The Impact of Neoliberalism on Latinos." *Latino Studies* 14 (2016): 11–32.

Martínez, Rubén O., and Raymond Rocco. 2016. "Neoliberalism and Latinos." *Latino Studies* 14 (2016): 2–10.

May, Vivian M. 2015. *Pursuing Intersectionality, Unsettling Dominant Imaginaries*. New York: Routledge.

McCammon, Holly J., Verta Taylor, Jo Reger, and Rachel L. Einwohner, eds. 2017. *U.S. Women's Social Movement Activism*. New York: Oxford University Press.

McCaughan, Edward J. 2012. *Art and Social Movements: Cultural Politics in Mexico and Aztlán*. Durham, NC: Duke University Press.

McGraw, Carol. 2013. "New Colorado Sex Education Law Adds Clarity." *Colorado Springs Gazette*, June 1.

McGreevy, Patrick. "2013. Signing Trust Act Is Another Illegal Immigration Milestone for Brown." *Los Angeles Times*, October 5.

McGregor, Sue. 2001. "Neoliberalism and Health Care." *International Journal of Consumer Studies* 25 (2): 82–89.

McLagan, Meg. 2006. "Introduction: Making Human Rights Claims Public." *American Anthropologist* 108 (1): 91–220.

Medina, Jennifer. 2018. "Migrant Photographed Fleeing Tear Gas Enters U.S." *New York Times*, December 19.

Menchú, Rigoberta. 1984. *I, Rigoberta Menchú: An Indian Woman in Guatemala*. Edited by Elisabeth Burgos-Debray. Translated by Ann Wright. London: Verso.

Menjívar, Cecilia. 2002. "The Ties That Heal: Guatemalan Immigrant Women's Networks and Medical Treatment." *International Migration Review* 36 (2): 437–66.

Menjívar, Cecilia, and Leisy Abrego. 2012. "Legal Violence: Immigration Law and the Lives of Central American Immigrants." *American Journal of Sociology* 117 (5): 1380–421.

Merry, Sally Engle. 2006. "Transnational Human Rights and Local Activism: Mapping the Middle." *American Anthropologist* 108 (1): 38–51.

Meyer, David S. 2002. "Opportunities and Identities: Bridge-Building in the Study of Social Movements." In *Social Movements: Identity, Culture, and the State*, edited by David S. Meyer, Nancy Whittier, and Belinda Robnett, 3–21. Oxford: Oxford University Press.

Mier, Nelda, Marcia G. Ory, Dongling Zhan, Martha Conkling, Joseph R. Sharkey, and James N. Burdine. 2008. "Health-Related Quality of Life among Mexican Americans Living in Colonias at the Texas-Mexico Border." *Social Science & Medicine* 66 (8): 1760–71.

Mignolo, Walter D. 2000. *Local Histories/Global Designs: Coloniality, Subaltern Knowledges, and Border Thinking.* Princeton, NJ: Princeton University Press.

———. 2011. *The Darker Side of Western Modernity: Global Futures, Decolonial Options.* Durham, NC: Duke University Press.

Milkman, Ruth, ed. 2000. *Organizing Immigrants: The Challenge for Unions in Contemporary California.* Ithaca, NY: ILR.

Milkman, Ruth, and Ed Ott, eds. 2014. *New Labor in New York: Precarious Workers and the Future of the Labor Movement.* Ithaca, NY: Cornell University Press.

Million, Dian. 2013. *Therapeutic Nations: Healing in an Age of Indigenous Human Rights.* Tucson: University of Arizona Press.

Mingus, Mia. 2010. "Changing the Framework: Disability Justice: How Our Communities Can Move Beyond Access to Wholeness." *Resist* 19 (6): 4–5.

Moncloa, Fe, Ada M. Wilkinson-Lee, and Stephen T. Russell. 2010. "Cuídate sin Pena: Mexican Mother-Adolescent Sexuality Communication." *Journal of Ethnic and Cultural Diversity in Social Work* 19 (3): 217–34.

Moore, Joan, and Raquel Pinderhughes, eds. 1993. *In the Barrios: Latinos and the Underclass Debate.* New York: Russell Sage Foundation.

Moore, Mignon. 2011. *Invisible Families: Gay Identities, Relationships, and Motherhood among Black Women.* Berkeley: University of California Press.

Moraga, Cherríe. 2002a. "Refugees of a World on Fire: Foreword to the Second Edition, 1983." In *This Bridge Called My Back: Writings by Radical Women of Color,* edited by Cherríe L. Moraga and Gloria E. Anzaldúa, 346–50. Berkeley, CA: Third Woman.

———. 2002b. "Theory in the Flesh." In *This Bridge Called My Back: Writings by Radical Women of Color,* edited by Cherríe L. Moraga and Gloria E. Anzaldúa, 21. Berkeley, CA: Kitchen Table / Women of Color Press.

Moraga, Cherríe, and Gloria Anzaldúa, eds. 1983. *This Bridge Called My Back: Writings by Radical Women of Color.* Berkeley, CA: Kitchen Table: Women of Color Press.

Morgan, Lynn M., and Elizabeth F. S. Roberts. 2012. "Reproductive Governance in Latin America." *Anthropology & Medicine* 19 (2): 241–54.

Morgen, Sandra, Joan Acker, and Jill Weigt. 2010. *Stretched Thin: Poor Families, Welfare Work, and Welfare Reform.* Ithaca, NY: Cornell University Press.

Morris, Sam, and Guardian US Interactive Team. 2018. "Mass Shootings in the US: There Have Been 1,624 in 1,870 Days." *The Guardian,* February 15.

Moss, Rebecca. 2019. "Tewa Women United: An Intertribal Network of Women Are Training to Be Doulas and Volunteers, Strengthening Cultural Knowledge and Healing Generational Trauma at the Same Time." *Vogue,* March 6.

Moynihan, Daniel Patrick. 1965. *The Negro Family: The Case for National Action.* Washington, DC: US Department of Labor.

Naber, Nadine. 2008. "'Look, Mohammed the Terrorist Is Coming!': Cultural Racism, Nation-Based Racism and the Intersectionality of Oppressions after 9/11." In *Race and Arab Americans before and after 9/11*, edited by Amaney Jamal and Nadine Naber, 276–304. Syracuse, NY: Syracuse University Press.

Naber, Nadine, and Junaid Rana. 2019. "The 21st Century Problem of Anti-Muslim Racism." *Jadaliyya Blog*, July 25.

Nagengast, Carole, and Terence Turner. 1997. "Introduction: Universal Human Rights Versus Cultural Relativity." *Journal of Anthropological Research* 53 (3): 269–72.

Nagourney, Adam. 2018. "'There Isn't Hope for Us': The Decline of California Republicans." *New York Times*, December 7.

NARAL Pro-Choice America. 2014. Mandatory Parental-Involvement Laws Threaten Young Women's Safety." Washington, DC: NARAL Pro-Choice America.

———. 2017. *Who Decides? The Status of Women's Reproductive Rights in the United States*. 26th ed. Washington, DC: NARAL Pro-Choice America.

Nash, Elizabeth, Olivia Capello, Sophia Naide, Lizmarie Mohammed, and Zohra Ansari-Thomas. 2019. "Radical Attempts to Ban Abortion Dominate State Policy Trends in the First Quarter of 2019." New York: Guttmacher Institute.

Nash, Jennifer C. 2019. *Black Feminism Reimagined after Intersectionality*. Durham, NC: Duke University Press.

National Academies of Sciences, Engineering, and Medicine. 2018. *Immigration as a Social Determinant of Health: Proceedings of a Workshop*. Washington, DC: National Academies Press.

National Economic and Social Rights Initiative. 2008. "Human Right to Health Care." New York City: National Economic and Social Rights Initiative.

National Latina Institute for Reproductive Health. 2011. "LGBTQ Latin@s and Reproductive Justice." New York: National Latina Institute for Reproductive Health.

———. 2013a. "At the Margins of Care: The Need for Inclusive Health Care for Transgender & Gender Non-Conforming Latin@s." New York: National Latina Institute for Reproductive Health.

———. 2013b. "Latinas and Cervical Cancer in Texas: A Public Health Crisis." New York: National Latina Institute for Reproductive Health.

———. 2013c. "NLIRH Strategic Plan, 2013–2018." New York: National Latina Institute for Reproductive Health.

———. 2015. "The Young Parents' Dignity Agenda." New York: National Latina Institute for Reproductive Health.

———. 2019. "Cabildeando por Justicia Reproductiva en Tejas." New York: National Latina Institute for Reproductive Health.

Nautiyal, Chandra Shekhar, Puneet Singh Chauhan, Yeshwant Laxman Nene. 2007. "Medicinal Smoke Reduces Airborne Bacteria." *Journal of Ethnopharmacology* 114 (3): 446–51.

Negrón-Gonzales, Genevieve. 2013. "Navigating 'Illegality': Undocumented Youth and Oppositional Consciousness." *Children and Youth Services Review* 35 (8): 1284–90.

———. 2014. "Undocumented, Unafraid and Unapologetic: Re-articulatory Practices and Migrant Youth 'Illegality.'" *Latino Studies* 12:259–78.

———. 2017. "Political Possibilities: Lessons from the Undocumented Youth Movement for Resistance to the Trump Administration." *Anthropology & Education* 48 (4): 420–26.

Nelson, Jennifer. 2003. *Women of Color and the Reproductive Rights Movement*. New York: NYU Press.

———. 2015. *More than Medicine: A History of the Feminist Women's Health Movement*. New York: NYU Press.

Nicholls, Walter J. 2013. *The Dreamers: How the Undocumented Youth Movement Transformed the Immigrant Rights Debate*. Stanford, CA: Stanford University Press.

Núñez-Mchiri, Guillermina Gina. 2009. "The Political Ecology of the Colonias on the U.S.-Mexico Border: Human-Environmental Challenges and Community Responses in Southern New Mexico." *Southern Rural Sociology* 24 (1): 67–91.

———. 2012. "Housing, Colonias, and Social Justice in the U.S.-Mexico Border Region." In *Social Justice in the U.S.-Mexico Border Region*, edited by Mark Lusk, Kathleen Staudt and Eva Moya, 109–26. New York: Springer.

Obama, Barack. 2016. "United States Health Care Reform: Progress to Date and Next Steps." *JAMA* 316 (5): E1–E8.

Ojeda de la Peña, Norma. 2007. "Transborder Families and Gendered Trajectories of Migration and Work." In *Women and Migration in the U.S.-Mexico Borderlands*, edited by Denise A. Segura and Patricia Zavella, 327–40. Durham, NC: Duke University Press.

O'Leary, Anna Ochoa, and William Paul Simmons. 2017. "Reproductive Justice and Resistance at the US-Mexico Borderlands." In *Radical Reproductive Justice: Foundations, Theory, Practice, Critique*, edited by Loretta J. Ross, Lynn Roberts, Erika Derkas, Whitney Peoples, and Pamela Bridgewater Toure, 306–25. New York: Feminist Press.

Omi, Michael, and Howard Winant. 2014. *Racial Formation in the United States: From the 1960s to the 1990s*. 2nd ed. New York: Routledge.

Oparah, Julia Chinyere, Helen Arega, Dantia Hudson, Linda Jones, and Talita Oseguera. 2016. "Battling over Birth: Black Women & the Maternal Health Care Crisis in California." Oakland, CA: Black Women Birthing Justice.

Orellana, Marjorie Faulstich. 2001. "The Work Kids Do: Mexican and Central American Immigrant Children's Contributions to Households and Schools in California." *Harvard Educational Review* 71:366–89.

———. 2009. *Translating Childhoods: Immigrant Youth, Language, and Culture*. New Brunswick, NJ: Rutgers University Press.

Orellana, Marjorie Faulstich, Lisa Dorner, and Lucila Pulido. 2003. "Accessing Assets: Immigrant Youth's Work as Family Translators or 'Para-phrasers.'" *Social Problems* 50 (4): 505–24.

Ortiz, Gabe. 2017. "10-Year-Old Rosamaria, Detained for Over a Week, Has Been Released." *Daily Kos*, November 3.

Paley, Julia. 2001. *Marketing Democracy: Power and Social Movements in Post-dictatorship Chile*. Berkeley: University of California Press.

Pallares, Amalia. 2015. *Family Activism: Immigrant Struggles and the Politics of Nonciti-zenship*. New Brunswick, NJ: Rutgers University Press.

Paltrow, Lynn M., and Jeanne Flavin. 2013. "Arrests of and Forced Interventions on Pregnant Women in the United States, 1973–2005: Implications for Women's Legal Status and Public Health." *Journal of Health Politics, Policy and Law* 38 (2): 299–343.

Pardo, Mary. 1998. *Mexican American Women Activists: Identity and Resistance in Two Los Angeles Communities*. Philadelphia: Temple University Press.

París-Pombo, María Dolores. 2008. "Health Promotion and Gender Power in the Oaxaca Mixteca." *Agricultura, Sociedad y Desarrollo* 5 (1): 53–69.

Passel, Jeffrey S., and D'Vera Cohn. 2018. "U.S. Unauthorized Immigrant Total Dips to Lowest Level in a Decade." Washington, DC: Pew Research Center.

Passel, Jeffrey S., D'Vera Cohn, and Molly Rohal. 2014. "Unauthorized Immigrant Totals Rise in 7 States, Fall in 14: Decline in Those from Mexico Fuels Most State Decreases." Washington, DC: Pew Research Center's Hispanic Trends Project.

Paz, Octavio. 1961. *The Labyrinth of Solitude*. Translated by Lysander Kemp. New York: Grove.

Pear, Robert. 2017. "Court Temporarily Blocks Rule Letting Employers Forgo Contraceptive Care." *New York Times*, December 16.

———. 2019. "States, Required to Cover Some Abortions, Flout Law." *New York Times*, February 18.

Peña, Milagros. 2007. *Latina Activists across Borders: Women's Grassroots Organizing in Mexico and Texas*. Durham, NC: Duke University Press.

Pérez, Emma. 1999. *The Decolonial Imaginary: Writing Chicanas into History*. Bloomington: Indiana University Press.

Pérez, Laura E. 2010. "Enrique Dussel's *Etica de la liberación*, U.S. Women of Color Decolonizing Practices, and Coalitionary Politics Amidst Difference." *Qui Parle: Critical Humanities and Social Sciences* 18 (2): 121–46.

Pérez, Miriam Zoila. 2015. "A Tale of Two Movements." *Colorlines*, January 22.

Pérez, Ramona Lee. 2014. "Las Fronteras del Sabor: Taste as Consciousness, Kinship, and Space in the Mexico-U.S. Borderlands." *Journal of Latin American and Caribbean Anthropology* 19:310–30.

Perreira, Krista M., Mimi V. Chapman, and Gabriela L. Stein. 2006. "Becoming an American Parent: Overcoming Challenges and Finding Strength in a New Immigrant Latino Community." *Journal of Family Issues* 27 (10): 1383–414.

Pesquera, Beatriz M., and Denise A. Segura. 1993. "There Is No Going Back: Chicanas and Feminism." In *Chicana Critical Issues*, edited by Norma Alarcón et al, 95–115. Berkeley: Third Woman.

Petchesky, Rosalind P. 2000. "Human Rights, Reproductive Health and Economic Justice: Why They Are Indivisible." *Reproductive Health Matters* 8 (15): 12–17.

Pew Research Center. 2014. "The Shifting Religious Identity of Latinos in the United States." Washington, DC: Pew Research Center.

Pierce, Sarah, and Andrew Selee. 2017. "Immigration under Trump: A Review of Policy Shifts in the Year since the Election." Washington, DC: Migration Policy Institute.

Pila, Daniela. 2016. "'I'm Not Good Enough for Anyone': Legal Status and the Dating Lives of Undocumented Young Adults." *Sociological Forum* 31 (1): 138–58.

Pilkington, Ed. 2017. "Why the UN Is Investigating Extreme Poverty . . . In America, the World's Richest Nation." *The Guardian*, December 1.

Polletta, Francesca. 2006. *It Was like a Fever: Storytelling in Protest and Politics.* Chicago: University of Chicago Press.

Potok, Mark. 2017. "The Trump Effect: The Campaign Language of the Man Who Would Become President Sparks Violence, Bullying, before and after the Election." *Intelligence Report* (Southern Poverty Law Center), February 15.

Potter, Joseph E., Amanda Jean Stevenson, Kate Coleman-Minahan, Sarah E. Baum, and Daniel Grossman. 2019. "Challenging Unintended Pregnancy as an Indicator of Reproductive Autonomy." *Contraception* 100 (1): 1–4.

Powell, Diane S., Batsche Catherine J., Jolenea Ferro, Fox Lise, and Glen Dunlap. 1997. "A Strength-Based Approach in Support of Multi-risk Families: Principles and Issues." *Topics in Early Childhood Education* 17 (1): 1–26.

Preston, Julia. 2013. "Women's Groups Rally for Immigration Reform, 115 Are Arrested at a Sit-In on Capitol Hill." *New York Times*, September 12.

Price, Kimala. 2010. "What Is Reproductive Justice? How Women of Color Activists Are Redefining the Pro-Choice Paradigm." *Meridians: feminism, race, transnationalism* 10 (2): 42–65.

———. 2011. "The Quest for Purity: The Role of Policy Narratives in Determining Teen Girls' Access to Emergency Contraception in the USA." *Sex Research Social Policy* 8:282–93.

———. 2017. "Queering Reproductive Justice: Toward a Theory and Praxis for Building Intersectional Political Alliances." In *LGBTQ Politics: A Critical Reader*, edited by Marla Brettschneider, Susan Burgess and Cricket Keating, 72–88. New York: NYU Press.

———. 2018. "Queering Reproductive Justice in the Trump Era: A Note on Political Intersectionality." *Politics & Gender* 14:581–601.

Pulido, Laura. 2006. *Black, Brown, Yellow, and Left: Radical Activism in Los Angeles.* Berkeley: University of California Press.

———. 2018. "Geographies of Race and Ethnicity III: Settler Colonialism and Nonnative People of Color." *Progress in Human Geography* 42 (2): 309–18.

Pyles, Loretta. 2018. *Healing Justice: Holistic Self-Care for Change Makers.* New York: Oxford University Press.

Quealy, Keven. 2018. "All the People, Places and Things President Trump Insulted on Twitter in 2018." *New York Times*, December 31.

Quesada, James. 2011. "No Soy Welferero: Undocumented Latino Laborers in the Crosshairs of Legitimation Maneuvers." *Medical Anthropology: Cross-Cultural Studies in Health and Illness* 30 (4): 368–408.

Quesada, James, Laurie Kain Hart, and Philippe Bourgois. 2011. "Structural Vulnerability and Health: Latino Migrant Laborers in the United States." *Medical Anthropology: Cross-Cultural Studies in Health and Illness* 30 (4): 339–62.

Quijada, David Alberto Cerecer, Caitlin Cahill, and Matt Bradley. 2013. "Toward a Critical Youth Policy Praxis: Critical Youth Studies and Participatory Action Research." *Theory into Practice* 52 (3): 216–23.

Quijano, Anibal. 2000. "Coloniality of Power, Eurocentrism, and Latin America." *Nepantla: Views from the South* 1 (3): 533–74.

Ramírez, Gabriela Arguedas, and Lynn M. Morgan. 2017. "The Reproductive Rights Counteroffensive in Mexico and Central America." *Feminist Studies* 43 (2): 423–37.

Ransby, Barbara. 2000. "Black Feminism at Twenty-One: Reflections on the Evolution of a National Community." *Signs* 25 (4): 1215–21.

Ransford, H. Edward, Frank R. Carrillo, and Yessenia Rivera. 2010. "Health Care-Seeking among Latino Immigrants: Blocked Access, Use of Traditional Medicine, and the Role of Religion." *Journal of Health Care for the Poor and Underserved* 21 (3): 862–78.

Reddy, Diane M., Raymond Fleming, and Carolyne Swain. 2002. "Effect of Mandatory Parental Notification on Adolescent Girls' Use of Sexual Health Care Services." *JAMA* 288 (6): 710–14.

Reed, Adolph L., Jr. 1992. "The 'Underclass' as Myth and Symbol: The Poverty of Discourse About Poverty." *Radical America* 24 (1): 21–40.

Reed, Adolph L., Jr., and Merlin Chowkwanyun. 2011. "Race, Class, Crisis: The Discourse of Racial Disparity and Its Analytical Discontents." *Socialist Register* 48:149–75.

Reese, Ellen. 2005. *Backlash against Welfare Mothers: Past and Present.* Berkeley: University of California Press.

Reichard, Raquel. 2015. "Why We Say Latinx: Trans & Gender Non-conforming People Explain." *Latina*, August 29.

Renfro, Paul M. 2019. "Why Dianne Feinstein Was Wrong to Dismiss Child Activists as Political Pawns." *Washington Post*, March 5.

Reuters. 2019. "U.S. Immigration Agents Arrest 680 Workers at Mississippi Plants." *New York Times*, August 8.

Richards, Cecile. 2014. "A Response to an Open Letter on Reproductive Justice and 'Choice.'" *RH Reality Check*, August 5.

Rios, Elsa A. 2015. "Building Leadership for Social Impact." Bayside, NY: Strategies for Social Change.

Rios, Victor M. 2008. "The Racial Politics of Youth Crime." *Latino Studies* 6:97–115.

———. 2011. *Punished: The Criminalization of Black and Latino Boys.* New York: NYU Press.

Riotta, Chris. 2017. "GOP Aims to Kill Obamacare yet Again after Failing 70 Times." *Newsweek*, July 29.

Roberts, Dorothy. 1997. *Killing the Black Body: Race, Reproduction, and the Meaning of Liberty.* New York: Vintage Books.

Roberts, Sarah C. M., Liza Fuentes, Rebecca Kriz, Valerie Williams, and Ushma D. Upadhyay. 2015. "Implications for Women of Louisiana's Law Requiring Abortion Providers Have Hospital Admitting Privileges." *Contraception* 91 (5): 1–5.

Robnett, Belinda. 1997. *How Long? How Long? African-American Women in the Struggle for Civil Rights*. New York: Oxford University Press.

———. 2002. "External Political Change, Collective Identities, and Participation in Social Movement Organizations." In *Social Movements: Identity, Culture, and the State*, edited by David S. Meyer, Nancy Whittier and Belinda Robnett, 266–85. Oxford: Oxford University Press.

Rodriguez, Cassaundra. 2016. "Experiencing 'Illegality' as a Family? Immigration Enforcement, Social Policies, and Discourses Targeting Mexican Mixed-Status Families." *Sociology Compass* 10 (8): 706–17.

Rodríguez, Roberto Cintli, Verónica Castillo Hernández, Maestra Angelbertha Cobb, Luz María de la Torre, Paula Domingo Olivares, Tata Cuaxtle Félix Evodio, María Molina Vai Sevoi, Francisco Pos, Alicia Seyler, and Irma Tzirin Socop. 2014. *Our Sacred Maíz Is Our Mother: Indigeneity and Belonging in the Americas*. Tucson: University of Arizona Press.

Rodríguez, Sylvia. 1994. "Review: Subaltern Historiography on the Rio Grande: On Gutiérrez's 'When Jesus Came, the Corn Mothers Went Away.'" *American Ethnologist* 21 (4): 892–99.

Romero, Diana, and Madina Agénor. 2017. "The Welfare Gamily Cap: Reproductive Rights, Control, and Poverty Prevention." In *Radical Reproductive Justice: Foundations, Theory, Practice, Critique*, edited by Loretta J. Ross, Lynn Roberts, Erika Derkas, Whitney Peoples, and Pamela Bridgewater Toure, 381–96. New York: Feminist Press.

Romero, Diana, Lisa Maldonado, Liza Fuentes, and Linda Prine. 2015. "Association of Reproductive Health Training on Intention to Provide Services after Residency: The Family Physician Resident Survey." *Family Medicine* 47 (1): 22–30.

Rosa, Jonathan, and Yarimar Bonilla. 2017. "Deprovincializing Trump, Decolonizing Diversity, and Unsettling Anthropology." *American Ethnologist* 44 (2): 201–8.

Rosaldo, Renato. 1994. "Cultural Citizenship and Educational Democracy." *Cultural Anthropology* 9 (3): 402–11.

———. 1997. "Cultural Citizenship, Inequality, and Multiculturalism." In *Latino Cultural Citizenship: Claiming Identity, Space, and Rights*, edited by William V. Benmayor and Rina Flores, 27–38. Boston: Beacon.

Rosay, André B. 2016. "Violence against American Indian and Alaska Native Women and Men." *National Institute of Justice Journal* 277:1–5.

Roschelle, Anne R. 2013. "Why Do You *Think* We Don't Get Married? Homeless Mothers in San Francisco Speak Out about Having Children outside of Marriage." *Advances in Gender Research* 17:89–111.

Rose, Tricia. 2003. *Longing to Tell: Black Women Talk about Sexuality and Intimacy*. New York: Farrar, Straus and Giroux.

Ross, Loretta. 2005. Transcript of interview by Joyce Follet. Voices of Feminism Oral History Project, Sophia Smith Collection, Northampton, MA.

Ross, Loretta, Sarah J. Brownlee, Dazon Dixon Diallo, and Luz Rodriguez. 2001. "The SisterSong Collective: Women of Color, Reproductive Health, and Human Rights." *American Journal of Health Studies* 17 (2): 79–88.

Ross, Loretta J., Lynn Roberts, Erika Derkas, Whitney Peoples, and Pamela Bridgewater Toure. 2017a. Introduction to *Radical Reproductive Justice: Foundations, Theory, Practice, Critique*, edited by Loretta J. Ross, Lynn Roberts, Erika Derkas, Whitney Peoples, and Pamela Bridgewater Toure, 11–31. New York: Feminist Press.

———, eds. 2017b. *Radical Reproductive Justice: Foundations, Theory, Practice, Critique*. New York: Feminist Press.

Ross, Loretta J., and Rickie Solinger. 2017. *Reproductive Justice: An Introduction*. Berkeley: University of California Press.

Ross, Luana. 2009. "From the 'F' Word to Indigenous/Feminisms." *Wicazo Sa Review* 24 (2): 39–52.

Roth, Benita. 2017. "Women's and Feminist Movements in the United States: The Contradictory Effects of Class-Based Success." In *Women's Movements in the Global Era*, edited by Amrita Basu, 241–64. Boulder, CO: Westview.

Roth, Rachael. 2017. "'She Doesn't Deserve to Be Treated Like This': Prisons as Sites of Reproductive Justice." In *Radical Reproductive Justice: Foundations, Theory, Practice, Critique*, edited by Loretta J. Ross, Lynn Roberts, Erika Derkas, Whitney Peoples, and Pamela Bridgewater Toure, 285–301. New York: Feminist Press.

Rubin, Joel, and Paige St. John. 2017. "How a U.S. Citizen Was Mistakenly Targeted for Deportation. He's Not Alone." *Los Angeles Times*, November 29.

Sacchetti, Maria. 2017. "Trump Administration Targets 'Sanctuary' Cities in Latest Wave of Immigration Arrests." *Washington Post*, September 28.

Salazar, Layidua. 2018. "Activist's Detainment Reminds Us Immigration Is a Reproductive Justice Issue." *Rewire.News*, March 12.

Sampson, Steven. 2003. "'Trouble Spots': Projects, Bandits and State Fragmentation." In *Globalization, the State and Violence*, edited by Jonathan Friedman, 309–42. Walnut Creek, CA: AltaMira.

Sanchez, Corrine. 2016. "Herstories and the Braiding of Environment and Reproductive Justice to Protect Those Most Vulnerable." *Journal of American Indian Education* 55 (3): 48–71.

———. 2018. "Tewa Women United." *UNUM Magazine*. www.unummagazine.com

Sandoval, Chela. 2000. *Methodology of the Oppressed*. Minneapolis: University of Minnesota Press.

Sanger-Katz, Margot. 2019. "Struggling to Follow the Rules About Rules." *New York Times*, January 23.

Santa Cruz Feminist of Color Collective. 2014. "Building on 'the Edge of Each Other's Battles': A Feminist of Color Multidimensional Lens." *Hypatia* 29 (1): 23–40.

Santelli, John S., Leslie M. Kantor, Stephanie A. Grilo, Ilene S. Speizer, Laura D. Lindberg, Jennifer Heitel, Amy T. Schalet, Maureen E. Lyon, Amanda J. Mason-Jones, Terry McGovern, Craig J. Heck, Jennifer Rogers, and Mary A. Ott. 2017. "Abstinence-Only-until-Marriage: An Updated Review of U.S. Policies and Programs and Their Impact." *Journal of Adolescent Health* 61:273–80.

Santelli, John S., and Mary A. Ott. 2006. "Abstinence-Only Education Policies and Programs: A Position Paper of the Society for Adolescent Medicine." *Journal of Adolescent Health* 38:83–87.

Savransky, Rebecca. 2017. "ACLU Sues after Immigration Agents Detain 10-Year-Old Girl after Surgery." *The Hill*, October 31.

Sawatsky, Jarem. 2007. "Rethinking Restorative Justice: When the Geographies of Crime and of Healing Justice Matter." *Peace Research* 39 (1–2): 75–93.

Schmalzbaur, Leah. 2008. "Family Divided: The Class Formation of Honduran Transnational Families." *Global Networks* 8 (3): 329–46.

Schrooten, Mieke. 2012. "Moving Ethnography Online: Researching Brazilian Migrants' Online Togetherness." *Ethnic and Racial Studies* 35 (10): 1794–809.

Schwartz, Sarah, and Claire Brindis. 2011. "Uneven Progress: Sex Education in California Public Schools." San Francisco: Boxby Center for Global Reproductive Health.

Schwarzmantel, John. 2015. *The Routledge Guidebook to Gramsci's Prison Notebooks.* New York: Routledge.

Sharkey, Joseph R., Wesley R. Dean, and Cassandra M. Johnson. 2011. "Association of Household and Community Characteristics with Adult and Child Food Insecurity among Mexican-Origin Households in Colonias along the Texas-Mexico Border." *International Journal for Equity in Health* 10 (19): 1–14.

Silliman, Jael, Marlene Gerber Fried, Loretta Ross, and Elena R. Gutiérrez, eds. 2004. *Undivided Rights: Women of Color Organize for Reproductive Justice.* Cambridge, MA: South End.

Silver, Lauren. 2010. "The Politics of Regulation: Adolescent Mothers and the Social Context of Resiliency." *Voices: A Publication of the Association for Feminist Anthropology* 8 (1): 1, 8–11.

Simpson, Monica. 2014. "Reproductive Justice and 'Choice': An Open Letter to Planned Parenthood." *RH Reality Check*, August 5.

Simpson, Monica, and Cecile Richards. 2014. "Moving Forward: A Joint Statement from Cecile Richards and Monica Simpson." *Rewire*, October 9.

S.I.N. Collective. 2007. "Students Informing Now (S.I.N.) Challenge the Racial State in California without Shame . . . Sin Vergüenza!" *Educational Foundations* 21 (1–2): 71–90.

Singh, Gopal. 2010. "Maternal Mortality in the United States, 1935–2007: Substantial Racial/Ethnic, Socioeconomic, and Geographic Disparities Persist 2." Rockville, MD: Health Resources and Services Administration, Maternal and Child Health Bureau, US Department of Health and Human Services.

Small, Mario Luis, David J. Harding, and Michele Lamont. 2010. "Reconsidering Culture and Poverty." *Annals of the American Academy of Political and Social Science* 629 (1): 6–27.

Smith, Andrea. 2006. "Heteropatriarchy and the Three Pillars of White Supremacy: Rethinking Women of Color Organizing." In *The Color of Violence: The INCITE! Anthology*, edited by INCITE Women of Color Against Violence, 66–73. Boston: South End.

———. 2008. "Human Rights and Social-Justice Organizing in the United States." *Radical History Review* 101 (Spring): 211–19.

Solinger, Rickie. 2017. "Making Art for Reproductive Justice." In *Radical Reproductive Justice: Foundations, Theory, Practice, Critique*, edited by Loretta J. Ross, Lynn Roberts, Erika Derkas, Whitney Peoples, and Pamela Bridgewater Toure, 397–403. New York: Feminist Press.

Solomon, Danyelle, and Connor Maxwell. 2018. "52 Harms in 52 Weeks: How the Trump Administration Hurt Communities of Color in 2017." Washington, DC: Center for American Progress.

Soto, Lilia. 2018. *Girlhood in the Borderlands: Mexican Teens Caught in the Crossroads of Migration* New York: NYU Press.

Spade, Dean. 2013. "Intersectional Resistance and Law Reform." *Signs* 38 (4): 1031–55.

Speed, Shannon. 2006. "At the Crossroads of Human Rights and Anthropology: Toward a Critically Engaged Activist Research." *American Anthropologist* 108 (1): 66–76.

Speed, Shannon, and Jane F. Collier. 2000. "Limiting Indigenous Autonomy in Chiapas: The State Government's Use of Human Rights." *Human Rights Quarterly* 22 (4): 877–905.

Stacey, Judith. 1996. *In the Name of the Family: Rethinking Family Values in the Postmodern Age*. Boston: Beacon.

———. 1997. "The Neo-Family-Values Campaign." In *The Gender/Sexuality Reader: Culture, History, Political Economy*, edited by Roger Lancaster and Micaela di Leonardo, 453–70. New York: Routledge.

Steinberg, Marc W. 2002. "Toward a More Dialogic Analysis of Social Movement Culture." In *Social Movements: Identity, Culture, and the State*, edited by David S. Meyer, Nancy Whittier, and Belinda Robnett, 208–25. Oxford: Oxford University Press.

Stephen, Lynn. 2007. *Transborder Lives: Oaxacan Indigenous Migrants in the U.S. And Mexico*. Durham, NC: Duke University Press.

———. 2013. *We Are the Face of Oaxaca: Testimony and Social Movements*. Durham, NC: Duke University Press.

Stern, Alexandra Minna. 2005. *Eugenic Nation: Faults and Frontiers of Better Breeding in Modern America*. Berkeley: University of California Press.

Stevens, Patricia E. 1999. "Lesbians and Doctors: Experiences of Solidarity and Domination in Health Care Settings." *Gender & Society* 10 (1): 24–41.

Stevenson, Amanda, Imelda M. Flores-Vazquez, Richard L. Allgeyer, Pete Schenkkan, and Joseph E. Potter. 2016. "Effect of Removal of Planned Parenthood from the Texas Women's Health Program." *New England Journal of Medicine* 374 (9): 853–60.

Stewart, Katherine. 2012. *The Good News Club: The Christian Right's Stealth Assault on America's Children*. New York: PublicAffairs.

Strickler, Rachael, and Monica Simpson. 2017. "A Brief Herstory of SisterSong." In *Radical Reproductive Justice: Foundations, Theory, Practice, Critique*, edited by Loretta J. Ross, Lynn Roberts, Erika Derkas, Whitney Peoples and Pamela Bridgewater Toure, 50–57. New York: Feminist Press.

Strong Families, Basic Rights Oregon, Brown Boi Project, Center for American Progress, Equality New Mexico, Family Equality Council, Forward Together, Montana Women Vote, National Center for Lesbian Rights, National Gay and Lesbian Task Force, Raising Women's Voices, SPARK Reproductive Justice Now, Southwest Women's Law Center, Transgender Law Center, Transgender Resource Center of New Mexico, Western States Center, and Young Women United. n.d. "Where to Start, What to Ask: A Guide for LGBT People Choosing Healthcare Plans." Oakland, CA: Strong Families.

Strong Families, California Latinas for Reproductive Justice, and National Latina Institute for Reproductive Health. n.d. "Vota por Nosotros: La Guía de Participación Cívica de Strong Families." Oakland, CA: Strong Families.

Strong Families Network. 2017. "Reproductive Justice Reference Guide for Latinx Media: A Guide for Reporting on Abortion and the Latinx Community." Oakland, CA: Forward Together's Strong Families Network.

Strong Families New Mexico Working Group. 2014. "Strong Families New Mexico Legislative Report Card 2013." Albuquerque, NM: Strong Families Initiative.

Stubbs, Julie. 2009. "Restorative Justice, Gendered Violence and Indigenous Women." University of Sydney, Sydney Law School.

Sun, Lena H., and Juliet Eilperin. 2017. "CDC Gets List of Forbidden Words: Fetus, Transgender, Diversity." *Washington Post*, December 15.

Taft, Jessica K. 2011. *Rebel Girls: Youth Activism and Social Change across the Americas.* New York: NYU Press.

Taft, Jessica K., and Hava Gordon. 2013. "Youth Activists, Youth Councils, and Constrained Democracy." *Education, Citizenship, and Social Justice* 8 (1): 87–100.

Talavera, Victor, Guillermina Gina Núñez-Mchiri, and Josiah Heyman. 2010. "Deportation in the U.S.-Mexico Borderlands: Anticipation, Experience, and Memory." In *The Deportation Regime: Sovereignty, Space, and the Freedom of Movement*, edited by Nicholas De Genova and Nathalie Peutz, 166–95. Durham, NC: Duke University Press.

Tambe, Ashwini. 2017. "The Women's March on Washington: Words from an Organizer." *Feminist Studies* 43 (1): 223–29.

Tavernise, Sabrina, and Robert Gebeloff. 2016. "Immigrants, the Poor and Minorities Gain Sharply under Affordable Care Act." *New York Times*, April 18.

Taylor, Keeanga-Yamahtta. 2017. *How We Get Free: Black Feminism and the Combahee River Collective.* Chicago: Haymarket Books.

Texas Policy Evaluation Project. 2015. "Texas Women's Experiences Attempting Self-Induced Abortion in the Face of Dwindling Options." Austin and San Francisco: University of Texas Population Research Center, University of California–San Francisco, Ibis Reproductive Health, University of Alabama–Birmingham.

Terriquez, Veronica. 2015. "Intersectional Mobilization, Social Movement Spillover, and Queer Youth Leadership in the Immigrant Rights Movement." *Social Problems* 62:343–62.

Terriquez, Veronica, and Tiffany D. Joseph. 2016. "Ethnoracial Inequality and Insurance Coverage among Latino Young Adults." *Social Science & Medicine* 168:150–58.

Thomas, Dorothy Q. 2000. "We Are Not the World: U.S. Activism and Human Rights in the Twenty-First Century." *Signs* 25 (4): 1121–24.

Thomsen, Carly. 2013. "From Refusing Stigmatization to Celebration: New Directions for Reproductive Justice Activism." *Feminist Studies* 39 (1): 149–58.

———. 2015. "The Politics of Narrative, Narrative as Politics: Rethinking Reproductive Justice Frameworks through the South Dakota Abortion Story." *Feminist Formations* 27 (2): 1–26.

Thornton Dill, Bonnie, and Ruth Enid Zambrana. 2009. *Emerging Intersections: Race, Class, and Gender in Theory, Policy, and Practice.* New Brunswick, NJ: Rutgers University Press.

Toebes, Brigit. 1999. "Towards an Improved Understanding of the International Human Right to Health." *Human Rights Quarterly* 21:661–79.

Treuer, David. 2019. *The Heartbeat of Wounded Knee: Native America from 1890 to the Present.* New York: Penguin Random House.

Trujillo, Carla. 1991. *Chicana Lesbians: The Girls Our Mothers Warned Us About.* Berkeley, CA: Third Woman.

———. 1998. *Living Chicana Theory.* Berkeley, CA: Third Woman.

Trujillo, Michel L. 2009. *Land of Disenchantment: Latina/o Identities and the Transformations in Northern New Mexico.* Albuquerque: University of New Mexico Press.

Trujillo-Pagán, Nicole. 2018. "Crossed Out by LatinX: Gender Neutrality and Gender-blind Sexism." *Latino Studies* 16:396–406.

Turner, Terence. 1997. "Human Rights, Human Difference: Anthropology's Contribution to an Emancipatory Cultural Politics." *Journal of Anthropological Research* 53 (3): 273–91.

Ulloa, Jazmine. 2017. "More than Half of Californians Support 'Sanctuary State' Legislation, Poll Finds." *Los Angeles Times*, November 10.

Ulloa, Jazmine, and Liam Dillon. 2018. "California Leaders Rebuke Sessions as 'Going to War' over State Immigration Policy." *Los Angeles Times*, March 7.

Upadhyay, Ushma D., Katrina Kimport, Elise K. O. Belusa, Nicole E. Johns, Douglas W. Laube, and Sarah C. M. Roberts. 2017. "Evaluating the Impact of a Mandatory Pre-Abortion Ultrasound Viewing Law: A Mixed Methods Study." *PLoS One* 12 (7): 1–23.

Urban Indian Health Institute. 2016. "Community Health Profile: National Aggregate of Urban Indian Health Program Service Areas." Seattle: Urban Indian Health Institute.

Valladares, Ena Suseth. 2009. "Making the Case for Latinas' Reproductive Health and Justice Policy." Los Angeles: California Latinas for Reproductive Justice.

———. 2010. "Young Women Speak Out! Perspectives and Implications of Reproductive Health, Rights & Justice Policies." Los Angeles: California Latinas for Reproductive Justice.

———. 2016. "Young Fathers Speak Out!" Los Angeles: California Latinas for Reproductive Justice.

Valladares, Ena Suseth, and Marisol Franco. 2010. "Unearthing Latina/o Voices on Family, Pregnancy and Reproductive Justice." Los Angeles: California Latinas for Reproductive Justice.

Vasquez, Tina. 2016. "Family Separation, a Natural Byproduct of the U.S. Immigration." *Rewire*, May 6.

Vélez-Ibáñez, Carlos G. 1980. "*Se Me Acabó La Canción*: An Ethnography of Nonconsenting Sterilizations among Mexican Women in Los Angeles." In *Mexican Women in the United States: Struggles Past and Present*, edited by Magdalena Mora and Adelaida Del Castillo, 71–91. Los Angeles: UCLA Chicano Studies Research Center.

Ventura, Stephanie J. 2009. "Changing Patterns of Nonmarital Childbearing in the United States." NCHS Data Brief. Hyattsville, MD: National Center for Health Statistics.

Vidal-Ortiz, Salvador, and Juliana Martínez. 2018. "Latinx Thoughts: Latinidad with an X." *Latino Studies* 16:384–95.

Villanueva, Karen Muktayan. 2010. "Norma Wong: Stance, Energy, Awareness, and Rhythm." *transform: vision & practice for transformative social change*, September 20.

Villarosa, Linda. 2018. "Why Are Black Mothers and Babies in the United States Dying of More than Double the Rate of White Mothers and Babies?" *New York Times Magazine*, April 15.

Villela, Khristaan D. 2016. "Controversy Erupts over Peter Nabokov's Publication of 'The Origin Myth of Acoma Pueblo.'" *Pasatiempo* (*Santa Fe New Mexican*), January 15.

Villenas, Sofia. 2001. "Latina Mothers and Small-Town Racisms: Creating Narratives of Dignity and Moral Education in North Carolina." *Anthropology & Education Quarterly* 32 (1): 3–28.

Vizguerra, Jeanette. 2017. "Why I Will Not Leave." *New York Times*, February 24.

Waldstein, Anna. 2010. "Popular Medicine and Self-Care in a Mexican Migrant Community: Toward an Explanation of an Epidemiological Paradox." *Medical Anthropology* 29 (1): 71–107.

Walker, Alice. 1983. *In Search of Our Mothers' Garden: Womanist Prose*. San Diego: Harcourt Brace Jovanovich.

Wang, Chenchen, Christopher H. Schmid, Maura D. Iversen, William F. Harvey, Roger A. Fielding, John B. Driban, Lori Lyn Price, John B. Wong, Keran F. Reid, Ramel Rones, and Timothy McAlindon. 2016. "Comparative Effectiveness of Tai Chi Versus Physical Therapy for Knee Osteoarthritis. A Randomized Trial." *Annals of Internal Medicine* 165:77–86.

Ward, Kelly, and Lisa Wolf-Wendel. 2012. *Academic Motherhood: How Faculty Manage Work and Family*. New Brunswick, NJ: Rutgers University Press.

Warren, Robert. 2019. "US Undocumented Population Continued to Fall from 2016 to 2017 and Visa Overstays Significantly Exceeded Illegal Crossings for the Seventh Consecutive Year." *Journal of Migration and Human Security* 7 (1): 19–22.

Weis, Lois, and Michelle Fine. 2000. Introduction to "Part 1: Spaces for Identity Work." In *Construction Sites: Excavating Race, Class and Gender among Urban Youth*, edited by Lois Weis and Michelle Fine, 1–3. New York: Teachers College Press.

———. 2012. "Critical Bifocality and Circuits of Privilege: Expanding Critical Ethnographic Theory and Design." *Harvard Educational Review* 82 (2): 173–201.

West, Robin L. 2009. "From Choice to Reproductive Justice." *Yale Law Journal* 118 (7): 1394–431.

Western States Center. 2006. "Building a Movement from the Ground Up: A Report from the Family, Community & Sexuality Project." Portland, OR: Western States Center.

Weston, Kath. 1991. *Families We Choose: Lesbians, Gays, Kinship*. New York: Columbia University Press.

Wexler, Lisa Marin, Gloria DiFluvio, and Tracey K. Burke. 2009. "Resilience and Marginalized Youth: Making the Case for Personal and Collective Meaning-Making as Part of Resilience Research in Public Health." *Social Science & Medicine* 69 (4): 565–70.

White, Kari, Joseph E. Potter, Amanda J. Stevenson, Liza Fuentes, Kristine Hopkins, and Daniel Grossman. 2016. "Women's Knowledge of and Support for Abortion Restrictions in Texas: Findings from a Statewide Representative Survey." *Perspectives on Sexual and Reproductive Health* 48 (4): 189–97.

williams, Rev. angel Kyodo, and Lama Rod Owens, with Jasmine Syedullah. 2016. *Radical Dharma: Talking Race, Love, and Liberation*. Berkeley, CA: North Atlantic Books.

Williams, David R. 2012. "Miles to Go Before We Sleep: Racial Inequalities in Health." *Journal of Health and Social Behavior* 53 (3): 279–95.

Wilson, Richard Ashby. 2006. "Afterword to 'Anthropology and Human Rights in a New Key': The Social Life of Human Rights." *American Anthropologist* 2006 (1): 77–83.

Wilson, William Julius. 1987. *The Truly Disadvantaged: The Inner City, the Underclass and Public Policy*. Chicago: University of Chicago Press.

———, ed. 1993. *The Ghetto Underclass: Social Science Perspectives*. Newbury Park, CA: Sage.

Wooden, Cindy. 2016. "Health Care Is a Right, not a Privilege, Pope Says." *Catholic News Service*, May 9.

Woodward, Bob. 2018. *Fear: Trump in the White House*. New York: Simon and Schuster.

World Health Organization. 2012. "The Right to Health, Fact Sheet #323."

Woznak, Zachary. 2014. "'MAKE/ART/SPACE' Seeks to Change Controversial Illinois Abortion Law through Art." *Chicago Bureau*, July 21.

Wray-Lake, Laura, Rachel Wells, Lauren Alvis, Sandra Delgado, Amy K. Syvertsen, and Aaron Metzger. 2018. "Being a Latinx Adolescent under a Trump Presidency: Analysis of Latinx Youth's Reactions to Immigration Politics." *Children and Youth Services Review* 87:192–204.

Wu, Ivan H., and NiCole T. Buchanan. 2019. "Pathways to Vitality: The Role of Mindfulness and Coping." *Mindfulness* 10 (3): 481–91.

Yamin, Alicia Ely. 2016. *Power, Suffering, and the Struggle for Dignity: Human Rights Frameworks for Health and Why They Matter.* Philadelphia: University of Pennsylvania Press.

Yang, Guo-Yan, Li-Qiong Wang, Jun Ren, Yan Zhang, Meng-Ling Li, Yu-Ting Zhu, Jing Luo, Yan-Jun Cheng, Wen-Yuan Li, Peter M. Wayne, and Jian-Ping Liu. 2015. "Evidence Base of Clinical Studies on Tai Chi: A Bibliometric Analysis." *PLoS One* 10 (3): e0120655.

Yosso, Tara J. 2005. "Whose Culture Has Capital? A Critical Race Theory Discussion of Community Cultural Wealth." *Race Ethnicity and Education* 8 (1): 69–91.

YouthNet, Family Health International, and Advocates for Youth. 2005. "Youth Participation Guide: Assessment, Planning, and Implementation." Arlington, VA: Family Health International, YouthNet Program.

Zaleski, Nikki, Paula Martin, and Joy Messinger. 2015. "Given and Chosen: Youth-Led Research on Family-Supported Conversations About Sexuality." *Family and Community Health* 38 (1): 131–40.

Zavella, Patricia. 1997. "'Playing with Fire': The Gendered Construction of Chicana/ Mexicana Sexuality." In *The Gender/Sexuality Reader: Culture, History, Political Economy*, edited by Roger N. Lancaster and Micaela di Leonardo, 402–18. New York: Routledge.

———. 2003. "Talkin' Sex: Chicanas and Mexicanas Theorize about Silences and Sexual Pleasures." In *Chicana Feminisms: A Critical Reader*, edited by Gabriela Arredondo, Aída Hurtado, Norma Klahn, Olga Nájera Ramírez, and Patricia Zavella, 228–53. Durham, NC: Duke University Press.

———. 2011. *I'm Neither Here nor There: Mexicans' Quotidian Struggles with Migration and Poverty.* Durham, NC: Duke University Press.

———. 2012. "Beyond the Screams: Latino Punkeros Contest Nativist Discourses." *Latin American Perspectives* 39 (2): 27–41.

———. 2016. "Contesting Structural Vulnerability through Reproductive Justice Activism with Latina Immigrants in California." *North American Dialogue* 19 (1): 36–45.

———. 2017. "Intersectional Praxis in the Movement for Reproductive Justice: The Respect ABQ Women Campaign." *Signs: Journal of Women in Culture and Society* 42 (2): 509–33.

Zavella, Patricia, and Xóchitl Castañeda. 2005. "Sexuality and Risks: Young Mexican Women Negotiate Gendered Discourse about Virginity and Disease." *Latino Studies* 3 (2): 226–45.

Zimmerman, Kristen, Neelam Pathikonda, Brenda Salgado, and Taj James. 2010. "Out of the Spiritual Closet: Organizers Transforming the Practice of Social Justice." Oakland, CA: Movement Strategy Center.

Zimmerman, Marc A. 2013. "Resiliency Theory: A Strengths-Based Approach to Research and Practice for Adolescent Health." *Health Education & Behavior* 40 (4): 381–83.

INDEX

abortion clinics, 81–82, 90
abortions, 3, 7; administration of, 227n54; campaigns against, 78; Catholic Church condemning, 45–46; distress surrounding, 120–21; funding for, 242n20; laws for, 81; obtaining, 82, 96; opinions on, 46–47; opposition to, 143; as option, not failure, 222n77; politics to, 11; right to, 42–44; Ross on, 11; as self-induced, 78, 83, 121, 226n50; spirituality and, 100; support for, 209n6. *See also* Parental Notification of Abortion Act
Abrego, Leisy, 186
ACA. *See* Patient Protection and Affordable Care Act
Activist Women in Letters and Social Change (Mujeres Activas en Letras y Cambio Social) (MALCS), 32, 152
Activist Women United (Mujeres Unidas Activas), 96
acuerdos (agreements), 164
Admassu, Senait, 17
Adolescent Family Life Act (AFLA), 231n1
adultism, 108
Advocates for Youth, 115
affiliate rule, Texas, 81
Afiya Center, 62–65, 189
AFLA. *See* Adolescent Family Life Act
African Communities Public Health Coalition, 17
age, 9
agreements (*acuerdos*), 164

Agreements of Cooperation in Communities to Enhance Safety and Security, 243n33
Aguilar, Cristina, 11–12, 21, 32, 55; COLOR and, 165–67; on friendship, 79; on leadership, 136; on media, 116; resiliency training for, 168–70; togetherness encouraged by, 188; worries of, 192
alcoholism, 149, 155
Alvarez, Sonia, 70
American Civil Liberties Union, 120
American Indian Religious Freedom Act, 237n34
anchor babies, 36
Anderson, Katrina, 65, 84–88
Anzaldúa, Gloria, 16, 19, 37; insight from, 103; on spiritual activism, 145, 180, 228n76
Araz, Eneri, 175
Arredondo, Sophia, 175
Artists United for Reproductive Justice (AURJ), 41, 65
Asian Communities for Reproductive Justice, 72, 159
Asian Pacific Islanders for Choice, 2
assimilation, resistance to, 226n29
AURJ. *See* Artists United for Reproductive Justice
authoritarianism, 189
Avila, Elena, 152, 180
Ayala, George, 38

Barboa, Adriann: on Forward Stance, 160; on Panocha Pláticas, 174–76; Strong Families and, 54, 56, 71–77

ABOUT THE AUTHOR

Patricia Zavella is Professor Emerita in the Department of Latin American and Latino Studies at the University of California, Santa Cruz. She is the author of *I'm Neither Here nor There: Mexicans Quotidian Struggles with Migration and Poverty* and coauthor of *Telling to Live: Latina Feminist Testimonios.*